The Amityville Horror: An Inquest into Paranormal Claims

The Amityville Horror: An Inquest into Paranormal Claims

Frank R. Zindler

An Imprint of the
Global Center for Religious Research
1312 17TH Street • Suite 549
Denver, Colorado 80202

info@gcrr.org • gcrr.org

GCRR Press
An imprint of the Global Center for Religious Research
1312 17th Street Suite 549
Denver, CO 80202
www.gcrr.org

DOI: 10.33929/GCRRPress.2022.04

Typesetter: Katie Curlee Hamblen
Copyeditor / Proofreader: Jaclyn Prout
Cover Art Cartoon: Chris Dunne
Cover Design: Abdullah Al Mahmud
fiverr.com/mahmuddidar

Library of Congress Cataloging-in-Publication Data

The Amityville horror : An inquest into paranormal claims / Frank R. Zindler
p. cm.
Includes bibliographic references (p.)
ISBN (Print): 978-1-959281-02-3
ISBN (eBook): 978-1-959281-03-0
1. Amityville Horror. 2. Paranormal investigation. 3. Fraud and hoax. I. Title.

HV6751.F37 .Z563 2022

ὒ3

This book is dedicated to the memory of
James "The Amazing" Randi
(born Randall James Hamilton Zwinge)

August 7, 1928–October 20, 2020

Friend, mentor, and master investigator of occult, paranormal, and supernatural claims.

James Randi was an inspiration to me for nearly half a century. I lament the fact that he couldn't live to read and criticize this book.

James Randi (left) Sitting with Frank Zindler (right)
Photograph by Catherine E. Zindler

Advanced Endorsements

The Amityville Horror: An Inquest into Paranormal Claims is Frank Zindler at the height of his creative and analytical powers, a skillset honed over six decades of using science and logic to challenge supernatural claims. Using an investigative methodology that utilizes both scientific inquiry and historical analysis, Zindler systematically exposes the paranormal claims in Jay Anson's 1977 bestseller, *The Amityville Horror: A True Story*, as a fraud.

—Dustin Lawson
Author of *The Ghost of Democracy*
and *The Firing of Doctor Democracy*

Why a book today on a decades-old "true" supernatural story? First, the original 1977 account has continued to spawn movies as late as 2017. Second, Americans remain susceptible to "alternative facts," baloney, and bald-faced lies. In a series of meticulous and short readable chapters analyzing each day of the alleged events, Zindler deftly debunks the Amityville myth. Yet if anything, the abundance of such hoaxes and the nefarious branding of inconvenient facts as hoaxes by certain parties has further eroded the very notion of truth and demonstrated the peril of gullibility and credulity. In this way, Zindler's project is as timely as ever.

—Jack David Eller, PhD
Author of *Trump and Political Theology*
and *Introducing Anthropology of Religion*

Zindler's book is *precisely* the kind of thorough and proper investigation into the paranormal that pop culture has repeatedly failed to conduct in their complicit furtherance of hoaxes and frauds. Those who are adamant in their belief in the paranormal need to read this formidable work by a true master of skepticism so as to see a brilliant example of critical thinking at play.

—Darren M. Slade, PhD
Author of "Properly Investigating Miracle Claims"
in *The Case Against Miracles*

Acknowledgements

Special recognition must be given to my daughter, Catherine, who had the arduous task of converting the hand-corrected typescript produced in 1980 into the digital file needed for completion of this book. She was also the one who prepared the illustrations, with special credit to the reconstructed blueprints for the house at 112 Ocean Avenue in Amityville, New York. In a phrase, Catherine has been *sine qua non* for the appearance of a book that first began when she was still in high school.

Thanks also must be given to my friend Prof. Jack David Eller, who brought my unfinished project to the attention of his editor, Dr. Darren Slade. Thanks must be given to Dr. Slade for his decision not to allow the information in this book to slip unnoticed into the oblivion that has swallowed up so many of the efforts that have been expended in the cause of reason throughout history. Finally, I must thank Jaclyn Prout at GCRR Press whose editorial eye and sense of academic style has improved this book greatly.

A Selection of Publications by Frank R. Zindler

Thomas Paine, The Age of Reason, Part Three: Examination of the Prophecies (edited and annotated by Frank Zindler, American Atheist Press, 1993)

The Legend of Saint Peter: A Contribution to the Mythology of Christianity, by Arthur Drews (translated and annotated by Frank Zindler, American Atheist Press, 1997)

The Jesus the Jews Never Knew: Sepher Toldoth Yeshu *and the Quest of the Historical Jesus in Jewish Sources* (American Atheist Press, 2003)

Through Atheist Eyes: Scenes from a World that Won't Reason, Volume I. Religions & Scriptures (American Atheist Press, 2011)

Through Atheist Eyes: Scenes from a World that Won't Reason, Volume II. Science & Pseudoscience (American Atheist Press, 2011)

Through Atheist Eyes: Scenes from a World that Won't Reason, Volume III. Debates (American Atheist Press, 2011)

Through Atheist Eyes: Scenes from a World that Won't Reason, Volume IV. Omnium-Gatherum (American Atheist Press, 2011)

Bart Ehrman and the Quest of the Historical Jesus of Nazareth: An Evaluation of Ehrman's Did Jesus Exist? (American Atheist Press, 2013)

Confessions of a Born-Again Atheist: The Implausible Lives of a Godless Guy (American Atheist Press, 2019)

Mark 1:32
And at even, when the sun did set, they brought unto him all that were diseased, and them that were possessed with devils. 33 And all the city was gathered together at the door. 34 And he healed many that were sick of divers diseases, and cast out many devils; and suffered not the devils to speak, because they knew him.

Luke 8:26
And they arrived at the country of the Gadarenes, which is over against Galilee. 27 And when he went forth to land, there met him out of the city a certain man, which had devils long time, and ware no clothes, neither abode in any house, but in the tombs. 28 When he saw Jesus, he cried out, and fell down before him, and with a loud voice said, What have I to do with thee, Jesus, thou Son of God most high? I beseech thee, torment me not. 29 (For he had commanded the unclean spirit to come out of the man. For oftentimes it had caught him: and he was kept bound with chains and in fetters; and he brake the bands, and was driven of the devil into the wilderness.) 30 And Jesus asked him, saying, What is thy name? And he said, Legion: because many devils were entered into him. 31 And they besought him that he would not command them to go out into the deep. 32 And there was there an herd of many swine feeding on the mountain: and they besought him that he would suffer them to enter into them. And he suffered them. 33 Then went the devils out of the man, and entered into the swine: and the herd ran violently down a steep place into the lake, and were choked.

The names and some identifying details of several individuals mentioned in this book have been changed to protect their privacy.

—Declaration at the beginning of
The Amityville Horror: A True Story

Tam Mossman, the book's editor at Prentice-Hall, said that "the necessity was—and the author and I agreed on this—was to change the circumstances so that, yes, the book is not strictly true. And yet the intent of what was discovered, or alleged, still remained. But the facts had to be changed simply to protect the guilty or innocent so that Prentice-Hall and the authors were not sued. There are places here where we had to change the facts, alter the facts, or even ascribe them as happening to somebody else, because if we told them straight we would be saddled with a very unhappy private individual or even saddled with a[n]… invasion of privacy suit or even a libel suit."

—Interview with Alex Drehsler & Jim Scovel,
reported in *Newsday*, Nov. 17, 1977

Contents

Foreword by the Author

Those who can make you believe absurdities can make you commit atrocities.

—*Voltaire*

America and the wider world did not first enter a "Post-Truth Era" in 2016 with the election of Donald J. Trump as president of the United States. "Alternative facts" were not invented by U.S. Counselor Kellyanne Conway on January 22, 2017. "Alternative facts," such as those that characterize and define post-truth eras, have existed since early antiquity when, during the course of cultural evolution, science and religion became separate, competing approaches to acquiring knowledge about the world in order to understand the place and status of humanity within it. The first Post-Truth Era was born when deception had been developed into a tool that could be employed by certain classes and groups of people for the purpose of religious, economic, political, or military domination. For several millennia, human beings have had to live in two thought-eras at the same time: an era of scientific modes of enquiry—an era ultimately becoming justifiably describable as a "Truth Era"—and an alternative facts era characterized by reliance on beliefs and disinformation instead of facts—in other words, a "Post-Truth Era."

A Post-Truth Era flourished in what historians have aptly dubbed "The Dark Ages"—the Ages of Faith that followed the fall of the Roman Empire in the west and the suppression and destruction of Greco-Roman science by the early Christian emperors. With the closing of Plato's Academy by the Christian emperor Justinian in 529 CE and the destruction of the Library of Alexandria by Patriarch Theophilus near the end of the fourth century CE, a Christian Post-Truth Era commenced that held sway in the Western World for nearly a thousand years.

The Western World's millennium-long sleep of reason was disrupted by the rediscovery of Greco-Roman arts and sciences, thanks to Muslims who had preserved—and in many cases improved upon—the ancient scientific understanding of how the world works. The Renaissance marked the return of a Truth Era. As scientific understanding of the world expanded from astronomy and mathematics to physics, then to chemistry, agriculture, mining, and finally to biology and psychology, the sphere of "alternative facts" and religious explanations shrank in proportion. With the triumph of Darwinian evolutionary theory at the beginning of the twentieth century in Britain and Western Europe, it appeared that a Truth Era was about to supplant the Post-Truth Era that had perdured in force since the fall of the Roman Empire.

Unfortunately, Darwin's *On the Origin of Species* was not published in America in 1859; rather it entered the world of thought in England. The American Civil War began just two years later and lasted until 1865. When *The Descent of Man, and Selection in Relation to Sex* came out in 1871, many of the most important arguments in favor of the natural selection theory leading up to its publication had never been heard in America. Distracted by the Civil War, Americans paid little attention to Darwin, and acceptance of evolutionary theory in America lagged far behind its advances in England and Western Europe. This was to continue up to the present, when many Republican legislators—at both state and federal levels—are young-earth creationists. Since the Scopes "Monkey Trial" of 1925, Truth-Era understanding and acceptance of evolution advanced slowly until the early 1960s, when the National Science Foundation bankrolled the development of three related editions of a high school biology text. All three versions incorporated evolutionary theory into virtually every part of the course. The texts were wonderful, and I myself was among the first to use them during the three years that I taught high school biology (1963–1966).

The backlash was violent, and it endures to the present. Young-earth creationism, nearly laughed out of the public consciousness after the Scopes Trial, came roaring back to the public arena. Among its most skilled warriors were Henry Morris and Duane T. Gish, debaters skilled in the art of rhetorical fallacy who demolished—in the eyes of their uneducated audiences—famous scientist after famous scientist who had never had to deal with disinformation in any of their previous scientific disputes. With the unexpected success of creationist propaganda, fundamentalist forms of Christianity regained ground. Fundamentalist parochial schools were built, and home-schooling became popular as a means of shielding children from the facts of science. With the growth of fundamentalist belief in the literal inerrancy of their Scriptures came belief not only in a world-wide flood around 2,348 BCE, but a belief that Jesus had cured diseases—and still could do so—by casting out devils and demons.

Belief in devils and demons had never weakened all that much in Roman Catholicism as compared with the Mainline Protestant churches by the time that William Peter Blatty published his novel, *The Exorcist*, in 1971. When the movie version came out at Christmas in 1973, an entire nation was made to solidify opinions on the reality—or not—of demons and devils. The publication of Jay Anson's *The Amityville Horror: A True Story* in 1977 and the release of the film in 1979—and then, the release of the sequel books and films—brought Satan and his minions back into the consciousness of many millions of Americans. The foundation was laid for a "Satanic Panic" that would overwhelm the nation in 1983, when a preschool teacher was accused of subjecting one of his students to satanic ritual abuse. Not many months later, hundreds of children around the country were thought to have been abused in satanic rituals. Even psychologists and law enforcement agents became infected by the ensuing social contagion, arguing about the significance of "recovered memories" of abuse by Satan-worshiping daycare workers. The Satanic Panic led to one of the longest and most expensive criminal trials in American history, not being concluded until 1990, when the original daycare worker was acquitted of dozens of charges that had been leveled against him.

Although the Satanic Panic of the 1980s eventually died down, worries of satanic child abuse never fully disappeared from the list of things that Americans worry about. Then, in November of 2017—the first year of the presidency of Donald J. Trump—"Q Clearance Patriot" appeared on the right-wing message board 4chan, and QAnon was born. Suddenly, famous people—including nearly all present or past Democratic elected officials—were being charged with satanic sexual abuse of children. QAnon followers quickly became allied with President Trump and would become enthusiastic believers in the conspiracy theory that he won the election of 2020. Along with many evangelical Christians, they would figure prominently in the seditious attack on the Capitol of the United States on January 6, 2021. In their minds, the government of the United States had to be overthrown in order to save children from Satan.

Post-truth partisans nearly succeeded in bringing about the extinction of constitutional, representative democracy in America. But there is an even more ominous aspect of the near-success on January 6, 2021 of reality-denying, science-decrying, facts-denying believers in the existence of ghosts and goblins. Such beliefs can be traced back to a time before the development of scientific methods for the discovery of truth—before the dawn of what might be called the Truth Era. Many of the anti-democracy seditionists of 2021 were not just post-truth partisans—believers in "alternative facts"—*they were actually pre-truth thinkers*. Most surely, they were believers in demons such as those whose actions were depicted in *The Exorcist* and *The Amityville Horror: A True Story*.

In the pages that follow, I demonstrate beyond reasonable doubt that almost everything alleged in Anson's book is fictional—at least in the context described. Moreover, I show that there are extremely strong reasons to conclude that at least some degree of fraud was involved in the confection of an alleged "True Story." For evidence-driven thinkers who read this book, my exposé will be welcomed but obvious—perhaps even considered overkill. But for readers who still harbor worries that His Satanic Majesty just possibly might yet stalk the world, I offer this long-delayed inquest into paranormal claims as an anxiolytic—something to dissolve their anxieties and engage their minds in the pleasurable excitement involved in the pursuit of truth.

It is my wish that by demonstrating the falseness of the Amityville story—a story likely accepted as factual by QAnon-type thinkers and their fundamentalist allies—this book will encourage others to join the fight against the pre-truth "alternative facts" that now pose a truly existential threat to American democracy.

Preface

I didn't read ghost stories very often after reaching adulthood. Indeed, as an occasionally organized professor of psychobiology at Fulton-Montgomery Community College in Upstate New York, I rarely had time to read fiction at all. Until November of 1979, I'd had only the vaguest awareness of the existence—let alone the purport—of the book by Jay Anson entitled *The Amityville Horror: A True Story.*

In October of that year, I had just finished the task of shepherding a new course through the College's Curriculum Committee and had managed to convince get the faculty to adopt it into the curriculum. The new course, entitled "Science and Its Imitators," was designed to teach students how to research the facts and evaluate the evidence surrounding such subjects such as astrology, ESP, geometric figures in Bermuda, UFOs, biorhythms, and any other blends of fact and fancy which may someday crawl out of the parascientific woodwork.

No sooner had my course been adopted that it came to my attention that the College Union Board was going to pay nearly a thousand dollars to bring Ed and Lorraine Warren to the college to lecture on "The Amityville Horror." According to the publicity package sent in advance, Lorraine was a clairvoyant and Ed was "one of only seven leading demonologists in the United States."[1]

I was dismayed and delighted at the same time. I was dismayed to see the College lend the dignity of its name to such a presentation and waste so much money on such obvious humbug. But I was delighted because I would soon have a chance to give a public demonstration of the skills I hoped to teach in my new course. I reserved the College's Little Theater for December 6—the day after the Warren's lecture—and put up signs announcing that I would give a free, public lecture entitled "The Amityville Folly." I had not yet read Anson's book! I had barely two weeks to read the book, make some telephone calls to Amityville, check some microfilms of Long Island newspapers, and prepare to meet a demonologist for the first time in my life.

---

[1] I never was able to discover the criteria used to rank demonologists nor could I identify the agency that issues such ratings.

To my utter astonishment and glee, *The Amityville Horror: A True Story* fell apart almost immediately after I began to pry into its evidential crevices. I quickly was able to prove that much material had been copied from William Peter Blatty's novel, *The Exorcist* although I had not suspected that so much material in *The Amityville Horror* had been obtained from William Weber, the defense attorney for the murderer Ronnie DeFeo, whose murder of his parents and three siblings had taken place in the horror house prior to its occupation by the Lutzes. The actual encounter with the Warrens turned out to be a boring disappointment (I almost fell asleep during their presentation), but my lecture the next day was quite successful. I had such a mountain of evidence that my only problem was to avoid "overkill," lest I cause my audience to sympathize with these purveyors of the preposterous. After the dust had settled, I looked at the mounds of material I had collected while over-preparing for my lecture. I had collected enough material to write a book! After several visits to Amityville, I was struck by the realization that the *real* story behind *The Amityville Horror* was much more fascinating and curious than the fictionalized fatuities presented as fact in Anson's book.

I called the publisher of a major publishing house specializing in books and magazines examining paranormal and supernatural claims. I described my research and findings and asked if I might submit an article for publication in one of the publisher's magazines. My call was received with enthusiasm, and I was asked if I might have enough information with which to write a book. I had not yet been able to obtain the transcript of a civil trial held in in the United States District Court in Brooklyn, New York on September 10, 1979, in which the Lutzes—the major protagonists of the horror story—had been sued for fraud. I said that I was certain the information in the transcript of that trial would be crucial, but the transcript would cost about five hundred dollars.

I was asked if I could write in "a popular, journalistic style," and I replied that it was my normal writing style. Then the publisher informed me there were rumors that the new owners of the horror house were probably going to publish a debunking book, and it would be necessary to write with lightning speed in order to get the scoop on the new owners of the house. If I were to visit Amityville, I would have to avoid interviewing anyone who might tip them off about a possible rival.

The Christmas-New Year's winter recess at the college was coming up in less than two weeks. I was scheduled to teach a three-week "minicourse" in non-majors' biology, but I told the publisher I could get someone else to teach the course and would have twenty-one days to write full-time. Given how much was already written, I probably could have a completed book in about six weeks if I had the expected treasure-trove of damaging information to be found in the trial transcript. To my surprise, I was told that I would be reimbursed for the transcripts by a publisher's advance. After detailed discussion, I believed we had a verbal agreement, and I would receive not only a written contract but also a check to reimburse the cost of the transcripts.

After hanging up the telephone that Thursday afternoon, I immediately called the college Dean to find someone else to teach my course, thus forfeiting the take-home pay of about eight hundred dollars. I wrote a check for $500 and a letter to the Brooklyn court specifying the desired transcripts. My teaching schedule was such that I had no Monday teaching duties. So, if I left for Amityville the next day after my last class, I would have three full days to surveil the horror-house neighborhood, visit the Amityville Historical Society, the Amityville public library, the Amityville police department, a Catholic church, and other agencies and persons that figured prominently in the horror story. Unfortunately, I would not be able to inspect the inside of the house at 112 Ocean Avenue, nor could I interview the neighbors. Even so, I was confident that I could expose the fraud that even by then was yielding millions of dollars of profits to the Lutzes, Prentice-Hall, and the author of the horror book, Jay Anson.

As soon as I returned from Amityville, I began to write *The Amityville Humbug*. The first week of the mid-winter recess ended, and I realized I had not yet received either a written contract or a publisher's advance. I called the publisher's office but was unable to reach him. I made a number of calls over the next week, always to no avail. Nevertheless, I continued to spend twelve hours per day typing out my exposé on my portable electric typewriter. By the end of the recess, I had written about eighty percent of the desired book.

At last, I was able to reach the publisher. He didn't know who I was, or what book I was talking about! I was told that book contracts are never made on the telephone, and they never paid advances. I was invited to submit my manuscript to the editorial committee. Completely shaken, I did as I was bidden. About a month later, my manuscript was returned with a note explaining that they were an academic and scientific publishing house and that my book had been written in "a popular, journalistic style"—exactly what I had been commissioned to do!

I stopped writing my exposé and packed my manuscripts, interview notes, and reference books and materials into a large cardboard box—a box that would not be opened until more than forty years later.

Early in the spring of 2020, I began to sort through my libraries and file cabinets to see which books, manuscripts, records, and Freethought memorabilia needed to be transported to Cranford, New Jersey, to be deposited in the Charles E. Stevens American Atheist Library and Archives. I filled seventy-nine large crates for transport to New Jersey. One of them contained just the large cardboard box in which my unfinished *Amityville Humbug* manuscript had been placed, along with all the associated research materials. As I examined the contents for the first time since 1980, I was astonished at how much work had gone into my research. I had prints of many, many pages of magazine and newspaper articles; the 500-page transcript of the Brooklyn trial; notes of interviews with important sources in Amityville; day-by-day weather records pertaining to the events alleged in the horror book; correspondence with Amityville sources; evidence that I had actually been allowed to take notes from the auction catalog itemizing materials abandoned in the horror house and talk with the realtor who sold the house to George and Kathy Lutz, and much more. I even had a copy of the report of one of the two polygraph tests that the Lutzes had undergone in order to validate their claims!

I couldn't let all that research disappear into oblivion—especially now that in the intervening years the Amityville fraud had turned into an industry grossing hundreds of millions of dollars. I kept the seventy-ninth crate at home, vowing to complete the project before I cashed my chips in. Fortunately, I have managed to stall the Reaper long enough to be able to place *The Amityville Horror: An Inquest into Paranormal Claims* before the reader.

Introduction: Discourse on Method

"When anyone tells me, that he saw a dead man restored to life, I immediately consider with myself, whether it be more probable, that this person should either deceive or be deceived, or that the fact, which he relates, should really have happened; I weigh the one miracle against the other; and according to the superiority, which I discover, I pronounce my decision, and always reject the greater miracle. If the falsehood of his testimony would be more miraculous, than the event which he relates; then, and not till then, can he pretend to command my belief or opinion."

—*David Hume* On Miracles

My investigation of *The Amityville Horror: A True Story* was intended to make the most of a "teaching moment" and show students in my newly created course, "Science & Its Imitators," how to investigate claims of the paranormal and supernatural. Even before the investigation had been carried out—let alone completed—it was intended to be an evolving lesson in method. At the very beginning of the course, before the Amityville case became an issue of interest, I had lectured my students on the philosophy and methods of science.

The Meaning of Meaning and the Nature of Science

First, I discussed David Hume's principle that "…no testimony is sufficient to establish a miracle [*in the context of my course, any paranormal or supernatural claim*], unless the testimony be of such a kind, that its falsehood would be more miraculous [*i.e., more unbelievable*] than the fact which it endeavors to establish." Science by its very nature is biased against miracles.

Second, I discussed the "Falsifiability Principle" of the modern philosopher of science, Karl Popper, and the "Verifiability Principle" of A.J. Ayer and the Logical Positivists. I concluded with my generalization of their views, my "Testability Principle." I explained that science can only deal with claims and propositions that are—at least in principle—capable of being tested. Those that cannot be tested even in the imagination are scientifically meaningless. They cannot even be false.

To illustrate my philosophical method, I contrasted two propositions:

(1) The moon is made of green cheese.
(2) Undetectable gremlins inhabit the rings of Saturn.

The first statement is a proposition that could be tested at least in the imagination long before humans first set foot on the moon—or even before the advent of absorption spectroscopy. Without violating any known principles of science, one could imagine walking on the moon, picking up the substrate, and checking to see if it was green cheese or not. The first statement is scientifically meaningful. It is now known to be false.

The second statement, however, is fundamentally different. It cannot be tested even in the imagination. One could fly a rocket containing NASA's most sensitive gremlinometers to the rings of Saturn, but undetectable gremlins would, by definition, remain undetected. There is no way to "prove" that undetectable gremlins inhabit the rings of Saturn. The second statement is untestable and scientifically meaningless. It cannot even be false.

In my discussion of the scientific method, I explained that above all else, scientific explanations must avoid a fallacy first identified by Medieval philosophers: *ignotum per ignotius*, the act of trying to explain the unknown in terms of the even more unknown. To illustrate the problem, I discussed the American Enlightenment solution to the question, "What is lightning?"

Clergy at the time of the American Revolution considered lightning to be an instrument of God's wrath, a divine force wielded in judgement of wicked men and institutions. Why it struck church steeples more often than it struck oak trees seems to have remained an unsolved theological problem. The clerical explanation sought to explain an observable phenomenon in terms of something that was more inscrutable, more unknown, and more difficult to investigate—indeed, something unknowable—the will of an undetectable divine being.

Benjamin Franklin, as is well known, had done fundamental experiments trying to understand the nature of electricity and to discover the "laws" governing electrical behavior. After his kite experiment, he was able to show that lightning shared all the properties of electricity that were known at the time. He was able to explain an unknown phenomenon—lightning—in terms of something better known and understood at the time: electricity. On the practical level, Franklin's discovery led to the life-saving invention of the lightning rod. To be sure, we still haven't fully explained electricity, but all progress in science since Franklin has involved explaining the unknown in terms of the better known.

Finally, I explained that in formulating scientific theories—the highest level of scientific explanation—research had to be exhaustive. Every fact or phenomenon even remotely related to a hypothesis seeking to be elevated to theory level had to be accounted for. To become a theory, a hypothesis had to be able to account for everything known at the time. Then, if something was discovered later that did not fit into the theory, the theory would have to be amended wherever possible. If not, the theory would eventually have to be discarded.

Investigative Methodology

In order to investigate the paranormal claims of *The Amityville Horror: A True Story*, a series of important tasks had to be carried out. Since my Amityville investigation was to be as scientific as possible, my inquest had to be as exhaustive as feasible given the constraints both of resources and time. My findings had to explain the greatest number of facts possible. It had to deal with as many claims of the *True Story* as I could investigate.

Obviously, I had to carry out a very close reading of the book. The only edition of the book that was immediately available to me at the time was the seventeenth printing of the paperback version, and so that was the first version I read. As I read it, I underlined in red all sentences alluding to claims suitable and capable of investigation. That included names of persons, institutions, almanac and weather conditions, and anything else that seemed susceptible to fact-checking. Sometime after reading the paperback, I found an article that indicated numerous changes had been made between the early printings of the hardcover edition and the paperback edition. Unfortunately, the only hardcover copy I was able to obtain had already been changed to agree with the paperback, and I was limited to investigating the changes reported in secondary sources until I could examine an earlier printing of the hardcover edition. It was only after I was able to obtain a transcript of a Federal Court trial in which the Lutzes (the protagonists of the horror story) were being sued for fraud that I would come to understand the reasons for the changes in the text.

Among the changes noted in the early reports were alterations of the room assignments shown in the floorplans of the horror house. That, combined with references in Anson's book to blueprints for the house that I encountered as I tried to resolve spatial relations implied in certain episodes of the story, prompted a failed effort to obtain copies of the blueprints that I could study. Only in the Age of the Internet, forty years later, could I procure the authentic blueprints for the house that appeared in a slightly simplified form in the book.

Weather Records Crack Open the Case

As I read the book for the first time, I was struck by the extraordinarily violent or extreme weather conditions that were reported. It seemed significant that many of the episodes were crucially dependent upon weather conditions: pig tracks in the snow; extreme cold making it hard or impossible to start cars; hurricane-force winds knocking out power in Amityville, leading to the need for a candle during room-by-room exorcism of the horror house; heavy rain flooding the house through demonically opened windows; and so forth. It was easy enough—even in the modest library of the community college in which I was teaching—to make microfilm prints of *The New York Times* weather reports for the 28 days allegedly chronicled in the book. As soon as the daily records were compared with the corresponding dates in the book, many of the most frightening claims of the book fell apart. The first fabrication to fall were the alleged pig-tracks in the snow. There had been no snowfall. In fact, there had been almost no precipitation at all in the days prior to the alleged event.

Shortly after I had printed out the weather reports for the days the Lutzes claimed to have been living in the house, I faintly remembered reading something about the horror house in the pages of *The Skeptical Inquirer/The Zetetic* over a year earlier. I was a charter subscriber to the journal, and I possessed all the issues published before November of 1979. In the Spring/Summer 1978 issue of the magazine, I found a review of *The Amityville Horror* written by Robert L. Morris. It immediately corroborated my findings and pointed to a host of other issues that needed to be investigated.

Library Research

It quickly became apparent that I needed the resources of a much larger library in which to carry out an exhaustive search of periodicals carrying information about the book. And so, I went to the State University of New York (Albany) library to search for "Amityville," "*Amityville Horror*," and "Jay Anson" in *Readers' Guide to Periodical Literature* and the index to *The New York Times*. I made a list of all available references. With the aid of a reference librarian, I was able to discover the names of several newspapers that were not covered in *Readers' Guide*, including several covering the Amityville area. I listed them and made plans to go to Amityville to see if any of them had published anything about the horror story.

Once I had a list of all available references, I proceeded to find microfilms for all that were available, and then I made prints to take home for study. For articles in journals for which microfilms were not available, I requested photocopies from Interlibrary Loan at Fulton-Montgomery Community College (SUNY), my home college.

Once at home, I read everything, taking notes and underlining or highlighting in yellow key facts and references. I discovered that there were several published accounts of the Lutzes' experiences in the horror house that seemed to reveal earlier, simpler versions of more extreme episodes recounted in Anson's book. I made charts of all the contradictions, omissions, or additions discovered as compared to Anson's version. In several articles that were critical of Anson's book, I jotted down all the findings in the margins at their corresponding position in the paperback edition of *The Amityville Horror*.

The Exorcist in the Background

Various articles I obtained discussed Jay Anson's authorial history, including his prior work on a documentary about the filming of the movie version of William Peter Blatty's *The Exorcist*. I realized I needed to discover all I could about the author, hoping to find clues relating to the claims of his book. It immediately became obvious that I would have to read *The Exorcist* to orient myself in the experiential world of the author of *A True Story*.

Close Readings and Indexing Required

I obtained a paperback edition of *The Exorcist* and subjected it to the same close reading done with *The Amityville Horror*. Because of Anson's association with the filming of *The Exorcist*, I remained vigilant to see if there were any parallels between it and *The Amityville Horror*. In my close reading of *The Exorcist*, I noted all similarities to *The Amityville Horror*. Forty years later, when I had forgotten even the main plot of the novel, not only did I have to re-read the book, I had to make a coarse-grained, key-word index of the book to assist in finding further parallels to the Amityville novel.

Since several newspaper articles mentioned lawsuits involving the Lutzes, I had to find citations giving the legal style of the cases to see how the cases had been settled. That required a visit to the nearest law library and the help of a reference librarian. Since an important case alleging fraud had been settled out of court, I had to obtain the 500-page transcript of the trial that had been held in US Federal Court in Brooklyn, New York. Lamentably, because the case was now sealed, I could not examine the various depositions that had been made, nor could I examine the many exhibits presented at the trial.

A close reading of the trial transcript immediately showed that much of *The Amityville Horror: A True Story* was far from truthful. Forty years later, when I decided to complete this book, it was hard to relate material in the court transcript to specific parts of my manuscript that had been written decades ago. It was necessary to create a detailed key-word index to the transcript so that as I reworked the earlier manuscript, I could immediately find the relevant passages in the trial transcript.

Unfortunately, I quickly realized that over the course of forty years, I had completely lost control of the details of the horror story itself and had to make a detailed key-work index of *The Amityville Horror*, as well. Although this was a tedious and time-consuming task, it entailed another close reading of the Anson text—a reading that led to several hitherto overlooked problems.

One amusing problem was a detail I had overlooked between my first reading of page 77 and page 100. Page 77 deals with the events of Saturday, December 27, 1975, and it mentions that the Lutzes returned from the wedding reception of Kathy's brother, Jimmy, at three AM. By inference, her brother and his bride would have flown to Bermuda for their honeymoon sometime later that Saturday morning. Page 100 deals with events of Monday, December 29, 1975—just a bit more than two days after Kathy's brother left for Bermuda. Page 100 of the paperback tells us, "After George drove off that morning, Kathy's mother called to tell her that she had received a card from Jimmy and Carey in Bermuda…"

Why was this amusing? When we recall that postcards have the lowest priority of ordinary mail, that Bermuda is a foreign country, and that almost all post offices are closed on Sundays, it became apparent that the greatest paranormal event of the whole book had not been noted by Anson at all: the telekinetic transport of a postcard from Bermuda to a mailbox in West Babylon on Long Island, New York!

Time-Line Charting of *Amityville Horror* Claims, News Reports, and Trial Transcript Data

Since the book purported to be a day-by-day account of the Lutzes' stay in the house at 112 Ocean Avenue, I had to purchase a wide roll of shelf paper in 1978 on which to construct a time-line calendar, creating very large cells in which to note each day's events as alleged in the book, together with any contradictory evidence that might be collected during my research. After the trial transcript had been obtained, dates of events established at the trial were added to the time-line chart.

It quickly became obvious that just as there was an important relationship between *The Exorcist* and the *Amityville* story, details of the DeFeo murders and the trial of Ronnie ("Butch") DeFeo (the backstory of Anson's tale) might also prove to be intimately intertwined with the story alleged by the Lutzes. I had to go back to the university library to research the DeFeo murders and make microfilm prints as needed to understand possible relationships between the murder case and the horror story.

In addition to the time-line calendar made for the horror story, I made a similar time-line calendar for everything I learned about: (1) the events surrounding the DeFeo murders that occurred in the horror house; (2)

everything learned about how the *Amityville Horror* related to the DeFeo murders; (3) the persons (including lawyers) associated with the DeFeo trial; (4) everyone involved in the publishing of the horror book; and (5) all facts established in the fraud trial of the Lutzes.

Since many events in the book involved extraordinary claims about weather conditions and the phase of the moon, I zeroed in on all the places in the book where the events were ruled out by the actual weather conditions. Then, I had to try to figure out where Anson obtained his material to fill in the days where the events reported were ruled out by the weather records.

Numerous trips were made to Long Island to visit Amityville. I surveilled and photographed the horror house and familiarized myself with the neighborhood. Since my verbal publishing agreement stressed that I had to work in secrecy because it was thought the new owners were writing their own exposé, I was not allowed to interview the new owners or their neighbors. For financial reasons, my publisher needed to publish before they did, and so I was not able to request a personal tour of the house—a serious liability as contradictory floorplans had been published and I would only discover much later that several events alleged in the horror story were ruled out by the actual floorplan of the house.

Investigations in Amityville

Because of various claims alleged in *The Amityville Horror*, I needed to visit the Amityville Historical Society and The Amityville Free Library to interview staff and make copies of materials in their collections. At the Historical Society, I sought materials pertaining to the history of the house at 112 Ocean Avenue. At the Library, I was able to copy articles and clippings of stories pertaining to various claims of the horror bestseller and its author.

On one trip to Amityville, I sought interviews with the police, priests at the Catholic church closest to the horror house, and Edith Evens, the realtor who sold the house to the Lutzes. As it turned out, she had detailed knowledge not only of the layout of the house, but also of the furnishings. Best of all, she had a copy of the auction catalog listing the contents of the horror house when it was sold by the bank that reclaimed the house after its abandonment by the Lutzes. The catalog included a photograph of the ceramic lion alleged to have been telekinetically moved about in the horror house. Details of that photograph would prove to be convincing refutation of several events claimed to have occurred in Anson's book.

When I visited the house forty years later, I discovered that 112 Ocean Avenue had become 108 Ocean Avenue. The emblematic jack-o-lantern, quarter-moon windows at the front of the third floor had been replaced by ordinary rectangular windows. The dark-shingled exterior of the house had been painted white, the in-ground, heated swimming pool was gone, and a beautiful enclosed sunporch had been added to the back of the house, facing the water. Because the neighborhood is still plagued by parades of the preternaturally curious, parking is strictly prohibited in a rather large zone surrounding the house. I had to park more than a block away and walk back to the house in order to take the photographs printed in this book.

Explaining the Unknown with the Known

I have already explained how the research carried out for this book was originally intended to serve as a lesson in methodology for my course "Science & Its Imitators"—a demonstration of how to explore one type of claim of paranormal (supernatural) phenomena. A year after I discontinued work on this book, Richard E. Blowers, a student in my class, investigated *Amityville Horror* publicity claims touting a polygraph test allegedly passed by George and Kathy Lutz as they sought to bolster their credibility in the public and in the press. Mr. Blowers' term paper, "A Report on the Polygraph Test Administered to George and Kathy Lutz," along with the official report of the polygraph test, made it possible for me to write part of Chapter 37.

The investigative methodology acquired by my class by the end of the course was surprisingly common-sensical and unsophisticated. It was just one more example of needing to explain the unknown in terms of the known. Once the first facts about the case had been discovered, they led to new facts; those in turn led to further discoveries.

Once weather records had shown the impossibility of certain key episodes in the book, the problem of explaining the origins of the false episodes cried out for investigation. That led to investigation of Jay Anson's connection to *The Exorcist* and the discovery of earlier, simpler versions of various episodes. Discovery of the earlier versions led to a discovery of the lawsuit in which the Lutzes were sued for fraud. That led to a complete collapse of *The Amityville Horror* as "a true story." Only curious, small details yet remain to be explained by the obsessive author of this book.

Fig. 1 The Amityville house at 112 Ocean Avenue where Ronald DeFeo murdered his family on November 13, 1974, as it appeared the following day. (Photo by Stan Wolfson/Newsday RM via Getty Images)

Fig. 2 The Amityville house now at 108 Ocean Avenue as it appeared in November of 2020. It was repainted and remodeled after the abandonment of the house by the Lutz family in January of 1976. Photo shows west (Ocean Avenue) and south sides of house.

Fig. 3 Photo showing the north (rear) and west sides of the horror house and its distance from the neighbor on the north side. The narrow projection from the north wall is the rear entrance to the house.

Fig. 4 Photo showing the south (front) and west walls of the horror house and its distance from the neighbor on the south side. The main entrance that allegedly had a 250-pound wooden door is beneath the narrow triangular projection from the south wall.

Part I: The Background and The Back Story

The parades began as early as eight o'clock in the October mornings of 1977. The cars would slow to a crawl so passengers could gawk at the house located at 112 Ocean Avenue, Amityville, New York. They would then circle the block and come back for a second look at the attractive Dutch Colonial. Processions would continue sporadically throughout the day, increasing in numbers as the witching hour of 3:15 AM approached—the credulous straining to see if a red-eyed pig still haunted the place. More than forty years after *The Amityville Horror: A True Story*, the public's fascination with the house has not died down yet, although there are no more parades.

In order to understand the origins of the book that triggered all that excitement and curiosity, it is important to understand the backstory of the Ocean Avenue home. Many of the motifs and events of *The Amityville Horror* are predicated upon and incorporate elements of that story—the story of the DeFeo murders.

The DeFeo Murders

Long before the Lutz family "fled in terror" after 28 days in the horror house, it had already become well known to the public, its picture appearing in *The New York Times* as well as in the local Long Island newspapers. Its notoriety had begun on November 13, 1974, when in the early morning hours Ronald DeFeo Jr. killed his mother, father, two sisters and two brothers. The murders would not be soon forgotten, nor would the house in which they had occurred.

The day after the murders, *The New York Times* reported that all but one of the seven members of Ronald DeFeo's family had been found murdered in their sleep in Amityville, a posh community on Long Island's South Shore. The dead were listed as being Ronald DeFeo, Sr., 43; his wife Louise, 42; his daughters Dawn, 18 and Allison, 13; and his two sons Mark, 12 and John, 7. The Suffolk County police reported that all six bodies were wearing night clothes and that the victims had likely been killed in their sleep. *The Times* said that the bodies were discovered at about 6:15 P.M. on the thirteenth by the oldest son, Ronald Jr., 23. He supposedly had just returned home from "business." Police were quoted as saying that DeFeo Sr. had worked for several years for his father-in-law at Brigante-Karl, a large Buick dealership in Brooklyn where Ronald Jr. also worked.

The article contained a small map which showed how Ocean Avenue extends from Montauk Highway, the main east-west highway on Long Island's South Shore, to the Great South Bay, located several blocks south of the highway. It was noted that the DeFeo home had a swimming pool in the back yard and religious statuary in the front yard. Neighbors were reported as saying that the DeFeos had been very religious and attended mass regularly.

On the same day as *The Times* article, *Newsday* had a somewhat more detailed account of the murders. *Newsday* is perhaps Long Island's major news source, and so its first article on the massacre benefited from the input of six local reporters. Ronald "Butch" DeFeo Jr., it reported, had returned home from work at about 6 P.M. and, because of some mix-up with keys, had to climb through a window to enter the house. Finding the bodies, he drove to Henry's Bar, located half a mile away on Merrick Road (Montauk Highway). He then ran into the bar shouting, "My father and mother have been shot!"

Accompanied by four friends, Butch returned to the house and called the police. When the police arrived, they found each of the victims in bed, with "one bullet in the back." It was reported that the family had been killed "between 5:45 and 9 yesterday morning." One of the neighbors confirmed that at about 3 AM, the two DeFeo dogs had barked loudly and continuously for about 20 minutes.

The *Newsday* article was replete with a floorplan of the second floor of the house, showing the location of all the bodies with the exception of Dawn, the eighteen-year-old daughter, who was found on the third floor. The family had lived in the house for nine years, it was said, having come originally from Brooklyn. The statuary in the front yard was identified as being a lighted shrine of St. Joseph holding the infant Jesus, surrounded by three adoring angels.

DeFeo Charged as Slayer

By the following day, November 15, both newspapers were telling a somewhat different story: young Butch DeFeo himself was being held as the slayer of his family. *Newsday* showed pictures of the bearded Ronald "Butch" DeFeo, Jr., his sisters Dawn and Allison, and the three rifles which had been removed from the house. *The New York Times* carried a picture of the now infamous house, which showed a sign in the front yard reading "High Hopes" in Gothic letters.

According to *Newsday,* Ronald DeFeo had shot up heroin with a girlfriend after he had shot his family. The father and mother had been shot twice in the back, the two boys once in the back, and the two girls had each been shot once in the head. Then began a bewildering series of contradictory reports of how many times each victim had been shot and where the bullets had entered their bodies. Chief Mellon, heading an investigation that combined both Suffolk County and Amityville Police Forces, said there was no sign of any struggle.

As reconstructed by *The Times*, the events leading up to Butch being charged with the killings began on Tuesday, November 12, 1974. Mr. DeFeo Sr. and his son both reported for work at the Buick Dealership that Tuesday morning. It would later be reported that the two men were quarreling that day over an event which had taken place two weeks earlier, on November 1. On that day, Ronald Jr., while riding in his car with a garage mechanic, supposedly had been the victim of a hold-up. Butch claimed that some $19,000 of Dealership funds were lost to a person with a shotgun. It had become apparent to DeFeo Sr. that his son was more involved in the incident than he had admitted. This had led to quarrels, with DeFeo, Sr. exclaiming at one point, "I've got a devil on my back!"

Butch told the police that he had returned home late on Tuesday night and had gone straight to bed. Although he had slept in the house Tuesday night, he had not heard the shots which killed everyone but him. He awoke around 7 A.M. and went to work the next day. He claimed to have discovered the bodies only upon returning home at 6:38 P.M.

The elder Ronald DeFeo's absence from work that day had not seemed particularly unusual as he often went away on business without notifying his colleagues. Butch left work early, between noon and 1:00 P.M., and was seen by neighbors in the Ocean Avenue vicinity during the afternoon. He had made several appearances at Henry's Bar before his dramatic return shortly before 7 P.M, shouting that his parents had been shot.

The Suffolk County police arrived on scene by 7 P.M. and found the bodies of the elder DeFeos in addition to those of the four children. On the morning of Friday the 15th, Butch was arraigned on one count of second-degree murder (of his brother Mark) and was sent to the county jail in Riverhead to await trail.

DeFeo's Confession

Subsequent newspaper articles told how Ronald "Butch" DeFeo Jr. had confessed to killing his family Wednesday morning around 3:30 AM, how he had been under a special narcotics probation at the time of the murders, and how the previous April a girlfriend had turned him in as a drug user.

This was not Butch's first brush with the law. He had previously been convicted of stealing a $1,750 outboard motor in September of the previous year and had a reputation not only for using heroin but LSD and other hallucinogens, as well. Neighbors described him as an addict who drank and got into brawls in local bars.

DeFeo's Possible Motives

What was Butch's motive for killing his family? There were insurance policies possibly totaling $200,000, and the young DeFeo, as sole survivor, would have collected all the money. But by Sunday, November 17, 1974, the young DeFeo had been implicated in the theft of $19,000 from his grandfather's automobile dealership. The employee of the dealership who had been with DeFeo at the time of the "hold-up" had been charged with aiding and abetting in the theft, now believed to have been master-minded by the twenty-three-year-old Ronald DeFeo Jr.

There were reports that father and son had argued about the loss of the company funds, which Butch said had been taken from him at gunpoint. It was reported in *The Times* that the elder DeFeo had been skeptical of this account of the money's disappearance. It is, I think, extremely probable that DeFeo, Sr. had figured his son out.

Butch's friend, Robert Kelske, said he had witnessed father and son fighting over the robbery on the Saturday preceding the killings. On Monday the 11th, two days before the murders, a nine-year-old friend of John DeFeo had witnessed a fistfight between father and son in the basement of the house. The boy testified later that they had been shouting at each other about money. Earlier that same day, the elder DeFeo had left work early, telling his coworkers that he was going to have a confrontation with his son over the alleged payroll robbery.

Although an attempt was made later to show that DeFeo's motive was the theft of a cache of money and jewels hidden in the closet of the master bedroom,[1] it seems more likely that the precipitating factor behind the killings was Butch's fear of what his father intended to do about his involvement in the dealership robbery. The murders seem to have been the culmination of an inexorably escalating war between the junior and senior DeFeos. The remainder of the family was killed in the overflow of the bloodlust evoked by the killing of the father. Butch later confessed, "Once I started, I couldn't stop."

The first lawyer to represent Butch's defense had asked for a psychiatric examination of the young man but had been turned down. The lawyer then pointed out that DeFeo had fresh bruises, implying he had been roughed up during questioning. Then the murder weapon—a .35 caliber

---

[1] In the Epilogue of the 1981 book *High Hopes: The Amityville Murders* written by Gerard Sullivan, the prosecutor in the DeFeo trial, and Harvey Aronson, there was credible testimony that DeFeo had indeed stolen the jewels and $200,000 in cash and buried it in a small park less than two blocks away from 112 Ocean Avenue. Sullivan says that a shovel was found in the trunk of DeFeo's Buick.

Marlin hunting rifle—was found near the DeFeo home in the Amityville Creek[2] at the foot of Ocean Avenue, twenty to twenty-five feet from the dock.

For security purposes, DeFeo's arraignment had taken place on Friday, November 15, 1974 in the chapel of the county jail. Meanwhile, the police lab in Hauppauge confirmed that the bullets in the gun matched the ones found in the six bodies.

According to an article appearing in *Newsday*, the bodies of the slain DeFeos were taken to a funeral home in Deer Park where George Lutz was living at the time. It is interesting to speculate that this possible initial encounter with the DeFeo tragedy may have had a lasting, unconscious effect upon Mr. Lutz, preconditioning him toward a horrific interpretation of his own experiences later when he moved into the DeFeo house. However that may be, the DeFeo funeral was held at St. Martin of Tours Roman Catholic Church in Amityville on Monday, November 18. The entire parochial school attended the funeral. Their burial followed at the St. Charles Cemetery in nearby Pinelawn.

A Lingering Mystery

There are many episodes in *The Amityville Horror* that reflect a puzzle never completely solved: How was DeFeo able to carry out all the shootings without at least some members of the family awakening and leaving their beds. Why weren't bodies found all over the house, instead of all in their beds, face down, with their hands raised over their heads? And why did none of the neighbors hear the gunshots?

It was initially reported that Butch had perhaps drugged his family at supper and later killed them leisurely while they were in a drugged condition. The Medical Examiner, however, was unable to demonstrate any trace of such drugs in the bodies.[3]

There are two possible reasons the neighbors did not hear the shots. Firstly, a neighbor reported loud barking of the DeFeo dogs which, in conjunction with closed windows and storm windows, could have effectively prevented neighbors from being aware of the sound of shots. Secondly, I was told by several members of the Amityville Police Department that there were very strong, noisy winds at the time of the killings. Of course, the large size

---

2 The body of water confusingly referred to as a creek, canal, or river is actually a triangular, narrow embayment of saltwater, with its base along the shoreline of the Great South Bay, and its apex touching the south side of Merrick Road, north of the horror house. The DeFeo property extends from the western shore of this embayment on the east to Ocean Avenue on the west.

3 Later evidence made it clear that Mrs. DeFeo had indeed awakened after her husband was shot, and that one of DeFeo's sisters had even gotten out of bed. It was also clear that all the bodies had been placed face-down in ritual positions after being killed.

of the house itself would have assisted in muffling the shots significantly. The neighboring houses are also not very close to the murder house, and the neighbors would have been deep asleep at the time of the gunshots. The muffled sounds of the shots had most likely not have been loud enough to awaken them. Apparently, only the sound of barking dogs was loud enough to do that.

Whatever the real explanation may prove to be if in fact the family did sleep through their execution, both *The Amityville Horror: A True Story* and a later book by the ghost-hunting Hans Holzer, entitled *Murder in Amityville,* implied that a supernatural explanation was necessary. According to Holzer, only a supernatural, soporific force could have held the victims motionless, in ritual positions, until Butch got around to deciding just which bullet he should place where.

THE DEFEO TRIAL

The murder trial of Ronald DeFeo, Jr. was the longest in the history of Suffolk County at the time. To some, it could also be considered one of the most interesting. Between the beginning of the pre-trial hearing (which began on September 22, 1975) and Ronald DeFeo being sentenced to six consecutive life-terms (on December fourth of the same year—just two weeks before George and Kathy Lutz were to move into the horror house), enough words were written, spoken, shouted, and read in connection with the affair to write a decently-detailed history of the world.

Presiding over the trial, which took place in Riverhead, Long Island, was State Supreme Court Justice Thomas Stark. The attorney for DeFeo's defense was Mr. William Weber, and the prosecuting attorney was Mr. Gerard Sullivan, the Assistant District Attorney.[1]

The scale of the proceedings was worthy of a Cecil B. DeMille production. There was a "cast" of more than fifty witnesses and a veritable mountain of evidence was displayed on a tabletop in the Riverhead courtroom. Included among the 150 items were the .35-caliber Marlin rifle, which had been identified as the murder weapon, and color photos of the victims' bodies. Fortunately, only a small portion of the trial's material is needed as background for understanding the case's relevancy to *The Amityville Horror: A True Story*.

Although there was little doubt from the beginning of the proceedings that Ronald DeFeo had indeed killed his family, there was a dispute as to the circumstances under which he had signed his confession. An attempt was made by Mr. Weber, the court-appointed defender, to show that Ronald had been denied the counsel of a lawyer at a critical, early stage in the proceedings, and that he had been beaten into signing a trumped-up confession. But neither assertion held up under scrutiny.

DeFeo claimed that he had been beaten, blackjacked, and slammed into a wall by interrogators during an all-night ordeal after the bodies of his family had been discovered. He did, however, admit that he had initialed

[1] In 1981, with the assistance of Harvey Aronson, Attorney Sullivan published *High Hopes: The Amityville Murders* (Coward, McCann & Geoghegan, New York), a book considered to be the definitive account of the DeFeo murders.

diagrams showing where he had dumped bloody clothing, spent cartridges, and the murder weapon. Medical records were cited to show that DeFeo had bruises on his body and face immediately after the confession. However, a witness later testified that DeFeo was in a fist fight with his father the day before the murder, and that the bruises had been caused by his father, not by detectives.

The Confession

As described in chapters six and seven of Prosecuting Attorney Gerard Sullivan's book, High Hopes: the Amityville Murders, the manner in which Detective Dennis W. Rafferty of the Suffolk County Police Department led DeFeo into confessing was a classic demonstration of the interrogator's art. While consoling Butch on the loss of his family, Rafferty led him to speculate that the shootings must have occurred between 2:00 and 4:00 o'clock in the morning—while DeFeo says he was sleeping in the TV room.

"Butch," Rafferty said, "you must have heard something. We have a lot of shots. You had to hear something. How about the dog? Did you hear the dog barking? Did you hear any shots at all?" DeFeo said he heard no shots.

At that point, Detective Dunn picked up the interrogation. He ventured that DeFeo must have heard something but was ashamed to admit it. He must have been very scared. Butch then admitted he did hear two shots, and Rafferty resumed the questioning, asking him when he heard the shots. He replied, "About 4:00 o'clock I was lying in there on the floor in the TV room, and I heard what appeared to be two shots. And I was scared. I just waited for about 20 minutes, and then I left. I got up.... I just left....Then I left and I went to work."

Rafferty chided him about hearing two shots but leaving the house without checking to see if anyone was wounded and needed help. He said he found that very unbelievable. If he heard two shots he must have heard more since more than two shots had been fired. DeFeo conceded he did hear more than two shots. With prodding, he admitted to hearing seven shots, relating each one to the rooms of the victims. Rafferty said he must have been terrified when he heard this, and Butch said he "was scared shit" and he stayed in the TV room for about twenty minutes, then went upstairs, got dressed, and left the house.

"You just went out of the house?" Rafferty asked. "Now you hear seven shots. You now know your family is wiped out, and you just leave the house? You didn't even check them?" Butch said he was scared. "You should have seen me driving." Rafferty chided him again, "You didn't know they were dead. Maybe they needed help. Maybe they were only wounded, or at least maybe some of them, or one of them was wounded?"

DeFeo admitted that he did check his mother and father before fleeing the house. "Butch, you didn't check any of your brothers and sisters?" Rafferty needled him further. "You just went out the door after checking your parents?" Butch said that's all he did. Rafferty pressed on, "Your whole family has been shot by a .35 caliber. How do you explain that? It's your gun they were shot with.... It's unbelievable, it's totally incredible that you would just check your parents and not your brothers and sisters and just go out the door."

DeFeo started to cry as he admitted he did check on them. "First I checked my mother and father, then I went down and I checked Allison. She got it in the head. Then I went and checked Mark and John's room. They got it in the back. *And John's toes were shaking. They were still shaking and moving when I was there* [emphasis added]." At this point, Rafferty realized that DeFeo must have been present at the shooting if he had been able to see the neuromuscular response.

Butch continued by saying he did go upstairs to see that his sister Dawn "got it in the neck," and then he left and went to the city. Rafferty pressed him further. "Butch, that's no good. That's unbelievable. They have all been shot with your weapon. We know it's your gun." DeFeo started to cry again—admitting the gun was his because he saw .35 caliber cartridges on the floor, but still said he didn't commit the crime. He claimed he was being framed by someone using his gun.

DeFeo remained silent for a while, then continued, "I went to my room, took a pillow case, put the rifle and the cartridge in it." He said he changed his clothes at that point and put them in the pillowcase because he had gotten blood on them when he went into Allison's room. He also said there were two pillow cases. He says he went through the house and collected all the shells.

He then said he retrieved the keys from his mother's pocketbook, left the house, and went down to the dock at the end of Ocean Avenue where he lived. Prior to that, he said, he had taken a 30.06 rifle from his room and had put that in the pillowcase, too. He said he drove down to the end of Ocean Avenue, where he threw one of the rifles in the bay. He believed that one to be the 30.06. The other rifle and the pillowcases with the cartridges and clothes were thrown into a sewer.

Rafferty asked him where the sewer was located, and Butch drew him a map. Rafferty pressed DeFeo, insisting that there had to be more to the story. He had to know who did it or seen something, or certainly see more than he had admitted. It was his rifle that was used—the .35 caliber weapon, the bullets. "You won't believe me," Butch replied. Rafferty reassured him. Butch said he was being framed by a Mr. M. and another man who came into the room that night.

DeFeo said Mr. M. pointed a .45 handgun at his head and told him he "was going to live with this." When DeFeo was asked what the other man looked like, he could not describe the person at all, indicating to Rafferty that "the man" was most likely fictitious. Instead of pointing this out immediately, Rafferty prompted DeFeo to continue his story, saying, "They must have made you shoot at least one of them, or some of them." DeFeo said they made him shoot his father and his one brother, John.

"Butch, how did they make you shoot your father, who was first, and then your brother, who was fourth on down the line? I don't buy that you just had to shoot one. I don't think they were there.... Butch, I know there is more to it."

DeFeo was silent, then blurted out, "It just started and it went so—it went so fast I couldn't stop. It just started and it went so fast I couldn't stop."

After regaining a degree of composure, DeFeo stated that he awoke about 3:30, went up to his room, got his .35 caliber weapon, loaded it, went downstairs, shot his father twice, his mother once, then went into Allison's room, shot her, then shot the two boys, then went upstairs to Dawn's room and shot her. But she awoke, he said, and the dog was "screaming" loudly. He said that after he shot them, he went to his room and retrieved the two pillowcases and tried to collect all the cartridges. When he went to Allison's room to get that cartridge, it was floating in a puddle of blood on a shag rug. He picked up the cartridge—which is how he got the blood on his hand and pants.

He then said he went back to his room, changed his clothing, and went downstairs with his pillowcases in hand, inside of which were the two weapons, the seven cartridges, and his clothes. He went as far as the front door and realized there was a mix-up in the keys. He put the pillowcases down by the door, went back upstairs to his parent's room and grabbed his mother's keys to the car, then left the house. He drove to the dock in Amityville, dropped what he assumed was the 30.06 into the water, then drove into the city and dumped everything else in a sewer. There was no house key on his mother's keyring, which was why he had to break into the house upon his return.

"At that point I ceased my interrogation," Rafferty testified at the trial. "I was certainly satisfied."

The Trial Continues

Failing to get the confession suppressed, Weber then proceeded to claim that his client was insane at the time of the murders. In response, the prosecutor had to prove DeFeo was sane and that robbery was his motive.

It was brought out that since childhood, Ronald DeFeo, Jr. had a history of irrational, violent behavior. He had been repeatedly expelled for fighting from numerous schools,. Mr. Weber attempted to show that DeFeo had been kept out of military service for psychiatric reasons; however, it turned out that DeFeo's exclusion from military service was due to his history of heroin and other drug abuse.

Although multiple examples of DeFeo's reckless—if not downright murderous—use of guns came to light during the trial, one of the most significant was an event which had transpired about a year before the murders in September of 1973. On that occasion, DeFeo's parents had a fight. Ronald Jr., in an attempt to break up the fight, put a shell in his shotgun, aimed it at his father and fired twice—but the gun jammed. The elder DeFeo considered the failed shooting to be a miracle and became intensely religious. The house and grounds were soon overrun with religious pictures and statues, and a priest from Montreal, Canada was imported monthly to conduct masses at the house.

Weber presented ample testimony at the trial to show that Ronald DeFeo, Jr. was insane in the sense that he was an amoral, psychopathic, violent personality whose condition was made even more antisocial by his abuse of hallucinogenic drugs and heroin. So, to counter Weber's argument that DeFeo was insane, prosecutor Sullivan presented a surprise witness—DeFeo's cellmate, twenty-eight-year-old John Kramer, who testified that DeFeo had boasted about trying to beat the murder charges by pleading insanity. Evidently, his plan was that after a few years of psychotherapy, he would be able to collect $200,000 in insurance and estate money and then move to Hawaii with his girlfriend. Kramer also testified that DeFeo had confided that he had staged a phony payroll robbery to cover up embezzlement from his grandfather's car dealership. This led to several violent fistfights between father and son, and—Kramer alleged—the night before the murders DeFeo took a large amount of cash from the family strongbox and buried it.

Sullivan then had two Suffolk County jail guards also testify that DeFeo had told them he planned to feign insanity. The guards said that DeFeo had quizzed them repeatedly concerning how other inmates who had pled insanity had acted when they were in jail. After they told him how other inmates had attempted suicide, pretended to forget people's names, or burned things, DeFeo began to perform the same activities and demanded that his behavior be recorded in the logbooks. Weber was unable, it would seem, to repair the damage done by this testimony.

When DeFeo himself testified, he gave a performance worthy of a high school thespian. He was alternately morose and agitated, threatened to kill the prosecutor and the remainder of the DeFeo-Brigante family, and said he had felt "extremely good" after killing his family. Moreover, he asserted, he had killed "more than a dozen others," and had killed his family "in self-defense."

To appear schizophrenic, DeFeeo—with a little leading by Weber—also said he regularly heard voices, which *The Amityville Horror: A True Story* included, stating that he heard voices which made him commit the murders. In court, DeFeo testified in this regard: "For months before the incident, I heard voices, and, whenever I looked around, there was no one there. So, it must have been God talking to me" [*AH*-pb, p. 14].[2,3]

It is ironic that it was Ronnie DeFeo himself who, later, ultimately laid to rest the myth of voices directing him to demolish his family. Hans Holzer, the famous ghost hunter and parapsychologist, published a book in 1979—two years after *The Amityville Horror*—which was even more absurd, slipshod, and inaccurate than Anson's book. Titled *Murder in Amityville,* the book is mostly padded out with pages of testimony taken out of context from the DeFeo trial. Nevertheless, Holzer performed a great service by visiting Ronald DeFeo at Dannemora prison and publishing a transcript of his interview with him.

Hoping to get support for his theory that Ronald DeFeo was possessed, Holzer brought up the question of when DeFeo had first heard "the voices." Probably to Holzer's surprise, DeFeo replied, "I'll be honest with you. I never heard any voices" [Holzer, *Murder in Amityville*, p. 258].

When Holzer tried to lead him to a different answer by reminding him he had testified that he had heard voices, DeFeo replied, "I tried to convince the psychiatrist that I was insane….I had to convince the psychiatrist I was crazy before I could go before the court and convince a jury" [Holzer, *Murder in Amityville*, p. 259].

The trial ended on Wednesday, November 20, 1975. On Saturday, November 22, *Newsday* reported that DeFeo was found guilty of murdering all six members of his family, stating: "The only hint of any emotion from the stocky, mustached defendant … came when court clerk John Roberts was taking his pedigree. 'Are your parents living?' Roberts asked. DeFeo gave a short, shrill laugh, and then answered calmly, 'No, sir.'"

---

[2] [AH-pb, p. 14] = *Amityville Horror*, paperback edition, page 14].

[3] While Anson's version of DeFeo's testimony is true to the context of what he said, it is not entirely correct. On pages 179–180 of Gerard Sullivan's book *High Hopes: The Amityville Murders,* DeFeo's prosecutor reports that what he actually said was "I honestly believe sometimes that I'm a secret agent for God. When asked "You thought you are an agent for God in what way?" he replied, "Them voices, they were voices always talking to me." "Whose voice would it be?" "I don't know. I told you in the beginning I used to turn around and look—who the hell is calling me? —and there would be nobody there… Maybe in my own mind I believed that God was trying to tell me to go out there and clean up this earth and get rid of all the bad people."

How *The Amityville Horror* Came to Be Written

Oh! What a tangled web we weave
When first we practice to deceive!
—Sir Walter Scott

To fully appreciate the following critique of *The Amityville Horror: A True Story,* it is necessary to understand the journey the book took to be written. It did not, like the Roman Goddess Minerva springing fully formed from Jupiter's forehead, erupt from Anson's cranium. Indeed, Anson originally would have been left out of the action (and the money) altogether. If we are to believe the Lutzes, the book was first meant to have been written by Mario Puzo. If we are to believe Attorney William Weber, the book was to have been written by a free-lance writer by the name of Paul Hoffman, who claimed he was originally supposed to write *The Golden Book.* Even after Prentice-Hall became involved in the project, Timothy Mossman, a senior editor at Prentice-Hall, first extended the offer to a man named Ronald Frey. Only after Frey turned the Lutzes' story away, Mossman said, did he call Jay Anson.

The circumstances surrounding the conception, gestation, and birth of *The Amityville Horror* are shrouded in confusion, deception, avarice, and—quite possibly—fraud. In September of 1979, more than three years after George and Kathleen Lutz had abandoned their house in Amityville, a lawsuit was tried in the Federal District Court in Brooklyn, New York. George and Kathy Lutz were the plaintiffs in the suit; Paul Hoffman and Attorney William Weber (along with the rest of his law firm) were the defendants.

For reasons which will be explained later, the Lutzes were suing the defendants for invasion of privacy, and the defendants were countersuing the Lutzes for fraud. Although the case was settled out of court (a *Newsday* article claimed the Lutzes paid everyone else's court costs), a great deal of testimony was produced which sheds light upon the book's genesis. Unfortunately, much of the testimony was often conflicting and the remainder was mostly unconvincing. The account which follows in this chapter is largely the result of weighing and sifting through the testimony given during the *Lutz v Hoffman* trial.

The start of this media circus began shortly after Ronald "Butch" DeFeo, Jr. was convicted of murder and had been sentenced to life in prison, when the Amityville house at 112 Ocean Avenue was purchased by George and Kathleen Lutz of nearby Deer Park. During the claimed 28 days of their occupancy, the Lutzes alleged they were subjected to malefic, supernatural influences. On January 14, 1976, they "fled the house in terror," abandoned all their possessions, and moved in with Kathy's mother in neighboring West Babylon.

By around July or August of 1976, the house had been reclaimed by the bank and the Lutzes had resettled in California, in the San Diego area. George Lutz sold his interest in the William Parry Surveying Company in Syosset, Long Island, and supported his family with the proceeds. In September of 1977, Jay Anson's book, *The Amityville Horror*: *A True Story*, was published with a movie version following later. By the time of the *Lutz v Hoffman* trial in September of 1979, the Lutzes had appeared on dozens of TV talk shows, had earned close to half a million dollars in royalties from the book and movie, and had purchased a $180,000 house in the San Diego sun—its exact address unknown, thanks to a protective court order.

Exorcism Instead of Imprisonment

In the Lutzes telling of their story, after abandoning their home and all their worldly possessions, their first concern was to procure a new trial for a convicted mass murderer! The extraordinary, preternatural things which happened to them at 112 Ocean Avenue, they allegedly believed, might have enabled Mr. Weber to secure a new trial for Butch DeFeo, wherein he could attempt to prove to a college-educated Judge and a presumably sane jury that Butch had been possessed by devils and demons at the time of the crime. They apparently felt that a garden-variety exorcism might do him more good than life imprisonment. It had never entered their minds, they said, that the incredible tale they told to Weber and Hoffman might have commercial appeal if done up in book form and marketed with a devil's tail and house flies on the cover.

According to the Lutzes, instead of using their highly personal story for the purpose of DeFeo's defense, the wicked Mr. Weber—in collusion with Mr. Hoffman (whom the Lutzes claimed had been introduced as a criminologist, not a writer)—used the Lutz story for crass, commercial purposes.

Naturally, Weber and Hoffman told a rather different story. At the time the Lutzes had come to them in late January, they claimed they were already in the process of putting together a book that was to tell the "inside story" of the DeFeo murders. Weber had already received oral permission from DeFeo to do this (DeFeo was to receive 5% of the royalties), and he had completed a title search on the DeFeo property going back to the 1600s in order to provide a provocative background for the plot of the book. The Lutzes' tale had obvious commercial possibilities if it were added on as a sequel to the DeFeo story, but all the nonsense about using the fable for DeFeo's defense was a premeditated attempt to stir up media interest.

Weber and his associates claimed that the Lutzes had verbally agreed to join in their project for a certain percentage, but secretly had no intention of making good on their oral commitment. Rather, the Lutzes already had plans to write a book by the time they came to "help out" with DeFeo's defense. Since Weber possessed an enormous amount of unpublished, confidential information concerning Ronald DeFeo, Jr. (which the Lutzes needed for their own book), they fraudulently misrepresented their intentions, agreeing to take part in the Weber-Hoffman book and stringing Weber along until they had obtained the DeFeo background material needed for their own book.

Who Is Being Truthful?

Which—if either—of these two conflicting interpretations is true is not easy to judge. Although the Weber-Hoffman version is in general more credible, credibility does not directly translate to truth. And even if the Lutz version were to be proven totally false, it would not necessarily follow that the Weber-Hoffman version is true. Federal Judge Jack Weinstein—having previously thrown out the Lutzes' claim of invasion of privacy—commented about the defendants' counterclaim of fraud on the part of the Lutzes and declared, shortly before the *Lutz v Hoffman* trial was abruptly settled out of court:

> THE COURT: ...as of now, I don't believe the defendants have established a case for the claim they made, nor have they made a claim for fraud. As I see it now, you have both sides trying to appropriate each other's ideas, and both sides being fully aware of what was happening.
>
> [*A dialogue then ensued between the Judge and Mr. Block, the attorney who was representing Mr. Weber and the rest of the defendants.*]
>
> MR. BLOCK: May I inquire to what extent, or which of the elements....of fraud you feel are lacking, so that I can have some guidance in terms of addressing—
> THE COURT: I don't think there was any misleading by each side. I think each side understood exactly what was happening. Certainly Weber understood. And I think the Lutzes did. The Lutzes right in the beginning, I believe, planned to write this book of fiction and were picking the ideas of as many people as they could. And the same thing was true of Weber. Certainly Hoffman got—through Weber's contact with the Lutzes—all of

> the information that he used in that article. That was not Weber's information, essentially, but the Lutzes'.
> MR. BLOCK: It seems to me there was disclosure of Weber's intention and Hoffman's intention, and Burton's intention to the Lutzes, but not the other way around.
> THE COURT: I don't believe so. Based on what was said, I can't believe that Weber didn't know that the Lutzes—
> MR. BLOCK: They were separately contemplating a book?
> THE COURT: Of course, their whole activity was commercial in nature.
> MR. BLOCK: I don't see anything in the case that suggests that at all. In fact, I see the contrary, that the Lutzes took pains to....fail to disclose that they were contemplating writing a book...
> THE COURT: That's my tentative hypothesis and my analysis of the case as it now stands. [*Lutz v Hoffman*, pp. 455–456]

After this jarring statement of the judge's opinion, the two sides decided to settle the case out of court. Judge Weinstein then was compelled to make it clear that the opinion he had just expressed was not a finding of fact:

> THE COURT: The parties have informed the Court that the case has been settled. The proceeding is therefore terminated. The Court has made no findings of fact or law. Any statements the Court made with respect to fact and law during the course of the proceedings were tentative for the purpose of the trial in order to assist counsel. Since the evidence was not fully developed and the law was not briefed, no findings of fact or law have been made. [*Lutz v Hoffman*, p. 458]

Although I lean more toward Weber's version of the dispute, I am not entirely confident of its veracity. Readers may form their own opinions on the basis of the "post-Exodus" sequence of events as I reconstruct them in the remainder of this chapter.

After the Exodus

In his testimony at trial, George Lutz did not rule out the possibility that he and Kathleen might have discussed the possibility of publishing a book about 112 Ocean Avenue even before they abandoned the house on January 14, 1976. He stopped short of admitting that they had done so. He did admit, however, that within a week or so of moving out, he tried to contact Mr. Weber through the agency of their friends, the Vetters.

Weber claimed that as early as January 15 or 16 (*i.e.*, as early as the day after the Lutzes left the house!) he was told by a Dr. Lieberman (a friend of the Vetters) that the Lutzes wanted to meet him to tell of their "ordeal" and provide information which might aid in Ronnie's defense. It is interesting to note that on the sixteenth, the Lutzes bought two cassette recorders and began to tape an oral reconstruction of their 28 days in the horror house. Of course, they claimed they did this as a means of personal catharsis only; but it is tempting to suppose they really did this to provide resource material with which a book might be written.

As a general rule, Weber and Hoffman dated critical events much earlier than did the Lutzes (who admitted, incidentally, that they had great difficulty with dates). For example, the Lutzes claimed that their first meeting with Mr. Weber took place on February 7, 1976. Weber, however, said he first met them sometime during middle or late January. All agreed, however, that the meeting took place at the home of Mrs. Conners, Kathleen's mother.[1] Lutz recalled the meeting "wasn't very long"—it was a chit-chat which lasted "maybe three hours at the most." At this meeting, the Lutzes claimed, they merely told ghost stories which Mr. Weber might later wish to retell in some court.

As Weber told it, however, he told the Lutzes at the very first meeting that he had an agreement with Hoffman to write a book regarding the DeFeo murders and suggested to the Lutzes that they might be able to contribute a "possession theme" to the book. Thinking such a theme might make the book sell better, Weber claimed that he had offered the Lutzes a share in the project equal to his own at the first meeting. It was his understanding that the tapes the Lutzes were making would be for Hoffman's use if he followed through as the book's writer.

Weber claimed further that he had had yet another meeting with the Lutzes in January—several days after the first meeting. At that meeting (also held at the Conners home) he made a revised offer to George and Kathleen, whereby five shares would be created out of the fifty percent of the profits which would be available; the Lutzes would have one share, and Mr. Burton and Mr. Mars (other members of the law firm) would also have shares.

A day or two later, the Lutzes called Weber and asked what Mars was doing for the project for him to earn a full share. After hearing Weber's explanation that Mars was the senior member of the law firm—Weber's boss in other words—Lutz suggested that they were entitled to two shares instead of one. This was agreed to by the other parties, and the Lutzes agreed to come over to the law office a day or two later to further discuss the project. I can find no evidence, however, that the Lutzes attended any meetings at the law firm prior to February 14, 1976—and even that date is disputable.

Although the Lutzes claimed they did not meet Hoffman until February 14, Hoffman himself said he first met the Lutzes on February 7 (the day the Lutzes maintained they had had their first meeting with Weber), and

---

[1] In the trial transcript, the name sometimes is spelled Connors and sometimes as Conners. The name is spelled Conners when the witness herself is introduced.

that besides Mr. Weber, the Lutzes, and Kathy's mother, two parapsychology students from Dowling College were also present. Using the information provided by the Lutzes and the two students during that meeting, Hoffman was later able to write the article which appeared in the *New York Daily News* on July 18 of the same year. (In this book we will have occasion to study that article very carefully, since it represents the earliest stage in the evolution of the myth of *The Amityville Horror*.)

It will be recalled that the Lutzes claimed that Hoffman's profession had been misrepresented to them at this meeting. Instead of being told that he was a free-lance writer, they said, he was introduced as a criminologist who would assist in the DeFeo defense. Hoffman, naturally, denied this, and claimed the Lutzes never told him he could not make use of the information they were providing in his writing.

At the time that Judge Weinstein ruled against the Lutzes' claim of invasion of privacy, he referred to this point specifically:

> THE COURT: I credit Mr. Hoffman's statement that the Lutzes never told him not to use the information. I think he is telling me the truth when he is telling, the surrounding circumstances…
> MR. DALEY: [*representing the Lutzes*] Well, the fact that Mr. Weber brought Mr. Hoffman to the meeting and misrepresented him to be something in Ronald DeFeo's …
> THE COURT: I don't believe he [*Lutz*] is a credible witness on this issue. I believe Mr. Hoffman. [*Lutz v Hoffman*, p. 155]

Inviting the Media In

During the second week of February (*i.e.*, three weeks after the Lutzes moved out), the story about the Lutzes leaving their house under strange circumstances broke in the Long Island newspapers. The Lutzes claimed that this was the first time they had privately discussed having a book written to clear up the "misrepresentations" in the press.

Laura DiDio, a program director for Channel 5 TV, wanted to join in on the story since she was doing a series of programs dealing with the paranormal. From the eleventh through the nineteenth of February, Miss DiDio was in daily contact with Mr. Weber in order to contact the Lutzes directly, and to aquire the exclusive story. Weber, of course, was using Miss DiDio for the purpose of "hyping" the story and laying the groundwork for a commercial publishing project.

Miss DiDio's testimony concerning her role in the gestation of *The Amityville Horror* is relevant at this point, and also provides an amusing insight into the world of "professional" students of the occult.

[*Miss DiDio being questioned by Mr. Daley.*]

A And the story broke on February 11th in the *Long Island Press* and *Newsday*, about this couple, Kathy and George Lutz, leaving their house in Amityville, which had also been the scene of mass murders because of some supernatural forces. There was no way to get in touch with the Lutzes, and the only name mentioned in the article was Mr. Weber, as the attorney for DeFeo, who was in contact with the Lutzes. So I called Mr. Weber at his office.

Q And in your first contact with Mr. Weber, what do you recall being discussed at that time?

A Well, basically I, like the rest of the New York Press Corps, wanted to get the story and wanted to get in touch with the Lutzes, and Mr. Weber told me well, he couldn't give me their number, that was confidential, but we discussed the possibility of my doing a story and getting into the house which at that time he said was not possible.

But he told me to call him back, which I did, for the succeeding week. And in ensuing conversations Mr. Weber told me that there was going to be a séance held at the house on February 28th, a Saturday night, in which Channel 7 Eye Witness News was invited, and this Dr. Steven Kaplan, who was a vampirologist from Long Island University, was going to be presiding—exorcising some white witches. So I said that sounded strange to me, and I called Dr. Kaplan up, and I spoke to him briefly, and I thought it sounded even stranger. I should mention that I have a background in parapsychology and the occult.

Q Let me ask what background and training you have, and education you have?

A Well, I have a B.A. from Fordham University, in communication with a minor in languages. And I had worked—I had taken courses in school and also on a non-matriculated basis—at the universities. I worked with Mr. Hans Holzer, Ed and Lorraine Warren, and other psychics before, and I had also done work with the New York City Police Department, stories where I covered the hypnosis unit, the police use of psychics in solving cases.

Q To the best of your knowledge, is that why you were selected by the news team you were working with at that time to make contact on this particular story?

A Oh, definitely. It was in conjunction with the fact that I was producing a series on psychic phenomena, and the story just happened to break at the same time, and I had the contacts and knowledge in the field.

MR. BLOCK: Do you intend to offer this witness as an expert witness on vampirology and parapsychology?

MR. DALEY: No, I am just laying a foundation as a news reporter reporting the thing.

MR. BLOCK: Then I'll not request a *voir dire* on the qualifications.
Q Now, do you recall anything else as far as the discussion at that time with Mr. Weber?
A Yes, basically I wanted the scoop on the story. So I told him, I said I really don't think, based on my knowledge, an exorcism by white witches is the right thing. I said I have some background, I know some people. Why don't you let me get in touch with Hans Holzer, who I worked with before. And he said that sounded like a good idea. And we had a very, very friendly, amicable discussion, and I let him know that I had some background in the field before. He related to me different things that were alleged to have gone on in the house by the Lutzes, and I said, Do you believe all this stuff? I said, What is your estimation? Because, look, I don't want to put these people on the air if they're crackpots, or if it's a hoax. Because that could be my job on the line. [*Lutz v Hoffman*, pp. 417–418][2]

While Miss DiDio was trying to reach out to the Lutzes, the Lutzes were discussing the possibility of having a book published:

Q Aside from your wife, did you ever discuss the possibility or prospect of having a book written by anybody about the Amityville experience at any time prior to February 14, 1976?
A Yes,
Q Who to?
A My cousin's husband.
Q Who are they?
A MacLaglan. Yes, I believe they live in Maine.

But less than a minute later, Lutz denied what he had just admitted:

Q You had thoughts [*between February 11 and 13*] and discussed the possibility of writing a book, at least, with your wife Kathy and with your cousins, the MacLaglans?
A My cousin's husband is an agent—a writer.
Q What is his full name?
A Robert MacLaglan. It had nothing to do with Kathy and I [*sic*] as such. We were discussing how books came about. [*Lutz v Hoffman*, pp. 107–108]

---

[2] Miss DiDio seemed to have been reassured when Mr. Weber told her that the DeFeos had had a mass said in the house and, with all the windows closed, a wind came up somehow and blew the candles out.

On February 14th or 15th, according to Weber, the Lutzes met briefly with the lawyers at the Mars and Burton law offices, at which time Weber and Burton confirmed that the Lutzes would each be receiving a share equivalent to 24% of whatever monies the corporation was going to earn. (A corporation had been formed for the purpose of handling the book venture.)

The Prentice-Hall Alternative

Although the Lutzes claimed that their first contact with Prentice-Hall occurred on or about March 9, and their first meeting with Anson took place on March 11, 1976, the *Lutz v Hoffman Defendants' Pre-Trial Memorandum of Law* (prepared by Attorney Block) told a very different story:

> The depositions of Tam [*sic*] Mossman and Jay Anson show, however, that plaintiffs [*the Lutzes*] must have begun an effort to find a writer and publisher in mid or even early February, while maintaining a pretense of cooperation with the defendant....*The first reference in a diary kept by Anson relative to his project with the plaintiffs was on March 9, 1976*. On that date, he had spoken on the telephone to a friend about the plaintiffs' story. Anson also testified that he had met with the Lutzes for the first time on or about March 1, 1976, *or even possibly as early as February 18, 1976*. [*Emphases mine*] [*Lutz v Hoffman Pre-Trial Memorandum*, p. 10]
>
> Tam [*sic*] Mossman also attended this meeting. Anson further stated that he was first told how to contact the plaintiffs by Mossman by the end of February....Mossman could not recollect any exact date for his first contacts with Al Carter [*a friend of the Lutzes whom they had asked to seek out a publisher for their book*]. He did recall, however, that he tried to interest a writer named Ron Frey in the plaintiffs' story before Anson was contacted. Mossman further stated that about a week transpired between his initial telephone conversation with Carter and his initial contact with Anson, and that he, the Lutzes and Anson then all met for the first time at Anson's office "at least a week to ten days" following Mossman's call to Anson. [*Lutz v Hoffman Pre-Trial Memorandum*, p. 11]
>
> Thus, *approximately 14 to 17 days prior to the meeting at Anson's office*, which took place sometime between February 18, 1976 and March 1, 1976, Carter, at the behest of the Lutzes, contacted Mossman to interest him and Prentice-Hall in the Lutzes' own book. Therefore, *as early as at least February 15, 1976*, the plaintiffs were actively, and unbeknownst to defendants, pursuing their own project. From the outset, therefore, plaintiffs' relationship with the individual defendants and their gratuitous representations about their desire to assist in the DeFeo defense and, later,

> to join with the defendants in writing the planned book, were knowingly false [*emphases mine*]. [*Lutz v Hoffman Pre-Trial Memorandum*, p. 11]

Although there was dispute among the parties as to the date of occurrence of every event so far discussed, we now come to Monday, February 16, 1976. On that date, all parties agreed, a press conference was held at Weber's offices in Patchogue. Of course, that's as far as the agreement went. The Lutzes claimed they had been threatened and coerced into attending the press conference, and the lawyers claimed that a half hour before the press conference, the Lutzes, Weber, and the others had made a tape recording reaffirming the publishing agreement they had made one or two days previously.

At the press conference, the Lutzes did not say very much, but they did say that there had not been any moving furniture, no wailing voices, and no mysterious power failures. They also denied that a local priest had attempted an exorcism of the house. (Neighbors of the Lutzes later told reporters they had seen George Lutz and a priest march around the house carrying a large crucifix, and that the two then entered the house, presumably to perform some sort of rite.) George said he had been back to the house twice, showing that he was not as terrified of the house as the public had been made to believe.

It would appear that with the completion of the news conference, the Rubicon had been crossed. The die had been cast, but unlike in the case of Julius Caesar, this die was being cast by people who believed that the throw of a die could be influenced by psychokinesis!

From then on, the pace of development of *The Amityville Horror* quickened. On February 18, 1976 Weber appeared on a TV news program to crank up media excitement over the Lutzes' story. On the twentieth, the Lutzes contacted Laura DiDio to discuss the TV program, and made an appointment to meet with her at Lutz' Syosset office on the following day.

On February 20, the *Long Island Press* carried an article saying that Dr. Kaplan (the vampirologist who was to have exorcised a brace of white witches on the twenty-eighth) was bowing out of the parapsychological investigation of the Lutzes' house.[3] The commercial overtones of the situation had made him suspicious that the whole thing was a hoax. He even asserted that the Lutzes might be friends of Ronnie DeFeo, and that DeFeo himself could have planned the whole affair.

---

[3] According to Dr. Kaplan's rival, Hans Holzer, Kaplan lectured on Dracula and other vampires, and was an expert in public relations. He was the head of the Parapsychology Institute of America, the Vampire Research Center of America, and—last but not least—the Ghostology Institute of America. All of these organizations were headquartered in Dr. Kaplan's Centereach home.

When the Lutzes met with DiDio on February 21, they told her they "had lost confidence" in Weber. "We would appreciate it if you really didn't tell Mr. Weber what we were doing," Lutz told DiDio, "because I am not really sure that we can trust him now." They were upset that Weber had been interviewed on the front lawn of their house, allegedly without their permission. Why this upset them so much was never really explained.

The Lutzes told DiDio they were giving her the "exclusive" on their story. According to DiDio, the Lutzes said they were taking a crash course in the occult and paranormal. According to a tape made by the Lutzes during that meeting, the Lutzes told DiDio

> We have done so far—we have done pretty close to 30, 45-minute tapes, different things about the house we found out through living there, things that took place immediately after visiting the house. Also, we're putting it all together and *are hoping to get a book together.* [*Lutz v Hoffman*, p. 119][4]

Again, according to the tape, the Lutzes told DiDio they had people researching the history of the house and the DeFeo family:

> We are the only ones who have really the whole thing… Bill Weber has the piece from the trial, but he really doesn't have much more than *he put together for us*, because we gave him a lot of pieces, but there are a lot of things he doesn't know, because there is no point in telling him. [*Lutz v Hoffman*, p. 121]

At the same time the Lutzes were telling DiDio about their own book and indicating they wanted nothing more to do with Weber, Hoffman—unaware of the Lutzes' duplicity—worked up an outline for a book. The book's "center of gravity," of course, was the DeFeo murder story. But the book was to have an epilogue devoted to the Lutz epic.

After her meeting with the Lutzes, Miss DiDio proceeded to arrange for psychics to carry out "research" in the house. She and Steve Bauman (also of Channel 5) tried to enlist Hans Holzer into their expedition into the house as Holzer had previously done a "documentary" for Channel *5,* and he wanted to do another half-hour program. However, when Holzer wanted to be paid for every minute of the program, Channel 5 balked. Miss DiDio next extended the offer to Ed and Lorraine Warren in Connecticut. They had also previously

---

[4] Although almost all tapes purportedly containing information damaging to the Lutzes' position had either been "lost" or destroyed by the time of the Lutz v Hoffman trial, this tape inadvertently must have escaped their scrutiny, since they sent it to the defendants when it was subpoenaed.

worked with Channel 5 News on several stories. They agreed to come down the next day, a Wednesday, February 25, 1976. (It will be recalled from the Preface of this book that the Warrens' lecture "The Amityville Horror" was the stimulus which led to the writing of this book.)

After five phone calls, DiDio secured permission to go into the Lutz house. So, on the twenty-fifth, Laura DiDio, together with a reporter by the name of Steve Campbell and the Warrens, visited the house. Lorraine Warren, a "light trance medium," went from room to room "just feeling her impressions." Needless to say, this exciting research was reported in the next news broadcast.

The next day, February 26, Weber received a written release which allowed him to use DeFeo's confidential story (with "Butch" receiving 5%). This crucial piece of paper made it possible for the lawyers to acquire their special corporation ready for business. On the twenty-eighth, according to the Lutzes, Weber and Burton met with them at the Conners home and made a proposal that the Lutzes take part in a corporation which was to produce three books and three movies. An attempt would be made—so the Lutzes say—to have Mario Puzo do the writing. The lawyers were asked to put their proposal in writing so that the Lutzes' attorney could study it.

Later that same evening, the Lutzes called and asked Laura DiDio to come to see them. After she arrived, they played for her a tape of the meeting they had just had with Weber and Burton and asked her for advice. Despite her other-worldly orientation, Miss DiDio's advice revealed a thorough knowledge of how things function on the terrestrial plane:

> They asked me what I thought they should do. I said, "The only partnership you should be worrying about at this point, if you're really upset as you say you are, is your marriage. What you do is, of course, up to you." [*Lutz v Hoffman*, p. 433]

Not long after the meeting on February 28, the Lutzes received a written copy of the proposal. The Lutzes claimed it had simply been left in Mrs. Conners' mailbox, but Weber claimed he had given it to them in person. During the first week of March 1976, Hoffman received and signed a copy of the agreement which had been given to the Lutzes. The Lutzes had not yet signed it, however, nor would they ever.

The Lutzes did not like the proposal. Although they may have been in contact with Anson as early as February 18, the latest possible date for their first meeting with him was March 1, 1976. At any rate, by the time they had received the written agreement, they had decided to proceed with Anson as their book's author. They did nothing to let Weber know that they did not intend to sign his agreement and they took pains not to let him know they were dealing with Anson.

Psychic D-Day

While Weber waited for the Lutzes to sign the agreement, the "research wing" of the enterprise was about to launch the parapsychological equivalent of the Normandy Invasion. D-Day was set for March 6, 1976. That day marked the second coming of Lorraine and Ed Warren (light-trance medium and demonologist, respectively), as well as the first advent of a passel of other paranormal notables. There were the psychics Mary Pascarella and Dr. and Mrs. Alba A. Riley, as well as the parapsychologists Jerry Solfvin and George Kekoris of the Psychical Research Foundation [*not "Institute" as stated in Anson's book*] in Durham, North Carolina. There was also Marvin Scott from Channel 5, who accompanied Miss DiDio, and Mike Linder of WNEW-FM.

Just in case the ectoplasmic entities might decide to emit photons in the visible or infrared range, or set up compression waves in the atmosphere, the "research" team also included a cameraman, Steve Petropolis, and a sound man, Richard Murphy. Tom Spring was the electrician. And for careful recording of the data, there was Mr. Dougherty of *The National Star*.

With the assurance of the psychic researchers that there were, indeed, evil forces dwelling at 112 Ocean Avenue, the commercial viability of the project must have seemed assured. In reality, of course, there were *two* projects: the Lutz-Hoffman and the Lutz-Anson projects. And only one was destined to survive. On March 9, Anson made his first notation in his diary of the already-progressing project, and Weber was still waiting for the Lutzes to sign their contract.

By March 20th, the Lutzes were getting on famously with Anson and Prentice Hall. It was then that they realized Weber still had a tape recording which contained the verbal proposal/agreement they had made with Weber. They had loaned it to him for the purpose of transcribing and turning into the written agreement they now possessed but did not intend to sign.

Without giving any indication that he was pulling out of the agreement, George Lutz went to Weber's house and retrieved the tape from Weber's wife (according to Weber's version, Weber was not at home at the time) or from Weber *and* his wife (Lutz version). The Lutzes claimed the single tape they retrieved was not the tape they wanted, while Weber claimed the Lutzes retrieved multiple tapes that included the only remaining tape of their agreement.

In this instance, it is possible to infer which version of this story is true. It is almost certain, I think, that the Lutzes did retrieve the agreement tape back, and that it met the same fate as the green slime from the keyhole in the playroom door. If Weber still possessed the tape during the *Lutz v Hoffman* trial, he surely would have used the tape as clear proof that there had been a verbal contract with the Lutzes. He could then have sued them for breach of contract.

The Lutzes, on the other hand, must have known that the material on the tape was potentially dangerous to their plans since they possessed—according to George Lutz's admission in the trial—a duplicate of the tape. Since *both* copies of the tape had disappeared by the time of the trial, the conclusion seems inescapable that the tape contained material damaging to the Lutzes' claims.

Why did the Lutzes break with Hoffman and Weber? Did they truly no longer trust Weber simply because he had visited the front yard of their house without permission, as they told Laura DiDio, and as they testified in court? Judge Weinstein seems to have perceived a different truth:

> The evidence shows fairly clearly that the Lutzes during this entire period were considering and acting with the thought of having a book published and enhancing their share of the book. They couldn't work out an agreement that was satisfactory to them with Hoffman and the law firm, because Hoffman's view was this was going to be an epilogue, and according to the contract proposed the Lutzes were to get a very small share.
>
> They worked out an arrangement with Prentice-Hall that was much more satisfactory, because it was *their* story which was critical, and the defendant was a subsidiary aspect, and they got a much larger portion of the rights. [*Lutz v Hoffman*, p. 156]

After retrieving the tapes on March 20, the Lutzes moved to sunny California as Weber and Hoffman waited for the signed contract to arrive in the mail. Finally, on April 13, 1976, Burton received a letter from the Lutzes' lawyer, Mr. Wachtel. In proper legalese, it said, "No dice."

Hoffman, notified of the collapse of the project, wrote up an article, based on his interview with the Lutzes on February 7, and sent it to the *New York Sunday News*. In May, Jay Anson received his first advance under contract with Prentice-Hall.

On July 18, 1976, Hoffman's first article, "Life in a Haunted House," appeared in the *New York Daily News Magazine*. The next day, someone at Prentice-Hall fired off a letter to Anson. Prentice-Hall was upset by the article, thinking that they had been given exclusive rights to the story. With the newly released article, there was a possibility that the publisher might cancel the agreement. But the dust eventually settled and the project continued.

On July 23, the bank which held the mortgage on 112 Ocean Avenue wrote to the Lutzes to tell them that vandals were invading the property as a result of the notoriety stemming from Hoffman's article. The house reverted to the bank, and the Lutz furnishings were auctioned off.

Last Séance in Amityville

By January 1977, Hoffman was trying—unsuccessfully—to find a publisher for his book. Since he no longer was in communication with the Lutzes, no one was interested. By this time Hoffman's contract with Weber had expired, and Weber had taken up with Hans Holzer. There was still a chance Weber could publish a book, but he needed parapsychological resources. So on January 13, 1977, the last grand séance was held in the house with the quarter-moon windows. Taking part in the "investigation" were Hans Holzer, his trusty trance medium Ethel Johnson Myers, Laura DiDio, William Weber, and Bernard Burton. There were also a couple of "psychic photographers" among the crowd. That last table-tipping provided material for Holzer's book, *Murder in Amityville*, which came out in 1979.[5]

In April of 1977, the bomb was dropped. Hoffman's article—tidied up for a gentler readership—resurfaced in *Good Housekeeping.* That almost blew the bottom out of *The Amityville Horror: A True Story.* The Lutzes had to convince Prentice-Hall that they weren't two-timing the publisher. In order to show that Hoffman did not have their permission to use their story, they had to initiate a lawsuit against everyone in sight, in order to protect themselves against cancellation by Prentice-Hall.

The lawsuit began in May 1977, in California. The venue was subsequently changed to Brooklyn, where the case came to trial in September of 1979. With the lawsuit's initiation as token of their good faith, the Lutzes were able to sign a healthy contract with Anson in August of 1977. The book with the flies on the cover was released a month later.

The Importance of the Lutz v Hoffman Trial

The importance of the *Lutz v Hoffman, et al.* trial for understanding not only the origins and content of Anson's horror book cannot be overstated. As we shall see in the next chapter, in the course of the trial, Attorney William Weber laid out the "overview" needing to be implemented in a joint effort with the Lutzes to implement the book to be written by Paul Hoffman—the project that was aborted after the Lutzes had obtained the information they needed for their own book that came to be written by Jay Anson. Excerpts from Attorney William Weber's testimony will make it abundantly clear: *The Amityville Horror: A True Story* was never intended to tell "a true story."

From start to finish, Jay Anson was putting on paper the "overview" contained in the previous project originally developed by Mr. Weber for

---

[5] To the extent that I can verify the facts, the only talent one requires in order to be a "psychic photographer" is the ability to take pictures without focusing the camera.

which Paul Hoffman would have been the author. As we shall see, in addition to all the DeFeo information and ideas obtained from Weber, Anson would flesh out the overview with material modelled after the horror novel *The Exorcist* to create his own "horror masterpiece".

Part II:
Critique of *The Amityville Horror*; The Prologue to the Amityville Tales

Channel Five News

Like its literary model, the novel *The Exorcist*, *The Amityville Horror* has a "Prologue." The Prologue of *The Amityville Horror* describes a program aired on February 5, 1976, by New York's Channel Five *Ten O'clock News.*[1] It tells of reporter Steve Bauman's investigation of the allegedly haunted DeFeo house in Amityville, Long Island, explaining the house being the scene of a mass murder, and it mentions the purchase of the house by George and Kathy Lutz and their moving in on December 18, 1975. After relating a number of preternatural experiences endured by the Lutzes, the Prologue goes on to say that

> before they left, Channel Five stated, their predicament had become known in the area. They had consulted the police and a local priest as well as a psychic research group. "They reportedly told of strange voices seeming to come from within themselves, of a power which actually lifted Mrs. Lutz off her *feet* [emphasis added] toward a closet behind which was a room not noted on any blueprints." [*AH*-pb, p. 4]

According to the Prologue, Steve Bauman discovered "that tragedy had struck nearly every family inhabiting the place, as well as an earlier house built on the same site." It claims that William Weber, Ronald DeFeo's defense attorney, "had commissioned studies hoping to prove that some force influenced the behavior of anyone living at 112 Ocean Avenue … after they [*the scientists being "commissioned"*] rule out all reasonable or scientific explanation, then it's going to be referred over to another group at Duke

---

[1] According to Lutz' testimony at the trial, this program aired on February 18 [*Lutz v Hoffman*, p. 115]. Since he claimed he had not even *met* Weber until February 7, and since Weber figured prominently in this program, either Lutz or Anson got the date wrong.

University, who will delve into the psychic aspects of the case." Weber "felt it might be the evidence he needed to win his client [*DeFeo*] a new trial."

Emissaries from the Vatican

The prologue winds up the account of the TV newscast by saying that in December (*i.e., while the Lutzes were still living in the house*),

> Two emissaries from the Vatican had arrived in Amityville … and were reported to have told the Lutzes to leave their home immediately. 'Now the Church's Council of Miracles is studying the case, and its report is that indeed 112 Ocean Avenue is possessed of some spirits beyond current human knowledge.' [*AH*-pb, p. 5]

The prologue ends by mentioning the press conference held on February 16, 1975, in the office of Attorney Weber, and saying that the Lutzes were now incommunicado, "feeling that too much was being overstated and exaggerated. It is only now that their whole story is being told."

What are we to make of all this?

Before discussing how Steve Bauman and Channel Five News came to make this program in the first place, let us examine some of the details of the report. It is alleged that the Lutzes' predicament "had become known in the area." The neighbors of the Lutzes deny, however, that they were ever, during the twenty-eight days, told of anything going bump in the night. Mr. and Mrs. James Mullaly, who bought the Lutz home in Deer Park, visited the Lutzes several weeks after they had moved in, and said they perceived no signs of distress. To the contrary, Mr. Mullaly told Alex Drehsler and Jim Scovel of *Newsday*,

> "I remember my wife saying as we left that if she were living in that house she wouldn't be in as good a mood as Mrs. Lutz was" [*because of the murders in the house*]. [Drehsler, "Fact or Fiction?" *Newsday*, Nov. 17, 1977]

Attorney Weber's "Overview"

The Amityville police department denied that there was any communication with the Lutzes before the Lutzes had "fled in terror," and Pastor William White of St. Martin of Tours (the local priest) told Drehsler and Scovel that the Lutzes never called him and never attended mass. As for the psychic research group consulted (the Psychical Research Foundation [*not "Institute" as in the text*] of Durham, N.C.), Gerald Solfvin, a senior research associate, told *Newsday* the organization did not investigate the case because "the phenomenon did not appear very measurable and the family had moved out," [Drehsler, "Fact of Fiction?" *Newsday*, Nov. 17, 1977].

We may note further that in the prologue's account of levitation, Mrs. Lutz is lifted right off her *feet* (*i.e.*, from a standing position). Nowhere in the book, and nowhere in Hoffman's account, is this tale repeated. In all the levitations mentioned (including the *Lutz v Hoffman* trial testimony), Kathy was asleep in bed when the alleged levitations commenced. It cannot be doubted that if this miracle did indeed occur, it would warrant an entire chapter in the book. Moreover, the "secret room not noted on any blueprints" alleged to be behind the bedroom closet which was the target of Kathy's trajectory, is also not mentioned again in the book. What we have here, of course, is the earliest appearance of an *Urmotiv*, the beginning of the "secret room" motif. In time, this will be transformed into the secret red room in the basement.

When one reads that "tragedy had struck nearly every family inhabiting the place, as well as an earlier house built on the same site," one might imagine a long line of accursed occupants. However, there were only two families who inhabited the house before the DeFeos, and there is no account of these previous tenants experiencing anything worthy of the word "tragedy." The previous house was not built on the site, incidentally. According to Mr. Seth Purdy, Jr., Director of the Amityville Historical Society, the house had been erected on Muncie Island in the Great South Bay, and later relocated to the Ocean Avenue site. In any event, both the previous structure and the present home were owned by the Moynahan (or Monahan) family. The house was then sold to the Rileys who, after getting a divorce, sold it to the DeFeos.

So far as I can ascertain, no real scientists were ever commissioned by anybody to make a study of the house. It is quite revealing to read that after the scientists "rule out all reasonable or scientific explanations, then it's going to be referred over to another group at Duke University..." It was a foregone conclusion that real scientists would be superfluous!

The Vatican Investigation That Wasn't

As for the two emissaries from the Vatican telling the Lutzes to leave their home immediately, we may ask how did the Lutzes manage to contact the Vatican in the first place? The Lutzes' phone hardly ever worked with ordinary priests on the other end. Imagine what electrogremlins could do to messages coming in from Vatican personnel! Considering the great lengths to which priestly trivia are expanded to chapter length elsewhere in the book, it is worth noting that Anson only mentioned the Vatican once.

Additionally, how would the Vatican have known what is going on at 112 Ocean Avenue, Amityville if the people residing at 100 Ocean Avenue did not? Considering that the "Council of Miracles" can take centuries in its deliberations, the allegation that as of February 5, 1975, it had already issued a report on the matter seems more miraculous than all the events of the book combined.

As a matter of fact, the possibility of Vatican involvement in December 1975 is totally ruled out by the statement on page 191 concerning the events of January 9, 1976:

> The Chancellors had confined any discussion of the Lutzes' case to scientific causes, and there would be a long period of investigation *before the church would acknowledge demonic influence* [emphasis added]. [*AH*-pb, p. 191]

Rereading the Prologue after having read the entire book, I was convulsed with laughter when I reached the bit about the Lutzes becoming incommunicado because they felt the press had "overstated and exaggerated" too many things. With the possible exception of the Council of Miracles tale just discussed, it is difficult to imagine what could be more overstated and exaggerated than the story actually presented by the book. As one looks through the media accounts which had appeared prior to the publication of Anson's book, one cannot find any accounts of the Lutzes story that exceed the incredibility of the book. Rather, one tends to find only the foreshadowing of the tales which later appear on the fly-spangled pages of *The Amityville Horror: A True Story.*

The DeFeo Connection

Leaving behind the details of the TV report, why was Channel Five News at the DeFeo house in the first place? It is most enlightening to examine part of Attorney Weber's testimony at the trial that took place in September of 1979:

> [*Weber is being questioned by his Attorney, Mr. Block, about an alleged agreement Weber had with the Lutzes to write a book.*]
>
> Q Mr. Weber, after your arrangement or understanding with the Lutzes was reached....did you then enter into elaborate discussions and conversations with the Lutzes during which you imparted certain information to them?
>
> A Yes. There was imparting of information by me to them, them to me and, together in certain areas we created stories.
>
> Q All right. And did any of this information that you imparted to them ultimately wind up in the book called THE AMITYVILLE HORROR—A TRUE STORY? [*sic*]

THE COURT: You said you created stories. I didn't understand that. What does that mean?
THE WITNESS: The Lutzes were going to participate in the "possession" aspect of the book. The book was a fiction, and it's indicated in Paul Hoffman's summary.
THE COURT: I see.
THE WITNESS: (continuing) We were going to take literary license with their experience, and basically we were going to convert certain ideas that came up during our discussions and translate them into what the public would consider para-psychic phenomena, to use that word.
Q The Lutzes knew that this was not going to be a true story, I take it?
A Absolutely. [*Lutz v Hoffman*, pp. 243*ff*].

[*After being asked to indicate all of his ideas which allegedly later found their way into Anson's book, Weber first tells of the general "overview" that was to be employed in advancing the project with the Lutzes (Lutz v Hoffman, p. 245) then continues*.]

Q I want you to, one by one, tell the Court each and every instance of the book [*The Amityville Horror*] which you contributed to the Lutzes, based upon information or thoughts that you gave to them.
A With the Court's permission, first I would like to discuss the three general areas … to show the approach that was presented.
Q This was a certain *overview* that was proposed? [*emphasis added*]
A Yes.
Q What was that?
A Based upon my discussion I had with other people, I told the Lutzes about how the project should be developed. Number one, the issue of credibility. I see there are hundreds, unfortunately, of mass murders. There are hundreds of horror stories and haunted houses. The difference between the good sellers and the bad sellers is where can you get credibility. We had to develop credibility. The credibility was developed, A, through—well, the Lutzes brought their priest into the story. [*Lutz v Hoffman*, p. 245]
Q So the concept of a priest attending to the house, and the possession of Ronald DeFeo, Sr., and his so-called mysticism was disclosed by you to the Lutzes as part of the overview of the joint effort that you were contemplating?
A Yes. That was one of the overviews. The other thing was to bring in outside forces, and to show their involvement in it, and to attempt to make it appear as if these outside forces were corroborating our story, and the outside forces that I, myself, brought in was the Laura DiDio situation. Laura DiDio was the program manager for Channel 5.

Q How did you propose that Laura DiDio and that situation would assist in the joint project?
A It assisted—not only did it assist in our project, but it actually assisted in THE AMITYVILLE HORROR [*sic*]. It appears in page 2 and 3. It's the classical curiosity approach that grabs the reader's attention and focuses the reader so the reader wants to go ahead.
Q What do you recall specifically that appears in the book that you put in motion?
A I set up an interview with Steve Bowman from Channel 5 News in front of the house….It was [*for*] general curiosity. Steve Bowman says to me, "I understand the Lutzes moved out." I said, "Yes. They told me there's certain forces in the house. We're considering it as a part of a possible defense for Ronald DeFeo." [*Lutz v Hoffman*, pp. 248–249]
Q You put that as a possible overview in motion?
A Yes … and the second curiosity approach, which again appears right at the beginning of their book, is the press conference that was held, and the press conference was held at my suggestion.
Q And so the press conference was your idea to also elicit some curiosity?
A Right. [*Lutz v Hoffman*, p. 249]

[*cross-examination by Mr. Daley*]

Q Did you at a later time, tell to the press at a news conference that you were contemplating an appeal….for Ronald DeFeo, based on some type of possession theory, based on what you had learned from the Lutzes?
A Not in words that you put it. But yes, the substance of that was said to the press.
Q So essentially, you lied to the press regarding the possession theory?
A No.
Q Of an appeal?
A No. Absolutely not. This was specifically discussed with the Lutzes, and it appears in their book at page two and three, I said we were *considering*, and will consider everything. Again, it was just baiting, if you can use that word, the news media to keep this information going. [*Lutz v Hoffman*, pp. 301–302]

[*After a few more questions, Judge Weinstein asks Weber to clarify his reasons for telling these stories to the media.*]

THE COURT: What did you say in substance with respect to the effect of the Lutzes' information on a possible new trial or appeal?

THE WITNESS: We said—I said that I was considering what the Lutzes were telling me, on a possible application for a new trial. At the time I said it, it was with a specific objective in mind. It was to develop the publicity on a commercial venture.

THE COURT: But you knew that the information that you and the Lutzes were developing was false?

THE WITNESS: No, I didn't, [*Lutz v Hoffman*, pp. 303–304]

THE COURT: With respect to the possession and with respect to these dreams and with respect to a lot of the material that was relied on to show possession, you knew that that was fictional, didn't you?

THE WITNESS: Judge, I believe it's fictional…

THE COURT: …you knew you weren't going to use any of this, at least for the basis of an appeal for a new trial.

THE WITNESS: Absolutely.

THE COURT: I don't understand why you misled the press and the public.

THE WITNESS: Your Honor, it was not a misleading of the press and the public the way I look at it. It was telling Mr. Bowman, right, that we were looking into what the Lutzes had told us.

THE COURT: For that purpose. But you knew you weren't using it for that purpose?

THE WITNESS: Yes, I did know I wasn't using it for that purpose. As was indicated before, I, from the very beginning of the Lutzes telling me, I felt if I ever attempted to go into a courtroom and use psychic phenomena as a basis for an application of a new trial, I would be laughed out of the courtroom. [*Lutz v Hoffman*, p. 305]

Preliminaries

Edith Evans

Edith Evans was a minor character in *The Amityville Horror*. She was also a real person. Just as it says on page eight of Anson's book, Mrs. Evans was a very pleasant, attractive, warm woman. Edith worked as a realtor for Conkling (not Conklin) Realty, Inc. and was the realtor who showed the DeFeo home to George and Kathleen Lutz in 1975. The book is correct.

Mrs. Evans told me that she did, indeed, say something to the Lutzes to the effect that "I wanted to show you how the 'other half' of Amityville lives." Examination of her records revealed that the closing on the house at 112 Ocean Avenue did, in fact, take place on December 18, 1975. It was further her recollection that the closing was in the morning, that the Lutzes did not immediately secure free title to the house, and funds, therefore, were placed in escrow. More amazingly, she verified an anecdote which previously seemed to be a perfect example of Anson's dramatic imagination: After the closing, everyone had in fact forgotten the keys to the house, and Edith had to go back to the office to retrieve them. She did deliver them to the Lutzes who were already at 112 Ocean Avenue with a U-Haul. The book is right again.

The Lutzes did obtain some furniture left from the DeFeo estate including a dining room set. This item, however, was still in the house at the time the Lutzes moved in and was not "in storage" as the book claims [*AH*-pb, p. 18]. Additionally, the Lutzes kept the DeFeos' refrigerator, two washers, two dryers, and a freezer which were also still on the premises and not in storage. This may seem like a small error, but even the slightest error can raise important questions concerning the general veracity of a story.

Moving into the House

On page seventeen we read,

> It was quite cold on the actual moving day. The family had packed the night before and slept on the floor. George was up early and singlehandedly piled the first full load into the biggest U-Haul trailer he

> could rent, finishing in barely enough time to clean up and get to the closing with Kathy. [*AH*-pb., p. 17]

We have already noted that the DeFeo items were already in the house, not in storage. But there are other problems with the story. The U-Haul trailer, we are told, was "the biggest he could rent." How was the big trailer pulled? We read on page eighteen that "Kathy followed with the children in the family van with their motorcycle in the back." There is no mention in the book of a second automobile owned by the Lutzes.

The mystery is compounded on two paragraphs later:

> At one o'clock, George rolled into the driveway of 112 Ocean Avenue, with the trailer crowded with their belongings, and the DeFeos' refrigerator, washer, dryer and freezer that had been in storage. [*AH*-pb, p. 17]

There still is no mention of how the trailer was towed and it is made clear that *all the Lutz possessions, including DeFeo items, were in the trailer*—even though it was only "the first full load" that had been piled into it. The problem of the biggest-possible trailer is resolved on page eighteen:

> Five of George's friends, young men in their twenties and husky enough to help move bulky items [*despite George having previously been able to load them into the trailer all by himself*], were waiting. Furniture, boxes, crates, barrels, bags, toys, bikes, *motorcycles*, and clothing were taken *from the truck* onto the patio at the rear of the house and into the garage [emphases added]. [*AH*-pb., p. 18]

So, it wasn't a trailer; it was a truck. The existence of the truck itself was attested by Father Pecoraro (the book's Father Mancuso) in the *Lutz v Hoffman* trial. Even so, the solution to one vehicular question raises a second. We have seen that Kathy conveyed one motorcycle in the back of the family van. But *motorcycles* were taken out of the truck. Did George Lutz own three or more motorcycles?

Regardless, the chapter continues to when the broker tells the Lutzes that the house formerly belonged to the murdered DeFeos. But she assured me she did not do it "without hesitation" as the book claims. To the contrary, she waited for an opportunity when the Lutzes' three children—Daniel, nine (actually, just turned ten, having been born on October 26, 1965); Christopher, seven; and Melissa, five—were occupied elsewhere and would not be upset by the gruesome story.

Happy Houses Only!

Moreover, Mrs. Evans was in a bit of a quandary about telling the Lutzes that this was *the* murder house for a very curious reason. Previously, when showing other houses to the Lutzes, they had instructed her to show them only "happy houses." They did not want to buy a house which had been the scene of unhappiness—let alone tragedy. George had explained that Kathy was sort of psychic, that she could sense if a house had been the scene of unhappiness. Apparently thinking that houses retain memories which could be perceived by her, and not wanting them to become her reality if they were negative, Kathy had told Edith, "Happy houses, only."

The problem was, it was a bad season of the year for real estate, and Edith had already shown them all the "happy houses" she knew of! She had delayed telling them the history of the DeFeo house when she first showed it, half expecting that at any moment Kathy would tell *her* which house it was! But there was no sign that Kathy was "picking up bad vibes." When the Lutzes were later told it was the DeFeo house, they were very surprised, according to Mrs. Evans. In fact, they seemed to take it as a good omen that Kathy had *not* perceived the truth about the house!

I believe this anecdote is of great significance in that it reveals an eccentricity in the psychology of Kathy Lutz and implies a high degree of suggestibility and a bias in favor of paranormal interpretations of the world. It also tends to discount the claim about the Lutzes "not being superstitious" [*AH*-pb, p. 4]. It explains why—even though George was supposedly a lukewarm Methodist—they decided to find a priest to bless the house. They apparently actually believed that holy water could change the house in some way. The stage for autosuggestion had been set long before the Lutzes moved into the house.

The "High Hopes" Sign

Contrary to what is said on page eight, at the time Mrs. Evans showed the house to the Lutzes, there was no sign in the front yard reading "High Hopes." During the *Lutz v Hoffman* trial [*Lutz v. Hoffman*, p. 254], Weber claimed he had shown the Lutzes an old portrait of the DeFeo house which showed a sign reading "High Hopes." He claimed that this was an instance of the Lutzes purloining special information originally intended for the Lutz-Hoffman-Weber book for Anson's writing. Weber said the reason for using the motif was to add a bit of dramatic irony to the story:

> There was never any sign on the outside of the house, and the name "High Hopes" was given to me. Again, "High Hopes" taken in context with this whole story… it's … counterpoint, if that's the right word….Here a

> family had been massacred, another family claimed to have fled, and now they look at the house and now there's a sign, "High Hopes." [*Lutz v Hoffman*, p. 255]

During the cross-examination, however, a news article dated November 14, 1974 (the day after the murders) was presented by Mr. Daley which clearly showed, in Gothic letters, the "High Hopes" sign in front of the house. Although Weber claimed the photo to be "doctored," the sign appeared in different photos, taken at various angles, which were published by many different newspapers.

Although knowledge of the sign was in the public record, it is still probable the Lutzes got the information from Weber. Their lawyer, Mr. Daley, admitted "I can have Mr. Lutz testify to the fact that he took that [*picture*] from news articles through the library a short while ago" [*Lutz v Hoffman*, p. 310].

The significance of this statement seems to have escaped the participants in the trial. If the Lutzes had done their newspaper research at the time it says they did in the book (December, 1975) they wouldn't have had to obtain it a short while before the trial (held in September, 1979). On page eight it says, "George ... noticed the neighbors' shades were all drawn on the sides that faced his house, but not in front or in the direction of the houses on the other side." According to the exposé by Alex Drehsler and Jim Scovel, however,

> Neighbors on both sides of the house, Diana Ireland and Stanley Milstein, denied that, as the book states, they had their blinds drawn on windows facing the Lutz house when the new family arrived. Both families said they do not even have blinds on ground-floor windows. [Drehsler, "Fact or Fiction?" *Newsday*, Nov. 17, 1977]

The Fireplace and Furnace

Page seventeen implies George did some work on the property prior to the closing: "Handy with his tools and equipment, George made good progress on many interior projects....He soon dropped everything to clean the chimney, then the fireplace" [*AH*-pb., p 17].

Mrs. Evans assured me that, though work *was* done in the house before the closing, Mr. Lutz was never allowed to work in the house. I was told that when Mrs. Evans showed the house, one of the first things George did was to turn up the thermostat to see if the furnace was working. The furnace promptly began to smoke and it was apparent that something was wrong with the heating system. At the expense of the DeFeo estate, workmen later were sent to replace a defective part in the furnace. Since difficulties with the heating system figure prominently in the story, it is significant to know that there may have been a very mundane reason for the anomalies which the Lutzes claim to have experienced with the heat. There may very well have been a defect remaining in the thermostatic system, according to Mrs. Evans. Although this information is merely suggestive, it accords with information which appeared in *Newsday* a month after the Lutzes left the house:

> One friend of Lutz said that the family left the house because they had used up all their money buying it and could not afford to repair the heating system, which failed when they moved in. [Carter, "DeFeo Home Abandoned," *Newsday*, Feb. 14, 1976]

As a matter of fact, George Lutz testified later that "we had the service people come in a number of times to fix the furnace" [*Lutz v Hoffman*, p. 183]. I am assuming, of course, that the workmen did not fully succeed in curing the furnace's ills. When one considers the great to-do made throughout the book of George Lutz hovering around the fireplace, fussing with the thermostat, repeatedly procuring "logs" to put onto the fire, it is strange that the visits of the service people are not mentioned in the book. After all, it would have been even spookier to have all the heating problems continuing in force after each service call's completion.

Thursday, December 18, 1975

Events of the Day

Weather claimed: "Quite cold, 6° by 11:00 PM."
Actual weather: Low of 23° at 7:00 PM; high of 39° at 12:01 AM

The Lutzes

Real estate closing in AM. George rolls into driveway with U-Haul at 1:00 PM. Keys forgotten, George calls Edith, who fetches the keys from her office.

Father Mancuso

Mancuso is introduced. He has awakened feeling uneasy, moves in a daze in the rectory. He has lunch with four friends in Lindenhurst and is told of DeFeo murders and told not to go to the house. He arrives at Lutzes after 1:30 PM and begins to bless the house. A voice says, "Get out?" He talks with Lutzes about DeFeo murders, then leaves for mother's house. He arrives at his mother's with black circles under his eyes.

The Lutzes

George completes first unloading around 4:00 PM, goes back to Deer Park. The Lutz dog, Harry, tries to run away. George returns to Amityville and chains Harry to dog compound after 6:00 PM.

Father Mancuso

Mancuso leaves his mother's house after 8:00 PM for rectory. On the Van Wyck Expressway in Queens his car is forced off road, the hood flies up, *etc.* He calls priest friend who helps with tow truck and is driven to rectory. An hour later he receives a call from priest friend telling him about the windshield wipers.

The Lutzes

George works inside. Harry chokes on his chain. At about 11:00 PM George burns cartons in the fireplace.

Dating the Beginning—Contradictory Accounts

Although the first chapter of Anson's book begins on December 18, and although Lutz, when testifying under oath, ultimately settled upon the eighteenth as the day he moved into the house, there is some uncertainty as to whether or not the Lutzes actually spent the night of December 18, 1975 in the house at 112 Ocean Ave. In the first hardcover printings of the book, the Prologue gave December 23 as the move-in date. Lutz's testimony in this regard is astonishingly imprecise:

Q Mr. Lutz, when was it that you first moved into the so-called Amityville house? On what date?
A I believe it was December 14th, a week before Christmas, 1975.
Q And when was it that you had purchased that house?
A That same day.
Q The actual closing was on December 14th?
A Well, it was exactly, if I remember right, seven days before Christmas. Around the 18th.
Q And you moved into the house with your entire family at that time?
A With my three children and my wife. [*Lutz v Hoffman*, p. 40]

In the face of such imprecision and uncertainty of recall, we may be forewarned that a healthy skepticism is in order when we consider Mr. Lutz's recall of other details! On February 14, 1976, A.J. Carter and Christopher M. Cook reported:

> *On Dec. 23* George and Kathleen Lutz bought the house in which six members of the Ronald DeFeo family were methodically shot to death the previous year, *and a few days later they moved in* [emphasis added]. Within 10 days they moved out. [Carter, "DeFeo Home Abandoned," *Newsday*, February 14, 1976]

As mentioned previously, when I asked Edith Evans to check her records concerning the date of closing, she showed me her records which gave December 18 as the date. So, in this regard, the book is correct and the newspaper account is in error. However, it is still by no means established whether the Lutzes stayed in the house the night of the eighteenth. The earlier account of the story written by Hoffman contains enough material to fill about two weeks. Throughout *The Amityville Horror,* one has the feeling that a great amount of inflation and stretching of incidents has taken place in its writing to fill up the space of a lunar month.

To proceed to the weather: "It was quite cold on the actual moving day....By eleven o'clock that night....it had grown colder outside, down to almost 6 degrees above zero" [*AH*-pb, pp. 17, 25].

According to the weather records in the *New York Times* for Dec. 19, 1975, the mean temperature for December 18 was 31°—with a high of 39° at 12:01 AM and a low of 20° at 11 PM. Although it may be argued that Amityville is about 35 miles away from New York City, and the weather may have been different from that reported in *The Times*, we may point out that both places have the same elevation and very nearly the same position with respect to the ocean. While we may allow for occasional microclimatic differences, over a month's time the weather records for the two places should average out about the same. The difference between six and twenty degrees above zero is significant and served the author as a warning that all weather alleged in the *True Story* had to be checked carefully.

There are a few minor errors in Anson's Chapter One. As we have seen, the realty office is given as "The Conklin Realty Office." In fact, it is "The Conkling Realty Office." Anson apparently picked up the incorrect spelling from a *Newsday* article. It is said that Ronald DeFeo killed his family "on the night of November 13, 1974." In reality, the murders took place in the *early morning hours* of November 13.

While these are picayune points, they nevertheless reveal that Anson was not one to check facts carefully. Only rarely did he go to primary sources. At no time, for example, did he ever call Mrs. Evans to check the accuracy of the Lutzes' story. Since he could not go into the house, and she *had* been in it, his not calling her seems tantamount to willful ignorance.

Anson's claim, on page 263, that "to the extent that I can verify them, all the events in this book are true" is underwhelming, to say the least. Robert L. Morris, reviewing *The Amityville Horror* in the pages of *The Skeptical Inquirer* [Spring/Summer, 1978] was of the opinion that the sentence should read "To the extent that I *bothered* to verify..."

Basement

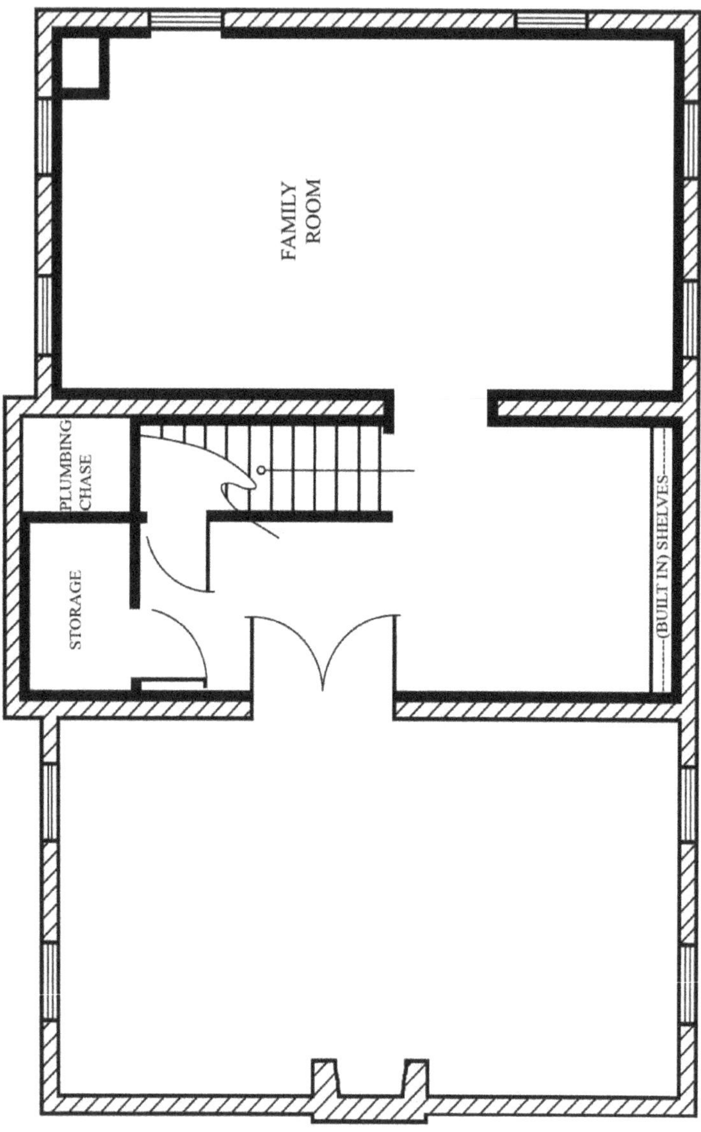

Fig. 5 Simplified blueprint of the basement of the Lutz-DeFeo house at 112 Ocean Avenue in Amityville, New York.

First Floor

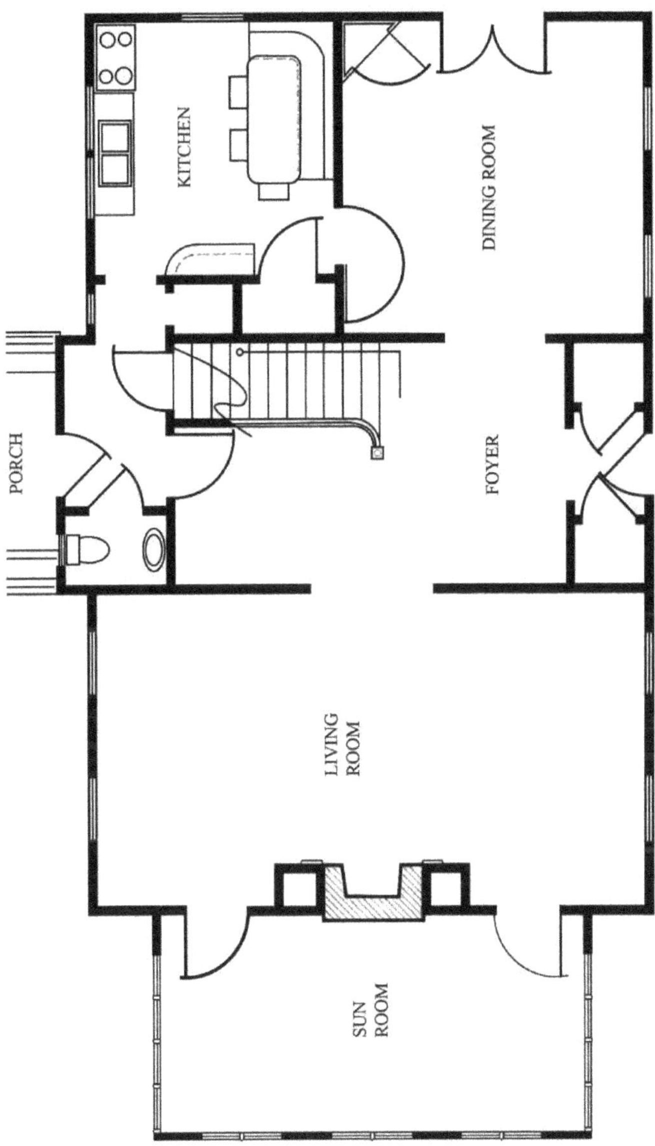

Fig. 6 Simplified blueprint of the first floor of the Lutz-DeFeo house at 112 Ocean Avenue in Amityville, New York.

Second Floor

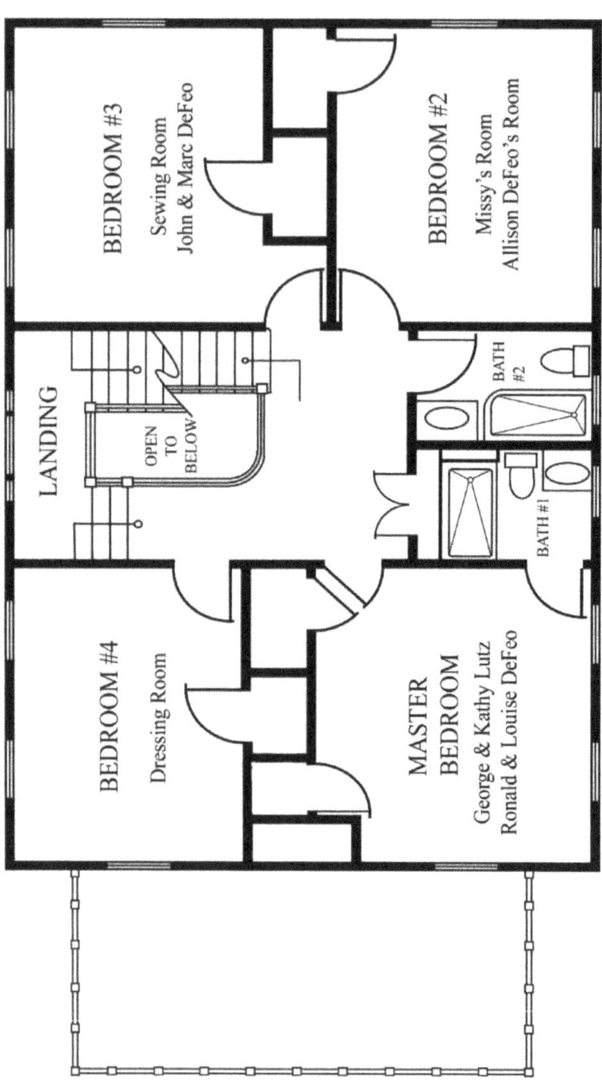

Fig. 7 Simplified blueprint of the second floor of the Lutz-DeFeo house at 112 Ocean Avenue in Amityville, New York.

Third Floor

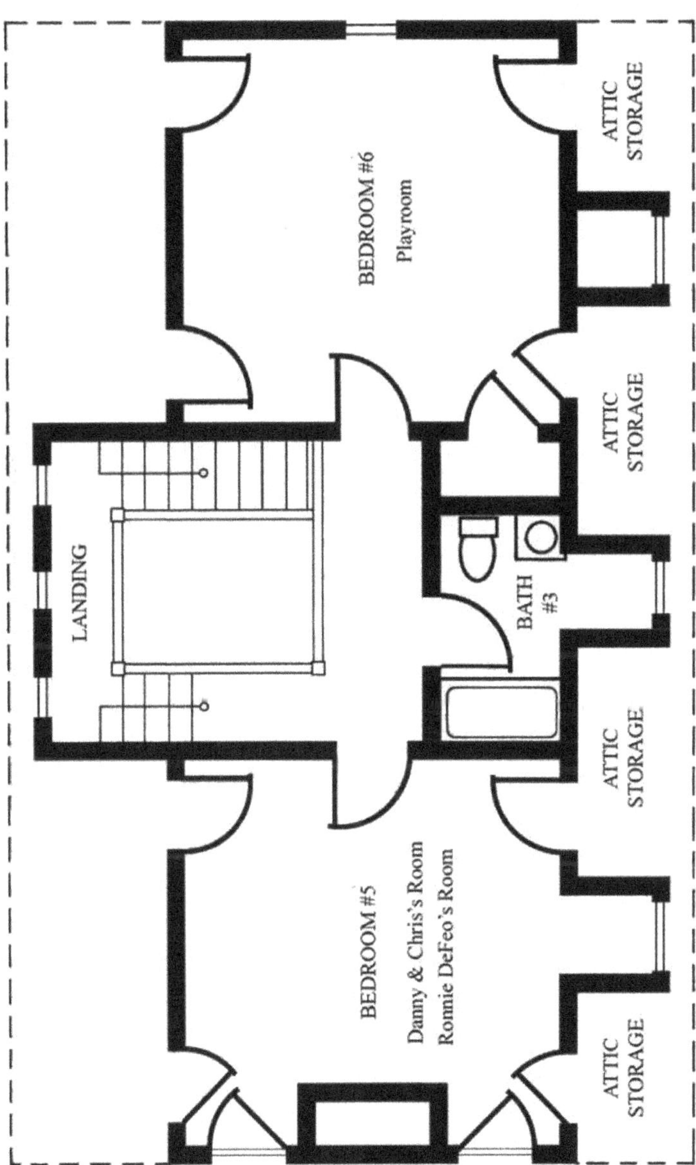

Fig. 8 Simplified blueprint of the third floor of the Lutz-DeFeo house at 112 Ocean Avenue in Amityville, New York.

Changes in Floor Plans

There are many interesting changes between different printings of the book. For instance, let us consider the floor plans of the house. In early hardcover printings, the "sewing room" is located at the southeast corner of the second floor (Allison DeFeo's room), and Missy's room is in the northeast corner (Mark and John DeFeos' room). In the paperback version, these two rooms are reversed. In the hardcover version, the third floor "playroom" is located at the front of the house (where Ronald DeFeo's room had been), and the boys' bedroom is at the back (Dawn DeFeo's room). These are also reversed in the paperback editions.

Although the floor plans change in the illustrations, the text of the paperback still reads as though the original floorplans were correct. For example, on page 38 we read:

> The fourth bedroom on the second floor—now Kathy's sewing room—has two windows [*although the illustrations show the correct number, three*]. One, which looks out at the boathouse and the Amityville River….The other faces the neighboring house to the right of 112 Ocean Avenue.

Now the house to the right of 112 Ocean Avenue would be the house on the south, if one is viewing the house from the street. Of course, to a viewer standing in the river it would be the house on the north side. Fortunately, we do not need to postulate such a strained point of reference. On page 39 we read about "the toilet in the second bathroom next to the sewing room." The room at the southeast corner is the only possible candidate for the sewing room.

What are we to think of an author who wrote about a haunted house but didn't seem to know for sure which room was where?

In a similar manner, though less clear-cut, the tale on pages 233–234 makes more sense if the boys' bedroom is directly above the master bedroom, rather than at the opposite end of the house. This is the story where George dreams he can see through the ceiling into Chris' room, and Chris claims he had been able to see through the floor into the master bedroom.

There would also be a good reason for having the playroom (one of the demonically "infested" rooms) be Dawn DeFeo's. Lutz admitted during the *Lutz v Hoffman* trial that he had received information about this room from Attorney Weber:

> [Weber] told us that the—Dawn DeFeo, the eldest sister, didn't want to sleep in the playroom. She used to go downstairs and sleep with her

younger sister. Her father would angrily wake up during the night on a regular basis and send her back up to the room. [*Lutz v Hoffman*, p. 187]

Which is the true floor plan for the *True Story*? I do not know. More importantly, did Jay Anson know? At the time he wrote the book, he had never actually been inside the house. It comes as no surprise, therefore, to find that he made many errors while describing the house at second hand. It is very perplexing to learn that although the Lutzes met Jay Anson as early as March 11, 1976, and the book did not come out until about a year and a half later, Anson never was allowed access to the house. An unconvincing explanation of this circumstance is given in the transcript of the *Lutz v Hoffman* trial, where Mr. Block is cross-examining Mr. Lutz:

[*Mr. Block is asking about what Mr. Lutz considers to be inaccuracies in the book, and how they came to be*.]

A For example, one of the requirements that we had with Mr. Anson was that he not go through the house personally.
Q Was there a particular reason why you did not want Mr. Anson or anybody else to go through the house?
A It wasn't the case of anybody else. There was certainly a reason for Mr. Anson. We felt that the kind of people that should be allowed to go there would be the people that dealt with such things, and knew about such things, or had experience in dealing with…
Q You wanted a person experienced in—
A What we called "super natural."
Q You wanted an experienced super natural person to go to the house?
A Yes. Someone to go to the house that would know exactly what.
Q Somebody experienced in ghosts and goblins?
A We didn't look at it as ghosts and goblins. [*Lutz v Hoffman*, p.45]

It must be said that this is a curious restriction to place upon the man selected to write the definitive *True Story* which will be used "to set the record straight"! When one considers the fact that Mr. Anson had just finished a project concerning the filming of the movie *The Exorcist* and was contemplating the writing of a book in collaboration with Father John J. Nicola (author of the Preface to *The Amityville Horror* and author of the book *Demoniacal Possession and Exorcism*), the case seems curiouser and curiouser, if we may quote Alice. A cynic might say that lack of first-hand knowledge of the house would allow for more "imaginative" use of the writer's talents. Moreover, if anyone should later point out errors, the writer could be used as a scapegoat, and the "true-but-unpublished real story" could still survive.

Priestly Changes

Floor plans are not the only things changed in the description of the events of December 18, 1975. There were changes affecting our understanding of who Father Mancuso was entirely. In the early hardcover version—and in the newspaper serializations of the book—it is said that:

> Father Frank Mancuso is not merely a cleric. In addition to properly attending to his priestly duties, he is a lawyer, a judge of the Catholic Court and a practicing psychotherapist.
>
> In the paperback version, this reads:
>
> Father Frank Mancuso is not only a cleric. In addition to properly attending to his priestly duties, he handles clients in family counseling for his diocese.

In the early version, Mancuso's mother lives in Queens; according to the paperback, she lives in Nassau. His apartment is first in the Sacred Heart Rectory, then in the Long Island Rectory (to be sure, the good Father is in a daze all morning in either case). As in the case of the changing floor plans, the text still supposes that Mancuso's mother lives in Queens. Toward the top of page 22, Mancuso refuses to have dinner with the Lutzes, "explaining that he planned to have dinner with his mother at her house in Nassau." Further on down the same page we read, "The priest nodded. Then with repeated goodbyes from the three children, the family watched as he drove off to Queens."

When Amityville's Horror commandeers his car, the priest is on "the Van Wyck Expressway in Queens"! This makes sense if his mother's home is in Queens, but it is utterly inexplicable if she lives anywhere in Nassau County. In the early version, the priest drives an "old, blue Vega." In the paperback, this becomes an "old, tan Ford." In this particular incident, Mancuso,

> found his car was literally being forced onto the right shoulder. He looked around quickly. There was no other vehicle within fifty feet of him! Shortly after driving back onto the highway and continuing on his way, the hood suddenly flew open, smashing back against the windshield. One of the welded hinges tore loose. The right door flew open! [*AH*-pb, pp. 23–24]

A reason for the change in the make of automobile has been suggested in an exposé by Dennis Hevesi: "Perhaps the transformation had something to do with the fact that hoods on all Chevrolet Vegas are hinged by the headlights and open away from the windshield" [Hevesi, "Haunted by Horror Story," *Newsday*, Sept. 17, 1978]. Although we may never know the reasons for the changes in floor plans, in the transcript of the *Lutz v Hoffman* trial I was able to find out why Mancuso details were changed.

[*Father Ralph Pecoraro, the real Mancuso, is being interrogated by Mr. Block*]

Q Are you involved in any business ventures with the Lutzes at the present time?
A No, I am not.
Q Were you ever involved in any business ventures with them in the past?
A I was involved in the law suit against them.
Q You were involved in a law suit against them?
A Yes.
Q Which law suit are you talking about?
A I had started a law suit against the Lutzes for what I felt was an invasion of privacy.
Q An invasion of your privacy?
A Privacy.
Q Yes. Continue.
A And against Mr. Anson.
Q Yes. Continue.
A Which situation was resolved out of Court....That's the only sort of business that I would have with them. [*Lutz v. Hoffman, pp. 347–348*]
Q Was there a cash settlement in that case?
A They agreed to change certain statements in the book in which I was involved, and to correct some statements, and that was amenable to me. And since that was done, then the case was settled. I had no further objections.
Q Which of the items in the book that you objected to were the subject of that law suit?
A The things I objected to in the book were obviously revelations of who I was, which I found extremely upsetting, because it interfered directly with my work as an ecclesiastical judge, and it's obvious that I have had to leave my practice as a judge in New York because of this problem....When my name appears in newspapers and when things are said about me that are not true, or that are grossly exaggerated, how in God's name can you expect these people to have any respect for me? [*Lutz v Hoffman, pp. 349–350*]

Did the Priest Lie?

Since Father Pecoraro's whereabouts had been kept secret even during the trial, I was not able to interview him with regard to what claims were false, exaggerated, or true. However, according to Peter Jordan and Rick Moran, whose report appeared in an article by D. Scott Rogo in the June, 1978 issue of *Human Behavior*,

> The priest who allegedly visited the house, for example made it clear to the writers that he was embarrassed by the book and denied ever witnessing anything supernatural there. He did have an automobile accident while driving in the neighborhood, he admitted. But, he added, it was caused by a blowout and nothing more. [Rogo, "Amityville Horror or Hoax?" *Human Behavior*, June, 1978, p. 55].

Nevertheless, the priest testified in court that he *did* bless the house, and that he *did* hear a "voice":

> A The strange occurrence, as far as I know, is to hear a loud *noise* informing me to get out of the house.
> Q Are you testifying now that you visited that house and that a voice told you to get out?
> A Yes. I'm testifying that I visited the house, and I did bless the house. Of course I did.
> Q Are you also testifying that you heard a voice tell you to get out on that occasion?
> A Yes, I did.
> Q Where did this voice come from and in what form did it take?
> A It took a very human form. My presumption was it was a man, and I looked around very startled.
> Q And nothing was there?
> A Nothing. There was nothing.
> Q Were the Lutzes there at that time?
> A The Lutzes, yes, of course they were. They were out unloading the truck.
> Q And you were there by yourself at that time?
> A I was, yes.
> Q No one else heard this voice but you?
> A No one heard it but me, and I really didn't pay much attention to that after that, because I thought it was nonsense, until some other situations occurred, and I was in communication with a friend of mine who was an orthodox Rabbi. [*Lutz v Hoffman,* p. 344–345]

Attorney Weber, being questioned immediately after the telephone testimony of Father Pecoraro (who, although his exact whereabouts were kept secret, was said by Mr. Lutz to be in the vicinity of San Francisco), testified to the contrary:

> A I asked him [*Pecoraro*] what was his involvement with this. He said that he had received a telephone call on several occasions from Mr. Lutz, and that he had spoken to the Lutzes after they had left the house. He told me—I asked him specifically if he had been in the house, and he said he was never in the house. [*Lutz v Hoffman*, p. 369]

Drehsler and Scovel also reported,

> Pecoraro admitted knowing Anson, Nicola (who wrote the preface) and the Lutzes. He said he had helped in annulling Mrs. Lutz' earlier marriage and in instructing Lutz in Catholicism. He said he has not read the book and was reluctant to answer questions about it. But he denied ever going to the Lutz home as the book has "Father Mancuso" doing. He said Lutz had telephoned him, complaining of psychic happenings and that he had referred him to the local parish. [Drehsler, "Fact or Fiction?" *Newsday*, Nov. 17, 1977]

Obviously, someone was not telling the truth. The Lutzes admitted that Pecoraro was Mancuso, and the priest claimed, under oath, that he did bless the house. Attorney Weber and the two *Newsday* reporters, on the other hand, claimed that Pecoraro denied blessing the house.

Memory Problems

The priest is supposed to have had lunch with four friends in Lindenhurst. They try to prevent him from going to the Lutz house after refreshing his memory of the DeFeo murders: "The priest tried to think back. He seldom read the news when he picked up a paper, only looking for items of special interest. 'No, I really don't seem to recall it'" [*AH*-pb, p. 21].

Although Father Mancuso's credentials are most impressive according to Chapter Two, it nowhere states that he is a Carthusian who has taken vows of blindness and deafness. Admittedly, the murders themselves had occurred thirteen months previously and had only filled all newspapers and TV and Radio news for several weeks. But the trial of Ronald DeFeo had taken place over the space of seven weeks *that same autumn.* Not only were there articles concerning the progress of the trial nearly every day in the local papers for seven weeks, DeFeo had been *sentenced* on December fourth of the same month as Mancuso's luncheon! He would have had to think all the way back from December 18 to December 5—the day the newspapers first reported the sentencing!

Amityville Rorschach Testing?

If the priest did in fact bless the house, and if he did in fact have lunch with ecclesiastical friends who warned him about the house, we may well imagine that the priest was very negatively "psyched" by the time he reached the house. People who actually believe in ghouls and ghosts can often be very convincing and terrifying as they describe the terrors that lurk in the bogeyman's bailiwick. The priest may have been expecting the worst, and when presented with the acoustical equivalent of the Rorschach Test, a Medieval state of mind could have projected itself into his sensorium.

The Rorschach Ink-Blot Test, it will be recalled, is the classical example of what psychologists call a *projective test*. The picture presented to the subject is, of course, just an ink-blot. However, the subject's nervous system—presumably guided by unconscious predispositions—creates order where none exists in the actual visual stimulus. The subject's interpretation of what is "seen" is actually a "projection" of unconscious biases upon the conscious perceptions.

An analogous phenomenon can be demonstrated in the auditory modality also. In this case, the subject is exposed to "white noise" at a volume just barely above threshold level. White noise is a random mixture of sounds of all audible frequencies and varying durations. Subjects who are told they are listening to a conversation will often report that they can identify various words, phrases, or even sentences. Again, there really are no words in the acoustical stimulus, but the subject's nervous system imposes an order upon the disorder, and the unconscious is projected into conscious perception.

It may also be noted that contemporary research in sensory neuropsychology has shown that the sense organs themselves routinely metamorphose vague or near-threshold stimuli into sharply-focused neural responses. In the visual realm, especially, there are numerous illusions known in which the subject "sees" lines which are not actually present in the visual stimulus. A similar acoustical illusion was exploited by J.S. Bach in his works for unaccompanied violin. There are passages where the listener will swear there are at least two violins playing at least two continuous melodic lines.

It is very revealing to note that Pecoraro's first description of the strange occurrence is of "a loud *noise* informing me to get out of the house." It is possible that he felt, at the time, that he had just experienced an acoustical Rorschach phenomenon. He went on to testify that "I really didn't pay much attention to that after that, because I thought it was nonsense."

It was only later, he said, after talking to an orthodox Rabbi that in retrospect he began to take the incident seriously. The fact that he ultimately became emotionally involved is shown by Weber's testimony that the priest (after denying that he had blessed the house) had told him, "as for me, I'm in abject terror of the mere mention of the house" [*Lutz v Hoffman*, p.361].

The Dog's Tale

On page 22 we learn that when George went back to Deer Park for his dog, Harry, and the remainder of the family's possessions, the dog "leaped out and would have made a getaway if he hadn't been snared by his head." This is supposed to have great occult significance. Animals, especially dogs, are not only especially sensitive to "entities," they are supposed to be telepathic and, in this case, exhibit the faculty of precognition. Despite his hardly-wrinkled cerebral cortex, that half-breed Labrador just knew, by jingoes, that no good would come of this move! Once the dog was chained up in the back yard, and night had fallen, the dog liked the situation even less:

> Harry began an awful howling outside....George ran out to the back fence to find the poor animal strangling. He had tried to jump over the fence and was now choking on his chain, which had looped across the top bar. [*AH*-pb, p. 24]

The probable source for this episode is to be found in Weber's testimony concerning the material he allegedly gave the Lutzes and which subsequently surfaced in Anson's book:

[*Weber is being questioned by Mr. Block.*]

Q Could you continue in terms of telling us where, thereafter, other material appears in the book on information which you imparted to the Lutzes?

A Well, page 19 [*hard cover*], the Lutzes have transposed a story which I told them about Ronnie DeFeo and his dog. Ronnie evidently did not get along with the family dog and made it a point on a number of occasions to fix it so that the dog would kill itself or strangle itself by jumping over the storm fence around the pool. [*Lutz v Hoffman*, p. 275]

The same story appears on page nineteen in Anson's book, but of course, this time it involves the Lutzes' dog, Harry.

Friday, December 19, 1975

Events of the Day

Weather Claimed: No weather mentioned.

The Lutzes

At 3:15 AM. George wakes to knocking seeming to come from downstairs, then across the hall. He goes to sewing room and hears a noise overhead. Danny and Chris are above him (*i.e.* at the back of the house). Something is moving down by boathouse. There is a shadow close to Harry. Another rap is heard from the direction of the boathouse. Kathy wakes as George returns to put on pants. Boathouse door is open.

A half hour later George is back in bed worrying about money. He falls asleep about 6 AM. Kathy wakes up *minutes later* [How could this have been reported?], goes down to kitchen, thinks about Transcendental Meditation, is surprised by Missy. George, unshaven, comes down after 9 AM. He unloads U-Haul and returns it to Deer Park. He hollers at the kids. He feels cold.

Kathy goes to bed at 11 PM. George is still in living room at fireplace with thermostat set at 75°. George goes to bed and falls to sleep immediately at midnight.

Although most chapters of the *Amityville Horror: A True Story* deal with a single day during the Lutzes' residence in the horror house, Chapter 3 of the book encompasses three days: Friday, December 19; Saturday, December 20; and Sunday, December 21. To the best of my ability, I have tried to assign specific events alleged for each separate day in this and the next two chapters.

Before examining Mr. Anson's description of the events of December 19 in detail, it is necessary that we become aware of the problems he had to solve in order to write this and other early chapters of *A True Story*. We have already seen that he was not allowed to inspect the house himself. Actually, this stipulation was only a minor impediment compared to the problem revealed in the following testimony, drawn from Mr. Block's cross examination of Mr. Lutz:

[*George Lutz is being asked about the title of the book*]

Q How about that portion of the caption of the book that said this was a true story? You had no objection to that?
A No.
Q In fact, what was written by Mr. Anson was in every sense a true story, was it not?
A Yes.
Q There was nothing in there that was fabricated or not correct, or not the truth?
A Well, if we were to look at the whole story and how it was related from the tapes, there were a number of things that Mr. Anson had to move around as far as exact dates. For example, he kept calling us or writing us and asking us to pin down exactly what happened on that date, and *we could not do that* [emphasis added].
Q You had a problem with dates from time to time?
A Certainly. We remembered the last week much clearer than the first week. Some events stood out more so than others. But there was no way to pinpoint exactly what happened on that date. [*Lutz v Hoffman, pp. 44–45*]

What, we may ask, can an author do to write a book chronicling 28 days of "horror" do when it's not possible to scare up even the memory of a goose pimple for the first week? Is there any textbook that can provide instruction? Is there any model that can help to pad the pages? In this case, I believe there existed a textbook which was as useful as the tape-recorded memories the Lutzes supplied to Mr. Anson: *The Exorcist*, a novel by William Peter Blatty.

The *Exorcist* Connection

Very early in my research for this book I came upon an article about Jay Anson in the *New York Times Book Review*. In the article, Judy Klemesrud had written,

> Mr. Anson ... said he had no knowledge of the supernatural until 1973, when he was assigned to write a short documentary "featurette" about the making of the movie, *The Exorcist*. On the set, he became friendly with the film's technical consultant, Father John Nicola, The Roman Catholic Church's occult investigator in America.…The two talked about doing a book to be called *Psychology of the Devil* for Prentice-Hall, but the

project never got off the ground. [Klemesrud, "Behind the Best Sellers," *New York Times Book Review*, 83:28, Jan. 22, 1978]

Could the material of *The Exorcist* have colored Mr. Anson's handling of the Lutzes' material? Could it even have colored the Lutzes' perception of events? While this was highly probable, I had never read *The Exorcist* before and so decided to remedy this. I had to evaluate my hypothesis that I would find similarities, if not actual borrowings, between one book and the next.

Before reading *The Exorcist*, however, I checked to make sure that the paperback version of the book had been available at the time of the Lutzes' "ordeal" and that the movie had played in their area of residence. I even came upon an article by Bill Mason in *Newsday* [Nov. 5, 1975] entitled "Books Cause Devilish Stir at School." It recounted how upset parents were about a teacher in Patchogue (about 20 miles from the Lutzes' home in Deer Park) who had recommended that her students read *The Exorcist*, *The Crucible*, and *Rosemary's Baby* for a unit on "Puritans, Salem, and Witchcraft."

Clearly, *The Exorcist* and things demoniacal were in the air during the Long Island winter of 1975. I began to read *The Exorcist*.

My attention was piqued almost immediately. On the first page after the Prologue (Anson's book also has a "Prologue"!), page eleven, my eyes fell upon the line which reads: "The beginning of the horror passed almost unnoticed..." Two lines later I read: "...perhaps not connected to the horror at all."

This seemed a bit of a coincidence, but by itself it certainly would not prove anything. One would expect to encounter the word "horror" in a book about exorcism. But later in the book, I read: "The stench was more powerful than the evening before. He closed the door. Stared. *That horror.* That thing on the bed" [*Exorcist*, p. 276].

I suddenly realized that here the word "horror" was being used to describe a *thing* which excites horror or dread. This is a bit different from our more common use of the word to denote "a painful emotion of fear, dread, and abhorrence," as Webster puts it. It hit me for the first time that the word "horror" in the title of Anson's book had been used in the *Exorcist* sense: it refers to *the evil entity* lurking in the lair at 112 Ocean Avenue. It does not refer to neuropsychology.

I then read on in amazement as I noticed the following similarities between the first chapter of *The Exorcist* and Anson's description of the Lutzes' first night in the house:

The Exorcist	*The Amityville Horror*
At approximately 12:25 AM. Chris [*the mother*] glanced from her script with a frown of puzzlement. She heard *rapping* sounds … the *rappings* persisted.	George sat up in bed, wide awake. He had heard a knock on his front door….It was 3:15 in the morning! Again a loud *rapping* … more from somewhere off to his left.
She got up to investigate. She went out to the *hallway* and looked around….She *padded* down the *hall* … and stepped into the *room* [*of her 12-year old daughter*].	George got out of bed, *padded* across the cold, uncarpeted floor of the *hallway* and into the sewing *room.*
She *padded* to the *window*. Checked it.	He looked out the *window* into the darkness.
Abruptly, she flicked a quick glance to the *ceiling*. There! Faint scratchings! *Rats in the attic*, for Pete's sake!	From somewhere over his head came a sharp crack… he… looked up at the *ceiling*. He heard a low *squeak*.
She felt oddly relieved. And then noticed the *cold*. The room. It was *icy*… she touched the radiator. Hot.	Barefooted and wearing only his pajama pants, *George was shivering now* [*i.e., before any windows are opened*]. He quickly lifted the window, and the *freezing air* hit him full blast.
She … padded quickly down to the *kitchen.*	Kathy… had too much to do in the *kitchen* and she had better get started before the kids get up.
Once, in the mountains of Bhutan, she had stared for hours at a Buddhist monk who was squatting on the ground in *meditation*, Finally, she thought she had seen him *levitate.*	It [*the kitchen*] might be just the place for her *Transcendental Meditation*, which George had been practicing for two years; Kathy, one.
[Chris' secretary is also "into" *meditation*, according to p. 30.]	[*We may remember that in the 1970s devotees of TM were paying extra for advanced courses designed to give them the power to levitate!*]

Scattered, these similarities would not be worthy of notice. But when condensed together as they are in the beginnings of both books, they are highly suggestive.

The similarities between the two books do not end here. In both books, there is a tendency for chapters alternately to describe the events in the life of a family and events in the life of a priest. Both books involve the possibility of murder being the result of demonic possession. In *The Exorcist*, the murder is actually fulfilled while in *The Amityville Horror* the suggestion is ever-present that Ronnie DeFeo was possessed when he wiped out his family. In fact, the Lutzes supposedly first went to Attorney Weber with their story for the alleged purpose of showing that DeFeo had been possessed and thus should have a new trial.

A little girl figures prominently in the stories of both books. Both girls paint or draw pictures of animals. Both spend increasing amounts of time alone by themselves. Both girls have imaginary playmates who take on a sinister reality as the plot unfolds. Regan's playmate in *The Exorcist* is named "Captain Howdy," whereas Missy has "Jodie the Pig." It is interesting to note that Regan occasionally had a real playmate named Judy. Could "Howdy" and "Judy" have become conflated into "Jodie"?

In both tales, unblinking eyes are seen at windows, drawers pop open, doors which had been shut are opened (and *vice-versa*), windows are shattered, objects and furniture become displaced, saliva drips from mouths, and there are "soundless shrieks for help."

But there is more! There are invisible, icy hands on the back of the neck, people's voices change and even speak in foreign languages, figures are seen in the little girl's window by observers outside the house, and cops keep lonely vigils in their cars parked outside infested houses. Both stories reference pigs. Things turn up missing, and a dead little boy, or spirit child, is mentioned. Both tales involve the odor of human excrement, things happen around three in the morning, followed by amnesia for the events the next day. Both homes have a "playroom."

Heroes in both novels stub their toes! There are dreams involving precognition and retrocognition. The mothers in both tales are suddenly startled by the previously undetected presence of another character (Kathy is startled by Missy, Chris is startled by her servant, Karl). In both novels, the hero develops from near atheist to devout believer in the noctibumpal world.

The priests of both books are psychiatrists, and both make trips to their mothers' homes. Both priests have problems with their superiors (Mancuso with his Chancellor, Karras with his Superior), and both are given reduced work assignments. Characters in both stories undergo changes in personality, disposition, and behavior. Insomnia, quarrelsomeness, and fits of temper are the order of the day. There is nausea, vomiting, and personal untidiness. Clairvoyant seeresses make visits to both houses ("Mary Jo Perrin" in *The Exorcist*, Eric's girlfriend Francine—alias Bill and Roz in Hoffman's account—in *The Amityville Horror*). "Psychic cold" is a prominent feature in both yarns, there are fireplaces, and guests leave early when visiting. A church is desecrated in *The Exorcist*, and a rectory attached to a church is stunk up in *The Horror*. Not to mention the inevitable crucifix is wont to move in both fables

The Exorcist as Textbook

Quite a catalogue. So much for the possibility of using *The Exorcist* as a model. How about using it as a textbook? On page 259 of *The Exorcist* we have a veritable recipe for developing a plot involving possession:

> Signs of possession may be the following: ability to speak with some facility in a strange language or to understand it when spoken by another; the faculty of divulging future and hidden events; display of powers which are beyond the subject's age and natural condition; and various other conditions which, when taken together as a whole, build up the evidence. [*Exorcist*, p. 259]

Several pages later, we learn how to expand the recipe for extra servings:

> [I]n case after case, irrespective of geography or period of history, the symptoms of possession were substantially constant. Some Regan had not evidenced as yet: stigmata; the desire for repugnant foods; the insensitivity to pain; the frequent loud and irrepressible hiccupping. But the others she had manifested clearly: the involuntary motor excitement; foul breath; furred tongue; the wasting away of the frame; the distended stomach; the irritations of the skin and mucous membrane. And most significantly present were the basic symptoms of the hard core of cases which Oesterreich had characterized as "genuine" possession: the striking change in the voice and in the features, plus the manifestation of a new personality. [*Exorcist*, p. 263]

I cannot, of course, prove that the Lutzes were carrying out self-fulfilling prophecies inspired by *The Exorcist*, or that Jay Anson was guilty of conscious and premeditated borrowing. Readers will have to evaluate the material presented in this book and draw their own conclusions. But let us return now to December 19, 1975, at 112 Ocean Avenue.

Let us first note that there actually are hot-water radiators in the house—just as in *The Exorcist* house. These could certainly provide a cacophonic chorus of knockings, rapping, banging and bumping. Nevertheless, we may never know for sure if George Lutz actually heard any knocking or rapping sounds that night. But we do know he did *not* "pad across the cold, uncarpeted floor of the hallway." According to Mrs. Evans, the second-floor hallway was carpeted at the time.

On page 29 we read, "Kathy turned off the light. 'Okay. Put your jacket on.' The next morning, she wouldn't remember having awakened at all [*AH*-pb, p. 29]. If this is supposed to be the beginning sign of incipient possession, I am unimpressed. My own wife could do that any night of the year! Moreover, many of my night students consistently developed amnesia for my finest and most edifying lectures. Especially during exams.

George goes out to the boathouse and finds a door open. Thus begins a behavior—never explained in the book—which is to be repeated night after night, if we are to believe Mr. Anson's account. From a dramatic point of view, the boathouse motif is poorly handled. It starts out well enough, and is used to increase tension in the reader as the epic progresses. But the boathouse motif is never woven into the harmony or counterpoint of the narrative. It goes nowhere. Still, the boathouse motif was discussed during the *Lutz v Hoffman* trial. When Lutz was asked about information he had acquired from Mr. Weber, he replied:

> A There were fights that had gone on in the kitchen, that there were personality changes that had taken place to the eldest boy Ronald DeFeo, and he used to spend a lot of time in the boathouse. And he felt that he was going to be invaded from the island.
>
> Q The boathouse played a prominent part in your book, did it not, ultimately?
>
> A Yes. [*Lutz v Hoffman*, p. 186]

It should be recalled that the so-called Amityville River, which is located to the rear of the Lutz property, is not a river at all, but is a narrow, V-shaped embayment connecting with the Great South Bay. There is a small island located a short distance from the boathouse.

Weber claimed that it was he who gave the Lutzes the boathouse motif, but the Lutzes claim they had the idea first and merely asked Weber if DeFeo had ever had a boathouse fixation. Since the Lutzes tape-recorded all their discussions with Attorney Weber, it should have been easy enough to determine who had it first. But alas, as in the Watergate affair, in the *Lutz v Hoffman* trial there was dispute about the genuineness and dates of the tapes which were presented as evidence, and perhaps as many as half of all the tapes had disappeared. Shortly before the trial was settled "out of court," Judge Weinstein was moved to declare:

> I am not going to allow these tapes to be further played. I am ruling, based on what I heard, subject of course to some explanation, that a number of

> the tapes have been withheld. Spoliation has therefore taken place and unless you can show why they're not produced I am going to assume that they were deliberately destroyed by your client [*i.e.*, *Lutz*]. [*Lutz v Hoffman*, p. 451]

Since the case was ultimately settled out of court, the Judge later had to point out that this and other statements he had made during the trial did not constitute findings either of fact or of law. It is rather revealing, however, that less than an hour later, the Lutzes decided to settle the dispute out of court!

Back to *The Horror,* after George goes back to bed, he is described as not being able to sleep due to money worries. Of course, this is quite possible—even probable. But we should keep in mind the fact that the Lutzes had *two* houses to sell at the time they decided to buy the Amityville property. Mrs. Evans was not certain of the location of the second house, but she was quite certain the Lutzes mentioned a second house which, for some reason, George said would be a bit more difficult to sell than the home in Deer Park.

The description of the Lutz family situation which is presented on page 30 is worth considering at this point. Anson mentions the fact that the three children were Kathy's by her first husband. Since George and Kathy had been married on the Fourth of July of the same year (according to the Hoffman articles), it may be expected that there would be a degree of readjustment and personality rearrangement in progress at the time of the story, regardless of the house in which they were living.

Later on in this book, as we consider windows and doors found open, and objects relocating in the house, we may want to remember that Danny (the eldest) was "into everything," and that Missy was "a little terror."

The discussion on page 31 regarding Transcendental Meditation is also of potential significance for understanding the Lutzes' experiences. If it is in fact true that both George and Kathy were involved in TM (*i.e.*, if the motif was not just borrowed from *The Exorcist*), it may be assumed that they were very suggestible persons. As a practicing hypnotist, I have had occasion to hypnotize a fair number of individuals who previously had practiced TM. Without exception, all proved to be excellent hypnotic subjects. Having been hypnotized, moreover, most reported that they now realized the meditative state was just a light stage of hypnosis. The hypothesis that the Lutzes were suggestible is further borne out by the fact that the Warrens said both George and Kathy had been interrogated under hypnosis.

The meaning of all this, of course, is that most of the preternatural experiences they are supposed to have undergone may be the result of both auto- and hetero-suggestion. With each one responding to the suggestive stimulation by the other, a sort of *folie à deux* could have developed. As we have seen, at the time they were looking at houses, they believed that bad memories residing in a house could "rub off" on new tenants. They later asked

Mr. Weber if the DeFeo family "had moved in happily and ended up very unhappily" in their last year. [*Lutz v Hoffman*, p. 191]

Kathy's meditation on meditation is followed by the scene where she is startled by the previously undetected presence of her daughter, Missy:

> Kathy sensed someone was staring at her. Startled, she looked up and over her shoulder. Her little daughter was standing in the doorway. "Missy! You scared me half to death....What are you doing up so early?" [*AH*-pb, p. 31]

This is, as I have said, very similar to the scene in *The Exorcist* where, *shortly after the first account of the rapping*—as also in Anson's book—the heroine is startled (in this case, by her servant).

Hygiene

Our discussion of the events of December 19 requires only a consideration of George's changes in personal hygiene to be complete. According to Anson's account, George Lutz underwent a degeneration in the course of the twenty-eight days with regard to his personal hygiene. On page 32 we read that after the first night in the house,

> Kathy looked at her husband whose big frame filled the doorway. She saw he hadn't shaved below his jawbone and that his dark blonde hair and beard were still uncombed. That meant he hadn't showered. [*AH*-pb, p.32]

The reference to George not having shaved is rather puzzling. In every photograph I have seen of him, he appears with a full beard which grows "below his jawbone" as well as above it.

Although absent from the prescription for possession quoted previously from *The Exorcist*, other parts of the book suggest that a possessed person initially becomes untidy, sloppy, and unclean. It seems relevant also to note that William Weber testified that he had given the Lutzes "confidential" information concerning Ronald DeFeo to the effect that he "would go for months on end, weeks on end, when he would refuse to take a shower" [*Lutz v Hoffman*, p. 277]. As we shall see in chapter 31, some people find this partial grounds for concluding Ronnie was possessed! Does DeFeo material undergo metamorphosis and emerge on page 33 of *The Amityville Horror*? William Weber thought so.

U-Haul Questions

We end this chapter by noting further complications of the U-Haul question discussed previously. On pages 32 and 33 we read:

> George sat down wearily at the table. "Nope. I still have to unload the *truck* and get it back out to Deer Park. We blew an extra fifty bucks by keeping it over-night." … George unloaded the U-Haul by himself, then drove it back to Deer Park, with his motorcycle in the rear so that he could get back to Amityville.

This leaves us with a number of questions:

1. Was it a U-Haul trailer or a truck?
2. Was the U-Haul unloaded by five husky young men, or by George Lutz alone?
3. Was there more than one motorcycle, and how did a specific one get to 112 Ocean Avenue from Deer Park, then to the patio behind the house, and then into the truck?

Perhaps we could add a fourth and fifth question: Did Jay Anson write more than one draft of his novel, and did his editor Tim Mossman at Prentice-Hall do anything that might be considered editing?

Saturday, December 20, 1975

Events of the Day

Weather claimed: No weather reported.

The Lutzes

George awakens at 3:15 AM and checks the boathouse. The boathouse is okay. The Lutz family begins to go through a collective personality change. George calls his office in Syosset and orders his men to complete some jobs over the weekend. George is preoccupied with the fireplace and boathouse.

Personality Changes

Since December 20, 1975 is early in the Lutzes' tenancy of the horror house, it is not surprising that there isn't much happening in the first chapter—perhaps the reason Anson had to bunch together three days into one chapter. About the only things to comment upon are the "collective personality change" the Lutz family is said to have undergone, the problem of the kitchen door, and the puzzle concerning the source of logs to burn in the fireplace.

Anson tells us, "Over the next two days, the Lutz family began to go through a collective personality change. As George said, 'It was not a big thing, just little bits and pieces, here and there'" [*AH*-pb, p. 33]. As with so much other material in the book, Attorney Weber claimed that he provided the *urmotiv* for this:

[*Mr. Weber is being questioned by Mr. Block*]

Q Could you continue in terms of telling us where, thereafter, other material appears in the book on information which you imparted to the Lutzes?

A Generally speaking, personality changes that the Lutzes referred to for the first time at page 25 [*hard cover*].

Q Where on page 25 are you referring?

A Well, the "little bits and pieces."
Q "It's not a big thing, just little bits and pieces"?
A That's correct. In fact, the little bits and pieces is a quote that Ronnie DeFeo told on two occasions to his psychiatrists, and he would explain to them how he had his personal difficulties when he was in the house. [*Lutz v Hoffman*, p. 275]

The Kitchen Door

Remembering that personality change is necessary for a diagnosis of demonic possession, we proceed to a question concerning the floorplan of the house. We read that "When George came out the kitchen door, Harry was still barking at the moving shadow. There was a length of two-by-four lumber lying against the swimming pool fence. George grabbed it and ran toward the boathouse" [*AH*-pb., p 29].

Although it is far from clear how a two-by-four just happened to be lying against the swimming pool fence in a posh, suburban neighborhood, it is quite clear that "the kitchen door" is an external door. George goes through the door into the yard between the house and the boathouse at the eastern end of the property. An examination of the floorplan published in all editions of *The Amityville Horror*, however, shows that there is no door on the east wall of the kitchen, only a window. The kitchen has only two doors—one leading into the dining room, and one leading to the foyer running between the main entry doors on the south and north sides of the house. The blueprints for the house confirm the absence of an external door between the kitchen and the back yard.

Unfortunately, the solution to the problem of the kitchen door turns out not to be so simple. The July 24, 1979 issue of the tabloid *The Star Magazine/Newspaper* carried an article about alleged further problems plaguing the "Horror Couple" three years after their abandonment of the house, as well as reporting their successful lie detector tests. It contained a picture of George Lutz displaying a number of photographs of the house taken at an angle that allows examination of the back wall. Examination of the provided photos with a magnifying glass raises the possibility that Anson's external kitchen door may have existed. In the photo taken from the boathouse that shows the swimming pool and the back door of the house, in addition to the double doors in the dining room wall, there appears to be a door immediately adjoining the kitchen window—right where the blueprints indicate a kitchen breakfast nook was located.

Unfortunately, the image is degraded in the photocopy of the clipping I was able to obtain, and the "door" may actually be a blurred image of a black shutter attached to the kitchen window. In the second photo of the back wall, taken from a more acute angle, there is nothing visible that would appear to be a door. It seems quite significant that the house in Lutz's pictures has been painted white with black shutters instead of the nearly black house with white shutters in which Lutz had been living. Subsequent owners have made extensive changes to the back of the house.

The Amityville Public Library has a clipping of an article in the tabloid *Star* dated January, 17, 1978 that shows Barbara Cromarty—the tenant immediately following the Lutzes—at the rear of the house. Clearly visible is a door beside the kitchen window—a three-component bay window! Significantly, at the time of the photograph the house had been painted white with black shutters—the exact opposite of the color scheme at the time of the Lutz residency. If—contrary to the original blueprints for the house—a kitchen door now exists, could it have existed at the time Anson's narrative needed it for a number of important episodes?

If there *had been* a kitchen door at the time of the Lutz residency, there could not have been a breakfast nook such as is shown in the blueprints. A breakfast nook figures prominently in the horrific events chronicled in *The Exorcist*, and it has seemed a happy accident that the house at 112 Ocean Avenue had one also. If, indeed, an external kitchen door existed in December of 1975, the breakfast-nook episodes of *The Amityville Horror* are further examples of borrowing from *The Exorcist.*

Whence Came the Wood?

We close this book's account of December 20, 1975, with an examination of questions raised by George Lutz's repeated feeding of "logs" into the fireplace in the living room of the horror house—an activity needed repeatedly throughout the book to document the "psychic cold" motif. We read that "George stayed down in the living room, feeding *log after log* into the roaring fireplace. Even though the thermostat read 75 degrees, he couldn't seem to get warm. He must have checked the oil burner in the basement a dozen times during the day and evening" [*AH*-pb., p. 33].

On the next page, Anson tells us, "George constantly complained the house was like a refrigerator and he had to warm it up. Stuffing *more and more logs* in the fireplace occupied almost his every moment, except for the times he would go out to the boathouse, stare into space, then go back to the house."

Where did George Lutz find the "logs"? There is no record of cords of wood remaining from the DeFeo residency, and Anson makes no mention of George bringing firewood from his home in Deer Park. (Did the former Lutz home even *have* a fireplace?) Since the entire function of all the fire-stoking episodes in the book is to emphasize the "psychic cold" required for demonic possession stories modeled on *The Exorcist*, it is necessary to examine all references to logs and firewood in Anson's book.

On the morning of Monday, December 22, 1995, we read that "George had still not gone to his office and was sitting in the living room, adding *more logs* to a blazing fire. Kathy was writing at her dinette table in the kitchen nook" [*AH*-pb, p. 35].

Later that same Monday, "George had brought in some more *logs from the cord stacked in the garage* and was sitting in the kitchen with Kathy. They began to argue violently about who should go out to buy the Christmas gifts" [*AH*-pb, p. 40].

By Tuesday, December 23, "the weather had begun to warm. A slight drizzle was enough to keep the children in the house. George still hadn't gone to work and was in constant transit between the living room and the basement, *adding logs* and checking on the oil burner [*AH*-pb, p. 46]. Consumption of firewood continued on December 24, 1975:

> Jimmy hefted the [*Christmas*] tree into the living room. "Boy! That's some fire you've got going there!" George explained that he just couldn't warm up; hadn't been able to since the day they moved in, and that he had already *burned ten logs that day*. "Yeah," Jimmy agreed. "It does seem kind of chilly around here. Maybe there's something wrong with your burner or thermostat?" [*AH*-pb, p. 55]

We then learn how much firewood had been consumed during the six days the Lutzes had been living in their new house: "Kathy threw up her hands. '...all he does is throw more wood on the fire! In one week, we've gone through almost a whole cord of wood.'"

Now a cord of wood is a lot of wood. It's 128 cubic feet in size, and weighs from two to three thousand pounds! Even so, by Christmas Day, George needed more firewood:

> George figured out that in the first week, he had burned over 100 gallons of oil and *an entire cord of logs*. Someone would have to go and buy *more wood* and a few groceries such as milk and bread....[*Kathy*] volunteered to go for *the wood* and food.... George heard Kathy return from her shopping. He could tell she was backing the van in because of the grinding sound the snow tires made in the driveway....He went out to meet her, took *two logs* from the van, put them into the fireplace, and then sat down in the living room, refusing to unload any more. Kathy fumed; George's attitude and appearance were getting on her nerves. Somehow she could sense they were heading for a fight....She took the bags of groceries from the van and left the *remaining logs* stacked inside [emphases added. [*AH*-pb, pp. 61-62]

The implausibility of this episode playing out *on Christmas Day* is enormous. Almost no stores of any kind were open on Christmas day during the 1970s, and we must remember that the Lutzes had only been living in Amityville for one week. How did Kathy know where to find a store open on Christmas day? More to the point, how did she know where to buy firewood? There is no mention of the Lutzes talking with their neighbors even once, let alone gaining practical advice from them regarding survival skills in Amityville. What was Jay Anson thinking when he had Kathy Lutz go shopping for firewood on Christmas Day?

A Lion in the Living Room

Firewood was needed again on Sunday, December 28, 1975, in order to have George enter the living room where he could trip over a ceramic lion telekinetically transported onto the living room floor:

> George left the kitchen for the living room. "I'd better put some *more wood into the fireplace*," he told Kathy. She watched her husband shamble out of the kitchen. Kathy began to get that depressed feeling again. Then she heard a loud crash from the living room. It was George!
>
> "Who the hell left this goddamned lion on the floor? It almost killed me!" [*AH*-pb, p. 98]

The next morning, we learn,

> George's ankle was stiff. He had taken a nasty tumble over the porcelain lion and fallen heavily against *some of the logs by the fireplace*. He also had a cut over his right eye, but it hadn't bled much after Kathy put a Band-Aid on it. What disturbed Kathy was the clear *imprint of teethmarks on his ankle*! [emphases added][1]

Logically, there are logs *by the fireplace*. However, it is hard to know how this is possible if there is also a table supporting a four-foot ceramic lion by it, as well as George's chair. According to the blueprints of the house, the

---

[1] The word "ankle" occurs only with low frequency in ordinary English prose. It is interesting to note that the word also occurs once in *The Exorcist* [p. 142]:

> Gliding spiderlike, rapidly, close behind Sharon [*the secretary*], her body arched backward in a bow with her head almost touching her feet, was Regan [*the little girl*], her tongue flicking quickly in and out of her mouth while she hissed sibilantly like a serpent.…Sharon turned and saw nothing. And then screamed as she felt Regan's tongue snaking out at her *ankle*.

In both novels, the ankle is not broken, sprained or twisted; *it is attacked orally by an entity at floor level.*

space between the fireplace and the doors on either side is about three feet, four inches.

More Wood!

Kindling wood, if not logs, was needed again on Wednesday, December 31, 1975 in order for soot "from his almost constant fires" to be available to form the demonic, hooded form that later would be seen in the fireplace:

> Then George began to feel a chill in the house. The thermostat automatically dropped the temperature between midnight and six in the morning. But now it was almost seven and the heat didn't seem to be on. George went into the living room and put some *kindling and paper into the fireplace*. Before the wood blazed up, George noticed that *the brick wall was black from all the soot accumulated from his almost constant fires* [emphases added]. [*AH*-pb, p. 111]

Logs are needed again on Friday, January 9, 1976: "Since his tirade, George had been completely uncommunicative, silently *staring at his blazing logs.* Kathy left him alone, realizing her husband was trying to resolve their dilemma in his own way" [*AH*-pb, p. 196].

On Tuesday, January 13, 1976, Lutz procures logs not from the "cord stacked in the garage," but from the basement:

> The dog stood, sniffed the air, then walked over to the unlit fireplace where George was sitting, and whimpered. His pathetic sounds broke his master's concentration on the van. George looked up and shivered. There was a definite drop in the house's temperature. A half hour later, the thermometer read 60 degrees. George *started for the basement to get some logs.* Harry trotted along behind him to the cellar door, but would not descend the steps with George.... With *several logs* in his arms, George climbed back upstairs and tried the telephone in the kitchen. It was still dead. He was all set to relight the *kindling wood* in the fireplace when he thought he heard Missy cry out [emphases added]. [*AH*-pb., p. 240]

Nowhere in the book is there any mention of George Lutz transporting logs into the basement from the original pile alleged to be in the garage. Indeed, there is no opportunity in the plot for it to have taken place. Furthermore, there is no logical or practical reason to store logs in the basement. The garage occupies the southeast corner of the property. The door to the basement steps is in the north foyer, opposite the entry door at the center of the north wall of the house. In order to move logs from the garage to the basement, George would have had to take it to the front door because the swimming-pool fence would have prevented transport of logs directly from the garage to the north entrance —the entrance opposite the door to the basement. Then, as he carried the wood past the living room doorway on his way across the foyer to reach the basement door, instead of walking fifteen feet more and stacking it beside the fireplace, we must believe he had unnecessarily carried perhaps a ton of wood down the steps to the basement and then carried it back upstairs when needed.

From the perspective of Anson's narrative, however, logs in the basement are important to demonstrate the ability of dogs to detect demonic entities and forces. While there is no reason to doubt that wood was sometimes burned in the fireplace, it seems most likely that "logs" generally served not to heat the house, but rather served to crescendo the psychic-cold motif.

Sunday, December 21, 1975

Events of the Day

Weather claimed: No weather reported.

The Lutzes

George awakens at 3:15 AM and worries about the boathouse and children. The children are misbehaving. Kathy is also tense. The children crack a window in the playroom. George undergoes personality changes. He doesn't shave or shower. Kathy and George beat their three children with strap and wooden spoon.

"The children bothered him too. Ever since the move, they seemed to have become brats, misbehaved monsters who wouldn't listen, unruly children who must be severely punished" [*AH*-pb, p. 34].

Problems with the Children

It would be rather extraordinary if George and Kathy were *not* a bit insomniac and tense, what with their financial concerns, their new house to put in order, and the plethora of problems that every newly-married couple faces while learning to adjust to each other. Certainly George, as the new father, would have some role problems to iron out with the three children. And what children would not be hyperactive, inquisitive, "into everything," and a bit boisterous after moving into a new house? Nevertheless, we are supposed to see here the sinister foreshadowing, the dark adumbrations, of *that Horror* which is to come. Robert L. Morris, in his book review in *The Skeptical Inquirer* analyzed this particular episode and made the following observation:

> [O]ne is given the impression that the Lutz children started to misbehave only after moving to the new house, and that the Lutzes were only now having discipline problems. Yet on page 86 [*p. 113 of paperback*] we read, "Later in the afternoon was the second time Danny and Chris threatened to run away from home. The first had been when they lived at

> George's house at Deer Park. He had restricted them to their room for a week, because they were lying to him and Kathy about small things. They had revolted against his authority: Both boys refused to obey his orders, threatening to run away if he also forced them to give up television." The following paragraph states that the children had run away from home but had returned and, "For a while, they stopped their childish fibbing." [Morris, "Review," *Skeptical Inquirer*, Spring/Summer, 1978]

The fact that the Lutz children are admitted to be liars should be kept in mind when strange things happen in the house and the children chime out, "We didn't do it!" Of course, lying is deemed a symptom of incipient possession in the world of *The Exorcist*. In the model novel, troublesome lying is one of the early signs of the young heroine Regan's developing possession.

The culmination of all this rebellion of the Lutz children is a child-beating: "On their fourth night in the house, she [*Kathy*] exploded and together with her husband, beat Danny, Chris, and Missy with a strap and a large, heavy wooden spoon" [*AH*-pb, p. 34].

Paul Hoffman, who published the first account of the Lutzes' 28-day adventure, describes the child-beating—minus Missy and subtracting the strap:

> Previously they'd rarely raised a hand to the children, but a few days before Christmas they took after the kids in *four hours of frenzy*—"yelling and swearing," Lee [*George's middle name*] recalls, "barking orders like a drill instructor." They smacked the boys with a wooden spoon and raised welts on their backsides. [Hoffman, "Life in a Haunted House," *New York Sunday News*, July 18, 1976]

As for the instrument used in this chastisement, I have been unable to discover any occult significance in wooden spoons, nor have I found any possible source for this curious detail. It is possible that it did in fact serve as an instrument of child abuse.

Little Bits and Pieces

It is necessary to note that chapter three of *The Amityville Horror* covers the alleged activities of three days—Friday, December 19, through Sunday, December 21, 1975. By the time Anson had to apportion activities to the third day, there appears to have been little left to mention. The only thing left to examine in the narrative for December 21, 1975 is the alleged personality changes the Lutzes undergo: "Over the next two days, the Lutz family began to go through a collective personality change. As George said, "It was not a big thing, just *little bits and pieces*, here and there" [*AH*-pb., p. 33].

Attorney William Weber, in his trial testimony, claimed that the "little bits and pieces" motif was part of the DeFeo material he had given them when it appeared they were going to join him in a book project to connect the DeFeo murders story to their alleged experiences in the house at 112 Ocean Avenue:

> In fact, the *little bits and pieces* is a quote that Ronnie DeFeo told on two occasions to his psychiatrists, and he would explain to them how he had his personal difficulties when he was in the house. How he had a compulsion to get out of that house, and that he couldn't understand why his father would always come out looking for him to attempt to bring him back to the house....Ronnie described his personality changes when the doctors asked him what he meant, and again, this was told specifically to George and Kathy, and it would go for months on end, weeks on end, when he would refuse to take a shower. [*Lutz v Hoffman*, pp. 275–276],

Repeatedly, from this chapter onward, deteriorating personal hygiene becomes ever more significant as a sign of George Lutz's personality changes. George is said to resemble Ronnie DeFeo physically, and Anson tried ominously to make him resemble him behaviorally as well.

Monday, December 22, 1975

Events of the Day

Weather claimed: Nor'easter and 8°, rising to 20° at 4 PM.
Actual weather: Low temperature 26°, high 32°, mean 29°; winds 6–21 mph; precipitation 0.02 inches by 7:00 AM, 0.00 by 7:00 PM.

The Lutzes

Kathy, in the kitchen nook, receives embrace of a motherly spirit. Chris discovers the third-floor toilet is black. Foul odors fill master bedroom, and the toilet on the second floor is also black. George opens windows on second floor. The window in the sewing room is found with hundreds of flies. George checks the furnace; Kathy tries to clean the toilets. George and Kathy squabble, during which Kathy erupts. There is a visit of a mysterious stranger with a six-pack of beer.

Jay Anson would have us believe that "Early Monday morning, it was bitter cold in Amityville. The town is right on the Atlantic side of Long Island, and the sea wind blew in like a nor'easter. The thermometer hovered at 8 degrees, and media weathermen were forecasting a white Christmas" [*AH*-pb, p. 35]. "By four o'clock in the afternoon....The outdoor temperature had risen to 20 degrees" [*AH*-pb, p. 39].

It is not clear which media were supposed to have predicted snow for that Christmas, but according to the *New York Times* for December 22, the extended forecast for Metropolitan N.Y., North Jersey, and Long Island read as follows: "Increasing cloudiness Wednesday, chance of *rain* Thursday [Christmas]; fair Friday. Daytime highs will average in the low 40's; overnight lows will average in the upper 20's, low 30's [emphasis added]." If the thermometer *was* hovering at 8°, it must have had a leak in its bottom. *The Times* recorded a low of 26 degrees with a high of 32 degrees at 11:10 AM. The mean temperature was 29 degrees.

The wind speeds of the "nor'easter" that roared through Amityville that day varied from a high of 21 m.p.h. out of the northwest at nine o'clock in the evening, to a low of 6 m.p.h. out of the north at five in the morning.

According to my almanac's classification of wind speeds, the winds recorded for the morning of December 22 varied from "light breezes" to "moderate breezes." Only later that night did the winds build all the way up to a "fresh breeze." It is odd that Jay Anson passed up the opportunity to elaborate upon the most unnatural event to occur in the entire 28-day period: a nor'easter out of the northwest.

The Motherly Spirit

The first major event of the day is Kathy's encounter with a "motherly spirit" which touches her. At least three variant versions of this episode are known. The earliest version, that of Paul Hoffman, appeared in the pages of *The New York Sunday News*, July 18, 1976:

> And one *evening*, as she sat before the *living room fire*, Kathy felt a hand clasp hers— "as a woman would take your hand to comfort you," she explains. She knew instinctively that it was Louise DeFeo's. "She's not with her kids," Kathy blurted. She has no idea what prompted the statement. On checking the next day, the Lutzes learned that Mrs. DeFeo's family was shifting her body from the DeFeo plot to another gravesite [emphases added]. [Hoffman, "Life in a Haunted House," *New York Sunday News*, July 18, 1976]

The second version is from Jay Anson's book. In that version, it is *morning*, and Kathy is in the *kitchen nook*:

> Something had come up from behind and embraced her. Then it took her hand and gave it a pat. The touch was reassuring, and had an inner strength to it. Kathy was startled, but not frightened; it was like the touch of a mother giving comfort to her daughter. Kathy had the impression of a woman's soft hand resting on her own! [*AH*-pb, p.36]

Perhaps because books tend to be larger than newspaper articles, what would appear to be the same episode is repeated on pages 70–71 (December 26, 1975, according to the book's chronology). On that occasion, however, the incident is extended and embroidered:

> Then the sweet smell became heavier….She started to gag, then tried to pull away from a grip that tightened as she struggled. Kathy thought she heard a whisper, and she recalls something deep within her warning her not to listen. "No!" she shouted. "Leave me alone!" She struck out at the empty air. The embrace tightened, hesitated. Kathy felt a hand on her shoulder, making the same motions of motherly reassurance she had felt the first time in her kitchen.

Recalling that Anson's book was published in September of 1977, we proceed to the third version of this goose-bumper—written by Kathleen Lutz herself. It is to be found in her article which appeared in the pages of *The National Enquirer*:

> The first time it happened I was in the kitchen when a ghostly presence took my hand and then held me around the waist—like a mother—giving comfort to her daughter. But the ghostly touch did little to comfort me. I often felt fear, depression and confusion. I always knew when I was about to be touched by the spirit. I would first smell the strange aroma of a cheap perfume. [K. Lutz, "Our 28 Days of Horror," *National Enquirer*, December 13, 1977]

As can be expected, Kathleen's version and Anson's are in essential agreement—differing only as to which came first, the hug or the hand hold. But both of these differ substantially from the earliest version, written by Hoffman from notes he had taken at a meeting with the Lutzes on February 7, 1975—just three weeks after they had abandoned the house.

Both time and place are changed in the later accounts, and the curious business about Louise DeFeo's body being moved—as reported in Hoffman's article—is absent in Anson's book. I discovered what I believe to be the reason for this omission quite by accident. When I was interviewing Mrs. Evans about her part in the selling of the DeFeo home, she told me she had almost sold it to some other gentleman a short while before the Lutzes came onto the scene. But at the time, Mr. Brigante (Mrs. DeFeo's father) had not wanted to have the house sold. He wanted, so it was said, to have the house sealed up and made into a monument to his daughter's memory.

Somehow, this had turned into a rumor that he was going to relocate his daughter's body. The would-be buyer went to talk to Mr. Brigante and asked him about the rumor. Brigante was furious that anyone would think he would separate the dead mother from her children. As of February 7 the rumor had not yet been squelched. But by the time the book appeared two years later, it was prudent to omit what would have been a marvelous example of what in *The Exorcist* is called "the faculty of divulging future and hidden events"—if only what had been divulged had been true!

The Power of Suggestion

But what if Kathleen did experience these ghostly grabbings and spectral odors? Is a supernatural explanation the only possible answer? Is it the best answer? I think not. One of the easiest phenomena to elicit during hypnosis is a distortion of the tactile sense. The hypnotist has but to suggest "You feel lice crawling behind your ear....they are wandering about on your scalp and eyebrows, under your nose," and the subject begins to scratch under the nose or behind an ear and display a most convincing discomfort. What is true for the tactile sense is true for the other senses as well. On numerous occasions, I have been able to cause someone to shiver—teeth chattering and all—on days when the temperature was in the 90s. On dozens of occasions, I have been able to transform the odor of an onion into the aroma of a rose. For many working hypnotists, it is a daily task to make the odor of a cigarette so repulsive that a client is brought to the point of retching when taking a drag on the forbidden pacifier.

I mention all this because it is my feeling that most people underestimate the power of suggestion. Indeed, most people think that "suggestion" is an over-worked, catch-all term used to explain away the otherwise unexplainable. Nevertheless, some of those very same people, if they have read the paragraph above—even without hypnosis—will by now have scratched their heads without even realizing they have done so.

Black Toilets

Checking back to our "Events of the Day," we see that the Lutzes' next misadventure involved the toilets. They all allegedly turned black on the inside. According to the book, the toilets were the only bathroom fixtures to be so sullied. But Hoffman's article is a bit broader, "Black stains appeared on the bathroom fixtures; no amount of cleansing could remove them." Assuming that either of these accounts had been true, are we forced to accept an occult explanation? Again, I think not. A natural explanation is probably to be found in the story itself: "She [*Kathy*] turned accusingly to the children. 'Did you throw any paint in here?' 'Oh, no Mama!' all three chorused' [*AH*-pb, p. 36].

Now it is obvious that the children must indeed have *had* paint they could have put in the toilet. Kathy would not have accused them of painting the toilets unless she knew that paint existed for them to use. As a matter of fact, later in the book we read "The room was a mess. Toys were scattered all over the floor, intermingled with discarded clothes. The tubes of an old paint set had been left uncapped, the pigments oozing onto the furniture and rug" [*AH*-pb, p. 114].

As for the angelic, three-part chorus, we are reminded that the parents themselves called their children liars. At any rate, it is far more parsimonious to believe we are dealing with the childish pranks of fibbing youngsters, than to postulate that septic specters are mocking Michelangelo on the walls of a pristine toilet. It also is possible that the mention of paint was just a subtle nod to *The Exorcist*, where a young girl's painting is a significant component of the plot. Indeed, analysis of her paint reveals the identity of the desecrator of an altar.

Where Were the Flies?

Although Mark Twain believed the common fly was God's favorite animal, most people have not agreed with him. To the contrary, flies and the odors that attract them have been consigned to the Devil by most persons who believe in His Satanic Majesty. In the Gospel of Matthew [12:24], Jesus is accused of doing his exorcisms with the help of "Beelzebub, the prince of the devils." In Hebrew, *Beelzebub* means "Lord of the Flies." Judging from the events alleged for December 22, 1975, the Lutzes appear to have shared the majority opinion:

> "George! Look at this!"
> The fourth bedroom on the second floor—now Kathy's sewing room—has two windows [*three windows in fact and according to the plans shown in the book*!]. One, which looks out at the boathouse ... was the window George had opened that first night when he had awakened at 3:15. The other faces the neighboring house to the right of 112 Ocean Avenue. On this window, clinging to the inside of the panes, were literally hundreds of buzzing flies! [*AH*-pb, p. 38]

We must remember that the floor plans have been changed in the paperback edition, so the sewing room ends up in the northeast corner of the house. As pointed out earlier, however, the text still reads as though the sewing room is in the *southeast* corner. The Lutzes are perplexed by the presence of flies in December. If the sewing room was on the south (*i.e.*, warmer) side of the house, and if the house had not been heated much before the Lutzes moved in, it is to be expected that in autumn the flies which had penetrated into the house would tend to filter toward the southern exposures. As the house became colder, the flies would become immobile, only to be reanimated when the furnace was turned up. Having already been drawn to the warmer, southern portions of the house, it is only natural the flies would appear in particular rooms but not in others.

I think, however, that there is more to the fly episode. In Hoffman's account, we read "In the *playroom* a sickening odor, like that of decaying bodies, came and went. Even in the dead of winter, flies clustered on the playroom windowpane [Hoffman, "Life in a Haunted House," *New York Daily News*, July 18, 1976].

Kathy Lutz, in her *National Enquirer* story, agreed with Hoffman, not Anson, that it is the *playroom* that was infested: "Strange things happened in the playroom, too. For some unexplainable reason, the window was covered with hundreds of flies—in the dead of winter. We used insecticides and swatted them until they were all dead. But every time we thought we had finally got rid of them, more would be back the next day" [K. Lutz, "Our 28 Days of Horror," *The National Enquirer*, December 13, 1977].

If the flies are accepted as being in the playroom (which in the case of both old and new floor plans has a south-facing window), then a portion of Weber's trial testimony gains in credibility. Weber claimed the Lutzes first got the fly-motif from him:

> WEBER: There are pictures of flies, but they also talk about flies on pages 25 and 26, and various pages after that in the book, and there was a very interesting scene that occurred during the [*DeFeo*] trial which I related to the Lutzes, and it was interesting to me because it seemed to convince me that the police, to me, personally, had rehearsed their testimony....Every police officer who was at the crime scene took the stand and testified that as they went in one room after another, when they finally went into the upstairs third floor bedroom of Dawn DeFeo [*i.e., the original "playroom"*] and saw her lying on the bed, that the first thing that struck their attention was flies and maggots and a terrible odor. I never believed the police when they said that, but yet, to a person, every police officer that testified in the trial managed to interject that in their testimony....I told them about the flies in the house. The flies, of course, constitute a substantial portion of their story.
>
> Q But you also told them about odors in the house?
>
> A Yes....In that one particular room, which is the third-floor bedroom. [*Lutz v Hoffman*, pp. 277*ff*]

Mysterious Stranger

The Anson saga proceeds from flies to the fly-by-night: the mysterious stranger who, six-pack in hand, wants to have a housewarming, then disappears never to be seen again. I am uncertain what to make of this item. It could, of course, be wholly imaginary. It could have been a wandering drunk or an unlicensed loony from a few blocks away. Or it could have been derived from information Lutz admitted receiving from Weber:

> Q As far as the boathouse, other than what has been previously indicated, has anything been denied or confirmed by Mr. Weber relating to Mr. DeFeo?
>
> A He told us that one of Mr. DeFeo's former friends kept his boat in the boat house, but that is all. [*Lutz v Hoffman*, p.192]

The tell-tale nexus in this case might be the tidbit dropped at the end of the Lutz episode: "He [*the stranger*] continued by telling the Lutzes that he kept his boat at another neighbor's boathouse, several doors down on Ocean Avenue" [*AH*-pb, p. 51]. Since the Lutzes, Weber, and Hoffman originally were working with an "overview" that involved an attempt to correlate DeFeo events with Lutz events, it is just possible that this represents a stillborn attempt to tie the Lutz superstructure into the DeFeo substratum. It was kept in the book because it added an element of mystery.

Tuesday, December 23, 1975

Events of the Day

Weather claimed: A cold spell; drizzle in PM.
Actual weather: Low 16° at 6:30 AM, high 23° at 2:40 PM, mean 20°; precipitation 0.00 inches all day; winds 3 mph to 16 mph.

The Lutzes

George awakens at 3:15 AM, goes downstairs and finds front door open, hanging from one hinge:

> So, when he woke once more at 3:15 in the morning … he was stunned to find the two hundred and fifty pound wooden front door wrenched wide open, hanging from one hinge [*AH*-pb, p. 41]….He pointed to the brass lock plate. The doorknob was twisted completely off-center. The metal facing was bent back as though someone had tried to pry it open with a tool, but from the *inside*! "Someone was trying to get *out* of the house, not in!" [*AH*-pb, p. 43].

Kathy awakens, joins George who is trying to close door. At two, children are kept inside due to drizzle. George not at work, instead he's building fires. Missy is humming to herself in her room; visiting sewing room, she asks "Do angels talk?" Boys are in playroom, fighting. Kathy resumes shelving. There is a sour smell in the walk-in closet in master bedroom, the crucifix is upside down.

Father Mancuso

That night, Mancuso comes down with the flu with a temperature of 103°.

Mr. Lutz did not call the police to report the incident with the front door. He didn't even call his insurance agent! It is this same door, we may note, that will be alleged to be "hanging from its hinges again" on the morning the Lutzes flee from the house. As we have seen previously in regard to spirit embraces, book-length exposition lends itself to theme-and-variation repetition. In his testimony at the trial in 1979, Lutz gave no indication that there was more than one un-hinging of the front door. In fact, his testimony at the time would seem to dispose of this entire episode:

[*Lutz is being cross-examined by Mr. Block.*]

Q Anything else you would like to tell us about some mistakes in the book?

A There's a reference in there about the front door, and I believe it's described as the heavy wooden door.

Q What was incorrect about the front door?

A In actuality, it was a heavy storm door that was in front of the house. It wasn't the wooden door. [*Lutz v Hoffman*, p. 48]

The transformation of a heavy wooden door into an ordinary storm door eliminates, of course, the rationale for calling in the "local locksmith" whom Anson needed in order to introduce the "fact" about the locksmith having previously come during the DeFeos' tenancy to fix the lock on the boathouse door. With there no longer being any reason for a repairman to come to the house, it is unsurprising that Peter Jordan and Rick Moran, when researching their article for *Human Behavior* [June, 1978], were unable to locate any local contractors and repairpersons who had ever been called to the house to do the repairs indicated in the book. Anson was, once again, following the model of *The Exorcist* where Chris, the mother of the possessed girl, exclaims "Boy, I'd better call a locksmith right away" to put a lock on her daughter's window. Just as George Lutz is obsessed with checking the locks on the house and boathouse doors, so too Chris frequently checks the latch on a window.

The fact that it is a storm door and not the actual front door of the house implies, of course, that the entire beginning of Anson's Chapter Five is apocryphal. If the door of the house is closed, there is no cold coming in, no need to check all the children only to discover them all sleeping on their stomachs.

Anson needs to have the children all sleeping on their stomachs, since all the newspapers had reported that the slaughtered DeFeos had all been found lying on their stomachs with their arms raised above their heads. Alas, this change in doors obliterates his chance to tie in DeFeo material. But no matter, for it turned out that at least two of the DeFeos (Louise and Allison) were not on their stomachs at the time they were shot, and an article in

Newsday on November 19, 1974, implied the bodies had been turned over into ritual positions after the fact.

Returning to the question of the front door—rather, the storm door—at 112 Ocean Avenue, a photograph was published as early as February 14, 1976, in *Newsday* (one month after abandonment of the house) clearly showing the storm door hanging from its upper hinges, its bottom broken into two pieces. But was the storm door broken before the Lutzes left the house four weeks earlier, or was it broken subsequently?

I have been told that the door was broken *after* the Lutzes left the house. However, I have not been able to establish this as a solid fact. If we postulate that the door was broken after the Lutzes abandoned the house, however, two other bits of information would seem to fit together. In the transcript of the *Lutz v Hoffman* trial, there is a puzzling section where Mr. Daley is cross-examining Mr. Weber. In his attempt to shake Weber's claim that the Lutzes acquired the door-motif from him, Daley introduces a tape recording of the Lutzes' reminiscences, allegedly dated February 7, 1976—three weeks after abandonment of the house. Part of the transcript of this tape was read aloud into the record. Apparently, George Lutz is speaking:

> There was only one that the boys would latch. The others I had hammered all shut. Every single door the next morning was wide open, and the furthest one away from the window on the most protected side of the house, was off its hinges, ripped off the bottom hinges. [*Lutz v Hoffman*, p. 324]

What can this refer to? There is nothing in the floor plan given for the first floor that can be matched to the layout implied in the quotation. Paul Hoffman's account, which only mentions the January 14 unhinging, gives us a clue:

> When Lee finally ventured downstairs after sunrise, he found that the front door, which he'd double-latched, was wide open. So was the basement door that he'd locked, even the doors on the *garbage shed*, including the one that had been nailed shut [emphasis added]. [Hoffman, "Life in a Haunted House," *New York Sunday News*, July 18, 1976]

Attached to the north side ("the most sheltered side") of the house there was a lean-to shed which, although it is not shown on the floor plan for the first floor, is indicated in the diagram of the property that appears on page nine of the paperback edition (and it was still visible when I visited the house in December of 1979). It would seem the door which became unhinged during the Lutzes' stay at 112 Ocean Avenue was, in fact, a door on the *garbage shed!* We can see the dramatic problem Mr. Anson had to face in dealing with the door-motif. It is eerie and thrilling to have the front door wrenched off its hinges by some demonic force which "was trying to get *out* of the house, not in!" But what drama can you create with devils in the *garbage shed*? Who has heard of any occult significance for garbage sheds anyway?

The Getting-Out Motif

The "trying to get *out*" motif was evidently borrowed from two parts of the DeFeo story. The first involved Ronnie DeFeo locking Shaggy, the family sheepdog, in the same shed before he murdered his family. DeFeo testified that the "dog was screaming" during the murders—the barking even waking up a neighbor boy. In his book, *High Hopes: The Amityville Murders*, Gerard Sullivan shows a picture (plate facing p. 225) of the scratching-eroded doors of the shed where the dog was *trying to get out*.

A second part of the getting-out motif was provided by Mr. Weber, who testified that about two weeks before the DeFeo tragedy Ronald had ripped the hinges off the storm door to get away from his father [*Lutz v Hoffman*, p. 327]. It is possible, then, that the Lutzes—attempting to correlate DeFeo material with their own "data"—transferred the story of the door on the garbage shed to the storm door, and a lucky "accident" befell the storm door (which, incidentally, can be made out hanging on its hinge in the frontispiece silhouette of the house!). It was broken in time to be photographed before the Lutzes' news conference on February 16, 1976. But both Hoffman and Anson, for dramatic or other reasons, turned the storm door into the heavy wooden front door of the house. Can the truth really be this much stranger than the fiction?

While it appears the unhinging of the front door did in fact come from the DeFeo story via Attorney Weber, it is worth noting that an unhinging motif can also be found in *The Exorcist*: "[I]n an instant she [Chris, the mother] and Sharon were racing from the study, up the stairs, to the door of Regan's bedroom, bursting in. They saw the shutters of the window on the floor, ripped off their hinges! And the window! The glass had been totally shattered!" [*Exorcist*, p. 390].

The Need for Rain

Let us now consider the weather report for Tuesday, December 23, 1975: "In the morning, the cold spell that gripped Amityville was still unbroken. It was cloudy, and the radio kept promising snow for Christmas" [*AH*-pb, p. 45]. "By two in the afternoon, the weather had begun to warm. A slight drizzle was enough to keep the children in the house" [*AH*-pb, p. 46]. According to the weather records from *The Times*, the "cold spell" was gripping the New York area with 30 degrees at five o'clock in the morning. It *had* warmed all the way up to 34 degrees by 2:05 PM, but no precipitation at all is recorded for the period between 7 AM and 7 PM that day.

From a dramatic point of view, rain is necessary so the children will be forced to stay indoors. Then Missy can communicate with her invisible playmate and the boys can have their "first fight, ever." There is no way of knowing how slight a drizzle would have sufficed to keep the Lutz children inside.

The notion that the episodes involving the children are apocryphal is consistent with the fact that neither the boys' fighting nor Missy's query about talking angels appears in Hoffman's first article. Interestingly, the talking angel item appears in Hoffman's later article in *Good Housekeeping*. But in his article the question is supposed to have been asked sometime after January 6, 1976.

In any event, it is difficult to find sinister significance in a child having an imaginary playmate. Only a mind which has rejected the post-Copernican world can interpret this as one of the tokens of demonic influence. From a compositional standpoint, however, the talking-angel motif serves as a foreshadowing of the advent of the invisible playmate Jodie, the demonic pig. Unsurprisingly, in *The Exorcist*, Regan the possessed child also receives messages from the invisible Captain Howdy and carries on conversations with a sinister, supposedly imaginary friend.

As for the assertion that December 23, 1975, was the first time ever that two brothers, aged seven and nine, had ever had a fight, this would seem to be needed more strongly to demonstrate the progressive changes in the whole family's behavior—an important prerequisite for demonic possession.

The Obligatory Crucifix

On page forty-eight, Kathy found another signifier of demonic possession in her new house:

> Kathy … continued on *into her own bedroom*….Kathy picked up a roll of shelf paper and opened the door to the walk-in closet [emphasis added]. Immediately a sour smell struck her nostrils….On the very first day the Lutzes had moved in, she had hung a crucifix on the inner wall facing the closet door … her eyes widened in horror. She began to gag at the sour smell, but couldn't retreat from the sight of the crucifix—now hanging upside down! [*AH*-pb, p. 48]

Sallyann Welford, writing in *The Star* on January 17, 1978, reported that there was no walk-in closet in the master bedroom—even though the floorplan shown on page twelve of the paperback (corroborated by the blueprints) shows a walk-in closet immediately on the right side of the bedroom door. If we are to take Ms. Welford's word that this walk-in closet was non-existent, where was the crucifix hung? In Hoffman's *Good Housekeeping* article, we read "Lee remained in the *sewing room* ... as he looked around the room, he saw Kathy's crucifix on the wall and stopped. He knew his rage would serve no purpose [emphasis added]." How could the sewing room and master bedroom have been confused? To Anson's credit, at least both rooms were on the second floor.

Location aside, crucifixes are overworked in contemporary horror literature. They are employed for purposes ranging from warding off Dracula to the masturbatory blasphemy seen in *The Exorcist*. It strains credibility to assert that anyone, at this late date, can still claim the patent rights on any particular use for crucifixes. And yet, I am inclined to believe—once again—Mr. Weber is the source of our crucifix story.

When testifying at the *Lutz v Hoffman* trial, Weber told how DeFeo Sr. regularly brought a priest down from Montreal to say masses in the house. Weber claimed the Lutzes came by the crucifix-motif from the following anecdote which he had related to them:

> I told them ... about a crucifix hanging upside down. Ronnie told me, and I told [the Lutzes], that on many occasions when the priest was in the house, Ronnie used to do this as a jest or maybe as an act of defiance with the priest, Father Gervault, when he used to come into the house. He used to turn the crucifix in the house upside down. He did it as a joke or as a prank. [*Lutz v Hoffman*, p. 281]

Wednesday, December 24, 1975

Events of the Day

Weather claimed: No snow is on the ground.
Actual weather: Low temperature 16° at 0:30 AM, high 23° at 2:40 PM, mean 20°; precipitation 0.00 inches all day.

The Lutzes

At 4 AM (?) Kathy is thinking about the sewing room.

Father Mancuso

At 4 AM Mancuso's temperature is 104°. He calls the pastor to his room and calls a doctor. He's thinking about the sewing room.

The Lutzes

After lunch, Danny and Chris get Christmas ornaments from the sewing room. George tests the lights and unwraps ornaments "for a few hours."

Father Mancuso

The doctor has come and gone. Mancuso calls George at 5 PM.

Lutz and Mancuso

George and Mancuso talk, Mancuso warns the Lutzes to stay out of the sewing room, the telephone goes berserk. Mancuso redials George. George dials Mancuso. At 8 PM the priest asks the operator to check the Lutz phone, then calls a friend in Nassau County P.D.

The Lutzes

Kathy is wrapping presents. The kids are in the playroom. Jimmy and his mother arrive with a tree. George has not bathed for a week. Everybody is cold. Men and kids are trimming the tree, women are in the "happy" room (kitchen). The window in the sewing room is open and the flies are back. George goes out to close boathouse door (almost 11 PM).

Sgt. Gionfriddo

Sgt. Gionfriddo watches George come outside door which "led from the kitchen" and he calls North Merrick.

Synchronicities and Authorial Omniscience

Although there were numerous reports that "Father Mancuso" denied any involvement in the Lutz affair beyond blessing the house and counseling them on the telephone, it is my opinion that he was more involved in the Amityville aberration than he wished to admit. Regardless, we shall play along for the nonce and take the story as it comes.

The book says, at 4 AM, Mancuso's fever is 104 degrees and he keeps "envisioning a room he believed to be on the second floor of the house." This detail isn't entirely impossible. When my brother was a little boy, he had a fever of only 103 degrees and clearly saw the Easter bunny peeking out from behind a curtain near his bed. Fevers do strange things to people, even if they do have degrees in theology, law, and psychology.

However, if it is true that Anson was able to determine that Kathy and Mancuso were thinking about the sewing room *at the exact same time*, we must ask how he ascertained that fact. The Lutzes have already testified that their memory for the first week is extremely hazy. Kathy did not keep a diary of her acts during the twenty-eight days, let alone a diary of her thoughts! Authors of novels have the God-like privilege of knowing the thoughts of their characters. Authors of nonfiction narratives, however, cannot claim to have such knowledge without the evidence of the testimonies of the characters involved. There are hundreds of places in *The Amityville Horror* where synchronicities between the lives of the Lutzes and Mancuso are alleged or implied, and even more cases where its author knows not only what they are thinking, he knows what they're thinking at the same time! Whenever Anson reveals the thoughts of his characters, we must ask what possible evidence he could have had to know them. In cases where it seems impossible for thoughts to be known, we must consider whether its fictional nature does or does not cast doubt on the truth of the episode in which it is embedded.

Although Father Pecoraro (Father Mancuso in the Lutz story) did testify in the fraud trial [*Lutz v Hoffman*, pp. 340–341] that he had spoken to Anson on the telephone and agreed "to verify some of the statements that the Lutzes had made" to him, there is no record of how many statements were "verified," let alone any possibility of covering all the synchronicities in thought and deed between Mancuso and the Lutzes alleged in the pages of *A True Story*.

To return to synchronous thoughts of the sewing room, we have no way of knowing just which room in the house we should take as the sewing room. Since the text of the book continues to assume it is the southeast bedroom on the second floor (despite the change in floor plans), we shall also assume that is the room intended. The sewing room—that sinister room periodically infested with flies—was previously Allison DeFeo's room. We may note again that the fly-motif was first associated with the *back* bedroom on the *third* floor—in Hoffman's early account and in Mrs. Lutz' article in *The National Enquirer*. It is more than a trifle amusing to see a photograph of the "sewing room" on pages 162–3 of the book *Murder in Amityville*, by the intrepid ghost-hunter, Hans Holzer. The caption for the picture reads, "Only Allison DeFeo's room seems free of psychic imprints."

Concealing Identities

A physician is summoned to Father Mancuso's side and despite the early hours the doctor arrives a short time later! Another miracle unremarked by Mr. Anson! We note that the doctor's identity is kept secret, as it well should be. Imagine what his colleagues would do to him if they found out he was making house calls in the 1970s! The topic of concealing identities brings us to note that several changes in this chapter are to be found in the paperback version. The Lutzes were sued for invasion of privacy not only by the priest, but by one of the Amityville police officers, as well.

At the very beginning of Anson's Chapter 6, Mancuso is troubled, but has not discussed his troubles with anyone:

> …not even with his Bishop (Hard Cover, p. 39)
> …not even with his Confessor (Paperback, p. 49).

Mancuso, told to stay in bed for a few days, is not pleased with the prospect of remaining idle, but he:

> …agreed that upcoming cases on his Court calendar could be put off … but some of his patients in psychotherapy … (Hard Cover, p. 41)
> …agreed that upcoming items on his busy calendar could be put off … but some of his clients in counseling … (Paperback, p. 51)

After the priest asks the operator to check the Lutzes' phone line and is told there's nothing wrong with it:

> He called a friend in the Nassau County Police Department (Hard Cover, p. 44).
> He dialed a number he normally used only for emergencies (Paperback, p. 55).

At the very end of the chapter, where a police officer is watching the Lutz residence at the time George goes out to close the door of the boathouse, considerable change is evident:

> "Cammaroto. This is Al. You can call North Merrick [*a village about 10 miles west of Amityville, in Nassau County*] back and tell them the people in 112 Ocean are home." Sergeant Al Gionfriddo of the Amityville Police Department was on duty this Christmas Eve, just as he had been the night of the DeFeo family massacre. (Hard Cover, p. 45)

> "Zammataro. This is Gionfriddo. You can call your friend back and tell him the people in 112 Ocean Avenue are home." Sergeant Al Gionfriddo of the Suffolk County Police Department [*which does not patrol Amityville*!] was doing a job this Christmas Eve, just as he had been on the night of the DeFeo family massacre. (Paperback, p. 58)

As far as I can figure, the reality implied by these altered passages was that Mancuso called his friend on the Nassau County Police Department, who in turn called a friend on the Amityville Police Force, who then checked out the house. Needless to say, the police forces mentioned in all versions of this episode denied that they ever conducted any surveillance whatsoever of the Lutz home. There is no reason to suppose the police-surveillance motif came from the DeFeo-Weber source of anecdotal material. However, it is worth noting that in *The Exorcist*, there are at least three occasions in which Lieutenant Kinderman conducts lonely vigils in his car as he carries out surveillance of a haunted house and a priest's residence.

Telephone Disservice

The reason "Gionfriddo" was supposedly watching the Lutzes was because the telephone call between Lutz and Mancuso had been mysteriously disrupted and terminated. Since one of the recurring themes in Anson's book is that of the malfunctioning phone, I shall discuss the Amityville telephone system at this point and be done with it.

To deduce whether or not there was any real malfunctioning of the telephones, we obviously would need to know how many calls (or attempted calls) there were between the two parties, and we would need to have some statistics regarding what fraction of calls in Amityville are likely to be disrupted as a general rule. According to his testimony in September 1979, Lutz said he managed to phone the priest three or four times. He did not indicate how many attempts he made, but did attest to difficulties with the phone:

[*Lutz being cross-examined by Block*]

Q When was it that you decided to leave the Amityville house after all these truthful experiences that you have related in your book happened to you?

A When the priest told us to get out. When we got a hold of him on the phone and he asked us what we were still doing there.

Q You were in constant consultation with a priest while you were in the house?

A Not constant. We had considerable problems staying in touch with him. *Every time we tried to call him, the phone was cut off*. He told us that he would call us about 1:30 that afternoon. [*Lutz v Hoffman*, p. 73]

Lutz' proclivity toward exaggeration shows up even in his court testimony. If *every* call was cut off, how did the priest notify him that he would call him at 1:30? Or was it customary for each call to be begun with the declamation, "If the demons cut us off, I'll call you back at X-o'clock"?

Father Pecoraro, in his testimony, indicated that George Lutz had called him "on several occasions," and that he had spoken with Kathleen "a few times," during the twenty-eight-day period. At no time in his testimony did the priest indicate that there was anything out of order with the phone service. In addition, although Mr. Weber acknowledged that he had spoken with the priest concerning the latter's telephone conversations with the Lutzes, he did not indicate that the priest had ever mentioned anything being out of the ordinary regarding the phone. Significantly, the first version of the story to be published, the Hoffman version, makes mention of three Lutz-Priest calls but never mentions any problems with the line.

I personally can add an amusing footnote to the question of "what fraction of calls in Amityville are likely to be disrupted as a general rule?" Of my first eleven Amityville calls (including both calls to Amityville from Upstate New York and calls made in Amityville), only two were completely free of interference. One call was so badly garbled that almost everything had to be repeated a second—or even a third—time. In fact, it became a joke among my colleagues at the college to say, whenever they had a bad connection, "I think I've got an Amityville line." Of course, my own data in regards to the phone service do not constitute a scientific proof of anything. Nevertheless, they allow me to scoff with greater conviction.

Other Noticeable Discrepancies

Within this chapter there remain a few odds and ends to discuss concerning the details of the Lutzes' Christmas Eve. The book says they unwrapped ornaments "for a few hours." Now that's a lot of ornaments! Considering the Lutzes later "fled in terror," taking only a few changes of clothing, some trace of all these ornaments should remain. But the catalogue for the sale at which all the Lutz possessions were auctioned off does not list any Christmas ornaments.

The problem of George's not bathing is mentioned again. If he was as cold all the time as he says he was, it might not be odd for him to be reluctant to bathe. Speaking of cold, there is one last datum concerning the heating problems:

> [*Lutz is testifying about what he had said at the press conference that had been held on Feb. 16, 1976*]
> "We explained [*to the press*] that we had a number of heating problems, that the house was not habitable, and that we expected to have that fixed and hopefully some time go back." [*Lutz v Hoffman*, p. 15]

The thirty words of that simple statement seem to me to say a lot more than Lutz thought he was saying. Not only would it dispose—once and for all—of the nonsense about "psychic cold" which allegedly plagued the inhabitants at 112 Ocean Avenue, but it also would seem to explain why, in reality, the Lutzes "abandoned" all their possessions in the house. If it is true that they intended to return, their possessions were not in any sense forfeit or "abandoned." Presumably it was not until later, after their tale had grown so tall that it escaped their control and assumed a life of its own, that they were forced to abandon their household. But as we shall see later, by that time this did not constitute much of a sacrifice, and there is evidence Lutz returned to the house at least once.

We conclude this chapter with a discussion of Kathy's "happy" room, the kitchen. On page 56 we read that the kitchen "was her 'happy' room, the one place in the new house where she felt secure." Considering the "fact" that it had been just two days before when Kathy had been grabbed by a ghost in the kitchen, it is little short of astonishing that she should now—of all places—feel secure in the kitchen. Why not the dining room? In the entire book, nothing *ever* happens in the dining room. Or why not the bathroom on the first floor? The only bathroom in the whole house, we are to believe, in which the toilet did not turn black. Possibly, Kathy still liked the kitchen because the embrace of the "entity" had not actually occurred.

Impossible Architecture

Anson seems to have had a great deal of difficulty in dealing with the anatomy of the dwelling's derrière. In the hardcover, the floor plan for the first floor shows a regular-size window in the kitchen and a triple window in the dining room, both facing the river. In the paperback's floor plan, the dining room's triple window is replaced by a door, and a curve-around-the-corner counter appears in the southeast corner of the kitchen. But there was a more serious architectonic difficulty raised by Anson's account of Sergeant Gionfriddo's surveillance of the horror house:

> A man [*Gionfriddo*] watched as George came out of a side door and ran toward the back of the house. He knew the door led from the kitchen because he had been at 112 Ocean Avenue before. He sat in a car parked in front of the Lutzes' home and observed George shut the boathouse door. [*AH*-pb, p. 58]

No such door is indicated in the floor plans of *any* edition of *The Amityville Horror: A True Story.* Nor could there be. There is no position on Ocean Avenue from which one could observe such a door. From no position on the street could any boathouse door or any door in the east wall (the back side) of the house be seen. The alleged kitchen door is said to be a side door from which George "ran toward the back of the house." Obviously, he would not have emerged from a door on the back (east) side of the house. It would have to be a door on the north or south side of the house from which he "ran toward the back of the house." As one observes the south side of the house (the dining room side), not only is there no door other than the main entrance, only the front of the garage is visible from the street. The boathouse is behind the garage, and it is impossible to observe anything happening in the back yard. From the north (kitchen) side of the house, not only has there never been a north door in the kitchen wall, nothing whatsoever can be seen behind the house, as can be confirmed by examination of the map of the property shown on page nine of the paperback.

Lonely Vigils

The account just quoted above is one of two *Amityville-Hor*ror episodes involving a policeman's lonely vigil observing the goings-on inside a haunted house. In the later account of January 9, 1976, Gionfriddo will carry out a lengthier surveillance of the Lutz home, watching as George Lutz opens all the windows in the house, which Kathy then proceeds to close. It is likely, once again, that the lonely-vigil motif was borrowed from *The Exorcist*. The novel describes Detective Kinderman's surveillance of the Jesuit residence:

> He [*Father Karras*] drove back toward Chris's house, but at a stop sign *at the corner* of Prospect and Thirty-fifth, he froze behind the wheel: parked between Karras and the Jesuit residence hall was Kinderman. He was *sitting alone behind the wheel* with his elbow out the window, *looking straight ahead*. [*Exorcist*, pp 310–311]

We may compare this scene to Sergeant Gionfriddo's surveillance of the Lutz home on page 196 of *The Amityville Horror*:

> Gionfriddo pulled up at the intersection where South Ireland Place cuts into Ocean Avenue [*i.e., at the corner* of South Ireland Place and Ocean Avenue], *directly opposite* [*i.e., straight ahead*] the Lutzes'. He turned off his headlights. Something was holding him back from getting out of his car and going up to that front door....Gionfriddo sat there and watched as a woman went around and shut all the windows in the house.

While verbal agreement between these two stories is sparse, imagining the scenes described shows them to be pretty much the same picture. Both take place at the intersection of two streets. In both, the policeman is alone and not exiting his car. In both, he is looking straight ahead. Both passages describe a police surveillance of a house inhabited by a major character in a possession story. As with many of the cases where Anson seems to have been following an *Exorcist* model, the differences between his texts and William Peter Blatty's show that he possessed considerable skill in the art of theme and variations.

Thursday, December 25, 1975

Events of the Day

Weather claimed: AM, cold enough to snow; at 6 PM wind whipping snow against the windows. Almanac: Full moon.

Actual weather: Low 17° at 12:01 AM, high 30° at 3:00 PM, mean 26°; precipitation 0.00 inches by 7:00 AM., 0:05 inches by 7:00 PM; winds 7 mph. to 8 mph. Almanac: moon at last quarter.

Father Mancuso

Mancuso's fever still 103, will still perform Christmas duties. Snowing has stopped at North Merrick where priest lives. His flu is worse, no heat in radiator.

The Lutzes

At 3:15 in the morning, George awakes. Kathy is sleeping on her stomach. "She was shot in the head!" Kathy yells. George checks boathouse. There is a full moon. George sees a pig behind Missy at her bedroom window. George runs into house and into Missy's room, sees no pig, but rocking chair is moving. At 9:30 AM George and Kathy compare notes in kitchen, but George doesn't mention the pig. The kids are in the living room with presents. Kathy tries to call Mancuso. She goes to buy wood and returns. The children are very curious about the sewing room ban. Jodie the pig enters the story. At 6 PM, snow begins. At 9 PM Kathy hears Missy talking to Jodie. The boys want to go to bed because the playroom is too cold. George and Kathy go to bed at midnight.

According to weather records for December 25, 1975, it *was* cold enough to snow. The high for the day, recorded at 5 PM, was 30 degrees. At 6 PM later that same day, Kathy allegedly stared at snowflakes "as the rising wind whipped the snow against the pane." [*AH*-pb, p. 63] The actual record shows the wind at 6 PM to have been NE at 8 mph ("gentle breeze") declining to 7 mph at 7 PM (a "light breeze"). Between 7 AM and 7 PM, a total of 0.05 inches of precipitation was recorded, hardly enough for a "White Christmas."

Divulging Hidden Events

On pages 60 and 61, Anson wrote,

> Kathy woke up … "She was shot in the head!" Kathy yelled. "She was shot in the head! I heard the explosions in my head!" … Filing his report after the initial investigation the night of the DeFeo murders, Gionfriddo had written that Louise, the mother of the family, had been shot in the head while sleeping on her stomach. Everyone else, including her husband who was lying right beside her, had been shot in the back while lying in the same position. This information had been included in the material turned over to the Suffolk County prosecution team, but never released to the news media. In fact, this detail had never come out, even at Ronnie DeFeo's trial.

On November 15, 1974, *The New York Times* reported "Mr. and Mrs. DeFeo had both been shot twice in the backs of their heads." Subsequent issues of *The Times* and the Long Island newspapers contained a bewilderingly contradictory series of reports concerning who was shot where. We must remember, before examining the facts further, just why Anson has Kathy waking up screaming, "She was shot in the head!" The recipe for possession given in *The Exorcist*, the reader will recall, requires that the candidate display "the faculty of divulging future and hidden events." It would seem, however, that in the episode quoted above Kathy was divulging past and public events. But there's more to the story. On October 16, 1975 (about two months before Kathy's dream), *Newsday* carried an article by Don Smith with the headline:

"Medical Aide Describes Death of Mrs. DeFeo"

> Riverhead—Louise DeFeo's last few seconds of life were described in a courtroom yesterday as terror-filled: She was awakened by the noise of the two shots that killed her husband, lifted her head off the pillow to look around, struggled to get out of bed, and was shot twice in the side.
>
> Deputy medical examiner Howard Adelman described the last seconds of Mrs. DeFeo's life in his testimony yesterday before the jury at the murder trial of Ronald DeFeo, Jr.…Adelman told the jury he could determine from blood spatterings on the sheet in two different places that Mrs. DeFeo had been awakened and tried to move before the bullets

ripped into her side, killing her instantly. [Smith, "Medical Aide," *Newsday*, October 16, 1975]

It would seem the Lutzes couldn't even prophesy backwards correctly! Of course, the Lutzes were not just filling an *Exorcist* prescription; they were also cooperating with Weber's "overview":

WEBER: The overview is how to relate their story to the DeFeos. That's the overview.
BLOCK: And what did you suggest in that respect?
WEBER: Well, it was the dreams that Kathy said she had, the nightmares. And I said, "Well, maybe we could connect them in some way."
BLOCK: The linkage with the DeFeo family, and what was happening?
WEBER: Right....We all agreed.
BLOCK: You say the Lutzes wanted that, as well?
WEBER: Sure ... this was the reason why they agreed to go along with the entire commercial venture.
BLOCK: What do you mean, specifically?
WEBER: They wanted to participate in a commercial venture....you see, initially Kathy had told me about a certain dream she had, and I didn't confirm them or deny them. Afterwards I confirmed some. I embellished a lot, and I told her to straighten out a few of her dreams, because they never occurred. [*Lutz v Hoffman*, p. 251]

Since his testimony matches the best evidence available regarding the episode under consideration, I shall once again allow Attorney William Weber to say the last word:

WEBER: Patrolman Geonfreda, page 47 and 48 of the hardcover book, it shows he had made an erroneous error in his initial report when he went to the crime scene. He was the first person who arrived at the crime scene. In his initial report he indicated that Louise was shot in the head. I told the Lutzes that it was just an honest error, because he was just running through the house when he got the initial report.
BLOCK: What is there in the book that refers to information which you gave to the Lutzes, Mr. Weber
WEBER: That Patrolman Geonfreda reported that it indicated Louise was shot in the head. No. That was never—that error was nowhere ever even introduced in the trial, no place.
BLOCK: That was information which you gave?
WEBER: Yes. I told him it was a mistake. Evidently it appears in the book that Patrolman Geonfreda told them she was shot in the head. In actuality, she was never shot in the head. [*Lutz v Hoffman*, p. 282]

The Pig in the Window

Proceeding from dreams that correctly repeat errors published in year-old newspapers, we come to the tale of the pig in the window.

> George circled around the swimming pool fence. The orb of the full moon was like a huge flashlight, lighting his way. He looked up at the house and stopped short. His heart leaped. From Missy's second floor bedroom window, George could see the little girl staring at him, her eyes following his movements....Directly behind his daughter, frighteningly visible to George, was the face of a pig. He was sure he could see little red eyes glaring at him! [*AH*-pb, p. 60]

For all sorts of occult reasons, a full moon is a desirable accessory for this incident. But alas, the almanac shows that on December 25, 1975, the moon was at last quarter. With such poor lighting conditions and the distance between George and Missy's window on the second floor, we must believe that George's eyes are possessed of incredible resolving power and sensitivity to be able to see Missy's eyes follow his movements!

Fortunately, readers will sleep a bit easier after they read Lutz' own true account of *A True Story*:

> Q And did you ever see the face of a pig looking into your daughter's window?
> A There was a time I was returning from the boat house in the middle of the night, where I saw from the boathouse, which is up to my daughter's, Missy's room, some kind of shape in there. I don't know exactly what that shape was....
> Q Mr. Lutz, you are familiar with the book that you authorized Jay Anson to write?
> A Yes.
> Q At page 48 I read to you this part in the book, "Directly behind his daughter, frightening, visible to George, was the face of a pig. He was sure he could see little red eyes glaring at him."
> Now, is that the truth?
> A That's not as I remember it.
> Q Then this is not a correct portrayal of your recollection that appears in the book?
> A Well, I remember it in a different way. I don't know what it was that I saw. I know it was much larger than my wife, and there was no way for there to be anyone else in the house at that time.
> Q So you were not sure that this was a pig or any particular form of animal?

A No, I wasn't.
Q Now, you read this manuscript before it was published, did you not?
A I read the galleys twice.
Q And the references to the pig were in the galleys?
A Yes.
Q Did you at any time tell Mr. Anson or anyone else that this was not the truth?
A Yes....
Q In any event, the pig is not the truth?
A No, it is not....
Q Your seeing a pig with little red eyes glaring at you, was that true or not?
A Well, the eyes were seen on a different occasion. As far as it being called a pig, my daughter called it that. She didn't know how else to describe it. When at first she talked about it, we considered it just a childhood fantasy, but she was so definite and positive about it, she eventually drew a picture.
Q On page 48 it says your [*sic*] seeing a pig?
A I saw no pig.

More *Exorcist* Parallels

But again, as we have seen before with other topics, pigs are ubiquitous in *The Exorcist*. Attorney Weber was quick to see that the commercial value of a pig was far greater than one could compute:

> [*As part of his "overview" to relate Lutz material to DeFeo material, Weber testified that he had given confidential DeFeo information to the Lutzes which became transformed into Jodie the Pig.*] [*Lutz v Hoffman*, p. 328]
>
> WEBER: When you mentioned the "pig" you reminded me of another incident that appears in the book that I say was the seed which was planted by myself to the Lutzes.
> DALEY: What was that?
> WEBER: Ronnie DeFeo's relationship with a neighbor's cat, who always used to perch himself up on the window sill or one of the back window sills. I think this was the kitchen sill. He would throw things at the cat and refer to the cat as a "Goddamned pig."
> DALEY: On tape 3 of the cassettes that have previously been entered, do you recall a conversation in which was related to you that "Missy, their daughter, came into the room with a picture she had drawn of her pet pig named Jody. Missy would ride her only in the rain and snow around the yard. The boys never saw her. The pig could carry on conversations with

> her. Missy said that the pig would just watch the house for burglars and fire." Do you recall that statement being made to you...?
> WEBER: Yes. I recall her [*Kathy*] saying that, but at the time she said it we both knew that it was part—that was part of a hoax. [*Lutz v Hoffman*, p. 330]

If George did not see a pig in the window, what *did* he see—if in fact the whole affair is not a lie? The quarter moon rose that day at 12:46 AM. Depending upon how much time George spent after awakening at 3:15 and comforting his wife after her nightmare, the moon may have been at an elevation of about 40 degrees. He could have seen an irregular reflection of the moon in the window. Since Venus rose in the sky at 3:56, he could have seen a double reflection (due to the storm window) of Venus rising.

The end of this chapter has both a change in the text between editions and another remarkable similarity to *The Exorcist*. Originally, page 65 of *Amityville Horror* read:

> "The snow had stopped falling in Amityville, as it had fifteen miles away outside the Sacred Heart Rectory in North Merrick. Father Mancuso turned away from his window."

The paperback version now reads:

> "The snow had stopped falling in Amityville, as it had fifteen miles away outside the windows of the Long Island Rectory. Father Mancuso turned away from his window."

On page thirteen of *The Exorcist*, we read that the heroine, standing in the "infested" room:

> "...then noticed the cold. The room. It was *icy*. She padded to the window. Checked it. Closed. She touched the *radiator. Hot*. [emphases added]".

Page 65 of *The True Story* reads:

> "When Kathy checked *in there* [italics original], she was struck by the freezing chill in the playroom. No windows were open, yet the room was *ice cold*... She felt the *radiator*. It was *hot*! [emphases added]" [*AH*-pb, p. 65].

Probably the eeriest scenes in this chapter is where, "from Missy's second floor bedroom window, George could see the little girl staring at him, her eyes following his movements....Directly behind his daughter, frighteningly visible to George, was the face of a pig. He was sure he could see little red eyes glaring at him!" We have already seen that George Lutz himself debunked the porcine portion of the scene. But there is still something unnerving about looking up to a second-floor window in the dark and seeing someone watching you.

Once again, I think the *Urmotiv* for this scene is to be found in *The Exorcist* in which Lieutenant Kinderman had just returned to his squad car after surreptitiously collecting a sample of the paint on the possessed child's artwork for forensic analysis. At this point in the story, readers are wondering if she might have pushed Mr. Demmings out her bedroom window while under demonic influence.

> When he'd entered the passenger side of the squad car, Kinderman turned and looked back at the house. He thought he saw movement at Regan's window [on the second floor], a quick, lithe figure flashing to the side and out of view. He wasn't sure. ... But he noted that the shutters were open. Odd. [*Exorcist*, p. 168]

Blatty later intensifies the dramatic tension, on page 211, when Kinderman asks the mother if Regan had been alone with Mr. Demmings on the night he was killed. Chris says no, and that her daughter had been heavily sedated at the time.

> "No, I told you before, she was heavily sedated and—"
> "Yes, yes, you told me; that's true; I recall it; but perhaps she awakened—not so? and ..."
> "No chance. And—"
> "She was also sedated," he interrupted, "when last we spoke?"
> "Oh, well, yes; as a matter of fact she was," Chris recalled. "So what?"
> "I thought I saw here at her window that day."
> "You're mistaken."
> He shrugged. "It could be, it could be; I'm not sure."

For Jay Anson, William Peter Blatty's novel *The Exorcist* was a gift that just kept on giving.

Friday, December 26, 1975

Events of the Day

Weather claimed: Slush from melted snow in the morning. Roads icy at supper time.
Actual Weather: Low 32° at 12:01 AM, high 53° at 12:15, mean 43°; precipitation 1.96 inches by 7:00 PM; winds 6 mph to 14 mph.

The Lutzes

Some previous night at 3:15 George had found Harry deep asleep. Early this morning George has diarrhea and nausea. Kids stay inside after breakfast. Danny and Chris rebel. Kathy receives second spirit embrace.

Father Mancuso

At 9 AM, Mancuso's temperature is still 103 degrees. At 11 AM, Mancuso's temperature drops to 98.6.

The Lutzes

George makes tenth trip to bathroom. Office in Syosset calls (successfully). The boys are fighting again. By lunchtime George has "showered and shaved" for first time in nine days. At 5:30 PM Jimmy comes to get Lutzes for wedding (they must be at Astoria Manor in Queens by 7). Jimmy's $1,500 disappears in the kitchen. As they are about to leave in Jimmy's car, Harry is asleep in his doghouse. At 6 PM George gets sick taking Communion before wedding ceremony, vomits, but feels okay during reception.

Snow and Ice

The weather alleged for December 26, 1975, can be inferred from the statement that Kathy "looked out of the window and saw the ground covered with slush from the melted snow," and from the statement that at 5:30 PM "The roads were reported to be icy from the recent light snow." Before this date there had been only 0.05 inches of precipitation that possibly could have fallen as snow which wouldn't make much slush. But Anson needed a reason to have the kids stay inside for the boys to have their second fight "ever," and for Missy to give Jodie-the-pig updates at dramatically opportune moments.

If Mr. Anson had bothered to check the actual weather record for this date, he would have found a more accurate reason for the kids to stay inside: during the 24-hour period ending at 7 PM there had been 1.96 inches of rain. The mean temperature for that day was 43 degrees, and by the time Jimmy arrives (quite appropriately, he is wearing a raincoat) the temperature has risen to 53 degrees before falling back to 52. Considering that Anson admitted that the snow had melted in the morning and the fact that temperature had risen steadily all day long, it is hard to understand how the melted snow could have later reappeared as ice on the highway.

Lying and Sleeping Dogs

Like a symphony of the Romantic Period, Chapter Eight of *The Amityville Horror* begins and ends with the same theme. The recurrent theme in this case is the "abnormal" behavior of Harry Lutz, the half-Malamute/half-Labrador member of the family. While poking around at 3:15 one morning, George finds Harry sleeping on guard duty. Again, at 6 PM (1.5 hours after sunset) on the day after Christmas, Harry is asleep at the switch again. Nowhere does the book state just which shift of guard duty it is that Harry is expected to be actively patrolling the perimeter. Nevertheless, we are to suppose that soporific spooks are sedating Harry, just as Ronnie DeFeo was initially thought to have drugged his family before he shot them.

The few photographs I have seen of Harry betray nothing of his alleged Malamute heritage. The dog appears to be more Labrador than anything else identifiable. But it is useful later in the book to have Harry be part Arctic sled dog when the weather is so bad that even a Malamute has to be brought in the house.

We are told, "When the Lutzes lived in Deer Park, Harry also had his own doghouse and slept outside in all kinds of weather. Normally he would remain awake, on guard, until two or three in the morning before finally settling down and going to sleep" [*AH*-pb, pp. 67–68]. We must wonder how the Lutzes knew Harry was generally awake at two or three in the morning—unless George's waking up at 3:15 in the morning was a habit which began before—not after—his moving into the Amityville house. The statement that Harry had "slept outside in all kinds of weather" implies that the dog is a seasoned veteran in braving all outdoor conditions. Laura DiDio, whom we met earlier as the Channel Five News authority on occult phenomena whom Weber had called in for "outside corroboration," mentioned Harry in her testimony at the *Lutz v Hoffman* trial. She had spoken with the Lutzes on February 21, 1976. On that occasion, she testified that the Lutzes:

> Described what had happened to their dog, who was a normally placid animal, they said. A year-old dog. He had suddenly turned to the point where he would either be sleeping all the time or he would be getting vicious. [*Lutz v. Hoffman*, p. 421]

If this testimony be true, it means that the Lutzes had had a new-born puppy "on guard, until two or three in the morning," during the latter part of the previous winter.

A Need for Diarrhea

From the initial discussion of the quadrupedal member of the Lutz family, the book proceeds to a discussion of a bipedal member with diarrhea. It is extremely significant that George has nausea and diarrhea, not some other ailment. Readers who are unfamiliar with *Exorcist*-like literature will simply assume that poor George has stomach flu. They will not realize that George's diarrhea has deep occult significance. Human excrement is always associated with the demonic, with the actions of "unclean spirits." In this case, diarrhea is the disease of choice.

It is recorded that at 11 AM George made his tenth trip to the bathroom. Although the starting point for this colonic chronical is not mentioned, I would suppose the first trip had taken place shortly after 3:15 AM. That would average out to be about one trip every 51 minutes and 40 seconds. How Mr. Anson ever managed to find out that George made his *tenth* trip, not his ninth or eleventh, at precisely 11 AM is an accomplishment unappreciated, I am sure, by Mr. Anson's readers.

At the exact same time as George was involved in his tenth "number two," Father Mancuso's temperature was back to 98.6 degrees. But we read in the hard cover edition [p. 56] that two hours before the fever broke, "At nine that morning, Father Mancuso had awakened in the North Merrick Rectory and taken his temperature. The thermometer had still read 103 degrees." In the paperback version, Mancuso awakens in "the Long Island rectory." Once again, we are witness to authorial omniscience allowing Anson to determine the synchronicities between the actions of the Lutzes and the priest.

Unholy Grail

Later that evening George vomits when the chalice is presented during Holy Communion, which is also supposed to have dark significance. Presenting a chalice to a man possessed is a form of "religious provocation," as the Warrens would have termed it. The "very blood of Christ" can be expected to rile up the spirits much more seriously than would a mere crucifix.

However that may be, the whole Holy Communion episode smells more than a bit fishy. First, it is improbable, in 1975, that a Catholic layman would have been given the chalice in the first place. And when we recall that George was still a Methodist at the time, his being offered the chalice by a Catholic priest is unthinkable. According to Anson, the Communion had taken place at Our Lady of Martyrs Roman Catholic Church, "a little church near the Manor." Having a mind to ask "Father Santini" (the priest who allegedly officiated) about this, I called Directory Assistance for Astoria (the "Manor" is the Astoria Manor). There *is* no "Our Lady of Martyrs" Church in Astoria.

Losing Things

In *The Exorcist*, the possessed child begins to "lose things"—a dress, her toothbrush, books, etc. Dramatically, a book about devil worship and occult phenomena disappears, only to be found later on under the child's bed. Readers are led to suspect that these items were never lost; rather, a poltergeist or demonic force has translocated them. In our *True Story* also, something disappears—a check in the amount of $1,500 needed to pay the balance on Kathy's brother Jimmy's wedding reception [*AH*-pb, pp. 73–74]. The check is never found, but readers are made to suspect the check wasn't really "lost."

Inconsistencies and Unmentioned Marvels

There are few happenings in the remainder of chapter fourteen which have not been touched upon in previous chapters of this book. However, I cannot resist bringing up how Anson details incredible happenings in *A True Story* that are not given the recognition deserved in a story of supernatural happenings. Such as on page 70, when we read about "The big freezer in the *basement*, one of the free items they had received from the DeFeo estate." Story wise, it makes sense for the freezer to be in the basement; Mr. Anson had to find some way to give Kathy an occasion to discover the "secret room". However, in the catalogue for the Lutz auction, the freezer is listed as part of the contents of the *garage*. Is it possible that *The Horror* teleported it from the garage to the basement after the Lutzes left, and that the world's most wondrous example of psychokinesis hitherto has escaped notice?

The topic of astounding impossibilities also has me bringing up the subject of George's poor hygiene one last time. At the top of page 73 we read,

"George came down a half-hour later. For the first time in nine days, he had *shaved* and showered." At the bottom of the very same page it says, "George came down, neatly clad in a tuxedo. His face was pale from the diarrhea, but he was freshly combed, his *dark blonde beard* framing his handsome face."

How could George have shaved—*i.e.*, not merely trimmed his beard— and still have his beard? In all photographs that I have seen of George Lutz, he is sporting a *full* beard—he hasn't even shaved his neck or the underside of his jaw. Anson seems to have missed an opportunity to underscore the supernatural implications of George's ability to grow a full beard within a few minutes.

Saturday, December 27, 1975

Events of the Day

Weather claimed: Bright and clear, temperatures hovering in the low teens. Actual weather: Low 34° at 3:45 PM, high 43° at 12:01, mean 39°; precipitation 0.00 inches all day; winds 5 mph to 13 mph.

The Lutzes

Sometime after midnight, George helps Jimmy pay for the reception at the Astoria Manor by writing a bum check. The party breaks up at 2 AM. Jimmy and Carey take a cab to LaGuardia to fly to Bermuda. George drives Jimmy's car to Amityville. Kathy goes to bed and George finds Harry asleep. All doors and windows are locked except the sewing room door, which is ajar.

George and Kathy make love for first time in the house. Kathy dreams of Louise DeFeo's "infidelity." Kathy takes the van and goes shopping. George takes the kids and Harry in Jimmy's car to get the mail in Syosset. Everyone is home after 1 PM. Kathy transports food to the freezer in the basement.

Her face ruddy from walking in the extreme cold, ex-nun Aunt Theresa pays a visit. Kathy is in the basement while George takes Aunt Theresa on tour of house. She balks at the sewing room and playroom. Kathy comes up and takes Aunt Theresa to the kitchen. A half hour after her arrival, Aunt Theresa leaves. Boys bring a friend home who won't go upstairs to play. A "secret room" is discovered in the basement. As George steers Kathy out of secret room, he glimpses the visage of Ronnie DeFeo at the back of the basement closet.

> "By then it was after one o'clock. The weather was bright and clear, the temperatures hovering in the low teens" [*AH*-pb, pp. 80–81].

The New York Times for December 27, 1975, predicted for the Long Island forecast that the rest of the day should be "variably cloudy through tonight," not "bright and clear" like the novel suggests. The actual temperatures recorded for the day showed a low of 34 degrees at 3:45 PM and a high of 43 at 12:01 AM. The temperature at 1:00 PM was 40 degrees, not "hovering in the low teens." Anson was correct that a ruddy face is in keeping with the weather for this date. However, the ruddy face should have been Anson's, not Aunt Theresa's.

Dreaming of a Lover

On page 80, we are granted insight into Kathy's mind after her and George's first-time making love in the Amityville house:

> That night, Kathy had a dream of Louise DeFeo and a man making love in the very same room she was lying in....Somehow Kathy knew that the man was not Louise's husband. It was not until several weeks after she and her family had fled from 112 Ocean Avenue that she learned from an attorney close to the DeFeos that Louise actually did have a lover, an artist who lived with the family for a while. [*AH*-pb, p. 80]

Considering the "fact" that it would be several days before George would come to know that the "visage" he sees in the basement closet belonged to Ronald DeFeo [whose picture had been in all the papers], it is hard to understand how Kathy would instantly know the woman in her dream was Louise DeFeo. In all the vast number of publications which I scrutinized before 1980, I had never seen a picture of Louise DeFeo. This fable appears to have been invented rather late in the creation of the novel, since it does not appear in Hoffman's articles. As usual, Weber claimed the "credit" for this purported example of "divulging hidden events":

[*William Weber is testifying*]

A A very important aspect which the Lutzes changed, page 63 of the book, they talk about Kathy having a dream that Louise had a lover. Now, the Lutzes asked me about that.
Q Louise, meaning Louise DeFeo?
A Louise DeFeo. Kathy asked me about that, and I told her that I had interviewed just about every neighbor for a least a block to a block and a half from that house, and even others, and to a person they all said as far as they were concerned, Louise DeFeo was a saint; that she had devoted her life to her children ... no, there was no way that Louise would ever contemplate anything like that....

Q How is that reflected in the book?
A Wait. But they felt that the father, or her husband, on occasions, had actually threatened the wife with his suspicions about this, and that was because the husband had hired a painter to paint portraits of the family and he had been in the house on many occasions, and it was just out of jealousy that the husband made those accusations. But there was actually nothing to do with it.
In the book on page 63 not only do they talk about Louise having a lover, but afterwards in that book....they say that they later on spoke with an attorney who corroborated that accusation. And first of all, it's a lie. I never corroborated it.
Q They were referring to you in the book as "the attorney"?
A Yes. They didn't mention my name in that paragraph, but I told them just the opposite. [*Lutz v Hoffman, p. 283*]

Coincidences do occur, even odd ones. An artist also makes an appearance in *The Exorcist.* Specifically, an art teacher who makes regular visits to the demon house to give art lessons to Regan, the possessed child. Regan sculpts, paints, and draws, just as Missy and her brothers have paints, and Missy draws a picture of the demon-pig that appears on page 249 of *The Amityville Horror*.

Short Visits

We come next to the case of Aunt Theresa, the ex-nun. Considering the temperature outside was in the forties, not the low teens, her arriving on foot is not *prima facie* too implausible. However, if she did indeed refuse to go into the sewing room and, when shown the playroom, say "No ... that's another bad place. I don't like it," we would be forced to diagnose a severe psychiatric disorder.

I have a strong suspicion, however, that Aunt Theresa is not the one with mental problems. Even though Hoffman also said she balked before certain rooms, the beginning of the Hoffman account of this incident seems eminently plausible: "Kathy's aunt, a normally placid ex-nun, came to visit and, according to Lee, "sat there and cut me down for three hours" [Hoffman, "Life in a Haunted House," *New York Daily News*, July 18, 1976]. We must remember that according to *The Amityville Horror: A True Story*, Aunt Theresa left the house after just half an hour.

Just as Aunt Theresa is leaving, the boys bring home a new playmate: "'This is Bobby, Mama,' Chris said. 'We just met him. He lives up the street'" [*AH*-pb, p. 83]. When the Lutzes invite Bobby to go upstairs (to the playroom?) to play, he turns very shy and says he'd just as soon play in the foyer. "For the next *half-hour*, the three boys played on the foyer floor, with

Danny's and Chris' new Christmas toys....That was the first and last time that the boy from up the street ever set foot in 112 Ocean Avenue" [*AH*-pb, p. 84].

Laura DiDio testified [*Lutz v Hoffman*, p. 421] that Kathy had told her how "*one* of her little boys had brought a playmate *home from school* [i.e., this could not have happened on Dec. 27] and the child wouldn't go any further than the foyer and left after *about five minutes*." Can it be another odd coincidence that in *The Exorcist* [pb, p. 81] two guests—a senator and his wife—"seemed edgy" and left a party in the haunted house, after being there only a short while? Whatever amount of truth there may be in this non-event, it is hard to see any paranormal significance in this shy little boy's behavior.

The Secret Room

In the previous chapter, it was noted that the DeFeo's freezer was first located in the garage at the time of the Lutz auction sale before miraculously being moved down to the basement. Of course, it could have originally been moved up from the basement for easy removal after the auction, but nevertheless, for dramatic reasons, it was absolutely necessary to have the freezer in the basement for the duration of *The Amityville Horror* so when Kathy entered the basement with her grocery purchases she was able to discover the "secret room" beneath the stairs. As Kathy is working in a basement closet, we read that the light from the bulb which illuminated the closet:

> shone through a small slit opening just enough to give Kathy the impression that there was an empty space behind the closet, under the tallest section of the stairs....[*George*] looked at the opening and pushed against the paneling ... "There isn't supposed to be anything back there," he said to Kathy. [*AH*-pb, pp. 84–85]

They discover a secret room:

> The room was small, about four by five feet. Kathy gasped. From the ceiling to floor, it was painted solid red. "What *is* it, George?"
> "I don't know," he answered...." maybe a bomb shelter....but it sure doesn't show up in the house plans the broker gave us." [*AH*-pb, p. 85]

A mildly macabre touch is added when, after George finishes "steering Kathy out of the secret room," she asks him, "Did you notice the funny smell in there?" "Yeah, I smelled it," George said. "That's how blood smells" [*AH*-pb, p. 85]. Whether or not George learned to recognize the odor of blood as part of his growing up in suburban Long Island or as part of his training in the marines, I do not know. I *do* know that despite the many times that I have shed my own blood in my very long life, I have never been able to detect any odor at all.

Readers who were completely awake when they read the quotation above describing the discovery of the secret room, must have had a good chuckle when they came to George's comment, "There isn't supposed to be anything back there." According to the floor plan given on page 87—as well as by admission in the text—the "secret room" is merely the area below the highest part of the basement stairs. Why shouldn't there be anything back there? Should it have been filled with concrete? He was expecting maybe a black hole? Even if it were a vacuum, that space would still have to be there! If it did not "show up in the house plans the broker gave us," we can only conclude that there must have been a rectangular hole in the paper.

It is also very amusing to notice that at one point George was "steering Kathy out of the secret room." It would be much more believable if the sentence said he was "prying Kathy out of the secret room." The "room" is a storage cubby and measures 2'4" wide, 3'6" long, and 3'6" high! Since the "secret room" is not mentioned in Hoffman's articles, again we may conclude that this plot device was included relatively late in the writing process.

Myths do not spring full-blown out of nothing. Myths grow from narrative seeds. As they grow, they turn and twist and transform until the final result is almost unrecognizable. Again and again, we have seen how seed-elements provided by Weber have grown and blossomed into episodes which seem to be intimately and originally part of the Lutz *mise-en-scène*. It would appear that Weber, once again, planted the mythopoeic seed for this "secret room" to spawn:

> WEBER: Almost everyone in Amityville would joke about Ronnie DeFeo, Jr.'s secret closet. That's because Ronnie DeFeo—and this I'm telling now to the Lutzes, too, about Ronnie—
>
> BLOCK: You told them about Ronnie DeFeo's secret closet?
>
> WEBER: Right. Ronnie DeFeo always had ample money in his possession.... Whenever Ronnie was asked where did he get the money, he got the money downstairs in his secret closet. Ronnie and his friend, Robert Kelsey, built that closet. It's just a partition between a large wide closet. [*Lutz v Hoffman*, p. 285]

We may remember that in the Prologue we first encountered the secret-room motif. There we read of Kathy being levitated "toward a closet behind which was a room not noted on any blue-prints." As we proceed from "Ronnie's secret closet" to the "room behind a closet" to the final secret room out of which Kathy is steered, we note both growth and transformation: a closet is transformed into a room, a small space growing into a large space.

Fleeting Vision

After George and Kathy have come out of the "secret room" and the closet in front of it, George, "turned out the light in the closet, shutting out the sight of the rear wall panel, but not obscuring the fleeting vision of a face he glimpsed against the plywood. In a few days, George would realize it was the bearded visage of Ronnie DeFeo!" [*AH*-pb, p. 87].

The last sentence of this quotation is rather specious. All the newspapers had printed pictures of Ronnie DeFeo not only at the time of the murders, but during the lengthy trial and sentencing as well. Pictures of DeFeo had appeared just a few weeks prior to December 27 from when he had been sentenced on December 5. When we later read about the supposedly startling similarity in appearance between George Lutz and Ronnie DeFeo, Jr., we may ask however did George conclude that the "fleeting vision of a face" which he had seen belonged to DeFeo? How could he be sure it was not a memory of his own "visage" in the bathroom mirror?

Sunday, December 28, 1975

Events of the Day

Weather claimed: Cold
Actual weather: Low 26°, high 35°, mean 31°

The Lutzes

George goes into Witches' Brew, reflects about children and Tax Assessor's Office. Bartender comments on George's resemblance to someone he used to know. He drops glass on the floor when he learns George lives at 112 Ocean Ave. Kathy waits in living room (afraid of kitchen). Around almost 4 PM, the boys watch TV in their room. Kathy thinks the ceramic lion has moved a few inches.

Father Mancuso and Gionfriddo

After mass, Gionfriddo visits Mancuso in the Sacred Heart Rectory. Gionfriddo recounts DeFeo murders and tells Gionfriddo about "a voice" and how Ronnie went to Witches' Brew. He talks about the rifle. Gionfriddo leaves rectory, throws up, passes Witches' Brew, and sees George enter. Priest works on Court work.

The Lutzes

At 6 PM George's phone rings, but all he hears is static. They have supper. George dials Mancuso's number. There is no answer. At 7 PM (by electric clock over kitchen sink), George trips over the ceramic lion on floor while on his way to the fireplace.

Father Mancuso

At 6 PM, the priest is hungry. His phone rings, but all he hears is static. At 7 PM, Mancuso's temperature is 102 degrees.

Hearing Voices

As we consider the conversation between "Sergeant Gionfriddo" and "Father Mancuso," the reader is reminded that all relevant agencies of the Roman Catholic Church repeatedly denied that any of the events ascribed to ecclesiastical persons ever happened. A number of reporters spoke with Father Pecoraro ("Mancuso") and said he denied any complicity in the affair (beyond blessing the house and hearing a voice say "Get out"). I feel the issue is not totally resolved, but after the *Lutz v Hoffman* trial he became incommunicado and I was not able to speak to him myself.

In his testimony at the *Lutz v Hoffman* trial, despite ample opportunity to do so, Father Pecoraro did not admit to any strange things happening to him, except for "the voice" at the occasion of his blessing the house. Though like the seeds Hoffman planted, it is probable that Father Pecoraro also said or did things that became wildly distorted and enlarged in the book. After all, he did complain about things that had been said about him "that are not true, or that are grossly exaggerated." In my experience, something first has to exist to be exaggerated.

In the alleged conversation between Sergeant Gionfriddo and Father Mancuso which is recounted on pages 90–91, the priest is quoted as saying, "I understand [Ronnie DeFeo] said he heard voices." Gionfriddo then replies, "At his trial, he did claim a voice told him to do it."

Now it *is* true that during the trial Ronnie claimed to have heard voices. Ronnie testified, "For months before the incident, I heard voices, and, whenever I looked around, there was no one there, so it must have been God talking to me" [Anonymous, "Summations Starting," *Newsday*, November 7, 1975].

However, in all the newspaper accounts of the DeFeo trial, not once was it reported that DeFeo claimed voices told him to kill his family. Moreover, in the trial transcript reproduced in Hans Holzer's book, *Murder in Amityville,* nowhere does there appear trial testimony saying any such thing. Considering that the entire purpose of Holzer's book (apart, of course, from making money) is to "prove" that Ronnie DeFeo was possessed, this omission seems odd and extremely significant.

The Witches' Brew

Gionfriddo then tells the priest that the police learned of the murders only later, "when Ronnie went into The Witches' Brew and told the bartender. The Witches' Brew is a bar near Ocean Avenue" [*AH*-pb, page 91]. I went to every bar in the vicinity of Ocean Avenue, but there was none under the name of "Witches' Brew." According to Mr. Weber, there never was such a place. The newspapers had reported that DeFeo had gone to *Henry's Bar* to report the murders. Thought I planned to visit Henry's and see if I could locate the bartender in question, alas, Henry's was no more. The bar had burned down sometime earlier in 1979.

On page 92 we read that Gionfriddo vomits immediately upon leaving the priest's apartment. As readers may suspect by now, nausea is always associated with the demonic and is one of the tell-tale signs of possession. We recall that *The Exorcist* also contains numerous accounts of nausea and vomiting.

We next are treated to a bit of imaginary geography. On page 92 it says that [*Gionfriddo*] "headed home, rolling up Amityville Road. He drove past The Witches' Brew on his right....Amityville Road, the main shopping street in town, was empty." Henry's Bar, for which Witches' Brew is being substituted, was located on Merrick Road (Montauk Highway), and so Gionfriddo had to have been on Merrick, not "Amityville Road" when he passed the bar. A possible reason for Anson's invention of a new address for the bar was so none of his readers could find the bar and interview the bartender. It is also possible that at the time he was writing his book, Henry's had already been sold and had a different name. If Anson had looked up "Henry's" in the phone book, hoping to find an address, he would have found nothing. In fact, one of the reasons for my first trip to Amityville was to track down the bar which, although the newspapers said it existed, could not be found in the phone book.

The description of George's visit to the bar makes a great to-do about the supposed physical resemblance between George Lutz and Ronald DeFeo. I was never able to see either of these men in person, but my examination of photos of both men revealed only two resemblances: their noses were similar and they both had beards. While I can accept the fact that, to many people, "all bearded men look alike," such generalized resemblance would hardly be cause for dropping a beer-glass on the floor. Hoffman's articles describe George as having "a shock of red hair," whereas Anson describes him as dark blonde. The photographs of DeFeo all indicate that his hair was fairly dark brown. Considering the fact that the episode described on pages 92–95 takes place in an imaginary bar at an imaginary address, have we any reason to doubt that the conversation too is unreal?

The Telekinetic Lion

The Exorcist has events involving "psychokinesis," and so does *The Amityville Horror.* The object used in *The Horror* involves a "huge, four-foot ceramic lion, crouched, ready to leap upon an unseen victim." Kathy had given it as a present to George, who "had thought it a pretty piece and had moved it to the living room, where it now sat on a large table beside his chair near the fire-place" [*AH*-pb, pp. 95–96].

Kathy thinks she sees the lion move a few inches toward her [*AH*-pb, page 96]. Of course if it had moved very far it would have fallen off the table. We are not told how large the table was which could accommodate a four-foot lion, but surely it could not have been much more than four feet long itself. There is a further problem: blueprints of the house show that there wasn't room for such a table on either side of the fireplace. It would project nearly two feet into the doorways flanking the fireplace on either side. It is possible that the table was placed perpendicular to the fireplace wall, with a pile of firewood and George's chair on the opposite side of the fireplace. (Recent photographs of the fireplace wall show four-foot-wide bookshelves flanking the fireplace, and it appears that a repositioning of the doors must have taken place at the time the house was remodeled to fill in the swimming pool and add the beautiful sunporch at the back of the dwelling.)

The lion did, in fact, exist. It was listed in the auction catalogue, and Mrs. Evans told me that it was, in fact, at least three feet long. I have seen a color slide of the lion, but unfortunately it was against a background which contained no objects with which to compare dimensions. The lion's mouth was open *with teeth projecting*. The latter point is important when, later, George stubs his foot on the lion (which, more appropriately, is on the floor) and Kathy finds tooth marks on his ankle. It is not accidental, I think, that Anson did not tell his readers about the ceramic lion having an open mouth with projecting teeth. It was not enough that his readers should suppose that an inanimate object was capable of locomotion; they must also imagine it was biting!

It must be admitted that having a ceramic lion be psychokinetically relocated is an improvement over the analogous incident in *The Exorcist*. In that story, the heroine stubs her toe on a piece of furniture which the demon has displaced. But dressers don't leave tooth marks. Unlike *The Exorcist* situation—where the dresser which relocates is much too big to have been moved by a little girl—in *The Amityville Horror* there were three excellent possible sources of energy for moving ceramic toys around the house! One was nine years old, one was seven, and one was five. Even so, for dramatic purposes it was necessary to have something be telekinetically moved around, and there was nothing in the catalogue of Lutz household possessions that could have served those purposes better.

There is also no indication that the lights were out in the living room at the time of George stubbing his toe. If we may assume normal lighting conditions, it is strange how Kathy could see the lion move an inch but George could not see it in the middle of the floor. A study of the blueprints of the house shows that for George Lutz to have left the kitchen through either of its doors, he would have passed through the large foyer of the house and entered the living room through a six-foot-wide archway. From the archway, he would have had a clear view of the fireplace on the far wall, as his goal was to put more wood onto the fire. Unless he were blind, he couldn't have missed the lion and "taken a nasty tumble over the porcelain lion and fallen heavily against some of the logs by the fireplace."

Telling Time

We may recall that Kathy still thought of the kitchen as her "happy" room, even after her first alleged encounter with a motherly ghost in that room. Now, however, after her second run-in, she is reluctant to be left alone in said room. She is in the kitchen only out of necessity, we may presume, at supper time and at 7 PM when, we read, George "looked at the electric clock over the kitchen sink."

According to the floor plan given on page eleven, there are windows above the kitchen sink, and we must suppose that the clock is above said windows.[1] Curiously, the auction list for the Lutz household did not list an electric clock for the kitchen. In fact, the only electric clock mentioned for the entire house is one in the "den." I have been unable to determine just which room is called the "den," but it is safe to assume it was not the kitchen. Of course, it is possible that there once was an electric clock over the windows over the sink and that the Lutzes took it with them when they left the house. If so, this puts into question the assertion that they fled "taking only a few changes of clothes."

---

[1] The only photograph I have seen of the kitchen sink is cut off below the middle of an obviously tall window, indicating that if there had been a clock above the window it would have been improbably close to the ceiling.

Monday, December 29, 1975

Events of the Day

Weather claimed: "With temperatures in the low twenties, George knew he could anticipate ignition problems" [*AH*-pb, p. 99].
Actual weather: Low 25°, high 37°, mean 31°

The Lutzes

George's ankle is stiff, and the tooth marks are still on his ankle. He has trouble starting his year-old Ford van. He goes to Syosset. Half-way there, on Sunrise Highway, one of the shocks falls off. Kathy's mother calls about receiving a postcard from Jimmy in Bermuda. Kathy lies down in the bedroom. She hears the window opening and closing in the sewing room.

Father Mancuso

Mancuso has redness in the palms of his hands.

The Lutzes

IRS inspector is waiting for George in Syosset. Everything is finished in Syosset by 1:00 PM. George stops at *Newsday*'s Garden City office. He studies microfilms of DeFeo murder, trial, and sentencing. He leaves thinking of coroner's report pinpointing 3:15 AM as the time of the DeFeo deaths. On his way back to Amityville, a wheel nearly falls off his car.

Car Problems

This is one of the few days of the chronicled twenty-eight where the weather Anson claimed is almost reconcilable with the actual weather recorded. Although the mean temperature for the day was 31 degrees, the low temperature, occurring at 6:10 AM, was 25 degrees. This is not exactly "in the low twenties," but we may be gracious and allow for microclimatic differences between New York City and Amityville.

We read on page 99 that George not only had difficulty in starting his 1974 Ford van (because of temperatures in the low twenties), but he *anticipated* ignition problems. Now of course from the vantage point of someone writing a book in 1977, a 1974 Ford may plausibly be considered to have passed the crest of the hill. But in 1975, the time of our incident, the van was only a year old and had only 26,000 miles on its odometer. At most, the van would have gone through one winter previously. Being brand new during that winter, there would be little likelihood of the vehicle having a history of ignition problems. So why should George anticipate ignition problems now, when the temperature is merely in the low twenties? And of course, we must wonder if George ever told Anson he was expecting ignition problems, or whether we have come upon just another example of the authorial omniscience of a novelist.

Although the dog that resides at 112 Ocean Avenue does not chase cars, someone—or some-*thing*—else residing at that address does! We have already read how it chased after Reverend Mancuso's car and nearly demolished it. We have also seen how it deranged the windshield wipers of the car belonging to the priest who aided Mancuso. And now *The Horror* has gone after a vehicle belonging to the Lutzes themselves:

> Halfway to Syosset, on the Sunrise Highway, George felt a bump in the back of the van. He pulled over and inspected the rear end. One of the shock absorbers had come loose and fallen off....He drove on again intending to replace the part once he returned to Amityville. [*AH*-pb, p. 100]

Evidently, even after the Lutzes leave for California, Amityville's Horror went on to attack a car carrying Anson's manuscript of his *True Story*, and—in Pennsylvania mind you—ran a car driven by the ghost-hunting Warrens off the road. With such long-range capability, it is a pity the Pentagon could not harness the force.

I do not know if the Lutz van did or did not lose a shock absorber on December 29, 1975. But even if it did, all the ordinary explanations are far preferable to any supernatural explanation. It should be noted, moreover, that *there is no mention of any automotive calamities in Hoffman's earlier account.* It is significant also that Anson's story makes no mention of how or if George replaced the shock absorber.

Unnoticed Miracle

Before pursuing paranormal automotive wonders further, it is necessary to note one of the most unbelievable events alleged in the entire book. On page 100, we read "After George drove off that morning, Kathy's mother called to tell her that she had received a card from Jimmy and Carey in Bermuda" [*AH*-

pb, p. 100]. Remembering that the wedding party had broken up in the early morning hours of Saturday, December 27, 1975, and that it was *a postcard*, not first-class mail, that arrived *just two days later*, on Monday, December 29 *from another country* we must wonder why Jay Anson didn't draw readers' attention to a happening worthy of Ripley's *Believe It or Not.*

Instead, Anson lets his readers know that Amityville's Horror is capable of bilocation. At the same time this supernatural force is pursuing George's van, it is also scaring the daylights out of Kathy by opening and closing the windows in the sewing room back home. Not that Kathy *sees* the windows opening and closing, nor does she open the door to the sewing room to make sure the sounds she hears aren't coming from the radiators. On page 100 it states that Kathy had been "dozing for about fifteen minutes when she began to hear noises coming from the sewing room." It is clear from the text that before she lay down to take a nap she was rather frightened about being alone in the house with just the children. Once again, we have excellent conditions for what I have called an acoustical Rorschach Test. If Kathy's mental set was one of supernatural expectation, all that would be needed would be a "white-noise" stimulus coming from any source, and she would project her fears onto the in-coming auditory stimuli.

In the present instance, the chances that the interpretation of the sounds given above is correct are greatly enhanced by the supposed fact that Kathy first heard the sounds while "dozing." In other words, she may not have been fully awake and may have been in what is called a hypnogogic state: a half-dreaming, half-waking condition which is characterized by extreme suggestibility. It is often very easy, in fact, to convert such a state into full-fledged hypnosis. Events "experienced" under such conditions may be extremely realistic and may compel very strong belief on the part of the subject. It is not impossible, in fact, for such a person's belief to be so strong that a lie-detector test can be passed with ease.

Of course, all this somewhat theoretical attempt at explanation assumes this episode occurred to begin with. I am conscious of the fact that there is nothing that evokes more mirth in the perpetrator of a hoax than the spectacle of "scientific experts" spinning out webs of hypothesis, stretching logic, and grasping for naturalistic explanations for phenomena that never occurred.

Researching DeFeo

After Amityville's Horror has removed the shock absorber from George's van, but before it managed to loosen the bolts on one of the wheels, George stops into the Garden City office of *Newsday* to check out the history of the DeFeo murders and Ronnie's trial:

"George only vaguely recalled the details of the way the son had slaughtered the whole family, but he did remember that the trial had been held in Riverhead, Long Island, sometime in the fall of 1975" [*AH*-pb, p. 102].

Worded this way, the event almost sounds like ancient history: "... sometime in the fall of 1975." In reality, news of DeFeo's conviction had appeared in the November 22, 1975, issue of *Newsday*, just five weeks prior to George's supposed visit to the microfilm department. News of DeFeo's sentencing appeared in the December 5 issue—in the same month as George's "research"!

On page 102 we read "The first articles told how Ronnie had run into a bar near his home, calling for help....With two friends, Ronald DeFeo returned to his house" The actual *Newsday* article referred to mentions *by name* four, not two, friends. Again, we see that Anson's research is characterized neither by accuracy nor by attention to detail. On page 103 it is claimed that George even read the account of how DeFeo had been sentenced to six consecutive life terms. George also read, we are told, "State Supreme Court Justice Thomas Salk [*should be Stark*!] called the killings the 'most heinous and abhorrent crimes.'"

Now, of course, I have read all those microfilms myself. But even before I checked the microfilms it had seemed odd to me that if George had, in fact, done the research he claimed, how is it he didn't know the name of the Judge? Upon examining the microfilms in the New York State Library, I noticed the reel containing the news of DeFeo's sentencing included issues of *Newsday* through December 15, just fourteen days prior to Lutz' alleged use of the microfilm thereof! A bit of checking with librarians familiar with microfilm purchasing revealed it normally takes one to two months to receive a given reel of microfilm. It seemed extremely improbable—though technically not impossible—that *Newsday* had received the necessary microfilm by the time of George's alleged visit.

To resolve the question, I placed a call to the librarian at *Newsday*, to ask her when, in fact, she had received the reel in question. To my amusement, before I could fully explain why I was calling, I was told by one of the librarians that she would be very happy to look up all the dates and pages for me, but I would not be allowed to use their microfilm collection myself.

"Our library facilities are not open to the public," I was told. "Is this a recent policy?" I asked. "No. We have not allowed public use for many years," she replied.

After explaining that I was trying to ascertain the validity of various claims in *The Amityville Horror,* I asked if there was a chance that a special exception might have been made in Lutz' case. The librarian said she was very sure there had been no exceptions to this rule, but she referred me to the head librarian, just to make sure. The head librarian denied the possibility of Lutz' visit even more firmly than had her assistant.

The Lutz visit to *Newsday* is thus an invention, created by Mr. Anson to develop several recurrent themes of his drama. Since *The Exorcist* prescription requires either precognition or the "divulging of hidden events," it had to be made to look as though Lutz sees his first picture of DeFeo *after* he hallucinates the latter's image in the basement closet. In actuality, DeFeo's face had appeared many times in newspapers during the year previous to the Lutzes' move to 112 Ocean Avenue, easily observable by George and the rest of the Lutzes'. That DeFeo was seen numerous times on TV news programs also cannot be doubted.

At 3:15 in the Morning

George's visit to *Newsday* was needed to establish the "fact" that the newspapers all said *all* the DeFeos had been shot in the back. It will be recalled that Kathy had a dream which "revealed" Louise DeFeo had been shot in the head, a "fact" known only to a few investigators. It was no accident, I believe, that Anson did not mention how, although the November 14 article in *Newsday* did say that all the DeFeos had been shot in the back, the November 20 issue of the same paper had reported (incorrectly) that all had been shot in the head. Nor would he have spoiled all the fun by mentioning that *The New York Times* had reported (again, incorrectly), as early as November 15, that Mr. and Mrs. DeFeo had been shot in the head.

The visit to *Newsday* also serves to develop the recurring 3:15-in-the-morning theme. George leaves the *Newsday* offices "thinking of the Coroner's report that pinpointed the time of the DeFeos' deaths at about 3:15 in the morning. That was the exact moment George had been waking since they'd been in the house! He would have to tell Kathy" [*AH*-pb, p. 103].

Nowhere in the pages of *Newsday*, at any time, did there appear a "Coroner's report" fixing the time of death at 3:15 AM. On November 14, 1974 *Newsday* reported the time of death as "between 5:45 and 9 yesterday." Later, it was reported that DeFeo had admitted killing his family "around 3:30 AM." Since a neighbor of the DeFeos had reported hearing the dogs barking furiously at around 3 AM, it seems Anson merely "split the difference," and arrived at the figure of 3:15 for the time of death. However, there is also the possibility that Weber had given the 3:15 AM pseudo-fact to the Lutzes on the basis of later, "confidential", information from DeFeo himself. The 3:15 figure also appears in the earliest published account of the Ocean Avenue Epic (that of Hoffman) which supports the hypothesis that Weber *was* the source of this notion. In fact, Hoffman admitted he heard the 3:15 figure from Weber who, as usual, claimed to be the source of the 3:15 figure when he testified in the *Lutz v. Hoffman* trial:

Q You've also indicated at the time of the murders that there was nothing, to your knowledge—and it was confidentially related by you that the murders occurred at three-fifteen, and that prior to that time, you had ascertained that from Ronnie DeFeo, confidentially; is that correct?
A What he told me was confidential, that's correct.
Q You indicated previously that there were reports that indicated that it could have been anywhere from 12 until four, I believe?
A In the trial no one was able to fix the date of death, the exact time of death. It was an approximation.

As we have no way of telling in which interview Ronnie DeFeo was—if ever—telling the truth, we can take our pick as to when the murders took place: 3:00 AM, 3:15 AM, or 3:30 AM. But no matter. George Lutz didn't always wake up at exactly 3:15 either:

A While we were in the house I—no matter what time I went to bed, I would repeatedly wake up at 2:15 in the morning and then again at 3:15 in the morning, if I got back to sleep, and … I was very tired of waking up at 3:15 in the morning because I would be unable to get back to sleep.
Q Do you wake up at 3:15 every night?
A Yes, or thereabouts, 3 o'clock, 3:30, but always in that vicinity. [*Lutz v Hoffman,* p. 67]

From the testimony just quoted, it appears that the *circum*-three awakening was a long-standing habit of Lutz which continued until the time of the trial. A urologist might have been better able to explain it than the "paranormalologers"!

18

Tuesday, December 30, 1975

Events of the Day

Weather claimed: No weather reported.

Father Mancuso

Mancuso has painful, red splotches on palms of hands and a high temperature.

The Lutzes

George gets information from the Amityville Historical Society, then gets information from the Real Estate Tax Assessment Office. The Lutzes go to bed early, George having first checked the sewing room.

Father Mancuso

Mancuso prays before retiring, his palms now beginning to bleed.

Stigmata Required

The prescription for possession given in *The Exorcist* calls for stigmata, and Anson served them up, *à la* Mancuso, for our delectation on December 30. Stigmata, according to Webster, are "bodily marks or pains resembling the wounds of the crucified Christ and sometimes accompanying religious ecstasy." Why it should be that signs which, on more than one occasion in the history of the Roman Catholic Church, have been grounds for elevation to sainthood, are also to be considered as signs of demonic possession quite escapes me. However that may be, we note that the severity of Father Mancuso's affliction lessened a bit between the hard cover and paperback editions. In the hard cover, the affliction was described in this scene:

> There was no logical or scientific explanation for Father Frank Mancuso as he prepared to go to bed. He had just prayed at his own altar in his

room, searching and hoping for an answer to the reason his palms were beginning to bleed. [Hard Cover, p. 82]

In the paperback version of this same episode, however, this became:

He had just prayed in his own rooms, searching and hoping for an answer to the question of why his palms were itching so terribly. [*AH*-pb, p. 107]

From bleeding stigmata to itching palms is quite a pull back, and we may well ask why this change was made. It will be recalled that Rev. Pecoraro sued the Lutzes and Anson because the scenes in *The Horror* using his "character" were not true or "grossly exaggerated." According to Pecoraro's testimony, the Lutzes and Anson "agreed to change certain statements in the book in which I was involved, and to correct some statements" [*Lutz v Hoffman*, p. 349].

It would appear, then, that Anson had transmuted the itching palms of a priest into the bleeding stigmata of a possessed prelate, only to be forced to reverse the metamorphosis after the lawsuit. It is then fair to assume, in light of the passage just examined, that all of the paranormal afflictions and accidents which befall Mancuso in the book were actually highly exaggerated transmogrifications of a reality that was about as hair-raising and heart-stopping as a hangnail.

The Shinnecock

As we have already seen, Chapter 11 not only tells us about the travails of Father Mancuso but also details George Lutz's systematic research into the history of 112 Ocean Avenue. It is said that on December 30:

the Amityville Historical Society had some interesting information for George, particularly about the very location of his house. It seems the Shinnecock Indians used land on the Amityville River as an enclosure for the sick, mad, and dying. These unfortunates were penned up until they died of exposure. However, the record noted that the Shinnecocks did not use this tract as a consecrated burial mound because they believed it to be infested with demons. [AH-pb, p. 104]

If this tale were true, it would be a most unique and horrifying bit of anthropological information. Fortunately, it is not true, and we do not have to believe that the first inhabitants of Long Island were so inhumane as to abandon their sick and dying without giving them—up to the utmost hour—the love, sympathy and encouraging support which have been always characteristic of human societies. If it be possible, the notion that a Native American tribe abandoned their members who were mad is even less believable. Madness, a condition apparently somewhat less common among "uncivilized" societies, was especially revered amongst most Amerindian groups. In many cases, schizophrenic individuals became shamans, and were believed to be capable of divining secrets and communicating with the spirit world.

Ketcham the Warlock

At the Amityville Historical Society, George also "learns":

> One of the more notorious settlers who came to the *newly-named* Amityville in those days was a John Catchum or Ketcham who had been forced out of Salem, Massachusetts, for practicing witchcraft [emphasis added]. John set up residence within 500 feet of where George now lived, continuing his alleged devil worship. The account also claimed he was buried somewhere on the northeast corner of the property. [*AH*-pb, p. 105]

In their *Newsday* exposé, "'Amityville Horror': Is it fact or fiction?'" Drehsler and Scovel reported:

> The Amityville Historical Society confirms that the Lutzes joined the society, seeking information on the house. But that happened Jan. 25, 1976, according to the curator, Seth Purdy Jr., a month later than the Lutz account's date and 11 days after the Lutzes purportedly fled the home in terror.
>
> Moreover, the society denied giving the Lutzes any information, as the book states, on either Shinnecock Indians once using the area to house insane or dying persons or about any "John Ketcham" or "Catchum" once practicing devil worship in the area, as the book states; the society has no information at all on that parcel of land. The Lutz version of the incident, Purdy says, is "completely erroneous." Beyond that, the Shinnecocks are a tribe that has always lived east of the Amityville area, which was inhabited by the Massapequas, a different tribe. Historical society officials in Massachusetts said they could not find any case of a "Ketcham" or "Catchum" practicing witchcraft in Salem. [Drehsler, "Fact or Fiction?" *Newsday*, November 17, 1977]

The Drehsler and Scovel article took care of the Shinnecock and Katchum business, or so I thought, until Ms. Draper, one of the librarians at my college, pointed out an item in *The American Indian, 1492–1976*. According to that reference work, Manhattan Island was sold on May 6, 1626, by Shinnecock Native Americans to the Dutch, under the leadership of Peter Minuit, for the equivalent of twenty-four dollars. Although several other reference works showed the Shinnecock to be farther out on Long Island—exactly where Mr. Purdy said they should be—I had a nagging suspicion that there might be more to this story than was apparent to Drehsler and Scovel.

This suspicion proved to be true almost immediately upon my first visit to Amityville. Before I even reached Ocean Avenue, I was startled to see a street sign saying "Ketcham Avenue." That told me that a Ketcham had existed, even if he had not practiced witchcraft and devil worship at 112 Ocean Avenue. Since the Amityville Historical Society was closed at the time of that visit (due to troubles with the heating system, of all things!), I did a bit of rapid research at the Amityville Public Library and the nearby Copiague Library.

I learned that up until 1697, the Massapequa Indians owned the land which later would become the central portion of the village of Amityville. In that year, John Ketcham and three other white men purchased the meadowland along the Great South Bay (that would have included not only the plot at 112 Ocean Avenue, but the entire neighborhood) because of the salt hay which grew there. This purchase was followed, a year later, by purchase of the neighboring uplands—the commercial center of the village today.

It will be recalled that Anson alleges that John Ketcham came to the "newly-named Amityville" after having been kicked out of Salem. Anson's information is off by 153 years, in this instance. The village did not take the name of Amityville until 1850.

And what of John Ketcham's roots? Edward Ketcham, the progenitor of the American Ketchams, emigrated from England to Massachusetts Bay Colony in 1635 where he settled in Ipswich, not Salem. It is possible that the Lutzes or Mr Anson knew this but decided that Salem would have greater occult significance than Ipswich. Once the history was safely written to include Salem, what could be more natural than the practice of witchcraft?

Regardless, Edward Ketcham did not stay in Ipswich. He died in Stratford, Connecticut, and his will was proved in 1655. The first of his descendants to show up on Long Island was John Ketcham, Sr. (father of the John Ketcham who purchased the meadowland at Amityville?), who is named as one of the grantees in the Nicholl's Patent of Huntington (1666). John Ketcham was *not* buried at 112 Ocean Avenue.

Native American Burial Ground?

Although we are told on page 105 that the Lutz property was *not* used as a Native American Burial Ground, on page 177, "Francine" (the psychic girl friend of the guy from the office) announces, "The house is built on a burial ground or something like that." A bit farther down the page we read "Francine stopped in front of the closets [in the basement]. 'There are people buried right here.'" Use of the term "burial ground" instead of "cemetery" would seem to imply Native Americans, and so we appear to have a clear contradiction.

Which is correct? George's "research" at the Amityville Historical Society, or the revelations of a psychic "born with a Venetian Veil"?

Mr. Seth Purdy, Jr., the Curator of the Amityville Historical Society Museum assured me that there was never a Native American Burial Ground on the site. According to Mr. Purdy, the water table is too high in the area to allow for any burial grounds south of the Montauk Highway. As for Ketcham practicing witchcraft, Mr. Purdy again assured me that he was "quite certain that witchcraft was never practiced on the site and that no structure existed there until the 1890s."

Doing Historical Research?

So, where did the Lutzes and Anson get the seeds for the tall tale about research at the Amityville Historical Society? The fable was evidently on its way to being formed by February 21, 1976, at least. On that day, Laura DiDio, the psychic expert from WNEW, interviewed the Lutzes at the William Perry Surveying Company in Syosset. Having told the Lutzes that she would have to try to verify their claims, she was told how to go about finding the confirmations. According to her testimony at the *Lutz v Hoffman* trial:

> [Lutz] said take a look, you know, some other people have had problems in living in this house before. It was not the first house that was on this property. He told me that the house was built in 1928 and that he himself had spent a lot of time going into the library looking at the old microfilms, things like this, trying to do research, and he said there was a man who was alleged to be a warlock who lived in the house and he told me go to Copiague Library, check the tax records, the Amityville Historical Society. If you're a good reporter you ought to be able to find the same things that I found. [*Lutz v Hoffman* , p. 430]

If Lutz did in fact tell Ms. DiDio that he had spent a lot of time looking at old microfilms in the local libraries, he most assuredly was pulling her leg. At the time of my early visits to Amityville in 1979, both the Amityville and Copiague Public Libraries' microfilm collections only carried films of a few magazines from recent years and *The New York Times* back to about 1965. No matter how "good a reporter" Ms. DiDio had been, she certainly would not have found anything about warlocks living at 112 Ocean Avenue from any of the places mentioned in George Lutz's advice to her.

Kathleen's mother, Mrs. Conners, testified at the same trial that she had been present during a meeting held at her house on February 14, 1976. The meeting involved Attorney Weber, the writer Paul Hoffman, the Lutzes, and two students from Dowling College. According to Mrs. Conners, one of the students brought up the name of John Ketcham and said that the house at

112 Ocean Avenue was on a Native American Burial ground. Since this meeting was tape recorded, and the tapes were supplied to Anson, elements of the myth appear to be derivable from this meeting. Lutz himself mentioned details of this meeting in his own testimony:

A Jay Perry [*one of the students*] was involved in research at the house that had been previously owned by John Ketchum in Buffalo, New York. There was a cross interest there about John Ketcham in that my wife and I had been in the—to the Amityville Historical Society and also been told by a friend of my mother-in-law's about John Ketchum.
Q Tell us about John Ketchum. Is he some sort of person you are interested in?
A John Ketchum was an earlier settler in the Amityville area. His name came up considerably in the records of the Amityville parcels of land. As I understand, to this day there is still a cemetery down there on Montauk Highway that Ketchum owned. [*Lutz v Hoffman*, p. 103]

I don't know if there is a Ketchum cemetery "down there on Montauk Highway." However, there *is* a Shinnecock Indian Cemetery further east on Montauk Highway, fifty miles farther east.

Prior to February 14, the Lutzes had already been in contact with Mr. Weber—since the middle or latter part of January 1976. Is it possible that their misinformation was largely or partly derived from information supplied by Mr. Weber?

Atty. Weber's Research

Before ever meeting the Lutzes, we have already discussed Weber's agreement with Mr. Hoffman to write a book about the DeFeo murders. While obtaining a general background for the book, Weber conducted a title search for information concerning the prior conveyances of the DeFeo property. According to his testimony, his title search went back to 1657. (I believe the date should be 1697, not '57; but I cannot be certain that the source from which I obtained the 1697 date for Ketcham's purchase of the meadowlands is accurate.)

Weber testified that he had discovered that the first known owner was John Ketcham, and that this information had been obtained from the Huntington Historical Society, not the Amityville Historical Society:

Q Was there a reason why it came from the Huntington Historical Society?
A Yes. The Lutzes have said that they went to the Amityville Historical Society and got this information. Well, the fact is that after or prior

to 1850 the area of Amityville now known as the Town of Babylon was part of the Town of Huntington, and all that information is not at the Amityville Historical Society. That was obtained from the Huntington Historical Society....

Q Did you cause any research to be conducted as to who John Ketchum was?

A Yes. I went, myself, to some occult shop in Hauppauge and got literature on it and asked some person—they called themselves the High Priestess of the Abraxas—well, first he told me the name Ketchum is very, very—it comes up very often in witchcraft or folklore, and the family probably emanated into Massachusetts, was one of the first families, and they knew that certain members of the family had come to Long Island, but he wasn't sure where.

Q Did there come a time when you imparted all that information that you obtained through your efforts with the title company and the research at the Huntington Historical Society, and what you learned about the name Ketchum, to Mr. and Mrs. Lutz?

A Yes. All the background on the house was placed on a tape by myself, and it appears in the book, except where it said the Lutzes went to the Amityville Historical Society and got this information... [*Lutz v Hoffman*, p. 237]

Q Referring to that portion on page 81 that talks about the Shinnecock being in the manor back in the late 1600s ... is that information which you gave to them...?

A Yes. Except I never said, "Shinnecock." I said Wyandanche.

Q I notice on page 81 the name of John Ketchum is also mentioned as somebody being forced out of Salem, Massachusetts, for practicing witchcraft....Is that the same John Ketchum that you uncovered in the title search?

A Yes.

Q Did you impart all that information, as well as your other investigations that you conducted to his name to the Lutzes, specifically?

A Yes.

Q And they didn't know about that from any other source but you?

A No. There's another episode in this book ... they talk about their discovering that the land where the house was situated on, or immediately adjacent to it, was an Indian burial ground. That information I had received from a local Amityville attorney.

Q Who was that attorney?

A I don't know his name. I've seen him in the criminal courts during trial, and he had just related that story to me.

Q That this property used to be a local Indian burial ground?

A Yes.
Q And did you, in turn, tell that to the Lutzes?
A Yes. [*Lutz v Hoffman*, p. 288]

Readers must forgive me for dragging them through the muddle of material presented on the previous few pages. I have presented information and testimony in the order as I first came upon it. To organize it into a fully intelligible exposition seems about as feasible as harnessing a flock of hummingbirds. However, I believe that it is from such muddled, inchoate hearsay that much of *The Amityville Horror: A True Story* was derived. In all fairness to the Lutzes, in the present instance, it appears much of the material had already been garbled, disjointed, and reconnected by the time Weber passed it along to them.

The Tax Assessor's Information

Returning to Anson's narrative, we learn on page 105 that after leaving the Amityville Historical Society, George goes to the Real Estate Tax Assessment Office, where he:

> learned that the house at 112 Ocean Avenue had been built in 1928 by a Mr. Monaghan. It passed through several families until 1965, when the DeFeos purchased it from the Rileys....There was no record of any improvements being made to the house that resembled the addition of a basement room. [*AH*-pb, p. 105]

Firstly, the house was built by a Mr. Jess Purdy *for* a Mr. Moynahan (or Monahan in some accounts), who became the first owner of the present structure. I have not seen the spelling "Monaghan" in any other source. As for the "several families" prior to the Rileys selling the house to the DeFeos, there weren't any besides the families listed. Confusion may have arisen when the house passed to one of Moynahan's daughters, whose married name was Fitzgerald. Nevertheless, only a total of three different families owned the house before the Lutzes took residence.

In various places in his book, Anson mentions George Lutz consulting blueprints for the house at 112 Ocean Avenue. Whether or not Lutz did in fact ever obtain or examine the blueprints for the house, it is quite certain that Jay Anson never saw them, even though he never was allowed to enter the house and needed as much information about the house as possible to write "a true story." We have already seen that he didn't understand how the kitchen's position related to that of the living room, and on page 106 we are given further evidence that he had no idea how the rooms were laid out at the time he wrote the book, and that the floor plans must have been added to the book after its completion:

> The couple had their arms around each other's waists as George turned out the light in the kitchen. They passed the living room on the way to the stairs. Kathy stopped. She could see the crouching lion in the darkness of the room. [*AH*-pb, p. 106]

It will be remembered that there are two doors through which one could leave the kitchen: one leading around to the entry foyer and one for entering the dining room. It is only reasonable to suppose that they would have taken the shortest route to the staircase they had to climb to go up to their bedroom, in this case taking the route through the dining room and into the foyer, since this would have taken them to the base of the stairs. They would not have passed the living room.

Even if the couple took the other door into the foyer, they would have immediately passed the door on their left leading down to the basement, then they would have turned left and walked along the side of the staircase in the foyer, turned left again to reach the foot of the staircase leading to the upper floors. At no time, in no meaningful sense, would they have "passed the living room on their way to the stairs." To be sure, the archway to the living room would have been only seven feet, eight inches away in the wall opposite the staircase when they reached the foot of the stairs. Even so, it would have been more reasonable to have written that the Lutzes "passed the staircase on their way to the living room."

The patently paranormal nature of Kathy's being able to "see the crouching lion *in the darkness of the room*" remains unexplained.

Adding a Room to the Basement

We end this rather tedious chapter on a somewhat lighter note. We must try to imagine just what it was that Mr. Lutz said to the people in the Tax Office as he endeavored to learn who had "added on" the mysterious red room not noted on any blueprints.

CLERK: Good afternoon, Sir. May I help you?

LUTZ: Yes. My name is Lutz, and I've just recently moved into the house at 112 Ocean Avenue....What I came here for is, I'd like to know if you have any record of the DeFeos ever adding a room on their basement.

CLERK: Adding a room on their basement? You mean did they ever finish off a room in their basement—paneling, that sort of thing?

LUTZ: No, I mean did they ever add on an extra room to their basement?

CLERK: [*Bewildered*] How do you add a room onto a basement?

Wednesday, December 31, 1975

Events of the Day

Weather claimed: Heavy snowfall at dawn, snow continuing through 10 AM. Radio predicting Amityville River will be frozen solid by nightfall.
Actual weather: Low temperature 37°, high 44°, mean 41°; precipitation 0.54 inches by 7:00 AM, 0.01 by 7:00 PM; winds 3 mph to 13 mph.

The Lutzes

George awakens at 2:30, not 3:15, and again at 4:30. He sees it's beginning to snow. He worries about money. He gets up at 6:30—cold again—and builds a fire. About 8 AM Missy gets up, delighted with the snow. At 10 AM snow is still falling. George goes out to boathouse to set up the air compressor to keep their water from freezing. Later in the afternoon the boys threaten to run away again. They fight again. At supper George says he'd rather stay home for New Year's Eve as it's too cold to go to a movie. After supper George takes the ceramic lion back up to the sewing room. The flies are back. By 10 PM Missy is asleep on living room floor while the boys watch T.V. George and Kathy watch Guy Lombardo salute the New Year with the kids in bed. One minute after midnight, Kathy sees a demonic image at the back of fireplace and screams.

Father Mancuso

All that morning, his hands are not bleeding, but blisters remain; his fever is 103 degrees. As the night wears on, Mancuso's hands worsen. He shows them to his doctor when he arrives. The doctor leaves for New Year's Eve party.

The Weather Report

If we are to believe Chapter 12 of *The Amityville Horror: A True Story*, the weather on December 31, 1975, was too cold for the Lutzes to go out to a movie. The mean temperature for the day was 41 degrees Fahrenheit. The low for the day (at 8:35 AM) was 37, and the high (at 12:50 PM) was 44 degrees. Cold, yes, but not outrageous for New Year's Eve in the northeast. Perhaps the Lutzes' year-old van had no heating system!

"The last day of the old year dawned on a heavy snowfall," we read on page 109. "At six-thirty, George finally gave up and got out of bed....It was still dark outside at that hour, but he could see the snow was beginning to pile up near the kitchen door." Later, on page 112, we read "At ten o'clock, the snow was still falling. Kathy called out to George from the kitchen that a local radio station had predicted the Amityville River would be completely frozen by night fall."

There *was*, indeed, some precipitation before 7 AM on December 31. However, with the lowest temperature of the day being 37, the 0.54 inches that fell did not fall as snow! After 7 AM, only 0.0l inches of rain fell, and with the high temperature for the day at 44 degrees, the chances of the Amityville River freezing are slim without even considering the fact that at the latitude of 112 Ocean Avenue, the Amityville River is *salt water.*

Anson needed to have the temperature be cold enough to freeze a salt water "river," because he needs to have George go out to the mysteriously alluring boathouse again, in this case to set up an air compressor bubbler system to prevent his yacht from being crushed by ice. The real reason for having the air compressor in the boat house, however, is to have a piece of equipment which can later be stopped dead by the mysterious "entities". Entities which—like the Norns of Nordic legend—spin a fateful web about the boathouse and entice, ensnare, or release whom they will, according to their whims.

Although the book does not mention the air compressor after the incident when it mysteriously ceases to function, it would appear to have suffered more than Anson ever knew. No air compressor was listed in the auction catalogue, and we know the Lutzes didn't take it with them when they fled in terror—taking only a few changes of clothes. It is just possible the entities ate it.

Because the Priest Sued Them

Although the chapter under examination deals with the on-going trauma of Father Mancuso and his stigmata, there isn't much to be said that we haven't already discussed. Let us then examine the changes which have been made as a result of the Pecoraro lawsuit:

Hard Cover

All that morning, Father Mancuso had been looking at his hands. His palms, which had begun to bleed the night before, were now dry, but angry red blisters remained.
The priest did not mention what had been happening to his hands. He kept them in the pockets of his bathrobe the entire time the Pastor remained in his rooms.
Father Mancuso thought about the stigmata, the marks resembling the wounds of the crucified body of Christ, said to be supernaturally impressed on the bodies of holy people. He stared at the ugly manifestation and became angry. The priest was prepared to give of himself in any way that God demanded, but if he was to suffer in that way, he thought at least, let it be to help humanity. With all his training, experience, devotion, and skill as a judge and psychotherapist, certainly he shouldn't have to settle for something as inconsequential as a house in Amityville.
The priest sighed and knelt at his private altar to thank God.
The doctor gave the priest some antibiotic capsules and assured him he'd have relief by morning. Then he left for a party.

Paperback

All that morning, Father Mancuso had been looking at his hands, which had begun to fester the night before. They were now dry, but angry red blisters remained.
The priest did not mention what had been happening to his hands. He kept them in the pockets of his bathrobe.
When the Pastor left his rooms, Father Mancuso stared at the ugly manifestation on his skin, and he became angry. All this suffering for just one appearance in an inconsequential house in Amityville? The priest was prepared to give himself in any way that God demanded, but at least, he thought, let it be to help humanity. With all his training, devotion, experience and skill, certainly there had to be some rational explanation he could apply to the enigma. At the moment he couldn't, and that accounted for his rage.
The priest sighed and knelt to thank God.
The doctor assured the priest that he'd have some relief by the morning. Then he left for a New Year's Eve party.

The Fevered Priest

Did Father Mancuso really spend the entire morning of December 31, 1975, looking at his hands? Did antibiotic pills really change hands that last night in 1975? Did he really have a high fever? A careful reading of *A True Story* shows that the priest had a fever of 103–104 degrees continuously from the evening of Tuesday, December 23 until 11:00 AM on the morning of Friday, December 26—*at least three full days*. His 102-degree fever returned at 7:00 PM on Sunday, December 28, rose to 103 degrees on Wednesday, December 31, and persisted until 3:00 PM in the afternoon of Monday, January 5, 1976—*almost nine days of high fever*!

Alas, we must believe that was not the last of his tribulations. His fever returned on Thursday, January 8, and it's not clear how long the third thermal assault on his brain persisted. Why wasn't he taken to a hospital? I suspect Jay Anson simply didn't understand the medical implications of his narrative.

The Fireplace Demon

Leaving unanswered the question of how Anson knew the Lutzes had watched Guy Lombardo on television, we must compare Anson's account with Hoffman's earlier report. Hoffman's article mentions that 1975's New Year's Eve was also George's twenty-ninth birthday. If this is true, it is odd that Anson made no mention of the fact, nor is there anything in the chapter to suggest the possibility of birthday festivity. Although *The Amityville Horror: A True Story* lacks an item of seeming significance found in the Hoffman articles, vice-versa, Hoffman's articles make no mention of the "demon with horns and a white peaked hood on its head" which the Lutzes allegedly saw burned into the sooty background of their fireplace:

> [*Kathy*] stared into the fireplace, hypnotized by the dancing flames … something was materializing in those flames….Kathy tried to open her mouth to say something to her husband. She couldn't. She couldn't even tear her eyes away from the demon with horns and a white peaked hood on its head….She saw that half of its face was blown away, as if hit with a shotgun blast at close range….George … saw it too—a white figure that had burned itself into the soot against the rear bricks of the fireplace. [*AH*-pb, p. 116]

During the cross-examination of George Lutz at the *Lutz v Hoffman* trial, Lutz was asked about this face in the fireplace:

Q Now, did you ever see, while you were in the house, Mr. Lutz, this fated house, a demon with horns wearing a white peaked hood, in the fireplace?

A There was a—I don't know how else to describe it. But something very ugly, a picture of something that was in the blackened back wall of the fireplace was in an outline of white. Again, when the researchers went in on March 6th, they came back to us and they said, "What was that? How did that get there?" We don't know how it got there. One day it was there.

Q You saw a demon with black horns?

A I wouldn't refer to it as a demon. It looked more like someone in a Ku Klux Klan outfit.

Q The book refers to it as a demon with horns.

A It also appeared in one part that the entire upper body was missing.

Q And you saw this in the fireplace?

A It was etched into the bricks somehow. It was white over black background.

Q And Mr. Lutz, how long did that etching remain on the bricks?

A I know it was still there on March 6th, when the investigators came, which was two months later....They came back and asked us what it was.

Q When was the last time that you saw the demon with the horns and the white peaked hood on its head?

A I never referred to it that way, sir.

Q That reference in the book was not correct?

A It's certainly correct. It's certainly a way of describing it that I don't necessarily agree with. The point is, it was there, it was still there two months later when other people went in and the last time I saw it, it would have been the last day we were in the house, which would have been January 14, 1976.

Q I'm going to read this passage from page 88 of the book and I'm going to ask you to testify as to whether this is a truthful portrayal or not.

"Kathy tried to open her mouth to say something to her husband. She couldn't. She couldn't even tear her eyes away from the demon with horns and a white peaked hood on its head. It was getting larger, looming toward her. She saw that half of its face was blown away as if hit by a shotgun blast at close range. Kathy screamed."

Is that a true account?

A Basically so, yes.

Q Your testimony is that is the truth?

A Yes.

So there you have it! Although the image was still in the fireplace during the next two weeks of the Lutzes' stay in the house, it only bothered them on New Year's Eve. Mr. Lutz assured us, under oath, that the image was still there when the Warrens (two of the "researchers" who came to the house on March 6) came to visit, even though the Warrens—who probably could have discerned a frightful, occult significance in an altered grocery list—make no mention of having seen the apparition when they visited the house. James and Barbara Cromarty, owners of the house at the time of my first visits to Amityville, saw only the usual, irregular negative-inkblot figure in the fireplace when they moved into the house.

What are we to believe? We end the year 1975 with George Lutz' assurance that there was a demon in the fireplace but are then told it wasn't much of a demon. He swore that "the entire upper body was missing." But with the upper half of the body missing, how could he know it was wearing a Ku Klux Klan costume and not a ball gown? It would probably be indelicate to ask just which anatomical features of the demon-but-not-really the Lutzes saw if the entire upper body was missing.

Lutz also swore that "half of its face was blown away." If half a face is missing from the missing half of a body, does that make half a face present? Do demons obey the algebraic rules for signs? Well, George Lee Lutz swore under oath that both claims are true.

Thursday, January 1, 1976

Events of the Day

Weather claimed: Gusts, gales, hurricane-strength winds; snowfall in the morning, driving hazardous, snow drifts.
Actual weather: Low temperature 31°, high 40°, mean 36°; precipitation 0.45 by 7:00 AM, 0.00 by 7:00 PM; winds 7 mph to 23 mph.

The Lutzes

George and Kathy go to bed at 1:00 AM. Five minutes later a howling wind rips the blankets off their bed. All windows are open. A gale is rushing between the sewing and dressing rooms. Missy's rocking chair is moving by itself. Missy's windows are shut and locked. Kathy takes Missy downstairs. George starts a fire. Winds diminish by 6 AM. By 9 AM the temperature inside the house is 75 degrees.

Father Mancuso

Mancuso gets out of bed at 7 AM. At 10 AM his palms are bleeding again. Medicine has no effect on his high fever.

The Lutzes

By noon George is at office in Syosset. Kathy calls Mancuso, but odor of perfume interrupts her call. She runs from the kitchen. George returns to snow-bound house and they have supper. Harry is brought inside, then taken out to dog-house and falls asleep. George checks the house. By 10 PM both parents are drowsy. Kathy screams. "Unblinking" red eyes are at living room window. Pig footprints are found in the snow.

Father Mancuso

Mancuso thinks about demonology.

Demonological Meteorology and Storm-Window Problems

Without a doubt, the weather is the major subject for discussion when we consider the alleged events of January 1, 1976. We learn that shortly after one o'clock in the morning, the Lutzes were awakened by a "howling wind roaring through their bedroom." Their blankets had been "virtually torn from their bodies," and the drafts were causing the bedroom door to swing back and forth. All the windows in the bedroom were completely open, and a cold "gale" was rushing between the sewing room and the dressing room. By 6 AM the "hurricane-strength winds" had diminished.

> The morning snowfall had made traveling on the roads hazardous. As the day wore on, it got colder, and cars began to get caught in drifts and skid on icy spots all over Long Island. But the snow had stopped falling while George was driving back to Amityville....The driveway of 112 Ocean Avenue was heavy with fresh snow ... [*so George*] parked on the street, which had been recently plowed by the city's snow trucks. [*AH*-pb, p. 125]

When George returned Harry to his compound, he is described as "wading through the snow that had piled up between the kitchen door and the compound" [*AH*-pb, p. 127].

At one o'clock in the morning, the actual wind speed recorded was 17 mph from the northeast. As seventeen mph winds being classified as a "moderate breeze," the description of "hurricane strength" seems a bit of an exaggeration. It is difficult to believe a moderate breeze could tear the blankets off the bed, even after the demons have opened the windows. For some reason, Anson has neglected to mention that the demons also would have needed to open the storm windows. There were, of course, storm windows for the house, and if George was as cold as the book claims he was, it is unthinkable that he would not have had the storm windows up. (Hoffman mentions the storm windows in his articles, albeit in a different context, and various photographs of the windows from the time of the DeFeos clearly show the presence of storm windows.) To understand the aerodynamic implications of this episode it is necessary to examine the full text more closely. On pages 117 and 118 we read:

> at one in the morning ... they were awakened by a howling wind roaring through their bedroom. The blankets on the bed had been virtually torn from their bodies....All the windows in the room were wide open, and the bedroom door, caught by the drafts, was swinging back and forth.

> George leaped from the bed and ran to close the windows....Both were breathless from their sudden awakening, and even though the door to their room had slammed shut, they could still hear the wind blowing out in the second floor hallway.
> George wrenched open the door and was hit by another cold blast. Flipping on the light switch in the hall, he was startled to see the doors to the sewing room and dressing room wide open, the gale rushing freely through the open windows. Only the door to Missy's bedroom remained shut.
> He ran into the dressing room first, fighting against the gale that hit him, and managed to force the windows down. Then he went to the sewing room and, with the cold now bringing tears to his eyes, closed one window. But George could not budge the open window that faced the Amityville River. He banged furiously on its frame with his fists. Finally it gave and slid to a close. [*AH*-pb, pp. 117–118]

Even though the existence of storm windows at 112 Ocean Avenue completely rules out the aerodynamic phenomena depicted in the long quotation above, let us ignore them temporarily and consider the physics of the scene. Consultation of the blueprints for the house shows that there is one window in the west wall of the master bedroom, and there are two in the south wall. Weather records show that the wind was blowing in from the northeast, and so the master bedroom was actually on the lee side of the house, sheltered from the assaulting "moderate breeze.

We are then told that "the bedroom door, caught by the drafts, was swinging back and forth." How was that possible? If we assume the door was closed at the beginning of the chaos, since all the bedroom doors open inwardly the force of wind rushing into the bedroom would simply have closed it more firmly, and the statement "George wrenched open the [*bedroom*] door" would fit reasonably into the scene. The door could not have been "swinging back and forth." On the other hand, if we assume the door had been open, flat against the bedroom wall at the start, perturbations of the door by air turbulence would have slammed it shut without any possibility for it to reopen and swing back and forth.

Then we read "George ran into the dressing room first, fighting *against* the gale that hit him ... with the cold now bringing tears to his eyes," and we encounter a similar problem. There's no indication that he had to struggle to open the door—remember it opens inwardly—but in fact it would have to have been shut if gale-force winds had been circulating in the dressing room.

Opening Windows and Windows Opening

Having considered the aerodynamic problems arising from the lengthy quotation above, we must turn our attention to the alleged source of all the aerodynamic problems: the open windows. An open window in a possessed child's bedroom figures centrally in *The Exorcist*, and in the story a lock must be procured for it. By contrast, Anson tells us on page 118 that the windows in Missy's room "were shut and *locked*" [emphasis added]. As implausible as it may seem to readers at this point, there actually may have been some problems with windows opening spontaneously—even though the aerodynamic problems could not have arisen due to the existence of storm windows. Rick Moran and Peter Jordan, in their article "The Amityville Horror Hoax" published in *Fate* magazine, wrote:

> As for the window that kept reopening "mysteriously," we have discovered there is a logical explanation. Because the counterweights in this window are too heavy, any vibration will cause it to open *if it is not locked* [emphasis added]. We have this information from people who were familiar with the house before the Lutzes lived there. We know also that the problem still exists because we caused the windows to open "mysteriously" ourselves by walking heavily across the floor of that bedroom. [Moran, "Amityville Horror Hoax," *Fate*, May 1978, pp. 43–47]

Pig Tracks in the Snow

Not only wind, but snow figures prominently in the meteorological portion of Anson's plot for the day. After all, without snow you can't tell if pigs have been running around your house in suburban Long Island. We are told that it continued to snow from morning until sometime in the afternoon. The recorded weather for this date states that *no precipitation was recorded after 7 AM*, and *most—if not all—of the 0.45 inches of precipitation that fell before that hour 7 AM fell as rain, not snow*.

The temperature for the previous day had averaged 41 degrees Fahrenheit, and it was only at 5 AM on January 1 that the temperature fell to slightly below freezing (31 degrees). Whatever small amount of snow may have existed at dawn, it surely would not have lasted long as the temperature rose during the morning. The mean temperature for January 1, 1976, was 36 degrees, with a high of 40 at 2 and 3 PM.

We can be sure that George did not "wade" through the snow when he returned Harry to his compound. And we can rest assured that he did not see a trail of pig footprints in the snow, if there was no snow on the ground to begin with. But even if there were snow so deep as to make a person "wade" through it, any pig footprints in it would not be recognizable as such. All that would be visible would be deep pits in the snow. As the animal lifted his foot off the ground, the actual imprint of the foot would be covered by snow falling from the walls of the cavity made by the animal's leg.

Theological Palmistry

From demonological meteorology, we turn to theological palmistry. We learn from the hard cover version that at 10 AM Mancuso's palms are bleeding again, although in the paperback version his "palms were smearing. The blisters looked as if they were about to burst." Curiously, although Anson tried to remove all indications of bleeding stigmata after the Pecoraro lawsuit, one passage appears to have escaped everyone's notice. On page 124 we read: "In the Rectory, Father Mancuso had been bathing his hands in the solution and found that the *bleeding* in his palms had stopped" [AH-pb, p. 124].

In the rest of the chapter, however, Mancuso's identity is more concealed in the paperback version, and his affliction less supernatural:

Hard Cover	Paperback
In an effort to concentrate on other things besides his mysterious affliction, Mancuso tried reading some of his medical journals, searching for articles on psychotherapy. In the three hours he had been out of bed, the priest had found over a dozen new and interesting items in this field. Then he noticed a reddish stain on the last magazine he had held… [p. 92]	In an effort to concentrate on other things besides his mysterious affliction, Father Mancuso tried reading some of his subscription magazines, searching for articles to divert his attention from his problem. In the succeeding three hours he read through over a dozen new and old periodicals. Then he noticed a slight discoloration on the last magazine he had held… [p. 122]

Back to the Doghouse

From priestly problems, we turn our attention next to Harry, the quadrupedal member of the Lutz family:

> [A] little after eight … George took Harry out to the dog-house. Wading through the snow that had piled up between the kitchen door and the compound, he tied Harry to the strong lead line. Harry crawled into his doghouse, turned around several times … and then settled down with a

> little sigh. While George stood there, the dog's eyes closed and he fell asleep.
> "That does it," said George. "I'm taking you to the vet on Saturday." [*AH*-pb, p. 127]

Once again, we are confronted with the allegedly abnormal behavior of Harry Lutz. On January l, 1976, the sun set at 4:37 PM. It was now almost four hours later. What was the poor dog to do? Bay at the moon? The moon had set at 5:05 PM.

The Unblinking Red Eyes—
of Evenrude

> She waited until George had poked out the last embers and had poured water over some still-smoldering pieces of wood. Then Kathy turned off the chandelier and looked around to take her husband's hand in the darkness. She screamed.
> Kathy was looking past George's shoulder at the Living room windows. Staring back at her were a pair of unblinking red eyes!
> George… also saw the little beady eyes staring directly into his. [*AH*-pb, p. 127]

In *The Exorcist*, Karras the priest sees eyes at his window, but they are presumably an illusion. In *The Amityville Horror: A True Story,* however, we are given to believe that these eyes belong to the real thing, since the Lutzes are alleged to have seen the tracks of a cloven-hoofed animal in the snow outside the window, and the tracks supposedly remained visible for several days. *The Exorcist* was a tough act to follow, and although many of the episodes in *The Amityville Horror* have their prototypes in *The Exorcist*, they generally appear in Anson's book bigger and better, fortified, and enriched.

We have already seen that George Lutz has disavowed seeing the pig in Missy's window. What about the eyes in the living room window? Robert L. Morris, in his review in *The Skeptical Inquirer* suggested the Lutzes saw the reflection of dying embers from the fireplace. That presumes, of course, that there ever were eyes to be seen in the living room window after George had put out the fire. Hoffman also has Kathy (and only Kathy) see red, beady eyes at the living room window; but in his account this occurs on January 12, 1976, after the visit of the psychics associated with George's office.

We have already seen that the Lutzes had been told of Ronnie DeFeo's run-in battle with the neighbor's Siamese cat, Evinrude, who would climb up on windows at the back of the house and peer into windows. The owner of the cat corroborated this fact, saying the cat frequently was to be seen perched on window ledges at 112 Ocean Avenue. Finally, the Cromartys told jokingly of the momentary scare they received shortly after moving into the house: they too saw eyes staring at them through a window one evening. But investigation showed that it was, indeed, just Evinrude. This suggests the possibility that the Lutzes did see these little beady eyes at a window. Their fright and great suggestibility would have done the rest.

Half-Way Through—
No Problems Reported

New Year's Day of 1976 was exactly two weeks after the Lutzes claimed they moved into the house. Now that we have read Anson's account of the day, we may compare it to the report of *Newsday* reporters Alex Drehsler and Jim Scovel:

> James Mullally, who bought the Lutzes' former home in Deer Park, said he and his wife visited the Lutzes about two weeks after they moved into the Amityville house, by which time various of the alleged psychic phenomena had occurred. He said Mrs. Lutz "gave us a tour of the place," made no mention of any sort of disturbance and seemed content. "I remember my wife saying as we left that if she were living in that house she wouldn't be in as good a mood as Mrs. Lutz was [because of the murders in the house]." [Drehsler, "Amityville Fact or Fiction?" *Newsday*, November 17, 1977]

Friday,
January 2, 1976

Events of the Day

Weather claimed: Light dusting of snow in the morning, rising wind, dangerous snow-and-ice-covered roads.
Actual weather: Low temperature 19° at 5:50 AM, high 32° at 2:15 PM, mean 26°; precipitation 0:00 inches all day; winds 5 mph to 13 mph.

The Lutzes

Pig tracks are still visible in the snow in the morning. The overhead door of the garage is nearly torn from its metal frame. George drives to his office. Kathy finds herself in a tug-o-war between two spirits in her bedroom and faints. George stops off at Witches' Brew, now located on Merrick Rd. Bartender tells of secret room and his dreams of ceremonial killings of dogs and pigs. George returns home in early afternoon. Lutzes compare notes.

Father Mancuso

Mancuso feels better in the morning. His "Superior" reduces his workload.

Lutz and Mancuso

Lutz calls Mancuso, Mancuso answers. George asks Mancuso to come back and bless house again. The telephone call is cut off.

The Lutzes

The Lutzes discuss possibility of getting parish priest to help. When Lutzes go to bed, George says he will go to police the next day.

Mancuso

Mancuso's hands are burning again.

More Problems with the Weather

According to Anson's account, on January 2, 1976 there was still snow on the ground from an imaginary, previous snowfall, and there was "a light dusting of snow" which had fallen in the early morning hours. In the morning, there was a "rising wind" and George had to maneuver his Ford van over "dangerous snow-and-ice-covered roads to Syosset."

A study of the actual weather records shows that there could not possibly have been any snow on the ground on January 2. The day before, there had been 0.45 inches of rain, and the mean temperature had been 36 degrees. The day before, December 31, 1975, there had been 0.54 inches of rain, and the mean temperature had been even higher at 41 degrees. On December 30, there had been a light drizzle, with a mean temperature of 36.

There was no precipitation on Friday, January 2, 1976, and the "rising wind" escalated all the way from 5 to 13 mph during the course of the day! Although it was cold enough on the second of January for snow to be on the roads to Syosset (mean temperature was 26 degrees), the roads were in fact clear, due to lack of precipitation. Anson's weather is utterly fictitious.

Don't Call the Police!

We read on page 129 "when George came out of his house in the morning, the cloven-hoofed tracks were still visible in the frozen snow. The footprints … ended at the entrance to the garage. George … saw that the [*overhead*] door of the garage was almost torn off its metal frame."

What does George do, now that he has concrete, physical evidence that he has not been hallucinating Beelzebubish boars possessed of portal-parting powers? Does he photograph the tracks in the snow?[1] Does he call the police or his insurance agent to report the vandalism? Does he board up the garage to prevent looting? Does he check with the neighbors to see if they saw who did it?

The correct answer is "none of the above." George simply takes off for the office. Almost as an afterthought, it would seem, "Before he'd left home, George had told Kathy about the garage door and the tracks in the snow." Since the door is "still broken" the next day, when Sgt. Cammaroto visits, it is clear nothing has been done to repair the devastation. Indeed, there is no indication in the book that the Lutzes *ever* repaired the garage door. Since the door is in perfect condition today, we must conclude that psychic forces beyond our ken have completely healed it.

---

[1] We know from the auction catalogue that George had both a Polaroid Land camera, and a 35-mm camera.

But of course, the real reason George did not photograph the pig tracks in the snow is because there was no snow. He went to work without boarding up the garage because there was no need to. He arrived safely at the office, because there was no snow or ice on any of the roads.

Aerobatic Fainting

While George is occupied at his office, Kathy is plumping up pillows on her bed. She is then caught in a tug-o-war between two spirit-forces and, while fainting, she executes a most wondrous aerobatic maneuver: although she must have been standing with her back to the bed (after her body had been turned around "to face the unseen presence"), she regains consciousness "lying half off the bed with her *head* almost touching the floor." Nijinsky at his greatest could not have done a flip like that!

The Bartender's Tale

Early in the afternoon, George returns to Amityville, and stops off at the "Witches' Brew," which is now located on Merrick Road (*i.e.*, where Henry's, the real bar, was located). The reader may recall that on December 28, the Witches' Brew was said to be located on the fictitious "Amityville Road." Another teleportation unremarked by Mr. Anson!

The bartender tells George of the secret room in his basement and confesses he had had nightmares of people killing dogs and pigs in it. As was noted in the *Newsday* exposé by Dennis Hevesi, "They would have had to be little people; the red room is 2 feet, 4 inches wide, 3 feet, 6 inches long, and 3 feet, 6 inches high" [Hevesi, "Haunted by Horror Story," *Newsday*, September 17, 1978]. Even so, Hevesi failed to note that in a room of such proportions, even Chihuahuas would be too large for the purpose of ritual sacrifice.

Two Overworked Priests

After allowing the Lutzes to compare notes on the events of the morning, Anson has them decide to call Mancuso again for help, and then he focusses his attention on events in the life of the priest. As in *The Exorcist*, the priest's workload is reduced by his Superior. As may be expected, changes have appeared in the paperback version to disguise the identity of the priest:

Hard Cover	Paperback
Father Mancuso's superior [singular] had been concerned with his health and had dropped by to look in on him. Father Mancuso told *the Bishop* that he felt much better that morning. They had decided to spend some time together to review the priest's workload. Most of the backlog was quickly cleared up and put in *the Bishop's* briefcase. His secretary would do the typing. Father Mancuso saw *his superior* to the building entrance and then walked back into his apartment. [emphases added]	Father Mancuso's superiors [plural] had been concerned with his health and had dropped by to look in on him. Father Mancuso told *them* that he felt much better that morning. They also decided to spend some time together to review the priest's workload. Most of the backlog was quickly cleared up and put in *a superior's* briefcase. A secretary would do the typing. Father Mancuso saw *the clerics* to the building's entrance and then walked back into his apartment. [emphases added]

But, as in the case where the location of the priest's mother's house was concealed, the cover-up is clumsy, and the very next paragraph of the paperback gives away the identity of the priest's superior: "[Mancuso] was still wearing the soft white cotton surgical gloves he had found in a drawer. The priest had explained *to the Bishop* that he had put them on his hands to protect them from cold, but his real motive was to hide the ugly rawness of his blisters [emphasis added] [*AH*-pb, p. 135].

The Lutzes call Mancuso, imploring him to bless the house a second time. As could be predicted from the formula which Anson apparently used in his writing, the phone call is interrupted by the gremlins, and Mancuso's hands begin to burn again. The Lutzes discuss the possibility of having the local parish priest come to bless the house, but decide not to do so, because "George recalled from the newspaper accounts that he was an elderly man who pooh-poohed the thought of 'voices' in the house telling Ronnie what to do. He wasn't much of a believer in occult phenomena." A more probable reason for the Lutzes not calling the parish priest is that they had never gone to church there and didn't know him at all. Besides, Mancuso seems to have been swallowing their bait, so why press their luck?

At any rate, the explanation given by Anson is utterly false. We have already seen that Ronnie never testified in the trial that "voices" had made him commit the murders; consequently, *Newsday* (the only newspaper George read, as far as we can tell) never had any articles telling of the parish priest's disbelief.

Bed-Time Daily Summary

As the Lutzes prepare for bed, they agree that they cannot "explain the horrible figure burned into the brick wall of the fireplace." Of course, they don't think to take pictures of it for documentation or show it to the neighbors. "Had they really seen a pig's tracks in the snow?" they ask themselves. Since the tracks supposedly lasted for three days, the Lutzes not only could have photographed the tracks, but they could also have made plaster casts and sent them to the Vatican! Or at least to *Outdoor Life*.

After they agree that there is a powerful, evil force in the house which could harm even them (by now they seem to have forgotten what "it" did to the 250-pound front door of the house and to the overhead door of the garage), what do they do?

They go to bed.

22

Saturday, January 3, 1976

Events of the Day

Weather claimed: Cold enough for snow to be on the ground.
Actual weather: Low temperature 32° at 12:01 AM, high 40° at 9:45 AM, mean 36°

Father Mancuso

In the morning of the third (not the second as in the text) Mancuso blesses the Lutzes' home by means of a votive mass at his church. He returns to his room, which smell of human excrement. He opens the windows, but the stench stays.

The Lutzes

In the morning, George takes Harry to the vet. In the afternoon, Sgt. Cammaroto visits the house and inspects the garage door and pig tracks. He wants "concrete facts." After he leaves, the compressor in the garage stops. George replaces the fuse in basement. There is an odor of human excrement in the red room. George vomits and by 11:00 PM he has cleaned up. The ceramic lion reappears in the living room.

Father Mancuso

At sundown, the rectory still stinks. That night, Mancuso and the Pastor quarrel.

When Exactly Was That?

Although Anson's Chapter 15 is supposed to include events of January 2 to 3, in fact almost none of the chapter's events take place on January 2, 1976. As is so often the case where Anson combined several dates in one chapter, we encounter more than the ordinary amount of confusion in regard to temporal sequences. In the chapter in question, the confusion commences on the second page of the chapter, page 140. There we read:

> On the morning of January 2, Father Mancuso again blessed the Lutzes' home. He didn't perform the ceremony in Amityville, but at the church and the Long Island rectory [Hard cover has "at the Sacred Heart Church in North Merrick"] [*AH*-pb, p. 140].

Of course, this could not possibly be true if the account in the preceding chapter of Anson's book is true. Chapter 14 reveals that the Lutzes were imploring Mancuso to re-bless their house on the afternoon of January 2. If the long-distance blessing had, in fact, taken place on the morning of the second—as Chapter 15 states—Mancuso would have mentioned it during his phone conversation with George later that afternoon. But not only does he *not* mention having just blessed the house, his conversation precludes such a thing having been done. Why would the priest have re-blessed a house before he was asked to do so?

If the events in question did, in fact, occur, they must have taken place on January 3, not January 2, 1976. With this chronological correction, we may proceed to evaluate the chronicle itself.

Sacrament or Excrement?

In *The Exorcist*, a church is desecrated by the placement of human excrement upon the altar. For a variety of reasons, it would not have been advisable for this to be exactly duplicated in T*he Amityville Horror: A True Story*. Quite prudently, I think, Anson settled for just the *odor* of human excrement, which he allowed to stink up a rectory, but not the church itself.

In describing the fouling of the rectory's air, Anson made a major contribution to the science of demonological pneumatics—to say nothing of what he had accomplished in the field of aerodemonics! On page 141, we read that in the morning, upon returning to his apartment, "[Mancuso] gagged but managed to throw open all the windows. The freezing air rushed in, providing momentary relief, but then the stench overpowered even the cold wind." Later, on page 143, we read "When the sun went down, there still wasn't very much relief from the stench at the Long Island rectory….Father Mancuso had left his windows wide open in the hope that the cold air would eventually drive the odor from his rooms. But that effort backfired: the inrushing wind had only blocked the smoke and smell from getting out."

Since air can rush into a room only if there is a difference in pressure, we are faced with a most peculiar situation. If the inrushing wind prevented the stench from escaping, we must conclude that the wind was coming in *all windows*, from *all directions*. For if there had been a cross-breeze, with wind coming in one window and going out the other, the stench would have been purged from the premises. But no, even though the wind was rushing into the apartment *all day*, there was no cross-breeze—no way in which the air could have escaped.

We must conclude, therefore, that there must have been a chronic center of low pressure in the middle of the rectory so no matter how much air was sucked in from the outside, the low pressure was perpetually regenerated. With all the air rushing in, and none escaping, something inside the rectory must have been devouring the very air itself!

It would be interesting to find out if Anson's aerophagous demon merely compressed the swallowed air into liquid form, or whether it annihilated it completely. If it annihilated it completely, we know from Einstein's famous equation, $E = mc^2$, that a vast amount of energy would have to have been released. But as I am unaware of any explosions in the million-megaton range being recorded anywhere on Long Island on January 3, 1976, we are forced to the conclusion that the inrushing air must have been compressed to liquid form. Although it is difficult to estimate how many tons of air would have been thus compressed in the course of a day, it is a puzzlement to know how the floors of the rectory ever supported its weight, and how so much liquid air could have escaped detection. No doubt about it, we are here confronted by a problem outside the purview of modern physics.

Olfactory Virtuosity

Leaving this problem in demonological meteorology unsolved, we proceed to consider a point in Anson's story which is almost inevitably passed over by casual readers of the book. On page 141 we read "After the votive mass, Father Mancuso returned to his apartment to find a stupefying odor of *human* excrement pervading his rooms!"

Without a lick of mental exertion, it would seem, Father Mancuso recognized the fecal fragrance as pertaining to *human* excrement. Considering the vast variability which exists with respect to human excremental effluvia, and considering the wide range of non-human *excrementa* which may mimic the aroma of the human variety we must stand in awe of the afflicted Father's olfactory virtuosity.

More Changes Ordered by the Priest

As we have seen in previous chapters, many changes have appeared in *The Amityville Horror: A True Story* due to the lawsuits brought against Anson and the Lutzes by Father Pecoraro and Sgt. Cammaroto. Since the activities of both individuals converge in Anson's Chapter 15, it is not surprising to find that the chapter has undergone the most extensive rewriting of any chapter in the Lutzes' *True Story*. At this point, we shall consider the changes which involve the priest.

Hard Cover	Paperback
Finally, the horrible odor *began to pervade* the entire Rectory. Other priests, *driven* from their rooms, gathered *in the lobby of the school building* across the yard. *The Pastor was* extremely upset over the incident and *suggested* that everyone burn incense to drive out the noxious stench.	Father Mancuso feared that the horrible odor *might begin to pervade* the entire rectory. Other priests *might be driven* from their rooms to *the school building* across the yard. The Pastor *would be* extremely upset over the incident. Finally, *Father Mancuso* decided to burn incense to dispel the noxious stench.
When the sun went down, there still wasn't very much relief from the stench at *the Sacred Heart Rectory.* The heavy smoke released by the burning incense had gotten *into everyone's eyes and lungs. The priests* who remained in the building were no longer able to tell whether they were nauseous from the smoke or from the original smell.	When the sun went down, there still wasn't very much relief from the stench at *the Long Island rectory.* The heavy smoke released by the burning incense had gotten *into the eyes and lungs of everyone who had entered Father Mancuso's rooms. His visitors* were no longer able to tell whether they were nauseous from the smoke or from the original smell.
Father Mancuso and the Pastor of *the Sacred Heart Rectory* had been friends for several years, ever since the priest *had been assigned to the parish.* With *Father Mancuso's rise in reputation* and prominence within the diocese, their friendship had ripened and the two priests had become close companions.	Father Mancuso and the Pastor of *the Long Island rectory* had been friends for several years, ever since the priest *had taken an apartment in the rectory.* Even with *Father Mancuso's heavy workload* and busy schedule within the diocese, their friendship had ripened and the two priests had become close companions.
On the night of January 3, all that changed. Depressed with the unrelenting, disgusting odor that permeated *his Rectory*, *the Pastor turned on Father Mancuso*, and their comradeship was irrevocably destroyed.	On the night of January 3, all that changed. Depressed with the unrelenting, disgusting odor that permeated *his apartment*, *Father Mancuso turned on the Pastor*, and their comradeship was irrevocably destroyed.

It started in the Pastor's office, where Father Mancuso had gone to pick up the reports that had been typed for him. He was about to return to his own rooms when the Pastor walked in with three other priests. *They had just finished dinner*—such as it was, with the clergymen unable to rid themselves of the odor that permeated their clothes. *The Pastor glared across the room at Father Mancuso,* who was standing beside a desk. "I don't know why *the Bishop assigns you all those cases,*" he barked. "*I'm a better Judge than you. I've got more experience*!"

Father Mancuso was stunned. He couldn't believe what he had just heard. Why, the man's jealous of me, he thought. "Yes, that's true enough," *Father Mancuso said gently in reply*. "But you've never objected to my work before."

The Pastor waved his hand at Father Mancuso in dismissal. The other priests had looks of amazement on their faces. He had never spoken like this, particularly about his close friend. The Pastor's next words puzzled them even more.

"Look at him, the great psycho-therapist!" The Pastor's face had become red with rage. "Judge! Doctor! How come *you're so smart, huh*?"

What had gotten into the man? *Father Mancuso* looked at the other priests. They were avoiding his eyes, embarrassed at being included in the outbreak. *Then Father Mancuso spoke up*. "I think this business with the odor is getting the best of you, my friend. It would be

It started in the Pastor's office, where Father Mancuso had gone to pick up some reports that had been typed for him. He was about to return to his own rooms when the Pastor walked in with three other priests. *Father Mancuso had just finished dinner*—such as it was, since he had been unable to rid himself of the odor that clung to his clothes. *He glanced across the room to the Pastor* who was standing beside a desk. "I don't know why *the stink is in my rooms only*," he barked. "*Why am I the only one chosen for this high honor*?"

The Pastor was stunned. He couldn't believe what he had just heard. Why, he thought, the man's completely irrational over the incident. "I'm sorry," *the Pastor said gently in reply*, "but I really can't give you a Logical explanation."

Father Mancuso waved his hand at the Pastor in dismissal. The other priests had looks of amazement on their faces. Father Mancuso had never spoken like this, particularly about his close friend. Now his face became red with rage. "How come you're *so nice to me eh?*"

What had gotten into the man? *The Pastor* looked at the other priests, who were avoiding his glance, embarrassed at being included in the outbreak. *Then the Pastor spoke up*. "I think this business with the smell is getting the better of you, my friend. It would be better if we talked at another time and in another place." He rose to leave the room.

better if we talked at another time and in another place." He rose to leave the room.

"Oh, no, your Honor!" cried the Pastor, moving quickly as if to block Father Mancuso's exit. "Let's get it all out now! We'll leave it up to the boys here to see just how big a fake you are!"

"That's enough, Pastor!" The youngest of the three other priests had stepped between the two antagonists. "Father Mancuso is right. We're all upset with this disgusting smell. We'd be better off trying to devote ourselves and energies to getting rid of it than adding to its stink!"

The sudden attack from an unexpected source *deflated the Pastor*. He retreated, but continued to *glare with hatred at Father Mancuso*. There was a look to his eyes, Father Mancuso is now convinced, that came from someone or something *within the Pastor's body*. *Something* had momentarily taken *possession of the priest* and was continuing to spew its venom at Father Mancuso, just as it had in *befouling the Rectory* with its excremental odor.

[deleted]

His determined calm *deflated Father Mancuso*. He retreated, but continued to *glare at the Pastor*. There was a look in his eyes that came from someone or something *within the priest's body*. *This emotion* had momentarily taken *possession of Father Mancuso*, just as something had taken possession of, and *befouled, his apartment in the rectory*.

Which "True Story" Is True?

Both versions of this clerical quarrel are alleged to be "The True Story," though given the massive amount of differences, it is not possible for both to be true. Did the priests leave the rectory and bivouac in the schoolhouse, or did they merely make evacuation plans? Did the nausea of uncertain etiology afflict priests who had stayed in the building to fight the fetor, or did it only afflict guests entering Mancuso's rooms? Had Mancuso been assigned to the parish, or had he merely rented a room there?

And who turned on whom? Did the Pastor turn on Mancuso, or *vice-versa*? Who had just finished dinner? Did the Pastor glare, or did Mancuso glance? And who was standing beside a desk? Weighty as these unanswered questions may be, they pale to insignificance when compared to the enigma arising from the endings of the two disparate accounts: Was it the Pastor's body or Mancuso's that was possessed by a venomous, Mephistophelian master?

Sergeant Cammaroto and the Police

> In the afternoon, Detective Sergeant Lou Zammataro [*hard cover has Pat Cammaroto*] of the Amityville Police Department went along with George, *saw the garage door* and *the animal tracks* still visible in the frozen snow[1] then went into the house....Even after George and Kathy showed him the red room in the basement, they sensed Zammataro's skepticism....[*He*] then asked the Lutzes whether they had *any concrete facts* to base their fears on [emphases added] [*AH*-pb, pp. 142–143].

No wonder Anson and the Lutzes were sued by Sgt. Cammaroto, considering the picture of investigative incompetence painted in the quotation above! Imagine a detective standing before a mangled and devastated garage door—*seeing it*— and asking for "concrete facts." Imagine a sleuth, supposedly trained in the art of tracking down criminals, not noticing that the pig tracks begin at the house and end at the garage with no signs of the peripatetic porker coming onto the property from any direction, nor that it had ever left the garage! No, the pig tracks won't do. The officer wants concrete facts.

Not only did Sgt. Cammaroto deny having made this visit to the house, the Amityville chief of police also denied that any of his men were ever on the Lutz property during their tenancy. And the *coup de grâce* was given to Anson's suffering creation by none other than George Lee Lutz himself:

> Q Now, did you report any of the incidents that happened *during the 28 days* that you were in the house *to the press*?
> A Yes.
> Q And who did you report those incidents to?
> A A number of different occasions we reported them *after we had left the house* to lieutenant Lowe and to Chief Bill Kay, *in the Amityville Police Department.*
> Q How about while you were in the house?
> A No.

---

[1] On January 3, 1976, the temperature all afternoon was about 38 degrees, down from a high of 40 degrees at 9:55 AM.

Q You reported none of this to *any authority at all* during the 28 days that you were living in the house?
A No. [emphases added] [*Lutz v Hoffman, p. 79*]

Blowing a Fuse

After the detective leaves, George notices that the air compressor in the boathouse (which previously we have concluded did not exist) has stopped. Anson has contrived to have the compressor blow a fuse, to give occasion for George to visit the basement of the house—where George will be given an opportunity to match Father Mancuso's olfactory virtuosity by identifying the odor of *human* excrement in the "secret room."

This causes George to throw up over himself, thus allowing us to check off one more "proof of possession." But unlike the undistinguished vomiting in *The Exorcist*, Anson here succeeded in taking a run-of-the-mill regurgitation and expanding it until it assumed epic significance. For although George vomits on himself sometime in the afternoon, it is not until 11 PM that "George had finally managed to clean himself up after the disastrous trip to the basement." We must infer that George had been stalking the halls, caked with clotted vomit, for six hours! Surely the most skeptical critic must admit that only a man possessed would do that.

But even if the above were insufficient to prove demonic influence, page 144 contains a proof of Satanic agency which makes everything in *The Exorcist* pale to insignificance:

> When he was halfway up the cellar stairs, George became aware of the smell....From his position on the stairs, George had been able to see almost the entire cellar. He sniffed and then sensed the foul odor was coming from the area near the northeast corner—by the storage closets that shielded the secret room.[2]

As the Cromartys—the subsequent residents at 112 Ocean Avenue—pointed out, from a position halfway up the stairs an ordinary mortal would only be able to see a few square feet of cellar floor at the base of the stairway. To see almost the entire cellar from that vantage point would require X-ray vision—a faculty possessed only by devils and deities. And if George's X-ray vision were not enough, we see that Mr. Lutz also possessed the power of smelling through walls in 3-D! As was the case with December 31, 1975, and

---

[2] Actually, on the basis of the plan of the basement given on page 86, the northeast corner of the basement would not be the site of the secret room, but rather the "Finished Paneled Playroom."

January 1, 1976, January 3 comes to an end with neither a bang nor a whimper. It ends with Kathy screaming.[3]

Lion Disposal

The reason for this particular screech is the reappearance of the ceramic lion, jaws bared, on the table next to Kathy's chair.[4] (It will be remembered that the infesting feline had been banished to the sewing room on December 31.) Do the Lutzes drag the children out of bed to interrogate them about the crockery ankle-biter? Do they beat them with wooden spoons until they get a confession from the culprit who dragged the piece down from the sewing room?

No. What *do* they do? Anson explained in the book how George "grabbed the lion off the living room table and threw it into a garbage can outside the house." He also says it took George "quite a while to calm Kathy down because he couldn't possibly explain how the porcelain piece had managed to come back down from the sewing room."

Just when, exactly, does Anson say that George chucked out the porcelain feline? The eviction is described on page 149, the first page of Anson's chapter dealing with January 4–5, 1976. So, we would conclude it took place sometime shortly after midnight, on January 4. But we shall prove a bit later on that there are *no* actual events in the book which are attributable to January 4. Since there is an unbroken series of events leading from the lobbing of Leo into the trash can up to events clearly intended for January 5, and since the entire chain of events takes place within the space of one day, we are forced to conclude that Kathy screamed shortly before midnight on January 3, George put the cat out shortly after midnight, on January 4, George then spent a little more than 24 hours (the "quite a while" referred to in the text) trying to calm Kathy down, and then—shortly after midnight on January 5—George and Kathy went to bed.

The only conclusion which is plausible is that George *never* threw the lion out at all. We know the lion was sold at auction along with the rest of the Lutz possessions. And the photograph of the beast which was in the possession of the Warrens showed the animal to be in mint condition—nary a tooth was chipped!

---

[3] Although much-ado has been made over the puzzle of why the DeFeos were not awakened by the first rifle shots, no one has yet tried to explain why the Lutz children never awaken when Kathy screams.

[4] Of course, the lion's jaws always were—and still are—bared. Anson mentions this fact only *after* the lion has "bitten" George, and he allows the reader to imagine that the animal is more menacing now than before.

Of course, there is always the possibility that the four-foot long cat didn't fit well in the garbage can and was pulled out by the tail by a wandering, red-eyed pig. It then could have reentered the house by means of the "well under the front stoop," and hidden, say, in the dining room until the Lutzes left the house. As we have seen previously, nothing *ever* happens in the dining room, and it would seem a logical place for a wily ceramic figurine to hide out.

Sunday, January 4, 1976

Events of the Day

For reasons to be discussed in the next chapter, a careful charting of events claimed for January third, fourth, and fifth shows that no events chronicled in *The Amityville Horror: A True Story* can be shown to have transpired on the fourth day of January, 1976, despite the fact that Anson's Chapter 16 allegedly documents both the fourth and fifth days of January.

Monday, January 5, 1976

Events of the Day

Weather claimed: low, fast-moving clouds; temperature at 7:00 AM in the low teens.
Actual weather: 19° at 5:30 AM, high 26° at 2:40 PM, mean 23°; winds 14 mph at 7:00 AM.

The Lutzes

Early morning, George grabs the lion, throws it in garbage can outside. George says he doesn't believe in spooks. Marching band strikes up. Kathy's first levitation. George doesn't tell her she's been flying. Daybreak.

Father Mancuso

Mancuso watches dawn from mother's house, 7:00 AM.

The Lutzes

By 10:00 AM, Kathy is still asleep. Amityville schools are closed due to a heating problem. At 11:00 AM, George calls Mancuso, but Mancuso is gone. Kathy comes down as the office calls.

Father Mancuso

Mancuso is roused at 3:00 PM by his mother. He calls rectory to learn the stink is gone.

Lutz and Mancuso

Mancuso calls George, tells him he's already blessed the house for a second time. George tells of Kathy's levitation. Loud moans on the line. Mancuso feels as if his face has been slapped.

Father Mancuso

After 8:00 PM, Mancuso returns to the rectory. At 10 PM he is frightened. His stigmata are gone.

The Lutzes

As Missy goes to bed, she bids "Jodie" good night. At 11:00 PM Kathy goes to bed. George goes out to find Harry asleep again. A marching band is in the living room again, the furniture moved and the rug rolled up.

It Didn't Happen on January Fourth

With the exception of George's eviction of the ceramic lion—an event which never occurred on *any* date—all the events alleged to have taken place on January 4 and 5 took place on the fifth. Assuming, of course, they actually happened! A careful outlining of the events listed in Chapter 16 of Anson's book shows an unbroken train of events leading from the concert by the marching band in the wee hours of the morning up to the cancellation of school (an event impossible on the fourth, a Sunday) after daybreak.

Imagining the Weather

We shall begin our analysis of Chapter 16 with a consideration of the weather claimed by the text. We may infer the weather existing at Amityville from the statement "The skies were laced with long streaks of white clouds. He noted they were *low* and *moving fast*. With the *cold spell* still holding in the *low teens*, that could mean more snow....It was only 7:00 AM [emphasis added]" [*AH*-pb, p. 152].

Considering that Anson has made up all his weather events out of pure imagination, it is difficult to know just how charitable to be on occasions where Anson's purported weather can be fitted to the facts if one is willing to do a bit of stretching. In the case in question, the temperature at 7:00 AM on January 5 was 19 degrees (not exactly *low* teens, but teens nevertheless). That happened to be the lowest temperature of the day (mean = 23 degrees, high = 26 at 2:40 PM), and was rather lower than the temperatures recorded on the previous day. Anson's "low teens" are supposed to be a continuation of a "cold spell," even though the previous day had averaged at a mild 30 degrees and had even been as high as a thawing 35. As for the high winds needed to propel the clouds so swiftly, the wind speed at 7:00 AM was a slow 14 mph.

No School Today!

Proceeding from the weather report to the report of the closing of the Amityville School System—due to lack of heat—we read "Danny and Chris had told their father that they had heard on their radio that the Amityville schools were closed because of a heating problem" [*AH*-pb, p. 152].

Being unable to imagine how a heating problem could close an entire school system, I telephoned the Amityville Public Schools attendance officer to check on this allegation. Quite expectedly, I was told that the schools were open on the day Anson says they were closed. Not only was the school system in general open, but every building in the system—on all campuses—was functioning as usual. Also, as expected, I learned that each building has its own heating plant, precluding the closing of the entire system due to any conceivable "heating problem."

Changing the Story

Leaving until later the major events of the day—the levitation and the band concerts—we will consider first a few miscellaneous items of interest: alterations in The Priest's Tale, and George's disbelief in "spooks."

As we have seen previously, Mancuso's mother is said to live both in Queens (Hard Cover) and in Nassau (Paperback). Consequently, on January 5 Father Mancuso awakens both in Queens and in Nassau. In addition, we now have two variant versions—both denied by the Rockville Centre Diocese—of Mancuso's alleged communication with the Chancellors' office:

Hard Cover	Paperback
Finally Father Mancuso picked up the telephone and called the Chancellors' office in the Rockville Centre diocese. He asked to see the Chancellors and was told to come in the next morning.	Finally Father Mancuso decided he would call the Chancellor's office in the diocese. He picked up the telephone, but thought he would go see them in the morning instead.

On page 150, we read that George, after throwing out the lion, told Kathy, "I just don't believe in spooks! No way, no how, no time!" Had George, then, lied to his wife on the evening of January 2, 1976, when according to page 140, "Kathy had her own opinions. When she had *said something had touched her*, had George thought it was just her imagination? He didn't."

If it wasn't spooks that were grabbing her, what did George think it was? And once again we must ask, if George didn't believe in "spooks," why would he be imploring a priest to come and *re-bless* his house? So much for the miscellaneous matters. On January 5 we have major happenings scheduled: two band concerts and a levitation!

The Marching Bands

> George dozed off, waking every once in a while to listen groggily for any unnatural noises in the house. He says that he has no idea how long he had lain there before he heard the marching music downstairs!
>
> His head was keeping time to the drumbeats before he realized he was listening to music. Glancing at Kathy to see if she had been awakened, he heard her breathe deeply. She was fast asleep.
>
> George ran out of the room into the hall and heard the stomp of marching feet get louder. There must be at least fifty musicians parading around on the first floor, he thought. But the moment he hit the bottom, step and turned on the hall light, the sounds ceased. [*AH*-pb, p. 150]

The concert described above was probably just a rehearsal for the main musicale which took place shortly before midnight on the same day:

> [*George is in the* backyard*, having found Harry asleep on duty again.*] George was about to reach down and shake the animal when he heard the marching band strike up in his house. He ran back in through the kitchen [*another change in the plans for the first floor*]. The drums and horns were blasting away in the living room. George heard the stomping of many feet as he tore through the hallway [*i.e., the foyer*].
>
> The lights were still on, but he could see there was no one in the room. The very instant he could see into the living room, the music had cut off. George looked about wildly. "You sonsofbitches, where are you?" he screamed.
>
> George took in great gulps of air. Then he realized there was something strange about the living room. Every piece of furniture had been moved. The rug had been rolled back. Chairs, couch, and tables had been pushed against the walls as if to make room for a lot of dancers—or a marching band! [emphasis added] [*AH*-pb, p. 157–158]

Was George having auditory hallucinations? Possibly. However, Hoffman's accounts of The Horror do not make any mention of Marching bands, making one suspect these episodes were fabricated sometime after February 7—the day the Lutzes told their tale to Mr. Hoffman. The notion that the episodes have been faked is reinforced by the ease with which Kathy Lutz, two years after leaving the house, claimed *she also* had experienced the concerts. In her *National Enquirer* article, she claimed,

On other nights, *we* were startled out of our sleep by the sound of a marching band. First we would hear the sounds of 50 marching feet and then the instruments. They never played a melody—it was as if they were just tuning their instruments.

The noise from their marching feet was as if the carpets had been rolled up and they were marching on the bare floor. But when George ran downstairs to check on the eerie music, the living room was exactly as we had left it—nothing had been touched....

[*On the final night*] From downstairs the horrible sounds of those mysterious voices and the marching band grew louder and louder. We could hear dozens of stomping footsteps mount the steps. [K. Lutz, "Our 28 Days of Horror," *National Enquire*, Dec. 13, 1977]

George Lutz' trial testimony concerning the marching band cleared up some aspects of the episodes, but befogged others:

Q You refer many places in the book, Mr. Lutz, do you not, to a marching band playing in the house at night?
A Yes.
Q And do you recall how many pieces were in the band?
A I never saw the band.
Q You heard the music?
A I heard what appeared to be a number of different instruments being tuned up, not necessarily any kind of music, as such. The only way I can relate to it was years ago when I was in school there had been a marching band, and when they got together and tuned up—
Q Was it a loud type of noise?
A Yes.
Q Can you estimate the number of pieces in the band for us?
A No.
Q How many occasions did the band tune up or play while you were living in the house?
A Distinctly, I remember three or four occasions. There was possibly more. [*This is distinct memory*?]
Q Did you ever go look to see whether the band was playing in the living room?
A Immediately.
Q When you went down there, what happened?
A The first time I thought that a clock radio had gone off downstairs. I didn't think it was anything that I couldn't find of real, physical—
Q Did you notice whether any furniture in the living room had been rearranged to accommodate the marching band?
A It had not been.

Q I call your attention to page 121 of your book, Mr. Lutz....I read to you this portion, and I ask you whether this is the truth or not: "George was about to reach down and shake the animal when he heard the marching band strike up in the house. He ran back in through the kitchen, but the drums and horns were blasting away in the Living room." Is that true, that the drums, and horns were blasting away in the living room?

A Every time I remember hearing it, I was in bed and my family was in bed at the time. I don't remember ever being in another part of the house.

Q You heard drums and horns blasting away?

A Yes.

Q "George heard the stomping of many feet as he tore through the hallway." Is that true?

A Not that I recall it that way.

Q That is not true? You did not hear the stomping of many feet?

A As I tore through the hallway?

Q Did you hear the stomping of many feet?

A I don't remember a hallway, as such, on the second floor landing. When I would get down to the second set of stairs going up, it would stop. The dog would still be asleep. The kids would come running out, and there would no way to understand how the sound came.

Q How about the stomping of many feet while the marching band was playing?....Did you ever hear the stomping of many feet?

A Yes.

Q That is true then?

A Yes.

Q Continuing on page 121, Mr. Lutz: "The lights were still on, but he could see there was no one in the room. The very instant he could see in the living room, the music had cut off. George looked about wildly. 'Son of a bitches, where are you,' he screamed." Do you remember saying that?

A Yes.

Q That's the truth, I continue:
"George took in great gulps of air. Then he realized there was something strange about the living room. Every piece of furniture had been moved." Is that true Mr. Lutz?

A No, it was not.

Q The furniture had not been moved?

A No, it had not been.

Q That is a false statement in that book, is it not?

A I am describing it on the tapes exactly, and what I said was, it was as if all the furniture had moved for that sound to be made down there. But in actuality, no furniture had been moved.

Q "The rug had been rolled back." Is that true?
A No. It was wall to wall carpeting.
Q "Chairs, couches and tables had been pushed against the wall as if to make a lot of room for the marchers"?
A No.
Q That is not true?
A No, it wasn't.
Q Thank you. [*Lutz v Hoffman*, p. 59*ff*]

We may note that as late as September of 1979, George Lutz still had made no mention of his wife being able to hear the band; but now we have the children also hearing the commotion, and a dog who is sleeping in the house instead of in the back yard. George mentions how he thought a "clock radio had gone off downstairs." No such item is listed in the auction catalogue, and it would be rather odd to have a clock radio downstairs, anyhow.

Auditory Hallucinations

The fact that Lutz says he was in bed every time he heard the noise is quite suggestive. It is hard to avoid the conclusion that he was dreaming or having an auditory hallucination while in a hypnoid state. Again, lest the reader think I am postulating hallucinations for simple want of any other explanation, I must assert that auditory hallucinations, although mercifully rare, *do occur*, and may be experienced by ordinary people. The conditions generally necessary for the generation of auditory hallucinations (apart from the use of drugs) include such things as general fatigue of long standing, lack of sleep, and sensory overload (*e.g.*, exposure to loud music, incessant noises, *etc*.).

At the risk of being thought overly self-indulgent, I must describe an auditory hallucination I personally experienced many years ago, when I was an undergraduate. I recount this tale simply to show how real—and terrifying—auditory hallucinations can be.

It was my first night at a dish-washing job at an all-night restaurant in my hometown. I had started work late in the evening and had worked with hardly any breaks until about three or four in the morning. Throughout the period that I was working, I had been bombarded by an unending barrage of rock music—something I detested even when I was a teenager. When I quit work and stepped out into the parking lot, a full symphony orchestra struck up and began to play the Mendelssohn violin concerto—all of it!

Although I had only heard the piece one or two times before, the clarity of the sound was astonishing: I could hear literally every note of every part. I could even separate the first and second violins—something I can rarely do even when I'm at a live performance. The sound was glorious! An important aspect of this story is the fact that I knew full well I was hallucinating. I even had a rough understanding of the sensory physiology which was causing it. Even so, *there was nothing I could do to make it stop.*

When I climbed into my car, the orchestra joined me, the soloist positioning himself behind my left shoulder. I arrived home as the first movement was ending. Thinking a cold shower might help, I froze myself through the second movement, and went to bed early in the third movement. As the third movement fiddled toward completion, I became absolutely terrified despite the exquisite beauty of the "performance." What was in store for me after the final cadence? I was afraid that some permanent damage had been done to my auditory system, and I feared I might be doomed to a life of auditory aberrations. But, to my great relief, when the concerto came to an end *approximately a half-hour after it had begun* the hallucination ended, and I went to sleep.

To return to the question of the marching band at 112 Ocean Avenue, we see that George was able to relate what he had experienced to something he had heard when he was in school—just as I had previously heard the Mendelssohn concerto. And although we have no evidence that George had been subjected to acoustical fatigue in the same way I had, there *is* reason to believe that the other two predisposing factors—general fatigue of long standing and lack of sleep—were present. All sane persons will agree, I think, that if George Lutz did in fact hear a marching band, he had to have been hallucinating.

The Levitation Claims

Turning now to the main event of the day, Kathy's levitation, I find that I must depart from the principle I have tried to employ throughout this book, namely, to deal with only one day's events in a particular chapter. In order to reconstruct the growth of the levitation fable, however, it is necessary to consider together all three levitations described in the book. As we shall see, we are faced once again with a trivial event which was inflated out of all proportion by the Lutzes, and then multiplied and varied for Anson's book-length exposition. Let us first reread Anson's account of the January 5 flotation:

> [George] raced back up the steps two at a time and into his room, turning on the light. There, floating two feet above the bed, was Kathy. She was slowly drifting away from him toward the windows!
>
> "Kathy!" George yelled, jumping up on the bed to grab his wife. She was as stiff as a board in his hands, but her drifting stopped. George felt a resistance to his pull, then a sudden release of pressure, and he and Kathy fell heavily off the bed onto the floor. The fall awakened her.
>
> When she saw where she was, Kathy was incoherent for a moment. "Where am I?" she cried. "What's happened?"

> George started to help her up. She could hardly stand. "It's nothing," he reassured her. "You were having a dream and fell out of bed. That's all." [*AH*-pb, pp. 150–151]

Leaving be the astonishment of George not telling his wife that she has just been imitating the Goodyear Blimp, we proceed to examine the second levitation, which is alleged to have occurred on the seventh of January:

> At 2 AM he began to yawn....[*Kathy*] was still flat on her back, her mouth open. Suddenly George had the urge to get up and go to the Witches' Brew for a beer....He turned to wake Kathy and tell her he was going out for a while.
>
> *In the darkness of the room*, George could see Kathy wasn't in bed [emphasis added]. He could see that she was levitating again, almost a foot above him, drifting away from him! Instinctively George reached out, grabbed her hair, and yanked. Kathy floated back to him and then fell back onto the bed. She awoke.
>
> George turned. He was looking at a ninety-year-old woman. [*AH*-pb, pp. 171–172]

The last alleged levitation—occurring not in the haunted house at 112 Ocean Avenue, but rather in the haunted house on Sixteenth Street in West Babylon—is an eerie, aerial *pas de deux*:

> George awoke first. He felt as if he was having a dream, because he had the sensation of floating in air! He was aware of his body being flown around the bedroom and then landing softly back on the bed. Then, *still in his dreamlike state*, George saw Kathy levitate off the bed [emphasis added]. She rose about a foot and slowly began to drift away from him.
>
> George reached out a hand to his wife. In his eyes, the movement was almost in slow motion, as though his arm was not attached to his body. He tried to call to her, but for some reason, he couldn't remember her name. George could only watch Kathy fly higher toward the ceiling. Then he felt himself being lifted, and again he had the sensation of floating.
>
> He could hear someone calling to him from a great distance. George knew the voice. It sounded very familiar. He heard his name again. "George?"
>
> Now he remembered. It was Kathy. George looked down and saw she was back on the bed, looking up at him.
>
> He began to drift toward Kathy, then felt himself slowly settling back down on the bed beside her. "George!" she cried. "You were floating in the air!" [*AH*-pb, pp. 252–253]

My belief that there was in fact only one "levitation event" which was expanded later for theme-and-variation use is somewhat corroborated by Kathleen Lutz's account of the levitations in *The National Enquirer*. Although her article is generally shy of specific dates, she did give a date for the only definite levitation described in the book. Instead of it being at 2 AM *on January 7*, she has it occurring at 2 AM *on January 6*. There is no hint of the January 5 event:

> My husband George was asleep in bed when he awoke and lovingly reached over for me. To his astonishment, he saw my sleeping body floating about a foot above the bed, drifting away from him. He pulled me down and quickly woke me up. Then he turned on the light ... and gasped....I had aged what seemed like 60 years! [K. Lutz, "Our 28 Days of Horror," *National Enquirer*, December 13, 1977]

Although Kathleen's article is too vague to pin much of anything down, she said that after the event described above, "At night I was afraid to fall asleep—never knowing what to expect. Sometimes when I was in the half-asleep, half-awake state *I'd find myself* floating a few inches above my bed" [K. Lutz, "Our 28 Days of Horror," *The National Enquirer*, December 13, 1977].

There is no mention by Kathy Lutz of her and George ever going flying together, and there seems to be a disagreement over just exactly what George's desires were when he reached over to wake her up! We are not surprised, however, to learn that Kathy did most of her flying while "half-asleep, half-awake." And we may note, before examining George's trial testimony, that Kathy was supposedly aware of her levitations—completely opposite the case in Anson's book where George goes to some length to keep her from finding out about her aerial high-jinx.

Although Kathy Lutz's article provides only weak support for the thesis that there was only one "levitation" which was then multiplied for public consumption, George Lutz's testimony in the *Lutz v Hoffman* trial makes it clear that there was only one levitation at 112 Ocean Avenue. For reasons not entirely clear, however, he did maintain that the double levitation at Mrs. Conners' home occurred.[1] George also places the date of the levitation on the night of January 11–12, contradicting both Anson and his own wife's accounts. If George's date is correct, it would mean the telephone conversation with Mancuso alleged for the fifth (where George tells Mancuso

---

[1] It should be remembered that the Lutzes supposedly had practiced Transcendental Meditation. As pointed out previously, many TM enthusiasts in the 1970s had deluded themselves into thinking that they could levitate.

of Kathy's levitation and Mancuso feels as though his face has been slapped) was a fabrication.

Lutz's Levitation Testimony Examined

Q Did you ever see your wife levitate off the bed at night while you were living in the Amityville house?
A Yes.
Q When was it that you saw her rise off the bed?
A It was about two nights before we moved out, which would have been the night of January 11th and 12th of 1976.
Q Was she sleeping at the time?
A Yes.
Q Can you describe for us what you saw, and what the truth was, on that occasion?
A Well, as it's described in the book, she levitated some two feet. In actuality, it was a number of inches just slightly above the bed. It wasn't two feet.
Q So the book referring to her levitating some two feet was not true in that respect?
A Well, she certainly levitated. She certainly was above the bed. She was not two feet high at that time. There was another time she levitated much higher.
Q How high was it the second time?
A About seven feet.
Q Were you with her?
A Yes, I levitated, also.
Q Was this in the middle of the night?
A Yes.
Q You were lying up in the bed?
A Not lying there. We were talking to each other, asking each other if we believed what was happening at the time. There was no way for us to relate to it. We were just trying to understand what was going on.
Q How long were the two of you hanging in the air?
A Less than two feet [*sic*].
Q After that, did you fall down to the floor together?
A No.
Q What happened to you? Did you rise higher or did you come down to earth?
A The next thing I remember, *we were back in bed again.*
Q You don't recall descending?
A *No.*

Q That was about what time?
A That was at my mother-in-law's house in West Babylon.
Q And that is the truth, is it not?
A Yes. [*Lutz v Hoffman*, pp. 57*ff*]

The testimony quoted above clearly states there was only one "levitation" event at 112 Ocean Avenue. Later in the trial, however, Lutz apparently forgot his earlier testimony and produced a somewhat muddled version of Anson's account—only to settle back to one levitation:

Q Mr. Lutz, at page 133 of your book, I'm going to read briefly from it and ask you whether or not this is all true…
"Suddenly George had the urge to get up and go to the Witches' Brew for a can of beer. He knew there were cans of beer in the refrigerator, but he kept thinking they wouldn't slake his thirst. It had to be the Witches' Brew and it didn't matter that it was 2 in the morning or it was freezing out.
"He turned to wake Kathy and told her that he was going out for a while. In the darkness of the room, George could see Kathy wasn't in bed. He could see that she was levitating again, almost a foot above him, drifting away from him."
Is that the truth?
A That's basically very close to what happened.
Q "Instinctively, George reached out, grabbed her hair and yanked." Is that the truth?
A Yes, that's correct.
Q "Kathy floated back to him." Do you remember her floating back to you?
A Not floating. I had to pull her.
Q And she was in the air at that time?
A She was *again*, a couple of inches off the bed.
Q A couple of inches off the bed?
A At no time did she just drift up. It was as if she was facing away from me, and it was as if she had become very, very straight and stiff. And yet, not flexible but not rigid. And I just pulled her back to me and held on to her and she stopped.
Q That wasn't the time that she was floating seven feet off the bed?
A That was at my mother-in-law's house.
Q That was another time?
A Yes.
Q Here she was floating a little bit off the bed?
A That's right.
Q "Kathy floated back to him." Is that the truth?
A I pulled her back to me.

Q "George turned on the nightstand light next to him and gasped. He was looking at a 90 year old woman, the hair wild, a shocking white, the face a mess of wrinkles and ugly lines, and saliva dripping from the toothless mouth." Is that true?
A Well, it didn't happen in that order, and it wasn't that way, but those things are definitely true. As I remember it, they happened on two distinct, separate nights. One time, Kathy lifted up a bit off the bed and started floating away from me. The other time when I got tired of waking up, and I was going to go out, and I was getting dressed, that's when I saw she had turned into someone other than who she normally is. [*Lutz v Hoffman*, p.72]

So, after flirting with a levitational double-header, Lutz apparently settled for one. But you never know. Mr. Lutz seems to have been a prime example of what the archeologist William Foxwell Albright once termed a "pre-logical thinker." Pre-logical thinkers are able to believe in three mutually exclusive propositions even before they've had breakfast. Mr. Lutz doubtlessly thought both his first and second levitation testimonies were true. He stated repeatedly that Anson's (contradictory) account was true. We cannot doubt that he also believed Kathy's (contradictory) article was true. And—most mind-boggling of all—he repeatedly affirmed the truth of Hoffman's utterly different version. Part of the reason for his ability to do this, I think, is the fact that he did not seem to realize that events which occur on two different occasions cannot be the same event.

Hoffman's Levitation Story

We shall end this chapter with an examination of Hoffman's version of the "levitation." Not only did Hoffman have only one levitation in his story, he also separated the levitation from the old-hag episode by having them occur on separate nights. Hoffman does not strain his reader's credulity too far—at least with respect to the "levitation":

> The next night, Sunday [i.e., Jan. 11—not the fifth, seventh, or sixteenth as Anson reported], Lee awoke to find Kathy sliding across the bed, *as if by levitation* [emphasis added]. He grabbed her, and switched sides with her so she wouldn't slide away again. Then he leaned back and closed his eyes. [Hoffman, "Life in a Haunted House," *New York Sunday News,* July 18, 1976]

Just as mighty oaks from tiny acorns grow, so too mighty tall tales can develop from unimpressive incidents. The Lutz aerobatic prodigies—including both the solo and co-piloted flights—developed, it would seem, from an event involving a hazard well-known to readers rich enough to own satin sheets: Kathy Lutz *almost* fell out of bed!

Amazingly, Anson did not even hint at the eerie thing Hoffman reported in the very next sentence following the above quotation:

> "Something came into the room right up on the bed," he says. "I had the impression of a cloven-hoof of a very light, big animal." He bolted upright and opened his eyes, but whatever it was had disappeared. The Lutzes sat up petrified the rest of the night. [Hoffman, "Life in a Haunted House," *New York Sunday News,* July 18, 1976]

Tuesday,
January 6, 1976

Events of the Day

Weather claimed: Yard has been cleared of snow; 10° after 6:30 PM, snow forecast by morning. Bitter cold at night.
Actual weather: Low temperature 17° at 6:30 AM, high 30° at 2:10 PM, mean 24°; precipitation 0.00 inches all day.

The Lutzes

After breakfast, Kathy takes the boys to school and goes to her mother's with Missy. George is in the basement. Nothing is left of odor which had made him vomit "the day before." He discovers a well in the basement under the front steps.

Father Mancuso

Mancuso talks to Chancellors. He receives lecture on possession and infestation. Mancuso calls George. George never hears the phone ring.

Lutz and Mancuso

George calls Mancuso at noon. Mancuso says he has talked to Chancellors, and George should hire "Psychical Research Institute" in North Carolina to investigate.

The Lutzes

George calls Kathy, who convinces him to do what the priest tells them. George goes to office on Harley Chopper to type a letter to parapsychologists, and calls Eric's girlfriend Francine, who tells George to look for a well. George calls Durham, N.C. Kathy picks boys up at school, has dinner at 6:30. Kathy wants to leave the house and stay at mother's house in "East Babylon." Harry kept inside due to cold. He's afraid of "Jodie." Boys go to bed without a fight. Kathy is asleep at midnight.

Father Mancuso

Mancuso has dinner from Chinese take-out. At 11 PM Mancuso receives call from priest who had helped him on expressway… "Tell the priest not to come back."

Diocesan Denials

The Roman Catholic Diocese of Rockville Centre repeatedly denied having any knowledge of what "Father Mancuso" was doing with the Amityville aberration. It denied that the Bishop had met with Mancuso, and was quite properly embarrassed by the recrudescence of superstitions which make Non-Catholics remember the Dark Ages and the Inquisition.

Of course, the ghost-hunting Warrens explained this by saying the Diocese has a policy whereby it routinely releases false denials in such matters. That Catholic officials might lie is not, of course, without precedent. However, it seems more parsimonious to assume that Anson was fabricating the meetings between Mancuso and the Hierarchy than it is to assume the entire Diocese was involved in a Watergate-style cover-up.

In view of the similarities already noted between *The Exorcist* and *The Amityville Horror,* it is interesting to note the similarity between the lecture given to Mancuso by the Chancellors, and the readings consulted by Father Karras when he diagnosed Regan's possession. Karras rules out such things as telepathy, suggestion, hysteria, and parapsychological phenomena in general. Like Mancuso, Karras learns that possession proceeds in stages:

The Exorcist

Moreover, in the chapter there was mention of the onset of possession in stages: "…The first, *infestation*, consists of an attack through the victim's surroundings; noises—odors—the displacement of objects; and the second, *obsession*, consists in a personal attack on the subject designed to instill terror through the kind of injury that one man might inflict on another through blows and kicks." The rappings. The flingings. The attacks by Captain Howdy… What's the answer, then?

The Amityville Horror

Chancellor Ryan picked up the thread. "Then there are the so-called extraordinary activities of the devil in the world. Usually these are material things around a person that are affected; that might be what you're up against. We call it *infestation*. It breaks down into different categories which we'll explain in a minute."

"*Obsession*," Father Nuncio put in, "is the next step, in which the person is affected either internally or externally. And finally there is *possession*, by which the person temporarily loses control of his

Genuine *possession*? A demon? [*emphases original*, *Exorcist*, p. 266]

faculties and the devil acts in and through him." [*emphases original*, *AH*-pb, p. 161]

Hoffman's Version

Although there would seem to be a *prima facie* case for Anson's having adopted ideas and materials from *The Exorcist*, all comparisons such as the one above can be no more than suggestive. It is rather interesting, however, to see just what kind of clerical conversations and priestly probings were alleged by Paul Hoffman—a writer who, unlike Anson, never had any professional association with the movie *The Exorcist*. Since Hoffman's article is short, we can easily examine all the passages where the (anonymous) priest is involved. As in Anson's account, the priest is first involved in the blessing of the house:

> On hearing the history of the house, a friend of Lee's insisted that he get it blessed by a Catholic priest. Lutz, a non-churchgoing Methodist, brought in the only priest he knew, a cleric in the chancery of the Rockville Centre diocese. The priest, who refuses now to be identified, performed the ritual. Before he left, however, he warned the Lutzes about one bedroom.
>
> "Don't use it as a bedroom. Don't let anyone sleep in there. Keep the door closed. Spend as little time as possible in there."
>
> The Lutzes took his advice. They made the room into a sewing room and kept the bottle of holy water the priest had given them in the closet. [Hoffman, "Life in a Haunted House," *New York Sunday News,* July 18, 1976]

Unused Holy Water

Although we shall never know why Anson passed up the opportunity to work the holy water into his account, if we consider Hoffman's account to be true—if in fact the priest at the outset frightened them about the sewing room—it could very well be the case that the Lutzes were merely the credulous, suggestible victims of a priest who thought he was still living in the Twelfth Century. Once he had convinced them there was something sinister about the house, their imaginations could then run rampant. With periodic stirrings and seasonings by the priest, the Lutzes would soon be swept into a witches' brew of illusions and delusions.

According to Hoffman, the second communication with the priest occurred on Monday, January 12, 1976 (Anson does not describe any such event on that date):

> On Monday morning, Lutz went to the office, phoned the priest and started telling him what had happened.
>
> "I'll talk to the local priest," the cleric said. Lutz poured out more details.
>
> "I'll talk to the bishop," the priest said. [Hoffman, "Life in a Haunted House," *New York Sunday News,* July 18, 1976]

If Hoffman was correct that the first call to the priest took place on January 12, it means that all Lutz-Mancuso interactions which we have considered up to this point (and beyond) were imaginary. We must not lose sight of how Hoffman's account was based on information obtained from the Lutzes *three weeks after they left the house*—before the myth had a chance to grow very much beyond the healthy bud stage. The next communication was on the very next day, January 13:

> During the day, Lee again called the priest, who said he'd been studying the subject and that the only way to purge the house was for a priest to stay there for three days and to say Mass each day, preferably at noon. But he refused to do it himself. He suggested that the Lutzes get a priest from England, where the clergy was more familiar with haunted houses. He recommended that the Lutzes leave the house immediately. [Hoffman, "Life in a Haunted House," *New York Sunday News,* July 18, 1976]

Hoffman's account bears no resemblance to anything in *The Exorcist.* It also bears no resemblance to Anson's account. According to Hoffman, the last Lutz-Mancuso communication took place on the fourteenth of January, the day the Lutzes "fled in terror": "Later that morning he called the priest again. 'What are you still doing there?' the priest asked angrily. 'Get out of there before the sun goes down!'" [Hoffman, "Life in a Haunted House," *New York Sunday News,* July 18, 1976].

Hoffman's "Little Christmas"

Although we have exhausted all of Hoffman's material pertaining to the priest's involvement in the fiasco, we are not through with Hoffman's version just yet. He has some interesting things to say about the events of January 6, the subject of the present chapter:

> Throughout the Christmas holidays the Lutzes remained baffled by what was happening, but they weren't afraid … yet. They stayed home on the night of Dec. 31 to welcome the New Year and Lee's 29th birthday. Then on Jan. 6—Epiphany or "little Christmas," as Kathy calls it—they took down the holiday decorations. After that … "havoc."

> That evening they had another pointless fight with the children, and a few hours later the noises increased—and then intensified over the succeeding nights. So did the mysterious opening and closing of doors and windows. [Hoffman, "Life in a Haunted House," *New York Sunday News,* July 18, 1976]

Readers may search in vain in Anson's account of January 6 (spread out through chapters 17 and 18) for signs of a fight with the children, and they will not read about taking down the Christmas decorations until Chapter 19 (January 8). "Little Christmas" is nowhere mentioned, nor is there any hint of doors and windows mysteriously opening or closing on Epiphany. More amazingly, George's twenty-ninth birthday is never mentioned in Anson's book at all!

Reflecting on the fundamental discrepancies between Anson's and Hoffman's accounts of the priest's involvement, and their total disagreement as to what happened on January 6, we ask, once again, which version is "The True Story"? Lutz, of course, said Hoffman's account was true but it was an invasion of privacy. Lutz later said that Anson's version was the authorized version which "sets the record straight."

Imaginary Weather in "East Babylon"

Before considering the many other events alleged to have occurred on Tuesday, January 6, 1976, it seems advisable to consider the weather conditions surrounding them.

> After they had finished dinner, Kathy told George she really wanted to return to her mother's until she felt the house was safe to live in. George reminded her that it was *ten degrees above zero outside* and snow was forecast by morning. Even though East Babylon wasn't too far up the road, he didn't think she could make it from her mother's house back to Amityville in time to get the boys to school in the morning. [*AH*-pb, p. 170]

Keeping in mind that there is no such place as "East Babylon" (Kathy's parents lived in *West* Babylon) and that this quotation is reporting the temperature at suppertime, we learn from *The New York Times* that the average temperature for the day had been 24 degrees Fahrenheit. The low (at 6:50 AM) had been 17 degrees, and the high (at 2:10 PM) had been 30. As for the expectation of snow the next day, *The Times* reported on Wednesday, January 7, 1976, there had been 0.27 inches of precipitation. However, the low for the day was 28 degrees during the first minute of the day, rising to 36 degrees less than an hour after noon. It then fell to 32 degrees by midnight. Not very close to "ten above"! Almost certainly, the precipitation fell as rain.

The actual weather does make the scene on page 165 more plausible, where we are told, "Finally George agreed, saying he would drive to his office on his Harley chopper and type out the letter to the people at Duke [*University*]. He didn't tell her he also wanted to talk to Eric, the young fellow at his office who said his girlfriend was a medium" [emphasis added] [*AH*-pb, p. 165].

While the actual weather would have made it possible to ride a motorcycle to Syosset in reasonable safety, problems relating to this excerpt remain—problems concerning Eric's girlfriend, the medium, that make it necessary to examine a rather lengthy excerpt.

Francine and the Well

> George rode to his office and mailed the letter to the parapsychologists....Then he telephoned Eric's girlfriend, Francine.
>
> She was terribly interested in what he had to say....she promised to come to the Lutzes' house with her boyfriend in a day or so.
>
> Then the young woman said something that really made George's ears perk up. Out of the clear blue, she mentioned that George should look around his property for an old, abandoned, covered-up well. He didn't admit that he had already found such a place, but asked instead *why* she wanted him to do the searching.
>
> Her answer shocked him: "I think," she said, "that your spirits may be coming from a well. You can cap it off, you know, but I bet if you do find a well under your house, there's a direct passage to it. And somchow, even if it's a tiny crack, that's all it takes. With that 'it' can climb out when it wants to." [*AH*-pb, p. 166]

"Eric and Francine" or "Roz and Bill"?

Before pursuing the complicated problem of the well under the front stoop, it is necessary to examine the contradictory account of this episode in Hoffman's much earlier account in the *New York Sunday News*.

> Later, Lutz mentioned the strange goings on to a woman in the office who supposedly possessed psychic powers. She asked if she and a friend could stop by that night. Lutz agreed. When the pair—Lutz will identify them only as "Roz" and "Bill"—arrived, there was a turbulence in the house, "like an elephant rolling over in its sleep," Lutz says. Except in the sewing room, where there was a "deafening silence." [Hoffman, "Life in a Haunted House," *New York Sunday News,* July 18, 1976]

The differences between Hoffman's and Anson's accounts are startling. Instead of a medium, Francine, the girlfriend of Eric who works in George's office, it's "Roz"—someone who herself worked in George's office along with her boyfriend "Bill." Instead of coming over "in a day or so," Roz arrives that same evening. She makes no mention of wells whatsoever. Instead,

> Bill examined the house and explained that it was haunted by the earth-bound spirits of those who had died in their sleep and didn't know they were dead. According to Lutz, "this was the first intelligent explanation of what was going on." [Hoffman, "Life in a Haunted House," *New York Sunday News,* July 18, 1976]

George Lutz and the Well

Bill then gives the Lutzes instructions of what to do and the incantations needed to expel the spirits—again something not finding an echo in Anson's *True Story*. But there is something Anson does include; the subject of the well. George doesn't "admit" to Francine that he has already found a well under the front steps. The account of his discovery is muddled, confused, and obviously has been written by someone who was not an architect:

> [*Lutz is in the basement.*] George had no success in finding any opening where the stench could have escaped, but under the area where the front steps to the house had been constructed, he did discover something interesting. When the contractor had laid the foundation for the house at 112 Ocean Avenue, it seemed he had covered over a circular opening with a concrete lid. By squirreling around the dirt piled up against this protuberance, George accidentally loosened some of the old gravel around the base and heard it fall into water far below. He flashed his light and saw the beam hit against a wet, black shaft. "A well!" he said aloud. "That doesn't show up in the blueprints. It must have been left from the old house that was here before." [*AH*-pb, p. 164]

It is true that there is no well—capped or uncapped—to be found in the blueprints for the dwelling at 112 Ocean Avenue, which is the *only* thing that is true in the paragraph above. The remainder of the quotation is either false or so incoherent as to be meaningless. If an intelligible claim can be inferred, it would merely be that Lutz discovered a partly cement-capped well under the front steps. Since George was supposedly *in the basement* of a posh suburban home on Long Island at the time of his discovery, we must grapple with the implications of his "squirreling around the dirt piled up against this protuberance". Does this mean the house had a dirt-floor basement—the basement into which George planned to move his surveying office? Where did the dirt come from? He's standing on the floor—at least six feet below the base of the front steps on the other side of the basement wall. There is no crawl space beneath the massive staircase opening. There is no place where he could have been "squirreling around in dirt" in his basement. Given where he was standing, there is no way he could have seen *anything* beneath the front steps. Had Anson been able to actually look at blueprints for the house, he would have seen that the wall adjoining the front steps is covered with floor-to-ceiling built-in shelves.

Weber's Well

Now that it has been demonstrated beyond doubt that there is no well under the front stoop at 112 Ocean Avenue, I can reveal the origin of the well-motif. In his testimony at the *Lutz v Hoffman* trial, William Weber testified under oath:

> A There is a talk about wells or water wells. In the book there's a well that appears either within the house or in the basement of the house. I explained to them I had told them a story of how Ronnie DeFeo, Sr., when they first moved into the house, had the pool renovated or repaired, and the workmen had discovered three manhole covers indicating wells or cesspools in the general vicinity, and that Ronnie DeFeo, Sr., always used to threaten his son that he was going to do away with him and throw him down one of the wells. One of these wells, one or more appear in the book and are talked about, and it's the demons emanate, according to the Lutzes, from these wells.
>
> Q And you told the Lutzes specifically that Ronnie DeFeo –
>
> A About the existence of the wells on the property. I don't have that name, the page number, but I know that it's in the book. I didn't write it down. [*Lutz v Hoffman*, pp. 291–292]

An "On Call" Priest

As is the case in many chapters of *The Amityville Horror*, events in the lives of the Lutzes and Father Mancuso are reported in parallel accounts, and phone calls between the two—successful or unsuccessful—are woven into the narrative. Anson's account of one of them is fraught with problems:

> George called the Rectory. The priest picked up on the first ring. George was surprised when Father Mancuso told him he had just called and that there was no answer at the house. Then George asked Father Mancuso when he was coming, and they got down to Father Mancuso's report.

> He said he'd been to see the Chancellors of his diocese and repeated their recommendation that George find an organization to conduct a scientific investigation of the house. Father Mancuso gave George the address of a Psychical Research Institute [*should be "Foundation"*] in North Carolina and suggested he get in touch with them immediately. George agreed, but pressed the priest to come to the house. [*AH*-pb, pp. 164–165]

We must note that Mancuso's meeting with the Chancellor is alleged to have taken place on Tuesday, January 6, 1976. By contrast, other than describing the blessing of the house on an unspecified date shortly after the Lutz move-in, Paul Hoffman's earlier article makes no mention of interactions between the Lutzes and the priest before Monday, January 12, 1976! Never, in Hoffman's article, does the priest tell the Lutzes to consult psychic researchers in North Carolina:

> On Monday morning [January 11, 1976], Lutz went to the office, phoned the priest and started telling him what had happened.
>
> "I'll talk to the local priest," the cleric said.
>
> Lutz poured out more details.
>
> "I'll talk to the bishop," the priest said. [Hoffman, "Life in a Haunted House," *New York Sunday News*, July 18, 1976]

We have already noted that the Diocese denied the bishop had been involved or that the priest had any interactions with the diocese at all. But it seems to me to be altogether probable that Father Pecoraro—a.k.a. Father Mancuso—was more involved in the Lutz saga than was admitted to in either of the trials in which he testified.

Canine Sensitives

According to paranormal wisdom—animals, especially dogs, are supersensitive to paranormal phenomena. This important "fact" finds no expression in the pages of *The Exorcist* but is developed quite masterfully in Anson's confection—especially when he needed to create episodes we now know would have been ruled out by the weather. Even though the mean temperature for Tuesday, January 6, 1976 had been 24 degrees Fahrenheit, it was necessary to have George say "it was ten degrees above zero outside" and "snow was forecast by morning," concluding that the dog should be kept inside for the night in order for several psychically significant events to occur:

> Harry had been in the kitchen with them while they were eating, and Kathy had given the dog all the scraps of meat left over from dinner.

> Before they went to bed, George thought that Harry might be better off staying inside that night. It was bitter cold out and would only get worse if the snow fell…
>
> While the boys did their homework, Missy took Harry up to her room to play. But Harry didn't want to stay there. He was nervous and sniveling, Kathy noted, particularly after Missy had introduced Harry to her unseen friend, Jodie. Finally the little girl had to close her door to keep Harry from running out. He crawled under her bed and remained there. Finally Chris came down for him. Harry scampered out of Missy's room and, with his tail between his legs, ran up the stairs to the third floor, where he remained the rest of the night. [*AH*-pb, 170–171]

In *The Exorcist*, the little girl's presumed imaginary friend Captain Howdy turns out to be horrifically real, and Anson needed to hint as strongly as possible that Jodie the Pig was just as real. So, he demonstrates how Harry, as well as Missy, could see Jodie even though Kathy and George couldn't. Of course, given the actual weather, Harry didn't *have* to stay inside that night. But how else would Harry and Jodie have met each other?

More Priestly Problems

Before closing this discussion of the misadventures of January 6, we must return to the travels of Father Mancuso one last time. On page 166 of *A True Story,* we read that the priest "ordered Chinese food from a nearby restaurant in the vicinity and wolfed the meal while reading some clients' case histories." On the next page, we are told:

> Father Mancuso, too, was on the telephone once more that night. [*His last reported phone call had been to order Chinese take-out for supper*.] The call came after eleven and was, surprisingly, from the priest who had helped him when his car fell apart on the Van Wyck Expressway [*I-678 in Queens*].
>
> Both clerics recalled the harrowing events of that evening and Father Mancuso asked the other priest whether he had encountered any further trouble after his windshield wipers had gone berserk. "No," his friend said. "That is, not until a few minutes ago." Father Mancuso's heart began to beat loudly against his chest. …
>
> "Frank," the other priest continued, "I just got a peculiar phone call. I don't know who it was, but he said 'Tell the priest [*you helped*] not to come back.'" …
>
> "He said, 'Tell the priest not to come back or he'll die!'" [*AH*-pb, p. 167]

It is easy to become excited about the narrative of a priest working out his work schedule with his superiors that one doesn't pause to ask how Anson discovered the fact that Father Pecoraro was eating Chinese take-out while reading the case histories of his psychiatric clients. Significantly, I think, Paul Hoffman's early account of the Lutz story does not mention the Chinese take-out, nor does it mention the priestly problems with automobiles or the threatening phone call. As we have seen, Hoffman *did* report that the priest had warned the Lutzes of a bedroom falsely supposed to have been that of Ronnie DeFeo, and that the Lutzes "made the room into a sewing room and kept the bottle of holy water the priest had given them in the closet" [Hoffman, "Life in a Haunted House," *New York Daily News Magazine*, July 18, 1976, p. 8]. Holy water figures prominently in *The Exorcist*, and Anson's failure to develop this important motif in Hoffman's account is hard to understand.

Although I have not been able fully to discover the origins of Anson's tale of two priests just cited above, it is worth noting that Rick Moran and Peter Jordan investigated the Van Wyck Expressway episode. In an article in *Fate* they observed:

> According to *Horror,* Mancuso enters the Lutz home, flicks some holy water around and suddenly hears a masculine voice shout, "Get out!" Later, as the priest is driving along the Van Wick Expressway in Queens, he finds his car forced onto the shoulder of the road. His hood flies open and smashes back against the windshield. The right door opens suddenly and as Mancuso attempts to brake the car it stalls.
>
> Father Mancuso, who is in fact associated with the Rockville Center Diocese (at least Anson has that much right), flatly denies ever having entered the Lutz home. He further denies that he heard a phantom voice command him to vacate the premises, which in any case he was never on. We also discovered that a fellow clergyman who was with Mancuso on the Van Wyck Expressway recalls that Mancuso experienced *nothing more than a flat tire* [emphasis added]. Our informant pointed out the Mancuso's car was old and in a state of disrepair. Neither man attributed the difficulty to anything but the car's obviously substandard level of performance. [Moran, "Amityville Horror Hoax," *Fate*, May 1978, pp. 45–46]

Father Pecoraro was lying to Moran and Jordan when he denied having been in the house. He testified on the telephone under oath for the *Lutz v Hoffman* trial that he had in fact blessed the house and had heard a noise that sounded like someone saying, "Get out!" But the *Fate* article reveals something that probably was true: the second priest was in the car with him at the time when it had a flat tire. Anson simply created a priestly sub-subplot to further amplify the anxiety of his readers.

Wednesday, January 7, 1976

Events of the Day

Weather claimed: Snowing at 1:00 AM, wind rising, whipping flakes about. Amityville river frozen. Bitter cold in the evening— "too cold out for even a rugged dog."
Actual weather: Low temperature 28° at 12:01 AM, high 36° shortly after noon, mean 32°; precipitation 0.00 inches by 7:00 AM, 0.27 inches by 7:00 PM; winds calm to 18 mph.

The Lutzes

George and Kathy are in bed at 12:00 AM. George is watching snowflakes whipped against his window at one o'clock. At two, he wants to go to the Witches' Brew for a beer. In the darkness, he sees Kathy is levitating again, almost a foot above him. She's a 90-year-old woman, saliva dripping from her toothless mouth, her lips burning hot. George wants to call Mancuso, Kathy does not. They check on the kids. Dawn breaks and George can barely make out Kathy's figure and face. Facial lines and old-hag features are gone.

Lutzes and Mancuso

George calls Mancuso early in the morning before mass, tells him he's called North Carolina. Jerry Solfvin has promised to have someone investigate immediately. Mancuso is aghast at second levitation and Kathy's face. He says they should leave the house for a while. George tells him about Francine the medium and the hidden well. Mancuso again urges them to leave the house. He says he'll talk to the Chancellors again to have them send a priest. He warns the Lutzes against Transcendental Meditation.

Father Mancuso

Mancuso calls the Chancery in Rockville Centre but can't reach the Chancellors. He prays. He gets violently ill and sneezes blood.

The Lutzes

That evening, Eric and Francine arrive. George hustles them "out of the bitter cold." In the living room, Francine can feel cold drafts, feels seats are warm from being sat on by a "lost spirit"—an old man and an old lady. They smell odors. She goes into basement toward the secret room, says someone was murdered or buried there, and thinks a new part of the house has been added on "over this grave." They leave the basement, go up to second floor hallway, where Francine has whirling sensation while holding onto banister. She goes into a trance, channeling the voice of Mancuso. The dog stays inside again for the night. As George goes up the stairs to go to bed, the banister has been "wrenched from its mooring."

Old Hag Problems

The most important event alleged to have occurred on January 7, 1976 is a double prodigy we have already partly considered in Chapter 24:

> At 2 AM he began to yawn....[*Kathy*] was still flat on her back, her mouth open.
>
> Suddenly George had the urge to get up and go to the Witches' Brew for a beer. He knew there were cans of brew in the refrigerator, but he kept thinking that they wouldn't slake his thirst. It had to be The Witches' Brew, and it didn't matter that it was two in the morning, or that it was freezing out. He turned to wake Kathy and tell her he was going out for a while.
>
> *In the darkness of the room*, George could see Kathy wasn't in bed. He could see that she was levitating again, almost a foot above him, drifting away from him!
>
> Instinctively George reached out, grabbed her hair, and yanked. Kathy floated back to him and then fell back onto the bed. She awoke.
>
> George turned. He was looking at a ninety-year-old woman. [*AH*-pb, pp. 171–172]

Although most of the problems with the levitation part of this story were exposed in Chapter 24, there are a few things remaining to be pointed out. First of all, Hoffman's earliest version of *The Horror* has the levitation and the transmogrification take place on separate nights. Secondly, there is the physical problem raised by Anson's claim that "*In the darkness of the room*, George could see Kathy ... was levitating again, almost a foot above him, drifting away from him!" [*AH*-pb, pp. 171–172]. How was George able to see in the dark? Perhaps by moonlight? Alas, the moon would not rise until later that morning at 10:22—when no one would be able to see it. Perhaps Anson is merely making use of his drama license? As we shall see from the account of the details of Kathy's demonically altered face, there had to be considerable light for Lutz to discern the details of her transformation. Without turning on a lamp,

> George turned. He was looking at a ninety-year-old woman—the hair wild, a shocking white, the face a mass of wrinkles and ugly lines, and saliva dripping from the toothless mouth.
>
> George was so revolted he wanted to flee from the room. Kathy's eyes, set deep in the wrinkles, were looking at him questioningly. George shuddered. It's *Kathy*, he thought, this is my wife! What the hell am I doing? [*All this has been seen "in the darkness of the room.*"]
>
> Kathy sensed the fright in her husband's face. My God, what does he see? [*She too sees in the dark.*] She leaped from the bed and ran into the bathroom, flicking on the light above the mirror. Staring at her own face, she screamed.
>
> The ancient crone George had seen was gone, her hair was upset, but it was blonde again. Her lips were not drooling any longer, nor was she wrinkled. But deep, ugly lines ran up and down her cheeks. [*What is the difference between wrinkles in the skin and "deep, ugly lines" that "cut deeply down Kathy's face"*?]
>
> George, following Kathy into the bathroom, peered over her shoulder at the image. He too saw that the ninety-year-old visage had faded, but the long, black slashes still cut deeply down Kathy's face. "What's happening to my face?" Kathy yelled.
>
> She turned to George, and he put his fingers up to Kathy's mouth. Her lips were dry and burning hot. Then he ran his fingertips gently across the deep ridges. There were three on each cheek, extending from just below her eyes down to just under the jawline. [*AH*-pb, p. 172]

Hoffman's Old-Hag Story

As just noted at the beginning of this chapter, Paul Hoffman separated the levitation from the transmogrification—the latter occurring not on Wednesday, January 7, 1976, but "On Saturday, Night—Jan. 10 [1976]":

> Lee woke and felt a compulsion to flee the house [*no thirst for beer, just fear*]. But he couldn't make himself leave until Kathy awoke. He yelled and shook her, to no avail [*no mention of how dark it was, she doesn't see the fear in his face*]. Then, *as he watched*, he insists, "she turned into a 90-year-old woman." Her hair, Lee says, became "old and dirty," creases and crow's-feet formed on her face; water dropped from her mouth until the sheets were sopping. It took several hours before she returned to her

> normal self. At sunrise, as always, "unseen forces" vanished. [Hoffman, "Life in a Haunted House," *New York Daily News Magazine*, July 18, 1976]

It is interesting to note that Hoffman makes no mention whatsoever of the old-hag transformation in the version of the story he published in the April 1977 issue of *Good Housekeeping*. We have already seen that his account of the "levitation" has Kathy sliding across the bed "as if by levitation." This phrase was repeated in the *Good Housekeeping* article, but the old-hag phenomenon was not. Was aging sixty years in a split-second too much for the editor of that wholesome periodical? Did Hoffman include it in the manuscript he submitted—only to have it be deleted by the editor?

Kathy's Old-Hag Story

Kathleen Lutz published a somewhat enhanced version of Anson's account in her article in the December 13, 1977, issue of the *National Enquirer*. She actually began her article with the episode. To understand the significance of the differences between it and other accounts, it is necessary to examine her version in its entirety.

> I stared into the mirror in sheer disbelief. "That's not me! That can't be me!" I screamed.
>
> I am a young blond-haired housewife with pale soft skin—but that's not what I saw in my reflection. I had turned into a disgusting-looking 90-year-old hag!
>
> My hair was white and scraggly. Ugly creases and crow's-feet scarred my face. I drooled all over my shriveled up, dried skin.
>
> It was the work of horrible evil spirits that plunged my family and me into chilling terror for 28 days. Swiftly and frighteningly, those powerful sinister forces turned our dream home into a hell house.
>
> I'll never forget that appalling night when I became a repulsive crone. It happened about 2 AM, Jan. 6, 1976, about two weeks after we first moved in.
>
> My husband George was asleep in bed when he awoke and lovingly reached over for me. To his astonishment, he saw my sleeping body floating about a foot above the bed, drifting away from him. He pulled me down and quickly woke me up. Then *he turned on the light* … and gasped [*ellipsis original*].
>
> I could see fright and bewilderment in his eyes—but I had no idea why. Then I noticed my reflection in the mirrored wall of our bedroom. What I saw stunned me beyond all human belief.

I had aged what seemed like 60 years! I ran my fingers down my craggy face and touched my dry lips. I shivered and broke out in a cold sweat. I burst into sobs.

The only way to describe it is that it was like looking through a Halloween mask. I knew where I was and what I should look like, but what I saw in the mirror was not me.

Slowly, my face returned to normal as if layers of makeup were being peeled off to reveal my true self. It took about six hours before the texture came back to my skin and my hair returned to its natural color.

George admitted to me later that he was so terrified he wanted to run out of the house. But he told himself, "That's my wife. I can't leave no matter what is going on." [K. Lutz, "Our 28 Days of Horror," *National Enquirer*, December 13, 1977]

Kathleen Lutz vs. Jay Anson

Apart from Anson claiming the transmutation occurred at 2:00 AM on Wednesday, January 7, 1976, and Kathleen Lutz saying it was at that time the day before, there are significant differences between the two accounts that allow us to estimate the amount of compositional license Jay Anson exploited in writing his *True Story.*

Firstly, in Kathy's version, there is no need for George to have the perfect night vision of a barn owl. Although he can see enough in the dark to sense that Kathy is levitating, he has to turn on the light to see the difference between blonde and white hair or to count the number of creases in her cheeks. With the light on, Kathy, too, no longer must be wearing infrared-sensing goggles to see the fear and bewilderment in George's eyes.

Secondly, Kathy doesn't need to take a trip to the bathroom to see herself in a mirror. She sees herself in the tacky, mirrored wall inherited from the DeFeos. At a minimum, Anson's account of her trip to the bathroom would seem to be fictional.

Thirdly, in Anson's account, by the time Kathy first sees herself in a mirror, her hair no longer is white, and Kathy herself never sees herself as a full-fledged hag: "Staring at her own face, she screamed. The ancient crone George had seen was gone, her hair was upset, but it was blonde again."

George Lutz himself added another version of the story in an article by Tsgt. George H. Roberts, Jr., a staff writer for the Pacific edition of *Stars & Stripes* [undated clipping from the time of the Lutzes' trip to Japan for the Tokyo premier of the movie version of Anson's story]:

> "One night I woke up and looked at Kathy who was still asleep," said Lutz. "Before my eyes she began to change into an old lady with gray hair and all. Then she began to raise up into the air. She was just floating there for a while. Then she woke up and caught a glimpse of herself in the

mirror and began to scream." [Roberts, *Stars & Stripes,* Pacific edition, undated clipping]

Sudden-Aging Story
Sworn under Oath

Recalling that in Anson's account Kathy already is an old hag when George first sees her, we also note that in neither of the Lutzes' accounts do we read of "saliva dripping from the *toothless* mouth," nor did Hoffman know of her momentary edentate condition. In fact, Lutz himself denied her dental deficit in his testimony at the *Lutz v Hoffman* trial. His testimony is so utterly confused and contradictory that I wish to present the relevant portion of it without analyzing it, leaving most of this amusing task to my readers.

Q. Now, Mr. Lutz, did your wife ever appear to turn into a 90-year-old woman with a hideously toothless, scarred and wrinkled face while you were in the house?
A. Yes.
Q. And when did this occur?
A. I believe it was the Sunday night before we moved out, the Sunday or Monday night before we moved out of the house in January [*i.e. on January 11 or 12, not on Wednesday, January 7, 1976*].
Q. And tell us what you observed on that occasion?
A. While we were in the house I — no matter what time I went to bed, I would repeatedly wake up at 2:15 in the morning and then again at 3:15 in the morning, if I got back to sleep, and by this time I was very tired of waking up at 3:15 in the morning because I would be unable to get back to sleep.
Q. Do you wake up at 3:15 every night?
A. Yes, or thereabouts, 3 o'clock, 3:30, but always in that vicinity. And I had become very aware than no matter what I did to get back to sleep I wouldn't be able to get back to sleep. So I took to getting up and walking around.
In that particular night I was getting up and was very tired, just knowing that I wouldn't be able to go back to sleep. I was going to go out. My normal way at that time was to get up and check on the children and then go back to bed and try to fall back to sleep. This night I was just, as I said, upset about constantly waking up at that time, and I intended to go out and go for a ride.
Q. Is that when you saw your 90-year-old wife?
A. I was going to wake her up to tell her I was going out. I looked down at her, and she — *her hair turned from blonde to black to eventually white*, and the creases *started to form* in her face, and she became

very, very old looking. It took me a considerable amount of time to wake her up [emphases added].

Q. Were there any teeth in her mouth at that time?

A. I would imagine so, yes.

Q. Was there any saliva dripping from her mouth at that time?

A. Yes.

Q. You woke her up at that time?

A. That's right.

Q. Did she return to her normal condition then?

A. *It took her about a day* [i.e., not 6 hours] [emphasis added].

Q. She spent the next day looking like a 90-year-old woman?

A. Most of the creases left after *about eight hours*, but we called her mom and her mom came over and sat with her and tried to calm her down [emphasis added].

Q. Did you see a doctor about that condition of your wife becoming a 90-year-old, wrinkled woman?

A. No. *From the time she woke up it started to go away*. Her first reaction to it when she saw herself, she was very besides herself [emphasis added].

Q. In any event, you did not think it was necessary to seek medical help for your wife's condition at that time or thereafter?

A. No. That wasn't a consideration. What was a consideration was to calm her down.

Q. And about a day or so later she returned to normal?

A. Later that afternoon she was much more coherent, and able to talk about it calmly. Both of us tried very hard to just dismiss it as a bad dream, *but the creases were still there*. There was no way to just deny that it happened [emphasis added].

Q. How about the white hair? Had it returned to the color that you have here today?

A. About a day later [i.e., long after her hair being blonde again when she first saw herself in the mirror].

Q. How long did it take for her hair to return to normal?

A. About the next day.

Q. She walked around for 24 hours with white hair?

A. No. As I said, by the time she woke up and saw herself, she began at that time to lose the creases, and the hair, even the texture of the hair changed. The texture began to come back. It wasn't an immediate thing, it was a very gradual thing.

[*The lawyer then reads into the record the pages in Anson's book dealing with the levitation/accelerated-aging episode. The pages dealing with the levitations have already been examined, so only the pages dealing with the old-crone allegation are repeated here.*]

Q. "George turned on the nightstand light next to him and gasped. He was looking at a 90-year-old woman, the hair wild, a shocking white, the face a mass of wrinkles and ugly lines, and saliva dripping from the toothless mouth." Is that true?
A. Well, *it didn't happen in that order, and it wasn't that way, but those things are definitely true* [emphasis added]. As I remember it, they happened on two distinct, separate nights. One time Kathy lifted up a bit off the bed and started floating away from me. The other time when I got tired of waking up, and I was going to go out, and I was getting dressed, that's when I saw she had turned into someone other than who she normally is.
Q. Without teeth? Toothless?
A. I believe she had teeth.
Q. She may or may not have had teeth?
A. I don't remember her teeth missing. [*Lutz v Hoffman*, pp. 67–73]

Polygraph Question Three

We'll end this critique of the old-hag episode by noting that when—for publicity purposes—the Lutzes underwent a polygraph testing by Chris Gugas and Michael J. Rice on June 21, 1979, George was not asked about the old-hag story, but Kathy was. According to the official report,

> [Question 3]
> While in that Amityville house did you actually see yourself as an old woman?
> The subject answered YES? [*sic*]
>
> After Mr. Rice evaluated Mrs. Lutz's charts, it was his opinion that she answered truthfully to all [five of] the critical questions listed above and that no deception was indicated to any of those questions. [Gugas, "Confidential Report," *Letter to Charles A. Moses*, April 17, 1980]

The Weather on January 7, 1976

I will defer discussion of the problems inherent in polygraph testing for a later chapter. Let us now consider the weather conditions existing on Long Island on Wednesday, January 7, 1976. As stated in *A True Story,* George, "first noticed the snowflakes falling outside the windows, he saw it was one o'clock on his wristwatch," and "the wind was rising, whipping the flakes about." Most amazing, "the [*Amityville*] river was frozen," so what he thought was the sound of a boat moving on the river had to be "ascribed … to the vagaries of the wind." Later that evening, when Eric from the office and his girlfriend Francine arrive, "George immediately hustled the young couple out of the bitter cold and into the living room to warm themselves in front of the big fire." Finally, once again, "Harry was staying with the boys since it was too cold out for even a rugged dog."

The actual weather record for January 7, 1976 shows that the winds for the day ranged between calm and 18 mph—a "fresh breeze" according to the Beaufort Wind Scale. At 1:00 AM, the wind that allegedly was "whipping the flakes about" was coming from the south at 11 mph—a "gentle breeze." Temperatures ranged from a low of 28° at 12:01 AM to 36° shortly after noon, with a mean temperature of 32°. While the temperature record shows that it would have been possible for it to snow at 1:00 A.M that day, there is no record of precipitation of any kind falling before 7:00 AM, when Lutz allegedly watches snowflakes falling outside his windows. Altogether, Amityville received only 0.27 inches of precipitation after 7:00 AM—all of it falling as rain.

Perhaps more significantly, "the bitter cold" from which Eric and Francine are escorted to the warmth emanating from the big fire in the fireplace actually would have been a temperature ranging from "the bitter cold" of 33° at 6:00 PM to a second daily high of 36° at 11:00 PM. Precipitation falling after 7:00 PM fell as rain. Since the weather records rule out at least a minor detail of Anson's report for Wednesday, January 7, 1976, it is necessary to see if there are any further problems with his account.

Eric or Roz "from the Office"?

Anson's account of the visit of Eric "from the office" and his girlfriend Francine—the medium born with a Venetian veil—constitutes a major part of Chapter 18 and is spread out from page 175 through page 179 of a ten-page chapter chronicling two days of the Lutz story. A major problem with this story, we have already seen, is that in Hoffman's account of what seems to be the same story takes place on Monday, January 12, not on January 7, and the visitors are "Roz"— "a woman in the office who supposedly possessed psychic powers"—and her friend "Bill," who does most of the talking.

Almost no detail of Anson's account has a parallel in Hoffman's telling of the tale. There is no feeling of residual warmth in seats just vacated by invisible spirits; no visit of the psychic to the basement to discover a burial site near the secret room; no unusual odors; no psychic chill; no hypothesizing of a "new part" that "has been added on" to the basement. The psychic does not go into a trance; does not experience a "whirling sensation" when grasping the banister in the second-floor hallway; no wrenching of the banister "from its moorings, torn almost completely off the floor foundation"; and no revealing of hidden knowledge of a crime committed in the house. There is no psychic channeling of the voice of someone of the opposite sex.

Conversely, Hoffman's account of "Bill's" instructions on how to exorcize the house and the Lutzes carrying them out finds no parallel in Anson's chapter:

> Lee and Kathy went through the house from the third floor to the basement, opening a window in each room. In each corner Kathy said a prayer. "God bless this house. God bless this room. This is our house. Whoever you are, get out." [Hoffman, "Life in a Haunted House," *New York Daily News Magazine*, July 18, 1976]

The Spirits Infesting 112 Ocean Avenue

Despite the nearly total difference between Hoffman's and Anson's accounts, there is one motif that seems to find expression in both. In Hoffman's version, we are told,

> Bill examined the house and explained that it was haunted by the earth-bound spirits of those who had died in their sleep and didn't know they were dead. According to Lutz, "this was the first intelligent explanation of what was going on." [Hoffman, "Life in a Haunted House," *New York Daily News Magazine*, July 18, 1976]

In Anson's version, Francine, not Bill, discovers the spirits:

> The girl headed for the kitchen, but hesitated before going into the breakfast nook [*an important feature in The Exorcist story*]. "There's an old man and an old lady. They are lost spirits. Do you smell the perfume?" Kathy's eyes widened. Quickly she looked at George, who shrugged. "Evidently these people must have had the house at one time," Francine continued, "but they died. Only I don't think they died in the house." … Francine had said she would rather draw her own conclusions after visiting the house and "talking to the spirits who live there." [*AH*-pb, pp. 176–177]

While a significant part of the activities reported for Wednesday, January 7 is attributed to Father Pecoraro (a.k.a. Father Mancuso), we have already noted that almost everything pertaining to him in *A True Story* has been denied and even litigated by the priest and the Rockville Centre Diocese. It is hard to know what kernels of fact gave rise to the tales told in Chapter 18, but given what we know of Anson's ability to sprout a mustard seed and grow it into an oak tree, I think it is safe to say that almost nothing alleged to have taken place on Wednesday, January 7, 1976, actually occurred.

Thursday, January 8, 1976

Events of the Day

Weather claimed: Late morning, weather allows Kathy to take the van to go shopping, but by 4:00 PM, "the icy roads … to East Babylon were still in a hazardous condition."
Actual weather: Low temperature 22° at 7:00 PM, high 35° at 12:01 AM falling below freezing at 11:00 AM, mean 29°; precipitation 0.20 inches by 7:00 AM, 0.04 inches by 7:00 PM.

The Lutzes

Jimmy and Carey return from Bermuda honeymoon and call Kathy from Mrs. Conners' house. The $1,500 check is still missing. George spends all morning repairing the banister's broken anchor posts. Kathy goes shopping with the kids in the van. George calls Eric, who says Francine never wants to visit house again. George Kekoris calls from North Carolina, says he'll try to visit next morning. George takes down the Christmas tree decorations.

Mancuso

Mancuso nurses "his new illness," "his recurrent case of flu," with fever up to 104° but no stigmata. He doesn't try to contact the Chancellor. He waits for Fathers Ryan or Nuncio to call and reads his breviary.

Lutzes

Kathy returns from shopping at 4:00 PM. They still have Jimmy's car. Kathy wants to drive it to pick up the honeymooners and bring them to 112 Ocean Ave. George vetoes it because of "icy roads." George picks them up instead, returning "within the hour." Jimmy and Carey will be spending night in Missy's room, she will sleep on couch in the "dressing room." Lutz shows Jimmy the damaged garage door. The two check all the doors and windows, then check the boathouse. All go to bed at 11:00 PM.

Problems Remembering Dates

As already noted, George Lutz testified that it was not possible to remember accurately the days on which alleged demonic happenings had occurred. More often than not, when Anson called the Lutzes for more precise calendar information, they could not provide it and he had to improvise—even to the point of inventing material modeled on *The Exorcist.* Whenever he dealt with the events of a single day in more than one chapter—or claim to be chronicling two days in one—we must be on guard and alert to possible obfuscation or even deception. Anson's Chapter 19 is devoted entirely to January 8, 1976, but he then claims in the chapter title of Chapter 20 to be reporting events of the eighth as well as those of Friday, the ninth. It appears, however, that nothing in Chapter 20 could have taken place on the eighth.

To see why this is so, we need to deal with the beginning of Chapter 20 before carrying out an analysis of Chapter 19. Chapter 20 begins with Mancuso's illness and communications with the Chancery concerning the need for the Lutzes to move out of the house immediately. He says he will call them to give them this advice. In the very next paragraph, we read that "In Amityville, Kathy and George were still shaken from *the previous night's* performances by the unseen chorus" [p. 190]. The "performances" had allegedly taken place after 3:15 AM on Friday, January 9, 1976.

The very next paragraph reports the telephone call from Father Mancuso as though it was shortly after the priest had ended his conversation with the Chancellor: "After speaking to Father Nuncio, Father Mancuso called George Lutz to tell him of the Chancellors' decision." Again, if the sick priest had done anything at all reported about him in Chapter 20, he would have done it on the ninth. Considering both the priest and the Diocese deny the entire story, we must suspect Anson's "Priest's Tale" to be as fictional as that of Chaucer. Unless the Lutzes had spent an intervening, eventless day remaining "still shaken," *nothing* in that chapter could have occurred on the eighth.

Icy Roads to "East Babylon"

Turning now to the subject of this chapter —Thursday, January 8, 1976— the only thing we are told about the weather for the day is that by 4:00 PM "the icy roads ... to East Babylon were still in a hazardous condition." Ignoring how there is no "East Babylon", therefore there are no roads to take to get there, how does Anson's weather report match actual records of the weather of January 8?

Temperatures fell from 35° Fahrenheit at 1:00 AM to 34° at 10:00 AM but by 11:00 AM had fallen to 30°, falling to 26° by 4:00 PM. By 11:00

PM the temperature had fallen to a very cold 15°. While the temperatures from very late morning on would have allowed for "icy roads" to exist, the precipitation records show that 0.20 inches of rain had fallen by 7:00 AM. Alas, between then and twelve hours later, only 0.04 inches had fallen. The roads to *West* Babylon—where Kathy's mother actually lived—would not have been icy either.

Banister Repair

Proceeding to the events alleged in Chapter 19, it appears that nothing particularly exciting had occurred earlier in the day. George repairs the banisters—which subsequent owners of the house claimed showed no signs of injury or repair—and one is left wondering how a surveyor just happened to have the tools and materials to carry out such exacting and peculiar a task. Were there splintered pieces of wood that needed to be glued and clamped? Was there damage to the floor needing to be repaired? How did Lutz even know *how* to repair uprooted bannisters? In Hoffman's article in *Good Housekeeping* [April 1977, p. 238] we are told "Only once did he and Kathy attend the home-improvement courses they'd signed up for." Not surprisingly, no other published accounts mention bannister battery at all, still less how the tort was settled.

D. Scott Rogo, in his *Human Behavior* article "Amityville Horror or Hoax?" nicely dispels the mystery attending not only the repair of the bannister but the repairs of the doors, door frames, windows, window frames, and garage:

> Peter Jordan and Rick Moran, two writers and part-time psychic investigators, have been hot on the trail of the Amityville horror from the start. After traveling to New York, cross-examining witnesses mentioned in the book and examining the house itself, Jordan and Moran found no evidence that any of the events described in the book ever took place....
>
> Despite Anson and the Lutzes claiming that the evil presences in the house broke down a door and otherwise wrecked the place, Jordan and Moran found the house in excellent repair. They also contacted local contractors and repairpersons in the area and questioned them about the house. None had even been called to the house to do any repair work. Not only that, Jordan and Moran examined the house closely and discovered no recent repairs had been done to it at all. The damage done by the ghost, they claimed, quite frankly never existed. [Rogo, "Amityville Horror or Hoax?" *Human Behavior*, June 1978, p. 55]

George Kekoris Calling

Anson briefly updates us on the goings on of his story's minor characters, Eric and Francine. Of course, the Eric and Francine material conflicts with Hoffman's account of "Roz from the office and Bill," and it appears to be a total invention. Anson then moves on to Father Mancuso and his fever that is "up to 104°. We have already commented on his reported fevers, one lasting three full days and another lasting almost nine!

Afterwards, on pages 182–183 we read:

> Then the telephone rang. It was George Kekoris, a field investigator for the Psychical Research Institute in North Carolina, who said he had been told to contact George and arrange to set up some scientific tests at the Lutz home. Kekoris also said he couldn't make it that day, since he was calling from Buffalo, but would try to get there the next morning [i.e., he would drive nearly the entire length of New York State in order to visit Amityville the next morning!].
>
> After speaking to Kekoris, George felt as if he had received a last-minute reprieve. Then, to pass the time until Kathy returned, he busied himself by taking down the Christmas decorations from the tree standing in the living room. Tenderly he placed the delicate ornaments on spread newspapers for Kathy to repack in cardboard boxes, taking special care of his great-grandmother's beautiful gold and silver piece. [*AH*-pb, pp. 182–183]

We already have seen that Hoffman's article reported "on Jan. 6—Epiphany or 'little Christmas,' as Kathy calls it—they took down the holiday decorations. After that … 'havoc.'" We also have noted that the auction catalog of the contents of the Lutz household mentions no ornaments. But what about the real person, George Kekoris? What is known about his involvement with *The Horror*?

The Psychical Research Foundation Investigation

In their critical report of *The Amityville Horror: A True Story* "The Amityville Horror Hoax" in *FATE*, Rick Moran and Peter Jordan reported that much of Anson's account of the séance reported in the Epilogue, which took place in the house after the departure of the Lutzes, was overblown:

> According to Solfvin, members of the Psychical Research Foundation [including Kekoris] did *not* [emphasis original] conduct a full investigation of the Amityville affair (despite what Anson says). They

> withdrew from the case for two reasons: one, the family had moved out of the house at an early stage (for reasons, incidentally, having nothing to do with the paranormal), reducing in PRF's opinion the probability of continued activity; two, the phenomena reported [to the investigators] were far too "subjective" to be measured reliably [Moran, "Amityville Horror Hoax," *FATE*: May 1978, pp. 43–47].

Nevertheless, Everything's Secure

Ignoring how a 250-pound wooden front door hanging from one hinge, a garage overhead door nearly destroyed, or a banister ripped from its mooring might be considered "subjective," we must then wonder what it might have been that George had told the psychic investigators when he talked to them on the telephone. At the end of the day,

> Everyone retired fairly early. Before turning in, George and Jimmy checked the house inside and out. George showed Jimmy the damaged garage door, but didn't offer any explanation beyond the theory that it was caused by a freak windstorm. Jimmy, who had been victimized of his money by an unknown source, was suspicious of something else [*i.e., something not a windstorm*], but he too kept silent and followed George as he checked the boathouse.
>
> Back inside, they continued their tour of doors and windows, until both were satisfied with the security of 112 Ocean Avenue. It was eleven o'clock when the couples said goodnight to one another [*AH*-pb, p. 185].

It's hard to understand how the men "were satisfied with the security of 223 Ocean Avenue" if the garage door that "was almost torn off its metal frame" [*AH*-pb, p. 129] was still broken open. Jimmy also doesn't ask if George's home-owner's insurance is going to cover the damage to the still-open garage door—or asked why he hadn't called his insurance agent. However, Anson's line that Jimmy was suspicious of "something else" damaging the door is curious, considering Anson never interviewed him. What kind of power allowed Anson to know what Jimmy was thinking as he meditated at the garage door remains a mystery.

Still, Jimmy's "suspicions" helped Anson to tie in the loss of $1,500 with the demonic force ever lurking in the subtext of Anson's prose. After all, there *had* to have been a demonic influence that must have prevented Jimmy from suspecting financially challenged George Lee Lutz of theft, causing him to suspect a supernatural agency instead.

Friday, January 9, 1976

Events of the Day

Weather claimed: Ice on Amityville River in boathouse. Howling winds at 10:00 PM.
Actual weather: Low temperature of 14° at 12:10 AM, high 22° at 2:05 PM, mean 18°; winds 7 mph to 22 mph.

The Lutzes

At 3:15 A.M, Carey wakes up in Missy's room screaming. George finds Jimmy and Carey huddled on the bed; Carey is sobbing. Something had been sitting on the bed and touched her foot. She saw a sick little boy seeking her help. She tells Kathy "He asked me where Missy and Jodie were!" Lutzes return to their bedroom, Kathy takes out crucifix from the closet. They proceed to bless the house, starting on the third-floor playroom, reciting the Lord's Prayer. They postpone blessing the rooms in which the guests and children are sleeping. At dawn, they finish in the living room and are interrupted by a loud humming and "jumble of voices" coming from the ceiling.

Father Mancuso

[*In Chapter 20*] Mancuso is too weak to celebrate mass. Father Nuncio calls from Chancellors' office, says he and Father Ryan could see him. He says he's too sick, asks to discuss Lutz affair on phone. Nuncio agrees Lutzes should move out, Mancuso says he won't return to the house, but he will relay information to them on the phone.

The Lutzes

[*In Chapter 20*] Kathy and George are "still shaken from the previous night's performance.... She had remained awake, sitting in their bedroom." George returns the crucifix to the closet. They wake the children at 8:00 AM, the newlyweds get up at 8:30.

Father Mancuso

After talking with Father Nuncio, Mancuso calls George just after Jimmy leaves for “East Babylon.” George tells of impromptu blessing, is warned against angering “whatever is in your house.” Mancuso remembers church would acknowledge demonic influence only after “a long period of investigation.” Call ends as Kathy screams from third floor.

The Lutzes

On every wall in the hall, green gelatinous spots ooze down from ceiling to floor. Kathy accuses children, they deny responsibility. George puts a bit on tip of tongue, says “it sure looks like Jello” … “but it doesn’t have any taste at all.” They go down to kitchen to eat.

Jimmy and Carey

Back in “East Babylon,” Carey says she felt creepy at 112 Ocean Avenue, declares, “I know I saw that little boy last night, no matter what anybody says.” She reminds Jimmy of money they lost while visiting the Lutzes.

Father Mancuso

The rest of the afternoon, Mancuso wonders what the scream was about, consider calling Sergeant Gionfriddo of Suffolk County Police to check on Lutzes. He calls Lutzes but receives no answer because they’re in the boathouse.

The Lutzes

They can’t hear phone because of noise of air compressor. They dump gobs of green jelly into freezing water beside their boat. It disappears beneath the ice. That evening, Kathy wants to leave the house. The Lutzes quarrel, George runs through house opening all the windows shouting, “Get out in the name of God!”

Sergeant Al Gionfriddo

Driving by house before going off duty at 9:00 PM., Gionfriddo sees a “madman” opening all the windows in the dead of winter. Watches spectacle for a while, then leaves.

The Lutzes

Heat returns after the windows are closed. At 10:00 PM Danny and Chris go to bed. Kathy goes to bed. George remains in front of fire in living room. Kathy is soothed by the "wind howling outside." She awakens, wanting to get crucifix from closet, but goes back to sleep. George gets her Bible and goes to living room to read about the cursing of the serpent—the Devil. Flames from the fireplace reach out for him! George is touched by icy fingers; a cold mist envelops him as he goes upstairs. Missy's windows are wide open. George takes her to Kathy to warm up. Windows in boys' room also open. *Still holding the Bible,* George carries them down to his bedroom. All five are in the same bed warming up.

Boathouse Disposal of Green Slime

The *True Story* tells us that sometime in the afternoon of Friday, January 9, 1976 Father Mancuso tried to call the Lutzes, but they didn't hear the phone ringing. That was because they all were in the boathouse, and George, Danny, and Chris were dumping gobs of green jelly into the freezing water beside their boat. The compressor hose kept churning the substance, mixing it with the icy water so it could be swept below the ice. [*AH*-pb, p. 194]

In the previous chapter, we are told the temperature the previous day had fallen from 34° at 10:00 AM to a very cold 15° by 11:00 PM. By 1:00 AM on Friday, it had fallen to 14°, but then rose to 22° by 3:00 PM before falling again to 14° Fahrenheit at midnight. As discussed previously, the "Amityville River" forming the eastern boundary of the haunted house is salt water—Atlantic Ocean water, which generally freezes at about 28.4°. So why—if the temperature had been as low as 14°—couldn't the green gobs of jelly have been swept under the water by turbulence caused by the air compressor?

Leaving aside for the moment the question of the reality of the green jelly, we have already noted that no air compressor was listed in the catalog for the auction that disposed of all but the, allegedly, most necessary possessions of the Lutz family. Despite ambient temperatures far below the freezing point of ocean water, there could not have been any ice in the boathouse due to the simple fact that the water in the boat house and the so-called Amityville River are in continuous circulatory communication with the Atlantic Ocean. It, in turn, was not frozen because of residual heat carried by currents such as the Gulf Stream from semitropical latitudes.

The Howling Winds

It was a lucky coincidence that the actual temperatures were low enough to make Anson's frozen river story seem plausible. Such was not the case, however, with his claim about the wind speeds for the day:

> In her bedroom [at 10:00 PM], Kathy left the lamp on George's nightstand burning. She undressed, slipped into bed, and closed her eyes. Kathy could hear the wind howling outside. The sound slowly relaxed her so that in a few minutes she began to doze off. [*AH*-pb, p. 197].

Kathy's hearing must have been extraordinarily sensitive if she could hear the "howling" of winds blowing at a speed of 11 mph—a "moderate breeze," according to the Beaufort Scale.

Green Slime Analysis—the Taste Test

Since it is now clear that the Lutzes could not have disposed of the green slime Jell-O under the ice in the boathouse, let's leave it to readers to deduce the ultimate fate of the stuff and study the "slime" itself, given the clues Anson (and Hoffman before him) have given us.

> George ran up the stairs to the third floor....he saw Kathy in the hallway shrieking at Danny, Chris, and Missy. George could see why: On every wall in the hall there were green gelatinous spots, oozing down from the ceiling to the floor, settling in shimmering pools of green slime....
>
> He went up to one wall and stuck his finger into a green spot. He looked at the substance, smelled it, and then put a little against the tip of his tongue. "It sure looks like Jello," he said, smacking his lips, "but it doesn't have any taste and all.".... He tried to get the feel of the jelly by rolling it against his finger tips. "I don't know what it is, but it sure leaves a mess." He looked up at the ceiling. "Doesn't seem to be coming from up there." [*AH*-pb, p. 192]

Literary critics probably aren't the only ones who will find the quoted passage "lacking in verisimilitude." George finds a mysterious green slime oozing down the walls and the first thing he does is taste it? How realistic is that? Then, after we have been clearly told that the stuff was "oozing down from the ceiling," George looks up at the ceiling and opines that it doesn't seem to be coming from there at all. How is that *possible*?

A Second Sliming

Green slime will reappear on Tuesday, January 13, 1976—one or two days before they "fled the house in terror," depending upon whose account we are following.

> After the playroom door had been damaged during the first storm, George had removed the lock. Now as he approached he saw the green slime was back, leaking from the open hole in the door and oozing onto the floor of the hallway. George watched as the pool of jelly-like substance slowly wound its way toward the staircase.
>
> He pulled off the pine boards nailed across the door and threw it open, half-expecting to find the room filled with the slimy material. But its only source seemed to be the empty lock hole in the door!
>
> George gathered some towels from the third floor bathroom and stuffed them into the opening. The towels soon became saturated, but the jelly stopped flowing. He wiped up the slime that had accumulated in the hallway and had managed to flow down the steps. George had no intention of telling his wife about this latest discovery. [*AH*-pb, pp. 238-239]

Let us leave aside for the moment the implausibility of Lutz not telling his wife that green slime had been emanating *ex nihilo* from the empty lock-hole of a door that Dennis Hevesi showed never had had a lock to start with [Hevesi, "Haunted by Horror Story," *Newsday*, Sept. 17, 1978]—in violation of the First Law of Thermodynamics. Let us not wonder why he didn't tell her it had even gotten to the staircase and had been oozing down the steps to fulfill who knows what demonic purposes. We must ask exactly how he disposed of all the tasteless goo that had flooded all the way across the hall from the playroom to the stairs and down the steps. He couldn't have taken it out to the boathouse without Kathy finding out about the reappearance of the devilish effusion. He couldn't have flushed it down the toilet, since it had been absorbed into towels. Did he wash out the towels in the bathtub? Did he sneak into the basement and throw it into the washing machine? One more question: Just how big was the hole in the door that he was able to stuff more than one towel into it? At least one inquiring mind would like to know.

Boards across Wrong-Way Doors

Anson has woven in a previous motif that he invented to raise anxiety levels—the motif of nailing boards across the playroom door to prevent "unseen foes" from coming out—mixing in the green-slime terror to create an even more horrifying episode. Unfortunately, consulting the blueprints for the house shows that the playroom door—like those of all the bedrooms—opens *inward.* Nailing boards across the door from the hallway side would be no barrier to "forces" coming *out* of the playroom. When Anson first introduces this motif, however, he claims:

> The locks to the sewing room and playroom doors he removed completely. In the cellar he found some one-inch pine boards that were perfect for his needs. The doors opened outward into the hallway, so George nailed the boards diagonally across both. For whatever might have remained in the two mysterious rooms, there was no longer a way out. [*AH*-pb, p. 215]

Alas, we can be quite certain: none of this ever happened. The bedroom doorways were never nailed shut with *deus-ex-machina* boards that just happened to have been left in the basement by the DeFeos. No nail holes remained in the woodwork to be filled in and repainted by the Cromarty family when it took up residence at 112 Ocean Avenue. Neither green slime nor green Jell-O ever emanated from empty lock holes of doors that never had had locks.

Origin of the Green-Slime Motif

So. How did this story begin? The answer is long and convoluted and requires an examination of variant versions of the green-slime motif. In her account of the *True Story* in the *National Enquirer* [12-13-77], Kathy Lutz wrote:

> Then came the slime. From some unknown source, thick green slime oozed out of the ceiling while black slime dripped out of keyholes of doors in several rooms. It hardened quickly and couldn't be washed or scraped off. [K. Lutz, "Our 28 Days of Horror," *National Enquirer*, December 13, 1977],

Kathy Lutz's account contradicts Anson's story in striking ways. The source of the slime is unknown. It emanates not from a ceiling or the lock hole of a single door; it's *keyholes*—not a lock hole—from several doors. It's not like Jell-O, but rather hardens into something that can't be scraped off—and couldn't be disposed of under the ice in the boathouse. More importantly, there are *two* kinds of slime: green and black.

Kathy Lutz's account was written nearly two years after the alleged events, and clearly seems to be a well-developed version of the story. Let us see what Paul Hoffman wrote long before Anson's inventions had been put to paper.

Black-Toilet Digression

We search in vain in Hoffman's article in the *New York Sunday News* [July 18, 1978] for any mention either of green slime or green Jell-O. But we *do* find the comment, "Black stains appeared on the bathroom fixtures; no amount of cleaning could remove them. Trickles of red ran *from the keyholes* on some bedroom doors" [emphasis added]. "Trickles of red" conjures images of "trickles of blood," and it's hard to understand why Anson passed up that far spookier motif for elaboration in his *True Story*. Perhaps he considered trickles of red to be *excessively* lacking in verisimilitude.

The brief quotation from Hoffman's article raises yet another issue that impugns the accuracy, if not the veracity, of Anson's account:

> [*Kathy*] ran up the stairs to her children. They were in their bathroom, looking into the toilet. Kathy saw the inside of the bowl was absolutely black, as though someone had painted it from the bottom to the edge just below the rim. She pushed the handle, flushing clear water against the sides. The black remained.
>
> Kathy grabbed toilet paper and tried vainly to rub off the discoloration. "I don't believe it! I just scrubbed this yesterday with Clorox!" She turned accusingly to the children. "Did you throw any paint in here?"
>
> "Oh, no Mama!" all three chorused.
>
> Kathy was fit to be tied; .... She looked into the sink and bathtub, but they were still gleaming from her scouring. She turned on the faucets. Nothing but clear running water. [*AH*-pb, p. 36]

The "Tale of Hoffman" has *all* the bathroom fixtures stained black, not just the toilet. Since possession stories such as *The Exorcist* and *The Amityville Horror* rely on excrement and diarrhea as signs of incipient demonic take-over, Anson's restriction of the blackening to just the toilet would seem to be an artful nod to Blatty's citation of the symptoms of possession as enumerated in the *Rituale Romanum* of the Catholic Church. And, of course, the mention of paints (we know that the children have a paint set) might make the demonological *cognoscenti* think of the importance of paint in the story of the possessed young girl in *The Exorcist.*

Green Slime under Oath

So, once again, if Anson didn't inherit the green-slime motif from Hoffman, where did it come from? The transcript of the *Lutz v Hoffman* trial gives us important clues.

[*George Lutz is being cross-examined by Mr. Block.*]

Q [Are there] any other essential basic parts of this book which are not true?
A I wouldn't have described the things in the book the way Mr. Anson did.
Q Is that a question of literary style or a question of substantive truth?
A I think accuracy as far as description. For example, the green slime that Mr. Anson refers to in the book was more like jello. It wasn't slimy, it was more like jello.
Q Are you telling us that all references to green slime on walls and doors in this true story of yours really was not the case?
A I remember it being on the floors. I don't remember it on the walls and doors.
Q And the green slime was more like jello?
A Yes. …
Q But there's no question that you saw this sort of slimy or jello-like green substance on the floors when you were in the house for those 28 days?
A Right. As a matter of fact, the stains were still on the floors and on the carpets when the investigators went into the house.
Q How would this green slime or jello appear from time to time?
A First time it happened we thought that the children had done it, that they had gone down to the kitchen and prepared something and spilled it around the house. The next time it happened the children weren't at home, and there was no way to blame them.
Q Did you actually see this oozing out from the floors or something of that nature?
A It was just there. One minute it wasn't there, the next minute it was there.
Q Where were you when this happened?
A We cleaned it up the first time.
Q Where were you, Mr. Lutz, when this was happening?

MR. DALEY: As to this line of questioning, I don't see where it has any bearing on it.

THE COURT: The line is proper. If he says he wasn't there, how would he know?

MR. BLOCK: I'm sorry. I believe he answered the question responsively, Your Honor.

THE COURT: All right. Let's take a short break.

[*The trial resumes after the* break.]

Q Now, Mr. Lutz, in respect to this – how do you refer to this, this gelatin, this slime? What language do you use for this green substance?
A Jello-like.
Q Did you see this on more than the two occasions that you have told us about?
A No.
Q Did you ever see this greenish-black substance or however you referred to it, coming up the stairs at your wife's mother's house?
A I believe the greenish-black substance you're referring to is what we saw coming from two particular key-holes, two rooms on the second floor of the house. Not at my mother-in-law's house.
Q This is at the Amityville house?
A Yes.
Q You saw this substance coming in through keyholes?
A It was on the bedroom door and the sewing room door.
Q Was this during the daytime or night time?
A [*Not answering the question*] At first it appeared very small, and then it got larger. By the time we left the house they were rather long. When the investigators came in, it was still there for them to see.
Q What size did this slime or green material ultimately take?
A It was more black than anything. It looked like epoxy, a drip.
Q How big was it?
A Like a tear drop.
Q Like a tear drop?
A Except it was eight inches long by the time we left.
Q Did you actually see this?
A We would go to bed at night and in the morning it would be a little longer.
Q That's related in your book, is it not?
A It's on the tapes. That I know. How it's in the book, I honestly don't remember since 1977 when I read it.
Q In any event, that is the keyhole; is it not?
A Yes.

THE COURT: These pictures, where were they taken? In the press conference?
THE WITNESS: Yes, sir.
THE COURT: And these are the reproductions from Newsday's print?
THE WITNESS: Yes, sir. I believe so.

[*A brief discussion of how* Newsday *and Prentice-Hall got permission to use the picture takes place, then the judge resumes*.]

THE COURT: These are not original pictures. These must have been taken right out of Newsday. They didn't even bother to get the original pictures. They must have just flipped them right out of Newsday.
THE WITNESS: I know they got permission from us. At least I was told they went to Newsday to get the negatives, themselves, but I don't know in actuality what they did.

Q You posed for those pictures?
A No. They weren't posed for. We objected to them when they were taken. [*Lutz v Hoffman*, pp. 48–54]

Despite the non-answering of questions and the chaotic logic of the above excerpts from the trial transcript, the pictures under discussion clearly had nothing to do with keyholes, doors, or green slime. Astonishingly, the only photograph of a doorknob and lock ever published in *Newsday* bears the caption:

> Green slime was oozing from the playroom door, the book says, "… its only source seemed to be the empty lock hole in the door." There is no lock hole in the door. There is no lock in the door. There is only an antique keyhole plate fastened over the spot where a keyhole might be drilled. [Hevesi, "Haunted by Horror Story," *Newsday*, September 17, 1978]

Nine Green-Slime Questions

Lutz's bewildering testimony leaves us with several unanswered questions and contradictions:

1. Was the slime George tasted green or "more black than anything"?
2. Was it slime or Jell-O?
3. What size was it? Was it the size of a tear drop that grew to be eight inches long, or did it cover the walls and floor from the playroom door to the staircase and down (or up) a number of steps?
4. Was it only on the floors, or also on the walls and doors?
5. Where did it come from? Did it come from the ceiling, from a door, or both? Did it come from the playroom door, the sewing room door, or a bedroom door? Was it one or two doors?
6. Did it come from an open lock hole, or from a keyhole? One or two keyholes?

7. Did it come from the door of the playroom (third floor) or the door of the sewing room (second floor, according to the paperback), or from two rooms on the second floor?
8. Did the stuff ever appear at a time the children weren't at home?
9. Did the stuff go up or down a staircase, and in whose house?

The Green-Slime Mystery—Solved

Fortunately, we do not need to leave our study of the mystery of the green slime with a long list of unanswered questions. William Weber's testimony at the *Lutz v Hoffman* trial seems to be able fully to account for the genesis of the gel.

> [*Mr. Block is examining Weber and asks what kinds of pictures he showed the Lutzes as they were expecting to collaborate on a book.*]

A Among the pictures that I showed them, there were – I mentioned the police crime scenes, the pictures of the doors, walls, etc., with what appeared to be on it a blackish-green substance. I told them that this was the fingerprint dust used by the police. They were very interested in that, but they didn't relate why they were interested. But I indicated to them it was in my opinion the fingerprint dust that the police had used when the pictures had been taken.
Q Was this by the keyholes?
A Yes. All around the keyholes, on the doorknobs, on some of the walls, on some of the doors, themselves. And of course, in the book, at page 147 and a couple of other places, that appears as green slime emanating from keyholes and doorknobs, etc. [*Lutz v Hoffman*, pp. 289–290]
Q So the material around the keyhole was information which you supplied?
A Was pictures.
Q Pictures that they received from you?
A Right. … Towards the end of this book a lot of this is repeated, the history of this, the history of the house, the green slime, the flies, the names of the demons. Those – well, I can't say for sure whether the Lutzes located those names or I located them, but I went to this occult shop [*after the Lutzes had left the house*] and purchased some books that had names of demons in them. [*Lutz v Hoffman*, p. 290]

Once again, we see how mighty oaks can grow from tiny acorns. A two hundred-fifty-pound front door can develop from the cupboard door of a garbage shed, and fingerprint dust can turn into a slime that covers walls and floors and is given an icy burial at sea.

Brother Jimmy and His Bride

A lot is alleged to have happened on Friday, January 9, 1976. Although most of the book centers attention on just the Lutz family and the priest "Father Mancuso," a few minor characters also play significant roles in the narrative. We have already encountered "Eric from the office" and his Venetian-veiled girlfriend Francine, and we have criticized the episodes in which they play a part in the horror narrative.

We have also encountered Kathy's brother Jimmy and his bride Carey and devoted some degree of critical attention to the parts they are alleged to have played in the story. There is a more perplexing episode in Anson's tale that involves them—an episode that raises the question of what *really* happened to them when they were sleeping in Missy's room. As we shall see, their role in the story will be found to reflect poorly on Anson's overall credibility. The *True Story* tells us:

> George knows that it happened at 3:15 AM …It was then that Carey woke up screaming.
>
> "Oh, God, not her too!" he muttered to himself. George leaped out of bed, ran to Missy's room, and snapped on the light. The young couple were huddled together in bed, Jimmy cradling his sobbing wife.
>
> "What's the matter?" George asked. "What's happened?"
>
> Carey pointed to the foot of Missy's bed, "S-s-something was sitting there! It touched m-m-my foot!"
>
> George approached the spot Carey had indicated and felt the bed with his hand. It was warm as though someone had been sitting there.
>
> "I woke up," Carey continued, "and I could see a little boy! He looked so sick! He was trying to tell me to help him!" She began to cry hysterically.
>
> Jimmy shook his wife gently. "Come on, Carey," he said soothingly. "You were probably having a dream!"
>
> "No, Jimmy!" Carey protested. "It wasn't a dream! I saw him! He spoke to me!"
>
> "What did he say, Carey?" George asked. …
>
> "He asked me where Missy and Jodie were!" [*AH*-pb, pp. 185–186]

Anson wraps up his account of Carey's apparition in the next chapter, in his account of the following day (Friday, January 9, 1976):

> Jimmy and Carey had arrived back in East Babylon. Carey was happy to be away from 112 Ocean Avenue, even if it meant being at her mother-

in-law's. "I felt creepy there, Jimmy," she said, as they got out of their car. "I know I saw that little boy last night, no matter what anybody says."

Jimmy reached out and patted his wife's behind. "Aw, forget it, baby," he said. "It was just a dream. You know I don't believe in that stuff."

Carey squirmed away from Jimmy's touch, looking around to see if any neighbors were watching. But as she was about to go in the door, he grabbed her arm. "Listen, Carey," he said, drawing her close, "do me a favor. Don't mention what happened in front of Ma. She gets very upset about such things. Next thing you know, we'll have a priest over here."

Carey stood her ground. "What about our money you lost at Kathy's? You say that was a dream, too?" [*AH*-pb, p. 193]

Cloven Hooves on the Bed

Readers may recall that in Paul Hoffman's early account of the demonic doings Lutz claims "Something came into the room right up on the bed," … "I had the impression of a cloven-hoof of a very light, big animal." Lutz bolted upright and opened his eyes, but whatever it was had disappeared. [Hoffman, "Life in a Haunted House," *New York Daily News Magazine*, July 18, 1976] Has Hoffman's account of a "very light, big animal" on his bed evolved into a little spirit-boy who disappears before others can see him? Have the cloven hooves of Hoffman's bed-sitter evolved into Jodie the pig? It seems probable to me. It is interesting to see the further evolution of this episode as related by Kathy Lutz in her article in *National Enquirer*:

> That murder [*the DeFeo murders*] began to haunt me—especially the times when I happened to pass an upstairs room and heard a child crying. They were very sorrowful cries. Whenever I whipped open the door, the room would always be empty.
>
> That wasn't the case for my sister-in-law who visited us one night. She was to sleep in Missy's room while Missy slept with me. My sister-in-law went upstairs to get ready for bed. When she opened the door to the room, she saw a strange little boy sitting on the bed. He looked sickly, and she had the impression somehow that everything around him was colored blue. She knew he wasn't real. She ran toward the stairs and called for us, but when we went to investigate, he was gone. Later, Missy told us that she had spoken to the boy, and he told her he had lived there—and had died there. [K. Lutz, "Our 28 Days of Horror," *National Enquirer*, December 13, 1977]

The differences between the two accounts are striking. Kathy, not just Carey, hears the voice of a presumed child. In Kathy's account, the crying comes from an unspecified room, albeit the apparition in both accounts appears in Missy's room—the room in which Allison DeFeo had been murdered. In Kathy's account, only Carey is spending the night at 112 Ocean Avenue, and she sees the boy on the bed when she is fully awake, not awakening from sleep. She calls the Lutzes who are downstairs for help, instead of them being in bed and being awakened by her scream. Whereas the boy seems to have simply come to visit Jodie and Missy in Anson's account, the child appears to be part of the permanent residents of the horror house and one more preternatural playmate for Missy.

The Real-Life Jimmy Conners

Although Jimmy Conners seems to be a minor character in Anson's book, he actually was an important player in its origin. In fact, he was summoned from military duty to be deposed in the *Lutz v Hoffman* fraud trial where he testified [pp. 137–139] that he had taken the Lutzes to a meeting in the offices of Mr. Weber and Mr. Burton—the meeting at which preparations were made for the press conference that would create publicity and excitement for the horror story were planning to write. Conners actually taped the meeting, and he testified that Atty. Weber told Lutz "If any questions come up, I will try to give you any advice you might need as far as whether you should answer it to the media or not." [*Lutz v Hoffman*, p. 138] It is likely that James Conners himself played some generative part in the creation of *The Amityville Horror*.

The Real-Life Mrs. Conners

I'll end this analysis of the spirit-boy episode in Anson's story on an amusing note. In the *True Story*, Jimmy Conners tells Carey, "Don't mention what happened in front of Ma. She gets very upset about such things. Next thing you know, we'll have a priest over here." It turns out that "Ma" —Johanna Conners—also played a role in the genesis of the *Horror*. She too was called to testify at the *Lutz v Hoffman* fraud trial [pages 444–450], and it became clear that much of the thematic material that later appeared in the book was first introduced at a meeting in her house between Weber, Hoffman, the Lutzes, and several parapsychology students from Dowling College who supplied allegedly historical information relating to the haunted house.

I have been unable to discover any germ of historicity underlying the episodes in which Jimmy Conners or his mother play a role in Anson's story. Unless they too had been at least slightly complicit in the deception, there would have been danger that they might have sued Anson for the things said about them in his book. My guess is that Anson would not have risked including them had they not been "in the know" about the entire project.

I will not examine any of the alleged activities of "Father Mancuso" as it has already been demonstrated beyond cavil that virtually nothing attributed to him in Anson's book can be documented beyond his blessing of the house on the first day and several telephone conversations. While it is likely that Father Pecoraro was more involved than he admitted, it is pointless to speculate what his involvement might have been—given the total absence of evidence outside the transcript of the Lutz vs. Hoffman trial.

Gionfriddo's Surveillance

As for "Al Gionfriddo's" surveillance of the Lutz home, readers may recall that the Amityville Police Department denied any interaction with the Lutzes before they vacated the house, and one of the policemen (either Geonfreda or Camerata) sued them for their allegations of his role in the story. Moreover, Atty. Weber testified, "Geonfreda and Camerata appear a number of places in the book, and they allegedly relate information to the Lutzes. The information that those people allegedly relate to the Lutzes is information that I gave to the Lutzes, not Geonfreda or Camerata" [*Lutz v Hoffman*, p. 282].

Holding Fast to the Bible

Chapter 20 of *The Amityville Horror: A True Story* ends with a flourish of activity that is as comical as it is implausible:

> George returned to his chair in the living room, opened the Bible and began at the beginning, the Book of Genesis. …
>
> George … felt a hot blast on his face, and he snapped his head up from the book. The flames of the fireplace were reaching out for him! George leaped off his chair and jumped back….then he was stabbed in the back by an icy finger.
>
> George whirled about. Nothing was there, but he could feel a draft… a cold mist coming down the staircase in the hallway!
>
> Gripping the Bible tightly, George raced up the steps toward his bedroom… George ran to Missy's bedroom and flung open the door. The windows were wide open, the below-freezing air pouring in. George grabbed up his daughter from her bed. He could feel her little body was icy and shivering. Rushing out of the room, he ran back to his bedroom and put Missy under the cover. Kathy woke up. "Warm her up!" George yelled. "She's freezing to death!"
>
> Without hesitation, Kathy covered the little girl with her own body. George ran out of the room and up to the third floor. The windows in Danny and Chris' bedroom, George found, were also wide open. The boys were asleep but burrowed completely under their blankets. He gathered both in his arms and staggered down the stairs to his bedroom.

Danny's and Chris' teeth were chattering from the cold. George pushed them onto the bed and got under the blankets with them, his body on top of theirs. All five Lutzes were in one bed, the three children slowly thawing out, the two parents rubbing their hands and feet. It took almost a half hour before the children's body temperatures seemed back to normal. Only then did George realize he was still holding onto the Bible. Knowing he had been more than warned, he flung it to the floor. [*AH*-pb, pp. 197–199]

I invite my readers to visualize George Lutz acting out the particulars of the above scene—never once putting down Kathy's Bible.

Not bothering to close Missy's windows and, apparently, holding the Bible in his left hand, George slides his right hand under the limp body of the sleeping child, scoops her up, clutches her to his side, and runs across the hall to his bedroom. With the Bible in his left hand and Missy clutched beside him under his right arm, he bends over Kathy, sliding the pinky and fourth finger of his right hand under the blankets covering her, squeezing Missy between himself and Kathy's body, with a whole-body swoosh and not falling over, he pulls the covers off Kathy far enough to make room for Missy, awakening Kathy. Still holding the Bible, bending over he lays the child beside Kathy without falling over.

Bible still in hand, Lutz runs up the stairs to the third floor to the boys' bedroom. Again without closing the open windows, he bends over Chris' body, grabs his covers with his right hand, pulls the covers off Chris, slides his right hand under the boy's body, scoops him up off the bed under his right arm, and stands up clutching him to his right side. Then, without putting down the Bible, Lutz transfers the boy to his left side, pressing him to the left side of his body and freeing his right arm for the next rescue.

With Chris clutched to his left side and the Bible gripped in his left hand, George turns and goes to Danny's bed. Once again, he bends over, grabs Danny's covers with his right hand and pulls them aside. Stooping down and bending over the bed, but not falling over and still holding Chris and the Bible, he slides his right hand under Danny's body, scoops him up in his right arm off the bed, and stands up—pressing him to his right side. Then he staggers down the stairs to his own bedroom.

Still holding the Bible in his left hand, he drops the boys onto his bed—apparently on top of the covers. Without ever setting the Bible down, he somehow gets the boys under the covers and covers them with his own body under the blankets. Without letting loose of the Scriptures, apparently no longer on top of the boys, he rubs the hands and feet of the children to warm them up. Perhaps he rubs the Bible against them to produce more frictional warmth? Could *that* have been what was needed to alert Lutz to the fact that he was still holding a Bible?

Saturday, January 10, 1976

Events of the Day

Weather claimed: Thunderstorm, "raining cats and dogs," trees swaying in the rising gusts. Icy rain wash away dirty piles of accumulated snow. Waters of river might "add to the frozen waters and overflow the bulkheads." Storm tore down a telephone pole, phones are out. Hurricane-force winds raging across South Shore. Winds whip front door back against the building. George has trouble trying to close door behind him. Still raining at 6:30 the next morning, through open windows.
Actual weather: Low temperature 13° at 7:10 AM, high 26 at 2:45 PM., mean 20°. Zero precipitation. Winds NW at 6–12 mph ("gentle to moderate breeze").

The Lutzes

In the morning, Kathy's in bed with red welts on her abdomen; she calls her mother to come help her. Mrs. Conners takes a cab to 112 Ocean Ave. Kathy is lying uncovered in bed as her mother examines her. Her mother burns her fingers when she touches the welts. The Lutzes don't call the doctor because "He'll think we're nuts!"

George leaves with the kids to go to a store and the library. At the Amityville library, he takes out a temporary borrower's card and gets a book on witches and demons.

Mrs. Conners has argument on phone with Jimmy. Kathy's welts begin to fade. When George returns with the kids, the welts are gone. Mrs. Conners wants the family to leave the house. George calls a cab to take her back to "East Babylon."

Lutz and Mancuso

After 8 PM, George has finished reading the book. He's made a list of demons and tries to pronounce their names. He calls Mancuso, who's alarmed they're still in the house. Lutz tells him he's learned how to call up the demons, and names Iscaron and Madeste. As he names more demons, Mancuso tells him never to do that. The phone goes dead.

The Lutzes

It appears to be after 8 PM when Kathy gets up and appears downstairs fully dressed for the first time that day. Her welts are gone. Kathy all day "had been in a languorous mood, as if she had been completely satisfied sexually," and had "visions of making love to someone. It wasn't George." She calls her mother (the phone is working) who tells her "it's raining cats and dogs there." The storm hits the house with lightning and thunder. Trees swaying in the rising gusts. The rain intensifies and Kathy sends Danny upstairs to close her bedroom window tight. Lutz runs out to bring Harry inside.

Danny cries out in pain from upstairs. The fingers of his right hand are trapped beneath the heavy wooden window frame. Lutz tries unsuccessfully to raise the window. Then, as he's cursing the unseen forces, the window opens by itself, freeing Danny's hand. Despite intense pain, he doesn't want to "open his fist" to show his mother his fingers. Except for the thumb, all his fingers are "strangely flat."

George tries to call "the Brunswick Hospital Center on Broadway in Amityville," but the phone is dead, due to the "hurricane-force winds" across Long Island. George takes Danny to the hospital. Although crushed flat, no damaged bones or cartilages in the fingers are found. Arriving home twenty minutes later, winds whip the front door back against the building, making it difficult to close it. They're trapped in the house for another night.

Refuted by the Weather Report

Few other chapters in Jay Anson's True Story can be refuted by the weather reports and forecasts of the *New York Times* so thoroughly as is the case with Chapter 21—January 10. Considering there was no precipitation at all that day means that nearly everything alleged to have happened after 8:00 PM—as well as during the horrific morning of the next day—never happened. Kathy's phone call disclosing rain in "East Babylon" never happened. (Anyway, Anson tells us the phone was out even before the storm hit, so how could Kathy have called her mother?) Kathy didn't have to tell Danny to run upstairs to close the window, eliminating the occasion for the miraculous crushing of his fingers and the trip to the hospital. There was no need to bring Harry inside. There was no need to worry if the Amityville River would overflow.

The gentle-to-moderate breezes that actually blew across Long Island also eliminate the possibility of power and phone lines being downed by hurricane-force winds. No whipping of the 250-pound front door (which actually opens inward) back against the house. Even if more than zero precipitation had been recorded for that day, with the temperatures ranging from a low of 13 degrees Fahrenheit to a high of 26 it could not have rained. *A fortiori*, another reason to not worry about an overflowing Amityville River.

The Burning Welts

Chapter 21 begins with a story so preposterous—so lacking in verisimilitude—that a prototype can be found neither in Paul Hoffman's account nor in William Peter Blatty's *The Exorcist*—the ultimate cookbook source for confections such as *The Amityville Horror: A True Story*. Kathy is lying in bed naked beneath her bathrobe with burning stigmata—welts on her abdomen—so hot that when Mrs. Conners or George touch them, they burn their fingers! A brief consideration of the physiological constraints on the conditions required for survival of living cells force the conclusion that such a sensation would have had to have been a miracle—unless it were a fraud, such as is apparent from the clumsy dialogue in which the tale is told:

> "Ow!" her mother winced, jerking a finger back from one of the welts on Kathy's stomach. "I burned myself!"
>
> "I told you to be careful, Mama!" Kathy cried. "It happened to George too!"
>
> Kathy's mother looked at him, and George nodded. "I tried putting some cold cream on them," he said, "but even that didn't help. The only way you can touch her is with gloves."
>
> "Did you call the doctor?"
>
> "No, Ma," Kathy answered.
>
> "She didn't want the doctor," George broke in. "She only wanted you." [*AH*-pb, p. 202]

There is no evidence that Mrs. Conners was a nurse or had any kind of medical knowledge beyond common sense. Is it possible to imagine anyone—enduring painful welts that are so hot they burn the fingers of those who touch them—preferring a mother's touch to a trip to the emergency room of the local hospital? Unbelievably, Anson's narrative sinks yet even deeper into absurdity:

> [*Kathy's mother is about to pick up the phone to call "Dr. Aiello."*]
>
> "No!" cried Kathy. She looked at her husband, her eyes wild. "George!"
>
> Kathy's mother was confused. "What do you mean?" she asked. "You can see she's burned all over her body."

> George was insistent. "But how are you going to explain it to him, Ma? We don't even know how it happened. She just woke up that way. He'll think we're nuts!" [*AH*-pb, p. 203]

Calling up the Demons

This awkwardly implausible episode is followed by an apparently trivial mention of something that will be needed to trigger a putatively scary episode in a later chapter: Lutz's trip to the library to get a book on witchcraft and demonology.

> At the Amityville library, George had been able to secure a temporary borrower's card and take out one book—on witches and demons. Now that his mother-in-law had gone home, he sat alone in the living room deep in the subject of the Devil and his works. It was after eight in the evening before George finished his borrowed book. …
>
> George had made notes while going through the book, and now he looked at what he had jotted down. On the pad was a list of demons, with names he had never heard of. George tried to pronounce them aloud, and they rolled strangely off his tongue. Then he decided to call Father Mancuso. … "[I] think I know how to lick this thing." He picked up the book from the table. "I've been reading about how these witches and demons work…" [*AH*-pb, p. 206]
>
> "And it says here if you hold an incantation and repeat those demons' names three times, you can call them up," George went on. "There's a ceremony in here that shows you exactly what to do. Isaron, Madeste!" George began to chant. "Those are the names of the demons, Father…"
>
> "I know who they are!" Father Mancuso blurted."
>
> "Then there's Isabo! Erz, erz—this one's hard to pronounce. Erzelaide. She has something to do with voodoo. And Eslender!"
>
> "George!" the priest cried. "For God's sake! Don't invoke those names again! Not now! Not ever!" [*AH*-pb, p. 207]

Certainly, nothing good is going to come from *that*! Paul Hoffman's article in *Good Housekeeping* informs us, "Lutz is convinced that the house is possessed by a number of spirits, 'some of whose names I won't pronounce, since merely to mention their names will bring them here'—to his mother-in-law's home" [Hoffman, "Our Dream House Was Haunted," *Good Housekeeping*, April, 1977, p. 242]. The probable reason for his belief is what Anson alleges happened immediately after the priest's command:

> "Why, Father?" George protested. "It's right here in this book. What's wrong with…." the telephone went dead in George's hand. There was an

unearthly moan, a loud clicking, and then just the sound of a disconnected line." [*AH*-pb, p. 207]

Origin of the Demonic Invocation Motif

Neither of Paul Hoffman's articles contains the invoking-the-demons motif, thus it is necessary to seek out its origins elsewhere. I was unable to find any evidence that Lutz had ever visited the Amityville Public Library before abandoning the house—leaving open the possibility of Anson's account of the library card and demonology book being true. When I was able to secure the transcript of the *Lutz v Hoffman* trial, however, the falseness of his account became clear:

[*Weber is being questioned about episodes in the book based on information he supplied to the Lutzes*]

A Towards the end of this book ... the names of the demons. Those—well, I can't say for sure whether the Lutzes located those names or I located them, but I went to this occult shop and purchased some books that had names of demons in them.
Q You gave that to them as well?
A Yes. There was another very important—
Q By the way, when you purchased those books, was that in accordance with your joint venture or joint arrangement that you then had with the Lutzes?
A Yes.
Q Did you spend your monies to purchase those books?
A Yes. Not much.
Q But it was monies that you laid out pursuant to this particular project?
A Right. [*Lutz v Hoffman*, pp. 290–291]

Crushed by a Falling Window

One of the more important episodes in this chapter is occasioned by a fearsome thunderstorm that Anson alleges besieged Amityville on Saturday, January 10, 1976:

> The rain was coming down much harder now, beating heavily against the windows and outside walls....with the coming storm, she [Kathy] wanted to play it safe. "Danny," she called. "Run up to my room and close the windows tight. Okay?"

[They hear Danny upstairs cry out in pain.]

Kathy raced ahead of George up the stairs to their bedroom. Danny stood at a window, the fingers of his right hand trapped under the window. With his left he was trying to push up the heavy wooden frame.

George pushed Kathy aside and ran to the boy who was yelling and trying to pull his fingers free. George tried to slide the window back up, but it refused to budge. He hammered at the frame but instead of releasing itself, the window vibrated, only hurting Danny more. In his frustration, George became furious and started to curse, shouting obscenities at his unseen, unknown enemies.

Suddenly the window came free on its own and shot up a few inches, freeing Danny. He grabbed his fingers in his other hand, cradling them and crying hysterically for his mother....Kathy screamed when she saw what his fingers looked like—all except the thumb were strangely flat. [*AH*-pb, pp. 208–209]

[They take Danny to "The Brunswick Hospital Center...on Broadway (actually 81 Louden Avenue) in Amityville, no more than a mile from the Lutz's house."]

The intern on duty was amazed at the condition of Danny's fingers, which were flattened from the cuticle to the second knuckle. But though they certainly looked crushed beyond repair, they were not broken, with no smashed bones or cartilage. He bandaged them securely, gave George some children's aspirin for Danny and suggested they return home. There was nothing more he could do. [*AH*-pb, p. 210]

Thanks to *The New York Times*, we know that the total lack of rain on January 10 obviated the need for Kathy to send Danny upstairs to close the window in her bedroom and provide the occasion for his fingers to be crushed by the falling window, followed by a trip to the hospital. Nevertheless, there appears to be a tiny element of fact in this sensational account.

Although Hoffman's early account of the Horror claims that this was the day on which Kathy Lutz turned into a ninety-year-old woman and makes no mention of Danny's fingers being crushed, he does provide an early account of the finger-crushing episode that allegedly occurred nearly four days later, on Tuesday, January 13, 1976. Rather than a hurricane-force storm laying the predicate for Danny's closing of the killer window, Hoffman asserts it was an impromptu exorcism:

But the Lutzes decided to stay. That night—Tuesday—Lee went through the house again, opening a window in each room, reciting the Lord's Prayer in each corner and telling the spirits, "Get out!"

> Afterward, they enlisted the aid of the children in closing the windows. Suddenly, Danny cried out with pain from the sewing room [not the master bedroom]. Lee and Kathy found that the aluminum storm window had fallen on his hands. But the pressure and pain, according to the Lutzes, were far greater than could be accounted for by the weight of the window. The grownups had difficulty lifting it.
>
> While Kathy took Danny downstairs to treat the slight cut he'd suffered, Lee remained in the sewing room. [Hoffman, "Life in a Haunted House," *New York Daily News Magazine*, July 18, 1976]

There is no mention of the fingers being crushed or flattened, no trip to a hospital for x-rays to check for broken bones. More importantly, it is the haunted *sewing room*—not the master bedroom—in which the event takes place. Most importantly, it is an aluminum storm window that falls. The fact that the windows are protected by storm windows shows that all the episodes obviated by winds and rains rushing through demonically opened windows are completely fictional.

Visions of Not-George

In *The Exorcist*, demonic sexual behavior, imagery, and vulgar sexual dialogue fairly saturate the pages of the last quarter of the novel. Curiously, it never seems gratuitous or salacious. Given the supernatural predicates of the story, it all fits naturally into the story. By contrast, there is very little dialogue or narrative with sexual overtones in *The Amityville Horror: A True Story*, and when we do encounter it, it seems contrived:

> George turned and saw Kathy standing in the doorway. No longer in her bathrobe, she had combed her hair and was wearing slacks and a sweater. Her face was slightly flushed....She felt strangely relaxed, almost sensual. Ever since she had the sensation of being stared at in her bed, Kathy had been in a languorous mood, as if she had been completely satisfied sexually. It had even carried over into her recent nap, she mused, when she had unconnected visions of making love to someone. It wasn't George.... [*AH*-pb. 207–209]

Are readers supposed to infer that it was Amityville's Horror that had satisfied her? In *The Exorcist,* demonic intercourse is common and frequent. Did Anson put this passage into his book for the sake of readers who had already read Blatty's novel? Certainly, they would have seen demonic sexual activity in this episode.

Sunday,
January 11, 1976

Events of the Day

Weather claimed: At 6:30 AM, rain is coming in through the bedroom windows, some frames are torn away from their jambs. Lutzes can hear wind and rain coming through in other parts of house. Windowpanes are broken. Doors on second and third floors are smashed open. Extensive water damage in house. Mud by Harry's compound. Steadily falling drizzle. Broken branches in street. Weather forecast: above freezing.

Actual weather: Low 20° at 12:01 AM, high 34° at 7 PM, mean 29°. Winds calm to 9 mph (gentle breeze). Precipitation 0.0 inches by 7AM; 0.15 inches by 7 PM.

The Lutzes

At 6:30 AM, George is awakened by rain falling on his face. Wind and rain are coming in through broken windows all over second and third floors, some "frames torn away from their jambs"; wind and rain are rushing into house; second- and third-floor doors have been "smashed open" despite being locked and bolted. There is extensive rain damage in house. Harry "the half-breed malamute" is "acting tough," howling at boathouse. Lutzes clean up house, tape heavy plastic sheets over broken windows, George nails windows shut with "heavy nails." He removes locks from doors of playroom and sewing room, nails pine boards across them from the hall side. George Kekoris calls, says he'd like to come to spend a night, says dogs are sensitive to psychic phenomena.

Father Mancuso

At 3:00 PM Father Ryan leaves Chancery in Rockville Centre, goes to visit "Long Island Rectory" to visit Mancuso—recovering from third attack of flu in three weeks, told "the decision would have to be his" to remain away from 112 Ocean Avenue or not. Father Mancuso says he wants to talk to the Bishop.

The Lutzes

Kathy's mother calls around 6 PM, asks if they're coming over to spend the night. Kathy says "no," as Danny and Chris had school next morning and were "missing too many days as it was." George and Harry tour the house. In the basement, Harry whimpers in front of the "red room," runs back to basement steps and up to the top. Won't go up steps to second floor. George drags him up. He hangs back in front of Missy's room and boarded up sewing room, won't enter Missy's room. On third floor, he enters boys' room, not playroom.

Father Mancuso

Mancuso confirms appointment with Bishop the next morning. His temperature is normal. High winds are in the forecast for the next day, but temperatures will be above freezing.

The Lutzes

At bedtime, all five are in the master bedroom, the children in the bed, George and Kathy in chairs beside the broken windows. Missy, then Chris, Danny, and Kathy drift off to sleep, followed by George [Anson knows this somehow]. "Very shortly" after, George is "rudely shoved awake" by Kathy. She says he was shouting "I'm coming apart!" [*In chapter 23*] He corrects her, claiming he instead said, "I'm coming unglued!" He remembers that he had felt a powerful grip lift the chair and slowly turn him around to see the hooded figure from the fireplace. (Events of January 11 and 12 now conflated).

Missy [no longer in bed of master bedroom) asks George to come to her room. "Jodie says he wants to talk to you!" She explains, "He's the biggest pig you ever saw." Lutz follows to her bedroom, no Jodie. "He'll be right back....He had to go outside for a minute." She points to window. George sees "two fiery red eyes! No face, just the mean, little eyes of a pig!" Kathy rushes in, grabs a play chair and swings it at the eyes, shattering the window. Loud squealing is heard heading for the boathouse.

Comparing Anson's Broken Windows with Blatty's

Many windows of the house at 112 Ocean Avenue were broken during the 27 or 28 days the Lutzes resided there—at least we are supposed to believe so. Not only were they allegedly broken, shattered, and ripped away from their jambs, but we are led to believe their demise came about by demonic forces—such as demon-driven hurricane-force winds. In no single case, however, do the weather records for Long Island during that accursed month allow for the *possibility* of such a physical agency, let alone its plausibility or probability. Not only do the weather records prove no such weather-related window damage ever occurred, but no contractors could be found who admitted to fixing any broken windows. Nor did the neighbors report seeing such work being done on the house. So, we must ask, why did Jay Anson have such a fixation on broken windows?

Recalling that the Amityville house had its storm windows up—making all the open-windows episodes impossible in the winter setting of the story—it seems likely (to me at least) that Anson was trying to outdo his model—*The Exorcist*, a story set in a warm season when storm windows would not be in place. A minor character in *The Exorcist* is hurled to his death through a demonically opened second-floor window and is found dead on the steps far below, and the hero of the story (Father Damien Karras) seems to have been demonically ejected through that same window and lies dead on the same steps. William Peter Blatty's single-window model was modest, compared to Amityville standards:

> Chris [the mother] knocked her drink over as she flinched at a violent splintering, at the breaking of glass, and in an instant she and Sharon [her secretary] were racing from the study, up the stairs, to the door of Regan's [the demonically possessed daughter] bedroom, bursting in. They saw the shutters of the window on the floor, ripped off their hinges! And the window! The glass had been totally shattered! [*Exorcist*, p. 390]

Jay Anson outdoes Blatty ten-fold in his account of the morning of Sunday, January 11, 1976:

> At six-thirty George … saw that every window in the room was wide open, some frames torn away from their jambs….Every room he went into was in the same condition—window panes broken, the doors on the second and third floors smashed open—even though every one had been locked *and bolted*! [emphasis added, *AH*-pb, p. 211]
>
> In the morning, they discovered that the battering rain and wind of the night before had left the house a complete mess. Rainwater had stained the walls, curtains, furniture, and rugs, from the first floor to the third floor. Ten of the windows had broken panes and several had their locks bent completely out of shape, making it impossible to shut them tightly. The locks to the doors of the sewing room and playroom were twisted and forced out of their metal frames; these couldn't be closed at all. [*AH*-pb, p. 213]

Repairing the Damage

George now must deal with the damage. After taping improbably available "heavy plastic sheets" over the windows, he proceeds to the devilishly difficult problem of locks:

> The locks on the windows and doors were a more difficult matter. George didn't have the hardware to replace the catches on the windows, so he used a pair of pliers to twist off the smashed pieces of metal. Then he hammered heavy nails into the edges of the wooden frames and challenged his unseen foes: "Let me see you pull those out, you sons of bitches!" [*AH*-pb, p. 215]

Since none of the bedroom doors *had* locks, it's hard to understand why their repair would be difficult. This is also the occasion when Lutz nails one-inch pine boards across the doors of the infested playroom and sewing room "which opened outward into the hallway." We already have seen via the blueprints that all the bedroom doors open *inward*, not outward, and they have no locks. *A fortiori*, they have no bolts. It appears this episode contains not even a scintilla of fact. In the midst of all this nonsense, George Kekoris of the Psychical Research "Institute" re-enters the narrative.

Kekoris Calling

> George Kekoris finally telephoned, saying he'd like to come out and spend a night. There was only one problem—since Kekoris had no equipment with him, the Psychical Research Institute would have to consider the visit an informal one. He would have to draw conclusions without the rigorous controls required for scientific evaluation.
>
> George said that didn't matter; he just wanted confirmation that all the weird events in their house weren't the product of his or Kathy's imagination. Kekoris asked George whether any sensitives had been there, but George didn't understand what he meant by that term. The field investigator said they would go into that when he came to visit.
>
> Before George hung up, Kekoris asked whether there was a dog in the house. George said he had Harry, a trained watch dog. Kekoris said that was good because animals were very sensitive to psychic phenomena. Again George was puzzled—but at least he had the first tangible evidence that help was on the way. [*AH*-pb, pp. 215–216]

There is no evidence to indicate George Kekoris ever tried to visit 112 Ocean Avenue during the period the Lutzes lived there, and this conversation would appear to have been concocted at least partly for the purpose of strengthening the motif of animal "sensitives." It is furthermore implausible that Kekoris could not—or would not—have defined what he meant by the term "sensitives." Clearly, the details are left out by Anson to inject a note of suspense.

What Didn't They Tell the Researchers?

We must remember that the publishing plan for *The Amityville Horror* called for "corroboration" by "outside forces." Timothy Mossman, Anson's editor at Prentice-Hall, when asked at the Lutz vs. Hoffman trial if he considered corroboration to be an important part of the book to be written—as much corroboration as could be obtained—replied "I would say it was desirable; not crucial, certainly desirable" [*Lutz v Hoffman*, p. 176].

It appears obvious that the Lutzes wouldn't have actually wanted the Psychic Research Foundation to study their house while they were still in it; the fraud would have been immediately apparent had they told the researchers about almost any of the events reported in Anson's *True Story*. Some of the original claims they made to the researchers were cited as vague and amorphous. Jerry Solfvin, the Project Director at the Foundation, told Rick Moran and Peter Jordan, "the phenomena reported were far too 'subjective' to be measured reliably" [Moran, "Amityville Horror Hoax," *Fate*, May 1978, p. 47].

Quite certainly, a wrecked overhead garage door and a 250-pound front door ripped off its hinges would not have been too subjective to measure! Unless Anson wanted to assure his editor that the Lutzes had at least *tried* to bring in outside forces to substantiate their claims, why would he have concocted an episode so absurd that he has George tell Kekoris, "he just wanted confirmation that all the weird events in their house weren't the product of his or Kathy's imagination"?

The Problem with Harry

Before moving on from our discussion of the alleged Kekoris phone call, it is necessary to tie up all Anson's accounts of the "sensitive" behavior of the canine member of the Lutz family. Whether it be Harry's attacks on the boathouse door, his refusing to go into certain rooms, whimpering, turning tail, and running out of the basement from the "secret room not on any of the blueprints," or his refusal to go up or down stairs—all these appear to have been invented to exemplify the sensitive-animal motif to reinforce the supernatural claims of the story. As if to say, "See, even the dog was aware of *The Horror* infesting the Dutch Colonial home on Ocean Avenue!"

Ecclesiastical Decisions

After the alleged phone call from George Kekoris, ecclesiastical forces reenter the story:

> At three in the afternoon, Father Ryan left the Chancery in Rockville Centre. The Chancellor was concerned about Father Mancuso's mental welfare in the Lutz case, and since one of his duties in the diocese was to minister to the rectories, Father Ryan decided that now would be a good time to visit the Long Island rectory. [*AH*-pb, p. 216]

> Father Mancuso finally said that before he made any more decisions in the case, for the Lutzes and for himself, he would like to talk directly to the Bishop. Chancellor Ryan recognized the urgency in the priest's request and said he would be in touch with the superior later in the day. He would call Father Mancuso that evening. [*AH*-pb, p. 217]

It is true that Father Ralph J. Pecoraro—the real Mancuso—was a member of the Rockville Centre Diocese. However, he did not live at "the Long Island rectory." He lived at the Sacred Heart rectory in North Merrick. Rick Moran and Peter Jordan interviewed the pastor of that parish in reference to the alleged stench in the rectory claimed for Friday January 2, 1976 [*AH*-pb, p. 142]:

> Father Alfred Casola, pastor of Sacred Heart, has dismissed as "pure and utter nonsense" the report of a pervasive odor in the rectory. Priests who were in the rectory at the time of the supposed disturbance have no recollection of any such stench and were not forced at any time to leave the building. [Moran, "Amityville Horror Hoax," *Fate*, May, 1978, p. 46].

Anson repeatedly claims that not only the Chancellors of the Rockville Centre Diocese were involved in the Lutz case, but even the Bishop himself. Pete Bowles, however, reported "The diocese has denied that any psychic incidents cited in the book as involving clerical officials ever took place" [Bowles, "Amityville Book," *Newsday*, Sept. 13, 1979, p. 25]. A healthy skepticism seems warranted here, and I am uncertain who was telling the truth.

A Lying Priest?

Moran and Jordan also interviewed "Mancuso," although they did not reveal his true name:

> Father Mancuso, who is in fact associated with the Rockville Center [*sic*] diocese (at least Anson has that much right), flatly denies ever having entered the Lutz home. He further denies that he heard a phantom voice command him to vacate the premises, which in any case he was never on. [Moran, "Amityville Horror Hoax," *Fate*, May 1978, p. 46]

At the *Lutz v Hoffman* trial [pp. 338–339, 341, 451] Father Pecoraro repeatedly admitted that he had blessed the Lutz home and had heard a noise that sounded like "Get out!" Which means he was lying to Moran and Jordan when they interviewed him. Curiously, it appears he also lied to Atty. Weber. While being cross-examined by Atty. Daley, Weber was asked about his conversations with the priest:

> Q Mr. Weber, I believe you previously indicated that you have talked to the priest and he had denied blessing the house or knowing the Lutzes; is that correct?
>
> A No. He denied blessing the house. … He said that he had received a telephone call on several occasions from Mr. Lutz, and that he had spoken to the Lutzes after they had left the house. He told me—I asked him specifically if he had been in the house, and he said he was never in the house. [*Lutz v Hoffman*, p. 360]

The Roman Ritual and Papal Exorcisms

Given the mendacity documented in the trial transcript, we must ask to what degree did Rev. Ralph Pecoraro credit the possibility of the house being demonically infested? The answer, probably more than he was ever supposed to admit. Volume II of the Roman Catholic handbook, *The Roman Ritual: Christian Burial, Exorcism, Reserved Blessings, etc.* [pp. 160-229], gives not only the proper instructions for diagnosing demonic possession but even the exact Latin incantations with which to exorcise them—as well as the plainchant notation needed for proper disenchantment. Amazingly, *The Amityville Horror: A True Story* begins with a preface by Father John Nicola, an expert on poltergeists and author of the treatise *Demonical Possession and Exorcism*.

During the 1970s there were widespread rumors that the Vatican itself had helped to finance the filming of *The Exorcist*, but I was never able to confirm or disconfirm them. It seems relevant that William Peter Blatty wrote the novel on which the movie was based at the suggestion of a high-level church official. In the "acknowledgments" paragraph at the end of the book, Blatty wrote that he "would also like to thank the Rev. Thomas V. Bermingham, S.J., Vice-Provincial for Formation of the New York Province of the Society of Jesus, for suggesting the subject matter of this novel."

Of even greater relevance to the question of clerical involvement at the heart of the Amityville story, however, are the seemingly credible reports that even the current pope still believes in demons and has himself performed an exorcism! Chris Roberts' article "Exorcism and Demonic Possession Are Now Tools in the Culture Wars" includes a YouTube video of Pope Francis apparently trying to exorcise two people. Roberts claims:

> More and more Catholics report seeking exorcisms, and as the BBC reported last year, 250 priests from 50 countries traveled to Rome for exorcist training. Francis is encouraging this: in 2017, the pope told priests that "they must not hesitate" to refer their parishioners to exorcists if they experience "genuine spiritual disturbances." [Roberts, "Exorcism and Demonic Possession."]

Overlooked Clues

In the course of studying this allegedly "True Story," it has frequently been the case that something that would seem to be utterly trivial and insignificant relative to the general arc of the narrative turns out to be crucial for critical understanding of what actually happened at 112 Ocean Avenue. In every good whodunit or mystery novel, a surprise ending is tied to a hint of foreshadowing dropped into the plot near the beginning. For example, in *The Exorcist*, the archaeologist-priest's discovery of a statue of the demon Pazuzu in Iraq suddenly explodes into the critical episode—many pages later, when the earlier scene had probably been forgotten by most readers—from which the novel earns its title: the archaeologist-priest is also an exorcist, who dies in the denouement of the story. In the case of Jay Anson's tale, such apparently trivial things need not be found at the beginning of the story, but for a critical investigator they can function as loose threads that threaten to unravel the entire narrative when one pulls on them.

One such case involves a detail completely unnoticed when I first read *The Amityville Horror* forty years ago. In fact, it escaped my attention even when I first resumed work on this book and reread the novel to refresh my memory:

> Kathy's mother called her around six o'clock, wanting to know if they were coming to her house to spend the night. Kathy took it on herself to say no: the house was still in a mess after the storm and she would have a lot of washing to do the next morning. And besides, Danny and Chris would have school, and *they were missing too many days as it was*. [*AH*-pb, p. 217]

After going through the story for the umpteenth time, it suddenly occurred to me that I couldn't remember any cases where the children had been forced to miss school because of the "forces" allegedly shaping the activities of the family. I had managed to obtain a digital copy of the book, and so I was able to perform a search for the word "school" to be exhaustive in my study. The first relevant mention of school relates to the day after the Lutzes moved into the house:

> Drinking coffee, Kathy sat at the table with a pad and pencil, making notes for herself on the jobs to be done around the house. Today was the nineteenth [*of December*], a Friday. The kids would not go to their new school until after the Christmas holidays. [*AH*-pb, p. 31]

The Christmas vacation apparently had ended by Monday, January 5, 1976, when we read:

> Kathy sensed someone was staring at her. Startled, she looked up and over her shoulder. Her little daughter was standing in the doorway. Danny and Chris had told their father that they heard on their radio that the Amityville schools were closed because of a heating problem. They were somewhat disappointed, *because it would have been their first day at their new school after the Christmas holidays and a chance to meet some new friends*. [emphasis added, *AH*-pb, pp. 152-153]

That same evening, we are told, "Evidently the heating problem had been solved, because the local Amityville radio station had announced that the schools would be open the next morning" [*AH*-pb, p. 157]. That is all we are told about the children's school attendance records. Nowhere does Anson tell us of demonic events preventing the children from going to school.

Escape, Thwarted

We now must ask why Anson put in the seemingly insignificant, false comment about the kids "missing too many days as it was." An important theme running through the book is the need for the family to flee the house as soon as possible. First, it is the ecclesiastical authorities who urge them to leave, at least temporarily. A bit later, Kathy's mother makes her own pleas. Then, the Lutzes themselves make plans to leave, but readers begin to suspect that "occult forces" are trapping them in the house in order to complete the process of demonic possession. Could it have been the Devil who made Kathy place her children's education above their very souls, keeping the family trapped in the house for yet one more horrific night?

And what a night it turns out to be! We don't realize what all happened on the night of Sunday, January 11, 1976, until we are on page

224—*in Anson's account of January 12,* 1976. Only after careful reconstruction of the temporal sequence of the family's travails do we discover what all happened when they were forced to spend another night in the horror house. Anson must have been hiding in the master-bedroom closet to document "One after another, they drifted off—first Missy, then Chris, Danny, Kathy, and finally George. Within ten minutes, everyone was fast asleep" [p. 220]. Shortly thereafter, George is awakened by Kathy who tells him he had been yelling "I'm coming apart!" Although the fact is not reported until the next chapter—Chapter 23, purporting to chronicle the events of Monday, January 12—George corrects her and says he had been yelling "I'm coming unglued!"

Remembering the Ku Klux Demon

Although the significance of George's correction eludes me, Anson has George immediately remember something of clear magnitude in the unfolding of the plot:

> Now he remembered he had been sitting in the chair when suddenly he felt a powerful grip lift up the chair with him in it and slowly turn him around. Powerless to move, George saw the hooded figure he had first seen in the living room fireplace, its blasted half-face glaring at him. The horribly disfigured features became clearer to George. "God help me!" he screamed. Then he saw his own face emerge from beneath the white hood. It was torn in two. "I'm coming unglued!" George yelled. [*AH*-pb, pp. 221–222]

Confronting Jodie the Pig

After a bit of argument between the adults, Missy breaks in with "Daddy … come to my room. Jodie says he wants to talk to you!" George asks Kathy, "Who's Jodie?" Kathy answers that Jodie is Missy's imaginary friend. "I told you, she makes up imaginary people. You can't see Jodie." Missy corrects her mother, saying, "I see him all the time. He's the biggest pig you ever saw." George rushes to the girl's bedroom but sees no pig. "Where's this Jodie?" he asks. "He'll be right back," she says, "He had to go outside for a minute."

A moment later, Missy shouts:

> "There he is, Daddy!"
>
> George looked down at Missy. She was pointing to one of her windows. His eyes followed her finger and he started. Staring at him through one of the panes were two fiery red eyes! No face, just the mean, little eyes of a pig!

"That's Jodie!" cried Missy. "He wants to come in!" [AH-pb, pp. 222–223]

In high melodrama, Kathy rushes in, grabs one of the little play chairs and swings it at the eyes in the window, shattering the window. "There was an animal cry of pain, a loud squealing—and the eyes were gone!" It sounds like the pig is headed for the boathouse.

Pigs in *The Exorcist*

None of this could have occurred if Kathy hadn't insisted that the boys shouldn't miss any more days of school (remember that the other excuse—having to clean up after the storm—is ruled out by the weather records.) All these events are needed to clinch a diagnosis of demonic possession in progress. The pig theme seems, once again, to be derived from *The Exorcist*, where swinishness is integral to the demon possessing the young girl. Although pigs are not mentioned in *The Roman Ritual* as being related to possession, all things piggish are integral to the demon inside the girl Regan. It seems to me almost certain that "Jodie the pig" is a character modeled after Blatty's demon, a.k.a. "Captain Howdy."

In the scene where Regan is masturbating with a crucifix, she addresses her mother as, "Aahh, little pig mother!" and croons, "with a guttural, rasping, throaty eroticism. 'Lick me, lick me, lick me! Aahhhhh!'" The demon calls Regan, "Ahh, there's my sow, yes, my sweet honey piglet, my piglet, my—" [*Exorcist*, p. 226] The pig motif reaches its climax during Father Karras' interrogation of the demon:

> "Are you saying that you *aren't* the devil?"
> "Just a poor struggling demon. *A* devil. A subtle distinction, but one not entirely lost upon Our Father who is in Hell. Incidentally, you won't mention my slip of the tongue to him, Karras, now will you? Eh? When you see him!"
> "See him? Is he here?" asked the priest.
> "In the pig? Not at all. Just a poor little family of wandering souls, my friend. You don't blame us for being here, do you? After all, we have no place to go. No home."
> "And how long are you planning to stay?"
> The head jerked up from the pillow, contorted in rage as it roared, "Until the piglet *dies*!" [Exorcist, p. 277]

Soot-Demon Testimony

Let us now return to Lutz's memory of being lifted into the air—chair and all—and rotated to see "the hooded figure he had first seen in the living room fireplace, its blasted half-face glaring at him. The horribly disfigured features became clearer to George.…Then he saw his own face emerge from beneath the white hood." First, let's recall what George and Kathy were alleged to have seen in the fireplace one minute into the new Year of Our Lord, One Thousand Nine Hundred Seventy-Six:

> [*Kathy*] stared into the fireplace… Something was materializing in those flames—a white outline against the blackened bricks—becoming clearer, more distinct.…She couldn't even tear her eyes away from the demon with horns and a white peaked hood on its head. It was getting larger, looming toward her. She saw that half of its face was blown away, as if hit with a shotgun blast at close range.…George followed her gaze and he saw it too—a white figure that had burned itself into the soot against the rear bricks of the fireplace. [*AH*-pb, p. 116]

Second, let's reread Lutz's confusing "clarification" of the exact appearance of the soot-demon:

Q Now, did you ever see, while you were in the house, Mr. Lutz, this fated house, a demon with horns wearing a white peaked hood, in the fireplace?
A There was a—I don't know how else to describe it. But something very ugly, a picture of something that was in the blackened back wall of the fireplace was in an outline of white. Again, when the researchers went in on March 6th, they came back to us and they said, "What was that? How did that get there?" We don't know how it got there. One day it was there.
Q You saw a demon with black horns?
A I wouldn't refer to it as a demon. It looked more like someone in a Ku Klux Klan outfit.
Q The book refers to it as a demon with horns.
A It also appeared in one part that the entire upper body was missing.
Q And you saw this in the fireplace?
A It was etched into the bricks somehow. It was white over black background.
Q And Mr. Lutz, how long did that etching remain on the bricks?
A I know it was still there on March 6th, when the investigators came, which was two months later.…They came back and asked us what it was.
Q When was the last time that you saw the demon with the horns and the white peaked hood on its head?
A I never referred to it that way, sir.
Q That reference in the book was not correct?

A It's certainly correct. It's certainly a way of describing it that I don't necessarily agree with. The point is, it was there, it was still there two months later when other people went in and the last time I saw it, it would have been the last day we were in the house, which would have been January 14, 1976. [*Lutz v Hoffman*, pp. 64–65]

Gone from the Fireplace

Exactly what, if anything, can be known about what the Lutzes saw in the fireplace? *Newsday* reporters Alex Drehsler and Jim Scovel tell us:

> Lutz tells of seeing the white figure of a demon's face burned into the gray, cinderblock, back firewall of the fireplace. The Cromartys [*the next owners of the house*], who said they had not used the fireplace since the Lutzes left, showed it to reporters. It does have a white pattern burned in—but one similar to those in many other fireplaces. [Drehsler, "Amityville Horror Fact or Fiction?" *Newsday*, November 17, 1977]

Even without the report of the burn marks in the fireplace, Lutz's testimony at the fraud trial reveals an ability to believe simultaneously in a demon with horns and a white, peaked hood on its head—as well as a demon lacking "an entire upper body." This argues that we must treat this either as hopelessly delusional thinking or as deceptive reporting.

Monday, January 12, 1976

Events of the Day

Weather claimed: [*end of chapter 22*] High winds forecast, temperatures to "remain above freezing." That morning, Mancuso shivers "in the cold, nippy air." No precipitation implied.
Actual weather: 23° at 4:30 AM, 35° at 12:15 PM. Mean 29°. Winds 3 to 12 mph (calm to moderate breeze). Precipitation: 0.04 by 7 AM, 0.0 by 7 PM.

The Lutzes and Mancuso

George and Kathy are still in their chairs dozing by the window, the children in the big bed. Mancuso drives to Rockville Centre through "cold, nippy air." He has a brief meeting with the Bishop, who has the Lutz file on his desk. The Bishop suggests Mancuso see a psychiatrist.

The Lutzes

Kathy wakes the children, gives them breakfast, and takes all three with her in the van to take the boys to school. When she returns, George is "still in a zombie-like state." He nails plywood over Missy's window. A call from Syosset says the IRS is due at the office at noon. After he leaves for the meeting, Kathy says she'll call a glazier in Amityville to fix their broken windows. She gives Missy lunch. Kekoris calls, says he's sick, but will be able to spend Wednesday night with the Lutzes.

Missy has secret conversation with Jodie under the kitchen table [breakfast nook à la Exorcist?]. Kathy asks her if Jodie is an angel. Missy says that's what Jodie told her. Missy tells her about the little boy who used to live in her room and died there. "Last night he said I was going to live here forever so I could play with the little boy."

The IRS session doesn't go well. George says he'll pick the boys up from school on his way home. Arriving home after 3 PM, Kathy's says they're going to go to her mother's house because of the Jodie conversation. They start to leave. Harry is barking. George goes to bring him inside, releasing him from leash. Harry rushes to boathouse, leaps against the door. They drag him by his collar back into house as Slavic-accented window repairman arrives in van. By 6 PM, all windows are fixed except for Missy's. He hadn't been harmed fixing windows in playroom and sewing room. It needs a carpenter. Lutzes have supper in kitchen nook.

Father Mancuso

Before going to bed, Mancuso concludes that the evil forces at 112 Ocean Avenue are demonic.

The Lutzes

The kids are set to sleep in master bedroom again, with Harry down in the cellar for the night!

What Day Is It—Actually?

We have already noted that the first four pages of "Chapter 22: January 12" actually pertain to events of January 11, 1976. When those events are removed from consideration, it turns out not much of narrative importance happens on Monday, January 12, 1976. Although the day's temperature was reported to "remain above freezing"—despite the mean temperature for the 12th being 29° and the mean temperatures for the previous two days also reported as below freezing—and Anson forecasted high winds with the actual winds as "calm to moderate breeze," nothing in the narrative is affected by the weather. The major events of the day are George's meeting with the IRS at his office in Syosset, Missy's conversation with Jodie "the angel," and the visit of a Slavic-accented window repairman.

Authorial Omniscience Issues

Of course, there are the usual, insidious problems concerning authorial omniscience. They arise in every chapter of the book and, by themselves, are strong signals of fictivity. How did Anson know that "George let out his breath" after being told Jodie "had to go outside for a minute" [p. 222]? How did he know "George had expected the worst when he heard the word 'pig'" [p. 222]? Had George read *The Exorcist*? Were the tapes Anson received from the Lutzes that detailed? Moreover, how did Anson know "George and Kathy were still dozing in their chairs, the children asleep in the big bed," at the same time "Father Mancuso bundled up and drove to Rockville Centre [p. 224]? How did he learn the details of the conversations between the Chancellors, Mancuso, and the Bishop [p. 224]?

How did Anson know that "before he retired Tuesday night" (why mention this in the chapter for Monday, January 12?), "Father Mancuso prayed that this evil force could somehow be reasoned with; that it should know what it was doing was totally insane" [p. 230]? How did he spy on the priest's thoughts to learn "the priest knew there was only one answer—it had to be demonic" [p. 230]? Anson had only a few phone interviews with Father Pecoraro; it is unlikely that the priest could have remembered the details of thoughts and prayers months later even if he had been asked about them. Moreover, Father Pecoraro could not possibly have known that the Lutzes were dozing in their chairs while he drove to Rockville Centre. Clearly, we are reading a novel, not "A True Story."

In an interview with *Newsday* reporter Alex Drehsler, Anson almost admitted as much:

> Anson said that "as a writer, I use a little literary license," specifically in reconstructing a purported dispute between Mancuso and the rectory pastor. Anson noted that he had stated in the book that the events were true "to the extent that I can verify them." But Mossman [*Anson's editor*] when questioned on the book, said that "the necessity was—and the author and I agreed on this—was the change the circumstances so that, yes, the book is not strictly true. And yet the intent of what was discovered, or alleged, still remained. But the facts had to be changed simply to protect the guilty or innocent so that Prentice-Hall and the authors were not sued. [Drehsler, "Amityville Fact or Fiction?" *Newsday*, November 17, 1977]

The Tax Man Cometh

From the viewpoint of the present investigation, the most important paragraphs in this chapter concern George Lutz's problems with the Internal Revenue Service, which were previously included as minor details in previous chapters. We first learn of the problems in the account of Monday, December 29, 1976:

> In Syosset, George found a caller waiting for him. The man introduced himself as an inspector from the Internal Revenue Service and explained he was there to examine the company's books and past tax returns. George called his accountant. The IRS agent spoke with him and made an appointment to return on January 7th. [*AH*-pb, p. 101]

Details of possibly actual importance appear in the account of Wednesday, December 31, 1975:

> George was beginning to choke with the pressures of mounting bills; for the house he had just taken on, and for the office, where he would shortly

> have a very serious payroll deficit. All the cash that he and Kathy had saved had gone toward the expense of the closing, an old fuel bill, and paying off the boats and motorcycles [plural]. And now the latest blow—the Internal Revenue Service. Small wonder that George dreamed of a simple magical solution to the bind he was in. [*AH*-pb, p. 1120]

While there are obvious problems with authorial omniscience in this paragraph, we shall see there are reasons to suppose the gist of the report is true, as well as that of the report for Monday, January 5, 1976:

> Kathy came downstairs just as the telephone rang. It was George's office, calling to ask when he was coming in. The Internal Revenue agent was due back and they did not know how George wanted to handle the situation. George squirmed. Finally he told his bookkeeper to call their accountant and postpone the appointment until the following week. [AH-pb, p. 153]

Then, on Monday, January 12, 1976, the problems become important enough for Anson to detail:

> Upstairs, George had just nailed plywood [how did he happen to have plywood?] over the shattered window frame to protect the room from damage by the weather when Kathy called up from the kitchen that his office in Syosset wanted him on the telephone. The company's accountant reminded George that the Internal Revenue Agent was due to come by at noon. Not wanting to leave the house, George asked the accountant to handle the tax situation himself, but the man refused. It was George's responsibility to determine how to pay the taxes. [*AH*-pb, p. 215] …
>
> George's session with the IRS had not gone well. The agent had disallowed deduction after deduction, and George's only hope lay in the appeal the agent said he could file. It was a temporary reprieve, at least. [*AH*-pb, p. 217]

Financial Pressures behind the "True Story"?

Could it be the Lutzes cooked up their *True Story* because of personal financial problems and business problems with the IRS? Curt Supplee of the *Washington Post* suspected as much. In his article "Dolors to Dollars: Big Bucks and Big Questions in the Tale of a House Possessed," he wrote that the obvious literary structuring of the story:

> provokes one to doubt [the veracity of the story], and the history of how the book came to be published is not reassuring. By his own admission,

> George Lutz was having financial problems *at the time he bought the house* [emphasis added], including potential trouble with the IRS over his business taxes. A short time after he and his family left 112 Ocean Avenue, one of Lutz's friends suggested that he tell his story to Prentice-Hall. [Supplee, "Dolors to Dollars," *Washington Post*, December 9, 1977]

In his *Washington Post* article "The Calamityville Horror," Michael Kernan reported some of the financial stresses George Lutz was experiencing:

> "Lutz thought he could just swing it by running his surveying business from his house and by putting his cabin cruiser and speedboat in the boathouse, thus saving marina fees" [Kernan, "Calamityville Horror," *Washington Post*, September 16, 1979].

According to the *Newsday* article "DeFeo Home Abandoned, Buyer Calls It Haunted," by A.J. Carter and Christopher M. Cook,

> One friend of Lutz said that the family left the house because they had used up all their money buying it and could not afford to repair the heating system, which failed when they moved in. But the friend would not deny that Lutz had talked about strange happenings in the house. [Carter, "DeFeo Home Abandoned," *Newsday*, February 14, 1976]

Two years later, Patricia Burstein and Sue Reilly wrote in *People* magazine that the Lutzes still were experiencing financial problems:

> George and Kathy Lutz feel abused. Having survived one set of horrors, they complain, they now find themselves plunged into debt and at the mercy of skeptical journalists. Though they are renting a $100,000 house outside San Diego, they say they can't afford a home of their own and must make do with one car—unusual in Southern California. Presumably they are using their royalties to pay off their debts, and George, who sold his surveying business after fleeing Long Island, has been looking in vain for a job as an air traffic controller. [Burstein, "Amityville Horror Lives On," *People*, February 13, 1978]

Three years after the Lutzes abandoned the house, Jerry Cassidy, in his *Daily News* article "Hosts of ghosts put Amityville tourist haunt on block" reported:

> "The Lutzes abandoned the house. The bank holding the mortgage took possession of the property, which subsequently, was purchased by Jim

> and Barbara Cromarty for a reported $55,000" [Cassidy, "Hosts of Ghosts," *Daily News*, February 16, 1979].

That same year, Kathy Lutz was quoted in an article in *The Star*:

> "So, we sought an isolated place to live with few neighbors and where we hope our past will make no difference."
>
> They are now planning to move from their luxurious duplex overlooking the ocean to a small farm in the southern part of the Golden State. But although the book has forced them to find a hideaway, *it also solved the financial crisis they faced after fleeing from Amityville* [emphasis added].
>
> Kathy said: "Having forfeited our $28,000 equity in the house and with George having given up his civil engineering business plus having received only about $1,800 from the auction of $45,000 of our things we just left there [*including the cabin cruiser, speedboat, and motorcycles*?], the idea of getting some income to keep our family going was not only appealing but downright necessary."
>
> George added: "Whatever monies we got, we never guessed that we would spend $70,000 of it on legal costs." [Anonymous, "We Just Wish It Would End," *The Star*, July 24, 1979]

I would differ with the anonymous author of this article in *The Star* concerning the timing of the financial crisis experienced by the Lutzes. It developed, I think, not "*after* fleeing from Amityville." Rather, it seems clear the financial crisis is what forced them to abandon the house in the first place.

More *Exorcist* Parallels

Anson's account of Monday, January 12, 1976, contains multiple episodes that strongly resemble their *Exorcist* model. In both novels, the possessed girl has conversations with an invisible friend. At first, the conversations are secret, overheard by the mother. Then the child reports the conversations to the mother. In both books, the friend turns out not to be so friendly. In *The Exorcist*, Regan is attacked by "Captain Howdy." In *The Amityville Horror*, the malignancy of the transformation is more subtle, but as ominous as could be without straining the credulity of even the most credulous readers. After Missy reports that Jodie the pig had told her about a little boy who had died in the house, she tells her mother, "Last night he said I was going to live here forever so I could play with the little boy" [*AH*-pb, p. 227] Very chilling, indeed.

Foreign Accents

Anson manages to parallel another, minor motif of *The Exorcist* in our *True Story*. In Blatty's novel, Karl (Chris' butler/factotum/handyman) is Swiss-German and has an accent and foreign syntax so strong it draws ridicule from Director Dennings—the first person to die in the house [*Exorcist*, pp. 39*ff*.] In the *True Story*, the Lutzes are unable to flee the house because of the arrival of a glazier:

> As [George] and the boys were drawing Harry into the house, a van pulled into the driveway. George saw that it was a window repairman. He and Kathy looked at one another. "Oh, my God," Kathy said, "I forgot all about having called him." They hadn't reckoned on this kind of delay.
>
> His pudgy face and broad accent gave away his Slavic descent. "I figured you folks needed the fixing right away," he said, "what with the bad weather we been having. Yah," he continued as he opened his rear doors, "better to fix now. If everything inside get wet because of outside, it cost you more money." [*AH*-pb, p. 229]

By six o'clock, all windows had been repaired except the one in Missy's bedroom that, after Kathy's attack with a toy chair, needed the skills of a carpenter. How the windows in the boarded-up rooms were repaired is not disclosed. George doesn't remove the boards from the door of the playroom until the following day.

Tuesday, January 13, 1976

Events of the Day

Weather claimed: Rain, lightning, thunder, a cold gust of east wind slams van hood down. Clouds broke "solid sheet of water." By 1:00 PM, "another storm of hurricane strength," 20 degrees, and sleet pelting Long Island: "enormous low-pressure system," electricity & phone are out. It's dark by 4:30 PM. Still storming at 6 PM. At 8 PM, "all the water in the world was being dumped on top of 112 Ocean Avenue." "Torrents of water were still smashing against the house."

Actual weather: Low temperature 24° at 2:10 AM, high 42° at 7 PM, mean 33°. Precipitation 0.0 inches by 7 AM; 0.01 inches by 7 PM; winds indeed from the east all day, but at 3–13 mph (calm to moderate breeze).

The Lutzes

At 3:15 AM, a marching band is again downstairs in living room. George dozes off in his chair, is wakened by Kathy because he's screaming in two different languages Kathy's never heard before. Then with different voice, he cries out "It's in Chris' room!"

From his position [boy's room and playroom reversed] he can see up through the ceiling to the boys' bedroom on third floor. He sees shadowy figure at Chris' bed. George is pinned to his seat by an invisible hand on his shoulder. He sees Chris is out of bed, wrapped in the dark shape. He wakes screaming "It's got Chris!" Kathy says Chris is with them there in bed. It turns out, Chris *was* upstairs. He'd woken up to go to the bathroom, but it was locked. So, he went up to the third floor. He says he could look through the floor and see George. They stay awake the rest of the night.

Lutz and Mancuso

In the morning Lutz calls Mancuso, who's just showered for first time in days, still has dark circles under eyes. Lutz tells him they're going to leave the house.

The Lutzes

Danny and Chris don't go to school. Lutz wants to call police to tell them they're leaving the house, but the phone is now dead. George brings Harry up from cellar, puts him in the back of the van. Van won't start. George takes "a look under the hood" of his 1974 Ford van. A gust of wind slams down the hood; thunder and lighting, and "a solid sheet of water ... drenched George immediately." They all run back into house as "Amityville was hit by another storm of hurricane strength." Power is out, 20 degrees and "sleet pelting all of Long Island."

George shoves towels into spaces in Missy's broken window where it separated from the frame. At 4:30 "it was as if night had already settled over 112 Ocean Avenue" [just nineteen minutes before sunset]. No lights in house, as "all the water in the world was being dumped on top of 112 Ocean Avenue." Heat rises throughout house, despite non-functioning furnace. Candle in hand, Lutz goes from room to room praying. Green slime is coming out of lock holes in playroom door. George pulls off boards from door, playroom is empty. By 8 PM torrents of water are still smashing against the house. Notes exact time on kitchen [electric?] clock. George puts everyone to bed.

George and Harry are alone in living room enduring the excessive heat. George thinks of going out to try to start van, but "its engine probably would be wet by now." The 90-degree heat breaks at 10:00 PM. It's 60 degrees a half-hour later. George goes to basement to grab logs for fire. Hears Missy cry, goes to her bedroom to cover her up. Kathy sleeping on her stomach "like a drugged person." George doesn't light fire. He brings Harry to master bedroom to block the door, kicks off shoes and joins Kathy and Missy in bed.

The Signs of Possession

In this chapter, our chronicle is now nearing its climax. Unfortunately, as we shall see, the actual weather conditions recorded in the *New York Times* rule out much of it. It is clear the crescendo of activity occurring in this chapter draws heavily from the rules for demonic possession enumerated in *The Exorcist*. Anson's model says that "Signs of possession may be the following: ability to speak with some facility in a strange language..." [p. 259]. Anson tells us "George must have dozed off in his chair, because Kathy awoke to hear him screaming. He was yelling in two different tongues—languages she had never heard before!" [*AH*-pb, p. 231].

The Exorcist model would have informed Anson that "Oesterreich had characterized as 'genuine' possession" a "striking change in the voice and in the features, plus the manifestation of a new personality" [p. 263]. Anson then records "George began groaning, and when Kathy touched him, he cried out in another completely different voice: It's in Chris' room!" [*AH*-pb, p. 231].

The model I believe Anson was imitating requires "the faculty of divulging future and hidden events; display of powers which are beyond the subject's age and natural condition" [p. 259]. This is beautifully fulfilled in Chapter 24 January 13"—not only by George, but by Chris as well: "George is positive he wasn't dreaming. From his position [in the second-floor bedroom] he was sure he could see clear to the boys' bedroom on the third floor. He had been watching a shadowy figure approach Chris' bed [*AH*-pb, p. 233]. When Kathy tells him Chris isn't on the third floor, but "here in bed all the time," Chris corrects her:

> "No, Mama. I had to go to the bathroom before."
> "I never heard you. Did you use my bathroom?"
> "Unh-unh. The door was locked, so I went upstairs."
> George went to the bathroom. The door *was* locked.
> "Upstairs?" asked Kathy.
> "Yeah," Chris answered. "But I got scared."
> "Why," his father asked.
> "Because I could look through the floor and see you, Daddy." [*AH*-pb, p. 234]

We shall never know how the bathroom door became locked with no one in it. Frustratingly, Anson never tells us whether the Lutzes could not use the bathroom for the remainder of their tenancy at 112 Ocean Avenue, or if George managed to unlock a door that usually locks and unlocks only from the inside. Anson, it seems, was checking off a list of requirements for demonic possession when he wrote this chapter. For good measure, he has Father Mancuso display the power of precognition:

> Even before he answered the telephone, the priest knew who was calling "Yes, George?" he asked.
> George was too preoccupied to notice that Father Mancuso had anticipated him. [*AH*-pb, p. 235]

As for Oesterreich's final stipulation that possession must involve "the manifestation of a new personality," from the early days of the Lutz habitation to the end, everyone in the family from George to Missy to Harry the dog are alleged to be undergoing personality changes. Indeed, personality change is the most frequently encountered possession motif in the entire book.

Looking under the Hood

Undoubtedly to heighten anxiety and tension in the reader, Anson has the Amityville Horror sabotage the family's 1974 Ford van—once again blocking their escape from the demon-infested domicile:

> George climbed behind the wheel of the van. He turned the ignition key but the motor wouldn't turn over. "George?" Kathy's voice quivered. "What's wrong?"
> "Take it easy," he said. "We got enough gas. Let me take a look under the hood"
> As he got out of the van, he looked up at the sky. The clouds had grown dark and menacing. George felt a cold wind picking up. By the time he lifted the hood, the first raindrops were hitting the windshield.
> George never got a good look at what could have caused the van to stall. A huge gust of wind blew in from the Amityville River in the back of the house, and the hood was slammed down. George had just leaped aside to avoid the falling metal when a lightning bolt struck behind the garage. The clap of thunder was almost instantaneous, and the clouds broke in a solid sheet of water that drenched George immediately. [*AH*-pb, p. 236]

Recalling the actual total precipitation recorded for the day had been 0.01 inches by 7:00 PM, and the winds had "gusted" all the way from 3 mph (calm) up to 13 mph (moderate breeze), it is immediately apparent that this episode is a total fiction. And poorly researched fiction at that. Of course, Anson was writing before Google was available, and so he could not easily know what my readers can determine with their smartphones: the hoods on 1974 Ford vans could not "slam down" or cause someone to leap aside "to avoid the falling metal." The "hood" of the van spans the width of the vehicle and is about fourteen inches high. It is just a steeply sloping metal flap at the front of the vehicle.

Anson's error in automotive anatomy is not the only thing wrong with the passage just quoted. Since Anson had never been allowed to inspect the house of which he was to write, he apparently did not know that the garage and the boathouse are actually a single, long, rectangular building. The garage constitutes roughly the front half of the building, the boathouse the back half bordering the Amityville River. If "a lightning bolt struck behind the garage," it would have hit the boathouse! Anson should have written "when a lightning bolt struck behind the *boathouse*..."

Anson's chapter dealing with Tuesday, January 13, 1976 contains a repeat performance of the marching band, the reappearance of green slime, heating problems in the house, and one last subtle reference to Ronnie DeFeo. Because the neighbors claimed to have not heard the eight shots of the murderer's rifle, it was supposed for a while that Ronnie had drugged his family so he could turn them all onto their stomachs and shoot them in the backs of their heads at leisure. Ominously, in this penultimate night in the demon-infested house, Anson tells us "Kathy, on her stomach, was sleeping like a drugged person, not moving or turning in bed" [*AH*-pb, p. 241].

Departure Delayed Again

Once again, because the "hurricane-force" storm has knocked the power out, Lutz must carry a candle so he could go "from room to room, asking the Lord to send away whoever didn't belong there" [*AH*-pb, p. 238]. Later, with the power still out and "torrents of water … still smashing against the house, he somehow knew they wouldn't be allowed to leave 112 Ocean Avenue that night. He picked Kathy up in his arms and took her to their bedroom, noting the time on the kitchen clock. It was exactly 8 PM" [*AH*-pb, p. 239]. I previously suspected the kitchen clock was an electric clock that would not have functioned with the power out, but I couldn't confirm the fact: no kitchen clock was listed in the auction catalogue when the Lutzes' household furnishings went up for sale.

Alas, Amityville's Horror is not yet finished with the Lutz family. There is one more night in its swinish scenario left to be played out in the Dutch Colonial house located at 112 Ocean Avenue on Long Island's South Shore.

Wednesday, January 14, 1976

Events of the Day

Weather claimed: At 1 AM there is a "raging storm outside"; "George felt he was freezing," no heat in house. The storm stops, the weather turns cold. The lightning storm returns, a thunderbolt strikes "close outside," "torrents of rain and wind lashing 112 Ocean Ave." Storm ends by dawn. (They flee the house at 7:00 AM).

Actual weather: Low temperature 35° at 7:00 PM, high 52° at 2:45 AM, mean 44°, 49° at 1:00 AM. Precipitation 0.39 inches by 7:00 AM; 0.0 inches by 7:00 PM. Winds SE 14 mph at 1:00 AM (moderate breeze), 20–25 mph from 3:00–5:00 AM (strong breeze).

The Lutzes

At 1:00 AM, George is freezing, a storm is raging outside. Kathy stands up, sleepwalks over to mirror to look at herself in candlelight. Harry prevents her from walking out of the bedroom. George seizes her and she collapses limp in his arms. He puts her back to bed. Harry vomits in doorway, the odor making Lutz gag also. The storm has stopped. Weather turns cold.

Noise above Lutz's head (the paperback floor plan is changed from original layout) because "The boys' beds were sliding back and forth!" Dresser drawers open and close in bedroom. Loud voices are heard downstairs, then the marching band starts again. George is thrashing back and forth on bed. The dog is undisturbed, as though drugged. Thunderbolt nearby. Storm is back. A silent scream as he lies held to his bed. Something with hooves steps on him.

At dawn, the storm over, George is awakened by the boys. They report a faceless monster in their room; Harry is growling at staircase. George finally can stand up, rushes into hallway and sees giant white hooded figure at top of stairs—the figure Kathy saw in fireplace. Danny carries Missy, George carries Kathy, they all rush out of the house to the van. Harry jumps in with them. Lutz prays, turns the key in the ignition and it starts. At 7:00 AM, January 14, 1976, they abandon the house.

Father Mancuso

As Lutzes are fleeing the house, Mancuso decides to leave town. At 11:00 AM he calls his cousin in San Francisco, saying he plans to come for a vacation, probably on Friday, January 16. He calls his office to have them reschedule his appointments. At 4:00 PM he receives call from Lutz, saying they're going to stay in "East Babylon" until the "scientific investigations" of the house are carried out. George tells him about the last night's terrors. Mancuso's stigmata return. He hangs up the phone.

The Lutzes

Missy gives Lutz a picture she had drawn of "Jodie the Pig." It includes "clouds" representing "snow … when Jodie ran away in the snow."

Father Mancuso

Mancuso changes his plans, decides to catch 9:00 PM TWA flight to San Francisco. Calls his cousin, tells his wife of changed plans. At the ticket counter, the stigmata have disappeared.

The Lutzes

To free up space in the Conners home for the Lutzes, Jimmy and Carey decide to spend the night at Carey's mother's house. Before they leave, all celebrate the abandonment of the haunted house. The Lutzes tell all about their horrifying experiences. After questioning Missy about her picture of Jodie, the Lutzes bathe early and "for the first time in almost a month, the Lutzes fell asleep in each other's arms."

"A Virtual Compendium"

Although Amityville's Horror has pulled out all the stops in its *fortississimo* performance during this last night in the house on Ocean Avenue, we shall see anon that it isn't finished with the Lutzes yet. Practically every paranormal sign of infestation and incipient demonic possession is to be seen in this chapter. Indeed, the psychic assaults are so numerous, intense, and varied that Rick Moran and Peter Jordan—themselves investigators of the paranormal—after listing some of the "events" of this and other chapters, observed:

> *Horror* is a virtual compendium of nearly every conceivable kind of psychic phenomenon. In short, the affair places uncommon demands on our credulity…. In all of our combined years of investigating such

> occurrences and studying the literature of the paranormal, we had never before heard of so much psychic activity concentrated in one area in such a short period of time. Indeed, the book reads like a primer of paranormal occurrences, with every conceivable type of experience reported. Either this was the most incredible haunting case on record, we thought, or Anson's book was something less than *A True Story*. [Moran, "Amityville Horror Hoax," *Fate*, May 1978, p. 44]

DeFeo and *Exorcist* Parallels

After all the criticism presented in previous chapters, there is little left to be said beyond the comments of Rick Moran and Peter Jordan. Nevertheless, it is worth enumerating *Exorcist* and DeFeo-story parallels that are found in this account of the last night in the demonic dwelling. There is the psychic cold, the nausea, and the vomiting so prevalent in Blatty's novel—even Harry the dog vomits in this *True Story*:

> [George] saw Harry [in the bedroom doorway] struggle to his feet, shake violently, and then begin to retch. The dog threw up all over the floor, but kept gagging and trying to force out something that seemed stuck in his throat. Restricted by his leash, the poor dog was only twisting the chain more tightly about his writhing body. [*AH*-pb, p. 242]

Not only does this passage repeat the *Exorcist* nausea/vomiting motif, the hard-to-visualize "twisting the chain" detail is something that followers of the DeFeo story would have recognized as a reprise of Ronnie DeFeo's attempts to make the family dog hang itself on the swimming-pool fence. Harry is made to reprise another DeFeo-story motif—the hypothesis that the DeFeo family had been drugged before they were killed:

> [*George*] saw the door to the bedroom swing wildly as though someone were yanking it open and then immediately slamming it shut. George could also see Harry lying outside in the hallway, completely undisturbed by the racket. Either that dog is drugged, George thought, or I'm the one who's going mad! [*AH*-pb, p 244]

To return to *Exorcist* influences, there is a reprise of Chapter Three's noise "from somewhere over his head"—Anson's first borrowing from Blatty the present author was able to discover:

> There was a noise above George's head. He looked up and listened. Something was scraping along the floor of the boys' bedroom. The noise

> became louder, and George could tell the movement was faster now. The boys' beds were sliding *back and forth*! [*AH*-pb, p. 243]

There is no exact parallel of beds sliding back and forth in *The Exorcist*, but motions of the bed of the possessed girl are so frequent and varied that bed motions lead to an effort to explain them as due to violent seizures or spasms. But it is Regan herself who first reports "My bed was shaking" [*Exorcist*, p. 50], and her mother reports "the matter of the shaking bed … had happened twice more and was always followed by Regan's insistence that she sleep with her mother" [*Exorcist*, p. 58]. Not only was the girl's bed shaking, but its mattress was quivering:

> Regan lay taut on her back, face stained with tears and contorted with terror as she gripped at the sides of her narrow bed.
>
> "Mother, why is it *shaking*?" she cried. "Make it *stop*! Oh, I'm *scared*! Make it stop! Mother, please make it *stop*!" [emphases original].
>
> The mattress of the bed was quivering violently *back and forth* [emphasis added]. [*Exorcist*, p. 93]

Is there a significant difference between a mattress moving "back and forth" and a bed doing the same? It would seem an easy thing to inaccurately recall a reciprocating mattress as a sliding bed. In fact, it is difficult to think of a mattress moving back and forth without the whole bed doing the same.

In *The Exorcist*, the demon telekinetically moves Regan's heavy bureau "halfway across the room," whereupon her mother finds "Regan in the kitchen complaining that someone had moved all her furniture during the night when she was sleeping" [*Exorcist*, p. 58]. Presumably, the child's bed had moved as well. Ultimately, Blatty has the demon cause entire the bed to levitate:

> Karras … looked back. And was instantly electrified. *The front of the bed was rising up off the floor* [emphasis original]! He stared at it incredulously. Four inches. Half a foot. A foot. Then the back of the bed lifted level with the front….The bed drifted upward another foot and then hovered there, bobbing and listing gently as if it were floating on a stagnant lake. [*Exorcist*, p. 358]

It appears Anson could have adopted the floating-bed motif with great effect in his *True Story*, and it is hard to account for its absence. Perhaps even he considered it lacking in verisimilitude? One or two people flying is one thing. But a *bed* flying? Who would believe *that?* But there's more telekinesis *à la* his *Exorcist* model:

> George managed to throw off his covers, but he could not lift his body out of bed....Now he heard the dresser drawers across his room begin to open and close. A candle was still on his nightstand and he could make out the drawers rapidly sliding back and forth. One drawer would fly open, then another, then the first would *bang shut* [emphasis added]. [*AH*-pb, p. 243]

Blatty's model narrative is much more frightening than is Anson's. Whereas Anson merely has telekinesis overheard at a distance, Blatty presents an up-close, sight-and-sound description of a conversation of a priest and the demon itself:

> Karras jerked around his head at a loud, sudden banging. A bureau drawer had popped open, sliding out its entire length. He felt a quick-rising thrill as he watched it abruptly *bang shut* [emphasis added]....Psychokinesis. Karras heard chuckling. He glanced back to Regan.
> "How pleasant to chat with you, Karras," said the demon, grinning. "I feel free. Like a wanton...."
> "You did that? You made the dresser drawer move just now?"
> The demon wasn't listening. [*Exorcist*, p. 278]

Clearly, Anson could not have sold a close copy of Blatty's model to even the most credulous of his readers as "A True Story." Even so, considering Anson used the unusual expression "*bang* shut" instead of "*slam* shut" to describe the sound of a violently closing dresser-drawer suggests at least a bit of dependence upon the *Exorcist* model.

If we recall that Jay Anson had been deeply steeped in Blatty's novel before writing *The Amityville Horror: A True Story* (he produced a documentary on the filming of the movie version of *The Exorcist*) the inescapable conclusion is he likely would have read the novel many times. He would have absorbed the sense and substance of the thriller to the point where his unconscious would have shaped his narrative, even if he was not consciously appropriating material from his model. He had almost no substantive, detailed materials with which to work, after all, and it seems likely that unconscious reflexes must have shaped the product of his pen to fill up an almost empty script. And what a script he produced to describe the family's last hours in the house!

Thunder and lightning return, shaking the house of horrors. George lets out "a horrible, silent scream. Somebody was on the bed with him!....Strong, heavy feet struck his legs and body....Oh God! He thought. They're hooves. It's an animal!" [*AH*-pb, p. 244]. George passes out. The storm stops. The boys awaken him. "'Daddy, Daddy!....there's something in our room!....It's a monster!' Danny cried. 'He doesn't have any face!'" [*AH*-

pb, pp. 244–245]. The hooded monster Kathy had seen in the fireplace is standing at the top of the stairs. George picks Missy up and gives her to the boys to take outside. He then picks a comatose Kathy up off the bed and carries her down the steps with Harry close behind. The front door is hanging by its hinges again as they make a run for the van. George says a prayer, turns the ignition key, the motor stars immediately, and the Lutzes are on their way to Kathy's mother's house:

> It was seven o'clock on the morning of January 14, 1976; the twenty-eighth day the Lutzes had lived in 112 Ocean Avenue. [*AH*-pb, p. 246]

A Possibly Better Ending

If Anson had checked an almanac before ending his description of the family's escape, he would have learned that their slated departure time was fifteen to twenty minutes before sunrise, and civil twilight had begun just ten to fifteen minutes earlier. How much more dramatic an ending he could have invented! After the final sentence previously quoted, he could have added some meteorological embroidery, such as:

> As the van shot backwards out of the driveway after the dark and stormy night, the storm clouds parted before them over the garage and the boathouse, revealing the approach of dawn. As they sped northward on Ocean Avenue, the winter sun's first warming rays shone through the passenger-side windows of the van, bathing Kathy's cheek in light and kindling a hopeful glow upon her pale countenance. They were on their way to her mother's house, where they knew they would be safe from *that horror*.

A Contradictory Account

Paul Hoffman—the first journalist to chronicle the Lutz's life at 112 Ocean Avenue—described the family's last day in the house much less dramatically. In both his July 18, 1976, article in the *New York Sunday News* and his *Good Housekeeping* article of April 1977, the exit plays out much more leisurely, and the sequence of events during the last two days is rather different. Quite notably, no extreme weather is involved in the plot. In fact, Hoffman never mentions weather at all in either of his accounts of the Lutz's travails. Although he agrees with Anson about the beds sliding back and forth on the night of Tuesday, January 13, 1976, the marching band's performance is replaced by "the noises [that] started again." Worthy of note, however, is while detailing the beds-sliding event, Hoffman has a Bible on the bedside table flip over precisely three times—a prodigy found nowhere in Anson's eclectic account.

After sunrise on Wednesday the fourteenth, George—not carrying a comatose Kathy—ventures downstairs to find:

> The front door, which he'd double-latched, was wide open. So was the basement door that he'd locked, even the doors on the garbage shed, including the one that had been nailed shut. [Hoffman, "Dream House," *Good Housekeeping*, April 1977, p. 242]

Long after seven o'clock in the morning when, according to the Anson account, the family fled from the house in terror, George calls the priest (Hoffman never calls him Mancuso, merely "a cleric in the chancery of the Rockville Centre diocese.") After the nameless priest tells him to "Get out of there" (the *New York Sunday News* article adds "before the sun goes down!"), Hoffman tells us:

> This time the Lutzes heeded him. When the children came home from school, they gathered them together, grabbed a few belongings and fled to the safety of Kathy's mother's home in West Babylon, N.Y. … never to return [ellipsis original]. [Hoffman, "Dream House," *Good Housekeeping*, April 1977, p. 242]

Not only does Hoffman *not* mention the boys being kept home from school the day before the exodus, he depicts a flight from the horror house so leisurely that they are sent to school as per usual. Only after school is over, on what is the most demonic day of Anson's tale, are we informed the family fled to safety!

Hoffman does not tell us what the Lutzes did later in the day on which they vacated the horror house. He merely says "In the weeks following their departure, the Lutzes took what they call 'a crash course' in mysticism and the occult to learn what happened to their house they had their astrological charts drawn, consulted a medium clergy, psychics and parapsychologists" [Hoffman, "Dream House," *Good Housekeeping*, April 1977, p. 242]. A cynic might say that all their "studies" were merely foraging for details with which to fill the tapes they were to give to Jay Anson.

By contrast, Anson tells us a lot about what happened when the Lutzes moved into the Conners' home. At least one important episode is alleged to have taken place on the day on which they fled the house—the episode in which Missy presents a picture she had drawn of Jodie the pig. A crude drawing of an animal running through bubbles is reproduced on page 149 of the paperback edition. Captioned "Missy's picture of 'Jodie' running through the snow," it allegedly was drawn by five-year-old Missy at the Conners home on the same day her family abandoned the house. There is no way to verify when or by whom the drawing was made, although it could very well have been drawn by a five-year-old child.

Father Pecoraro's Departure

Not only do the Lutzes flee from Long Island to California to escape Amityville's Horror. Father Ralph J. Pecoraro, a.k.a. "Father Mancuso," also moves to California. Unlike the Lutzes who move to the San Diego area in Southern California, the priest moves to San Francisco in the north. Although Anson gives precise details of the priest's departure for asylum in the west, there is no reason to suppose they bear any resemblance to reality. It is known from the transcript of the *Lutz v Hoffman* fraud trial that he did indeed flee to California, but we learn from his testimony under oath that it wasn't demonic forces which caused him to flee. Rather, it was Anson and the Lutzes who had threatened his career in the Rockville Centre diocese:

Q Were you ever involved in any business ventures with them [*the Lutzes*] in the past?
A I was involved in the law suit against them … for what I felt was an invasion of privacy….That's the only sort of business that I would have with them….
Q Was there a cash settlement in that case?
A They agreed to change certain statements in the book [in] which I was involved, and to correct some statements, and that was amenable to me.
Q Which of the items in the book that you objected to were the subject of that law suit?
A The things I objected to in the book were obviously revelations of who I was, which I found extremely upsetting, because it interfered directly with my work as an ecclesiastical judge, and it's obvious that I have had to leave my practice as a judge in New York because of this problem.
Q Why were you compelled to do that, Father?...
A Well, I think that as an attorney you are well aware that the first thing that a client does is depend upon your integrity and upon the entire sense of confidentiality that is going to exist in a relationship that you have with that client.

When I am trying a case I am trying it on ecclesiastical grounds and, therefore, my integrity—that association which I have with my client, with those who appear before me is going to have to be extremely strong.

When my name appears in newspapers and when things are said about me that are not true, or that are grossly exaggerated, how in

> God's name can you expect these people to have any respect for me? [*Lutz v Hoffman*, pp. 347–350]

"Not Smart Enough"

An attempt has already been made to assess the reliability of Father Pecoraro's testimony and the actual degree of his involvement in the Amityville epic. It is interesting to end discussion of the priest with his assessment of George Lutz. Speaking privately to Judge Weinstein, he confided his evaluation as follows:

> Your Honor, I'm speaking to you as one judge to another, and I speak to you in that capacity, and I say to you that I know Mr. Lutz. He is not smart enough to make these things up. He is really a very simplistic individual. [*Lutz v Hoffman*, p. 358]

At this point, the Judge cut him off, saying "I don't want to hear this." And so, it remains unclear whether this was supposed to mean someone else had to have made up the story, or whether the story was true because Lutz wasn't smart enough to have made it up.

Thursday, January 15, 1976

Events of the Day

Weather claimed: No weather reported. Almost everything in "Chapter 25: January 15" happens on the fourteenth. Levitations and sliming begin after midnight (supposedly).

The Lutzes

George and Kathy levitate off the bed. Kathy grabs George's arm and pulls him out of bed. "We've got to get out of this room!" At the head of the staircase, "Coming up the steps toward them was a snake-like line of greenish-black slime!" The Horror was following them, "wherever the Lutzes fled."

Planning Sequels?

As this investigation of the Ocean-Avenue saga approaches completion, it becomes clear that Anson and perhaps the Lutzes as well—realized the possibility of one or more sequels following after his tall tale. (As it turned out, there would indeed be many, many sequels to both the book and the movie.) But a more immediate problem had arisen for the author to solve: the problem of new owners of the house. They would surely report the complete absence of "psychic forces" or paranormal activities at 112 Ocean Avenue. Indeed, it is possible that the Cromartys, who had moved into the Horror House after the Lutzes fled, had already been rebutting media reports of preternatural happenings shorty before Anson finished writing his book. If Anson had Amityville's Horror move out of the house in pursuit of the Lutzes, he could have the basis for sequels and would give believers in the noctibumpal world a way to rebut the findings of future owners of the house.

From Acorns to Oak Trees

The eerie, areal *pas de deux* executed by the Lutzes at Kathy's mother's house has already been discussed, and it will be recalled that all the levitations reported by Anson are nothing but imaginative enhancements of Paul Hoffman's original report from January 11:

> "Lee awoke to find Kathy sliding across the bed, as if by levitation. He grabbed her, and switched sides with her so she wouldn't slide away again" [Hoffman, "Life in a Haunted House," *New York Sunday News*, p. 22].

The green-slime prodigy has also been examined in the light of the *Lutz v Hoffman* trial transcript. When asked if he had ever seen "this greenish-black substance" coming up the stairs at his wife's mother's house, Lutz replied under oath: "I believe the greenish-black substance you're referring to is what we saw coming from two particular keyholes, two rooms on the second floor of the house. *Not at my mother-in-law's house*" [emphasis added] [*Lutz v Hoffman*, p. 51].

Just as a 250-pound door coming off its hinges was an evolutionary development from the garbage shed door somehow becoming unhinged, and just as the levitations are an exponential amplification of the problem of sleeping on slippery sheets, so too the green slime turned out to be a mighty oak tree that had sprung from a tiny acorn. The green slime, it has been seen, is a transformation of the greenish-black fingerprint ink of Attorney Weber's crime-scene photographs that had so engaged the curiosity of the Lutzes. There never was any slime.

Bring the Kids!

It seems almost certain that *none* of the episodes reported in *The Amityville Horror: A True Story* ever happened—at least not in the way Jay Anson reported them in his runaway bestseller. Clearly, the Lutzes merely experienced a number of odd sensations and surprising phenomena, such as the second-floor window opening all by itself due to counterweights that were too heavy, which were blown far out of proportion. Exactly one month after abandonment of the house, *Newsday* reporters A.J. Carter and Christopher M. Cook reported:

> At William H. Parry Inc., 600 Jericho Tpke [Syosset] where Lutz works, the doors were locked yesterday. But employees of another firm in the same suite said that, in January, Lutz had brought his children into the office for several days in a row "because they were terrified about what was happening to them." They said Lutz then moved in with relatives in Nassau County [Carter, "DeFeo Home Abandoned," *Newsday*, Feb. 14, 1976 p. 6].

We know that by the time of the report, the Lutzes were already planning to write a book and were evidently taking "crash courses" in astrology and other paranormal studies. It is possible that bringing the children to the office was just part of their plan to build publicity. After all, we do not know if the children had been taken to the office during the days chronicled by Anson, who makes no mention of this undoubtedly true report. Moreover, Steve Bauman of Channel Five had already broadcast a report about the Lutzes on February 5—nine days before the *Newsday* report of bringing children to the office. However, it is also possible the Lutzes were experiencing fear aroused by unexplained sensations and phenomena. Almost certainly, however, whatever those stimuli might have been, they would have been orders of magnitude more trivial and insignificant than the horrific events reported by Anson.

"We Aren't Superstitious"

The oft repeated "we are not superstitious" comments the Lutzes routinely fed the press and broadcast media almost surely belied a superstitious reality. Given the ubiquity of publicity stirred up by the movie version of *The Exorcist* and other popular novels based on demonic themes, and given a suggestible personality and bias that allowed the Lutzes to believe that such things could possibly happen, it is reasonable to suppose they would reflexively interpret odd sensations and happenings as paranormal phenomena. If, then, a priest belonging to a religion that even today teaches that demonic possession can be real enters the picture, a sort of *folie à trois* could develop between the priest and the Lutzes. With financial pressures lurking in the background, and the lure of a future of wealth and fame, completely unremarkable days spent in the Dutch colonial house at 112 Ocean Avenue could be transformed easily and effortlessly into the twenty-eight days of terror of *The Amityville Horror: A True Story*.

The Epilogue

Like its model *The Exorcist, The Amityville Horror: A True Story* has an "Epilogue." In the model, all the surviving protagonists move to California at the end. By an odd instance of truth intruding into fiction, after the Lutzes flee Amityville, they also move to California. For good measure, the priest also relocates to California—something his *Exorcist* role-model couldn't do, due to death-by-demon. In the *Exorcist* epilogue, the atheist mother Chris confirms the demonic nature of the happenings in the house by professing belief in a devil. "As far as God goes," she says, "I am a nonbeliever. Still am. But when it comes to a devil—well, that's something else. I could buy that. I do, in fact. I do" [*Exorcist*, p. 400]. In *A True Story*, however, the demonic nature of the happenings is corroborated by an invasion of psychics whose séances save the day for the Devil:

> On February 18, 1976, Marvin Scott of New York's Channel 5 decided to investigate further the reports on the so-called cursed home of Amityville, Long Island. The mission called for spending the night in the haunted home at 112 Ocean Avenue. Psychics, clairvoyants, a demonologist, and parapsychologists were invited to participate. [*AH*-pb, p. 157]

Only Ten Days?

Those séances would have been just two days after the Monday, February 16 press conference held in Attorney Weber's law office [*Lutz v Hoffman*, p. 11, 12]. That same day, *Newsday* reporter Neill S. Rosenfeld wrote:

> On Saturday [February 14, 1976], it was reported that in December, *after having lived only 10 days at 112 Ocean Ave.* [emphasis added], George and Kathleen Lutz left the house in which Ronald DeFeo Jr. had shot and killed his parents, two brothers and two sisters in November, 1974….[The Lutzes] were said to be skiing in Vermont and could not be reached, but neighbors quoted them as having said that the house was filled with human shapes, strange sounds, eerie vibrations and unexplained power

failures [Rosenfeld, "The Curious Haunt the DeFeo House," *Newsday*, February 16, 1976].

Psychic Invasion

According to Anson's "Epilogue," Channel 5's Marvin Scott had previously contacted the Lutzes for permission to film activities in the haunted house. "George Lutz agreed and sat down at a meeting with Scott in a small pizzeria in Amityville. George refused to re-enter 112 Ocean Avenue, but said he and his wife, Kathy, would wait for the investigators the next day at the Italian restaurant" [*AH*-pb, p. 257–8]. The time and location of this meeting insinuates the Lutzes had returned from their skiing vacation in Vermont. But perhaps this is not the case. The *Wikipedia* article "The Amityville Horror [https://en.wikipedia.org/wiki/The_Amityville_Horror, accessed 1/24/21] cites sources claiming that the invasion of the psychics took place almost a month later, on the night of March 6, 1976.

> On the night of March 6, 1976, the house was investigated by Ed and Lorraine Warren, a husband-and-wife team self-described as demonologists, together with a crew from the television station Channel 5 New York and reporter Michael Linder of WNEW-FM. During the course of the investigation Gene Campbell took a series of infrared time-lapse photographs. One of the images allegedly showed a "demonic boy" with glowing eyes who was standing at the foot of a staircase.

This sounds very much like the February 18 event described in Anson's "Epilogue":

> The researchers held *the first of three séances* at 10:30 PM [emphasis added]. Present around the table were Lorraine Warren, a clairvoyant; her husband, Ed, a demonologist; psychics Mary Pascarella and Mrs. Albert Riley; and George Kekoris of the Psychical Research Institute in Durham, North Carolina. Marvin Scott also joined the group at the table....Then George Kekoris, the psychic researcher, also became violently ill and had to leave the table. Observer Mike Linder of WNEW-FM stated that he had felt a sudden numbness, a kind of cold sensation....As some people slept in some of the second floor bedrooms, a photographer shot infrared pictures in the vain hope of capturing some ghostly image on film [*AH*-pb, pp. 258–9].

Signs of Textual Revisions

March 6 being the correct date of the séances is possibly supported by what appears to be an aporia (compositional seam) resulting from revision of

Anson's text. On the day of the séance, George tells Marvin Scott that "he and his wife, Kathy, would wait for the investigators the next day at the Italian restaurant"—the day after the all-night séance. Alas, "When Marvin Scott returned to the little pizzeria, the Lutzes were gone. By March, they had moved clear across the country to California..." [*AH*-pb, p. 259]. Indeed, if the séances had been held on March 6, the Lutzes would indeed not have been able to wait for the reporter in an Amityville pizzeria. Best of all, they wouldn't have had to cut short a skiing vacation in Vermont on February 18.

There appears to be a second aporia in the text of the "Epilogue"—perhaps indicating hasty revision of the short chapter. On page 258 we read "The researchers held *the first of three séances* at 10:30 PM [emphasis added]." But then, on page 259—with no intervening second séance—the reader is told "At 3:30 AM, the Warrens attempted another séance. There was nothing unusual reported, no sounds or strange phenomena. All the psychics felt the room had been neutralized ... they definitely felt the house on Ocean Avenue was harboring a demonic spirit, one that could be removed only by an exorcist." That was it. Only two séances are reported to have been held.

Unsurprisingly, all the psychics reported feeling cold, nausea, and other symptoms needed for a demonic diagnosis. But the psychics aren't the only ones Anson claims suffered ill effects during their night in the haunted house:

> Then George Kekoris, the psychic researcher, also became violently ill and had to leave the table. Observer Mike Linder of WNEW-FM stated that he had felt a sudden numbness, a kind of cold sensation....Television cameraman Steve Petropolis, who had been assigned some scary assignments in combat zones, experienced heart palpitations and shortness of breath when he investigated the sewing room upstairs where the negative force was said to be concentrated. When Lorraine Warren and Marvin Scott went into that room, they both came out saying that they had felt a momentary chill [*AH*-pb, pp. 258–9].

Rick Moran and Peter Jordan, however, interviewed Jerry Solfvin, Project Director of the Psychic Research Foundation. Solfvin told the reporters:

> While the book's description of the séance is basically accurate, Anson tends to "select facts to support his own speculations." Anson writes, for example, that George Kekoris, who participated in the experiment at the Lutz home, suddenly became "violently ill" and was forced to leave the room. Although Solfvin concedes that Kekoris became momentarily "queasy," he thinks this is hardly surprising in view of the hot, stuffy, "emotionally-charged" situation. Moreover, the room was small—

approximately 12 feet by 15 feet—and more than 20 persons were present, including a film crew using hot movie lights [Moran, "Amityville Horror Hoax," *Fate*, May 1978, pp.46–47].

The Missing Séance

So, why did Anson say there were three séances if he only reported two? It is possible that an early draft of the "Epilogue" had included mentions of a third séance that took place on a different date. Laura DiDio—the Channel 7 Eye Witness News reporter who had unwittingly become a part of William Weber's "corroboration strategy"—when asked about her contacts with Attorney Weber mentioned a séance not included in Anson's epic of evil:

> Mr. Weber told me that there was going to be a séance held at the house *on February 28th* [emphasis added], a Saturday night, in which Channel 7 Eye Witness News was invited, and this Dr. Steven Kaplan who was a vampirologist from Long Island University was going to be presiding exorcising some white witches [*Lutz vs. Hoffman,* pp. 416–7].

Said séance never took place. According to the Wikipedia article "The Amityville Horror":

> Dr. Stephen Kaplan, a self-styled vampirologist and ghost hunter, was called in to investigate the house. Kaplan and the Lutzes had a falling out after Kaplan said that he would expose any fraud that was found. Kaplan went on to write a critical book titled *The Amityville Horror Conspiracy* with his wife Roxanne Salch Kaplan. The book was published in 1995 [*Wikipedia*, "The Amityville Horror"].

Though it is likely the text of Anson's "Epilogue" contained material in fact pertaining to a total of three séances, the reason for deleting the account of one of them seems obvious. Certainly, the aborted February 28 séance couldn't be used to corroborate the claims of *A True Story*! What such an account might have said will never be known.

Fulfilling Weber's Plan

When asked at the *Lutz v Hoffman* fraud trial if he had said anything to Anson or the Lutzes about "the value of obtaining certain corroboration about some of the material that was being proposed," Anson's editor Timothy Mossman replied:

> Mainly I would have said it to Mr. Anson because he and I worked more thoroughly on the book together. I said that whenever a newspaper

> account could be pulled in to back up or corroborate the facts in a story as George Lutz provided them, that this was all to the good. [*Lutz v Hoffman*, pp. 175–6]

It must not be forgotten how Jay Anson adopted the strategy of the "project" the Lutzes had worked out with attorney Weber concerning the need for outside forces to corroborate their claims. As we near the end of this book, it is worth reminding ourselves of what Mr. Weber told the Court in the fraud trial:

> The differences between the good sellers and the bad sellers is where can you get credibility. We had to develop credibility. The credibility was developed, A, through—well, the Lutzes brought their priest into the story. [*Lutz v Hoffman*, p. 245]
>
> The other thing was to bring in outside forces, and to show their involvement in it, and to attempt to make it appear as if these outside forces were corroborating our story, and the outside forces that I myself, brought in was the Laura DiDeo (phonetic) situation. Laura Dideo was the program manager for channel 5. [*Lutz v Hoffman*, p 248]

The multimillion-dollar industry that sprang from Anson's *True Story* is proof that Weber's "project" was successful—even if he never benefited from it beyond the out-of-court settlement he received at the conclusion of the *Lutz v Hoffman* fraud trial.

Anson's "Afterword: Note from the Author"

Functionally, there are three endings to *The Amityville Horror: A True Story*. The first ending is Anson's chapter 25, "January 15," at the conclusion of the demonic events at Kathy's mother's house. The second ending is the conclusion of the séances and paranormal investigations reported in Anson's "Epilogue." The third and final ending is the "Afterword: Note from the Author" which occupies the last pages of the book. It is nothing less than an *apologia*—a defense of the "True Story" subtitle of Anson's book. Anson himself might have realized his tale was so absurd, so implausible, and so unbelievable that it would take a great deal of effort to assure his readers his claims were completely in line with the best "research" done by investigators of the paranormal.

"To the extent that I can verify them, all the events in this book are true" [*AH*-pb, p. 263], the author assures his readers. "George Lee and Kathleen Lutz undertook the exhaustive and frequently painful task of reconstructing their twenty-eight days in the house in Amityville on a tape recorder, refreshing each other's memories so that the final oral 'diary' would be as complete as possible ... many of their impressions and reports were later substantiated by the testimony of independent witnesses such as Father Mancuso and local police officials" [*AH*-pb, p. 263]. Of course, this book has shown that both the priest and the police *did not* substantiate the claims.

The Missing Tapes

As for the tapes in question, the specific content on them is unknown because many were not provided to the court during the *Lutz v Hoffman* fraud trial. Judge Weinstein, the judge for the trial, sternly told the Lutzes' attorney Mr. Daily, "I am not going to allow these tapes to be further played. I am ruling, based on what I heard, subject of course to some explanation, that a number of the tapes have been withheld. Spoilation [*sic*] has therefor taken place and unless you can show why they're not produced I am going to assume that they were deliberately destroyed by your client" [*Lutz v Hoffman*, p. 451].

Minutes later, the fraud trial was settled out of court—before Jay Anson could be sworn in to testify under oath just exactly how true *A True*

Story was. It has already been demonstrated beyond cavil that virtually *nothing* reported in the twenty-eight-day chronicle ever happened—at least not in the manner depicted in *The Amityville Horror*. We have seen how Anson employed information regarding the DeFeo murders provided to the Lutzes by Attorney Weber, and extensive material was incorporated from *The Exorcist*.

Reverse Engineering from the Afterword

Further insight into how *A True Story* was fabricated can be gained by a study of material in the Afterword. By a sort of "reverse engineering" from what Anson wrote in the Afterword, it is possible to draw inferences concerning how he wrote the book. Anson had extensive knowledge of paranormal literature and could have used his knowledge for the purpose of inventing material not found in *The Exorcist*, as will be evident from reviewing his Afterword arguments.

Pages 264 to 266 of the paperback edition of *A True Story* provide a veritable checklist of things that had to be put into the book. Anson begins with the need for psychic cold: "The chilling cold that George and others noted is a syndrome repeatedly reported by visitors to haunted houses who sense a 'cold spot' or pervasive chill. (Occultists speculate that a disembodied entity may draw on thermal energy and body heat to gain the power it needs to become visible and move objects)" [*AH*-pb, pp. 264-265]. It is obvious that Anson's research was thorough, since he understood that principle of para-thermodynamics!

Next, Anson demonstrates why the family dog was made to play so important a role in the story: "Animals are often said to display discomfort and even terror in haunted surroundings. This was certainly true of Harry, the family dog, to say nothing of human visitors who had never entered the house before—Kathy's aunt, a neighbor's boy, and others" [*AH*-pb, p. 265]. This provided a reason to put those minor details into the book.

The arguments in the Afterword are specious efforts to cover compositional tracks, clearly evident in Anson's attempt to explain an episode that has been shown to be entirely false: "The window that slammed on Danny's hand has its echo in an English case in which a car door closed by itself, crushing the hand of a woman who was arriving to investigate paranormal reports. Minutes later, during the drive to the nearest hospital, her hand reportedly returned to its uninjured state" [*AH*-pb, p. 265].

It will be recalled that Paul Hoffman's early report indicated Danny's hand only suffered a "slight cut" when the sewing room "aluminum storm window had fallen on Danny's hands" [plural] and Kathy merely "took Danny downstairs to treat the slight cut he'd suffered" [Hoffman, "Our Dream House

Was Haunted," *Good Housekeeping*, April 1977]. There was no trip to a hospital, and there was no miraculous repair of a crushed hand. Anson does not tell his readers where this English "echo" of the crushed-hand motif had been published. Almost surely, the English case had been the "shout," not the "echo." It is altogether unbelievable that Anson himself dreamed up the episode in question; it had to have been modeled after something he had read.

Explication of His Own Text

Anson's next argument helps understand how the DeFeo-murder material Attorney Weber had provided to the Lutzes was molded into other episodes of *A True Story*, and it appears Anson was making sure his readers understood the paranormal implications of episodes in which no serious danger was evident:

> George's visionary glimpse of what he would later identify as Ronnie DeFeo's face, his repeated awakening at the time of the DeFeo murders, and Kathy's dreams of illicit lovemaking have their counterparts in a phenomenon called *retrocognition* [emphasis original], in which an emotionally charged site apparently manages to transmit images of its past to later visitors. [*AH*-pb, p. 265]

Anson certainly had done his research here, and he appears to be passing it on to his readers. In truth, this is nothing less than telling his readers how to interpret what he had written! He then proceeds to show that virtually all the happenings in his *True Story* are well-documented in the literature—the literature from which the episodes themselves must surely have been derived:

> The damage to doors, windows and banister, the movement and possible teleportation of the ceramic lion, the nauseating stench in the basement and Rectory are all familiar elements to readers of the voluminous literature about poltergeists or "noisy ghosts" whose behavior has been documented by professional investigators. The "marching band," too, is characteristic of the poltergeist, which is often reported to create dramatically loud noises. (One victim reported the sound of "a grand piano falling downstairs," but with no visible cause or damage." [*AH*-pb, p. 265]

In addition to his already demonstrated dependence on *The Exorcist* and the information provided by Attorney Weber, Anson might inadvertently have revealed his dependence also on the writings of Rev. John Nicola, the author of the preface to *The Amityville Horror: A True Story*:

> Most poltergeist antics seem childishly malicious, rather than vicious or physically harmful. But on the other hand, as Father Nicola points out in his *Demonical Possession and Exorcism*, poltergeists sometimes serve as the first manifestation of an entity ultimately bent on demonic possession. The inverted crucifix in Kathy's closet, the recurrent flies, and *odors of human excrement* are all characteristic of demonic infestation [emphasis added]. [*AH*-pb, p. 266]

It was hypothesized previously that Anson was considering the possibility of sequels when he had Amityville's Horror follow the Lutzes to Kathy's mother's house "in East Babylon." If this was true, it would appear he was working at cross purposes when he wrote his last argument in support of the veracity of his *True Story*. Quoting an unidentified, "experienced researcher into paranormal phenomena," he wrote:

> Evidently George Lutz was not the ideally passive 'horse' for a discarnate rider; the threat to his wife and children galvanized him to fight back. But neither were his unseen adversaries mere ordinary 'ha'nts.' Their unusual strength is suggested by their long-range attacks on Father Mancuso's car, health, and rooms, and by George and Kathy's levitation even after they had fled to her mother's. But why, then, have the Lutzes reported no further trouble after moving to California? Another old occult tradition—that spirits cannot extend their power across water—may have some significance here. [*AH*-pb, p. 268]

Alas for Jay Anson, two years after the present book had been begun, the Lutzes—with the assistance of John G. Jones—published *The Amityville Horror II*. The back cover of the Warner Books 1982 paperback edition of the book informed readers that "The Horror Continues." It then explains how "When the Lutz family left the house in Amityville, New York, the terror did not end. Through the next four years wherever they went, the inescapable Evil followed them. Now the victims of the most publicized house-haunting of the century have agreed to reveal the harrowing details of their continuing ordeal."

Perhaps only the Lutzes had been planning for a sequel.

Part III: Aftermath—Books & Films

Early Success

The Lutzes had relocated to Southern California by the time *The Amityville Horror: A True Story* was published in September of 1977. By February 1978, Patricia Burstein and Sue Reilly wrote that the Lutz's story "made *The Exorcist* pale by comparison." They reported how Jay Anson, 55, "working from 45 hours of taped interviews with the Lutzes, and additional hours ... with the priest who allegedly helped them ...wrote *Amityville* in three months." "Royalties are split with the Lutzes," they noted, "but Anson's share should make him wealthy. Now in its 12th printing, the book has been a best-seller since October. Paperback rights sold for nearly $200,000. He will be paid an additional fee for writing the screen-play.

[Burstein, "Horror Lives On," *People Magazine*, Feb. 13, 1978]
Anson was thriving. As for Anson's plans, Burstein and Reilly reported that he:

> would like to buy a villa on the island of Majorca. Otherwise, he says, the money will not change his life. "I'm not one for Rolls-Royces," he says. "I'll probably just buy more cashmere sweaters." As for the authenticity of the book that has made him a fortune, Anson enjoys playing the tease. "I'm a professional writer," he says with a shrug. "I don't believe and I don't disbelieve. I leave that to the reader." [Burstein, "Horror Lives On," *People Magazine*, Feb. 13, 1978]

The film version of *The Amityville Horror* was released in 1979, with James Brolin as George Lutz, Margo Kidder as Kathleen Lutz, and Rod Steiger in the role of the priest—renamed "Father Delaney" for the screen. By that time, the Lutzes had appeared on television and radio talk-shows all over the country and even in Japan publicizing their story. Jay Anson had become wealthy from the sales of his *New York Times* bestseller—sales that Wikipedia reports were to total around ten million copies of the book's various editions [Wikipedia, "The Amityville Horror"].

"Dead on West Coast"

Sadly, Jay Anson's enjoyment of the financial triumph did not last more than a year after the smashing success of the film. On Friday, March 14, 1980, C. Gerald Fraser published an obituary in *The New York Times* titled "Jay Anson, 58, Writer of 'Amityville Horror,' Dead on West Coast":

> Jay Anson, whose book about supernatural occurrences in a Long Island home, "*The Amityville Horror*," was a bestseller and was made into a movie, died Wednesday after heart surgery at Stanford University Hospital in Palo Alto, Calif. He was 58 years old and lived in Roslyn, L.I. Mr. Anson had been working in California, completing the screenplay of his second book, "666," another account of psychic phenomena. The book will be published next year by Simon & Shuster and the film will be distributed by Orion....Mr. Anson is survived by his wife, Leona Anson, and two children by previous marriages, a daughter, Lisa, and a son, Andrei [Fraser, "Jay Anson, 58," *New York Times*, march 14, 1980].

Lawsuit over the Subtitle

Shortly before *The Amityville Horror* film came out, James and Barbara Cromarty—the new tenants at 112 Ocean Avenue—had sued Prentice-Hall for $1.1 million in damages, seeking to have them remove the subtitle "A True Story" from the book. They claimed the subtitle had led to property damage and harassment being carried out by fanatical believers in the veracity of Anson's account. Even the crowds of merely curious readers had become a serious nuisance. Long before their lawsuit would be settled out of court in late February of 1982 (*i.e.*, two years after Anson's death), it had become painfully clear: much more corroboration of the true-story subtitle claim was urgently needed. Miriam Pawel would report that the settlement reached by the Cromarty's with Prentice-Hall, the Jay Anson estate, Bantam Books, and American International Pictures had amounted to something between one- and five-hundred thousand dollars [Pawel, "Old ghosts at Rest," *Newsday*, Feb. 21, 1982]. The subtitle, however, was allowed to remain. The initiation of the Cromarty suit was a wake-up call; more corroboration had to be obtained. The Lutzes decided to submit to a polygraph test of their claims.

Polygraphy Publicity

Even before the movie version of the Lutz story came out, numerous claims of fraud and deception had been published—claims that could seriously damage the financial future of the "project" the Lutzes had allegedly purloined from Attorney William Weber. Much more than the subjective, unimpressive reports of psychics and demonologists was needed to save the supernatural enterprise from financial ruin. The Lutzes decided to take lie-detector tests to probe the truth of their implausible claims. The tests were carried out at the Professional Security consultants—Polygraph and Security Specialists office in Beverly Hills, California, on June 19, 1979. Chris Gugas examined George Lutz, and Michael J. Rice examined Kathleen Lutz. They submitted their report to the radio executive and movie publicist Charles A. Moses of the Charles A. Moses agency on June 19, 1979. (With great difficulty, and having overcome many obstacles placed in his way, my student Richard E. Blowers, Jr., was able to obtain a copy of the report in 1980. It was stamped "PERSONAL AND CONFIDENTIAL," and return of the original document was requested.)

The report was signed by both Mr. Gugas and Mr. Rice. Mr. Gugas concluded, "After reviewing the charts containing the above critical questions, it is the opinion of Mr. Gugas, that Mr. George Lee Lutz answered truthfully all his critical questions asked in his examination." In similar manner, Mr. Rice concluded, "After Mr. Rice evaluated Mrs. Lutz's charts, it was his opinion that she answered truthfully to all the critical questions listed above and that no deception was indicated to any of those questions" [Gugas, "Letter to Charles A. Moses," June 21, 1979].

Questionable Questions

Each of the Lutzes was asked five test-questions. Curiously, George and Kathy were asked completely different questions—the possible significance of which may become clear shortly. Many of the questions seem to have been tailored to be impossible to be checked. For example, Mr. Gugas asked George "Are the details you gave me on your frightening experiences at the Amityville house true?" Nowhere is there any record of what Lutz told the examiner before the test, so the significance of his truthful answer to this question cannot be assessed. For all practical purposes, it is meaningless.

Similarly, the significance of one of the questions Mr. Rice asked Kathy cannot be determined. Rice asked her "To the best of your ability did the events of that Amityville house *as recorded on your tapes* [emphasis added] actually happen?" The question was asked more than six months after the cross-examination of the Lutzes in the *Lutz v Hoffman* fraud trial. It will be recalled how many of the most crucial tapes containing the supposed memories of the Lutzes were not produced for the judge—leading to his opinion (albeit not his "finding") that those tapes had been willfully destroyed. Since no tapes existed at the time of the testing, the significance of Kathy's truthful answer also cannot be evaluated. Rice also asked her "Are all the events discussed in your interview today true and correct?" As in the case with George, there is no mention of what had been discussed prior to testing.

Other questions were trivially subjective or insignificant. George was asked "When you fled your Amityville house, were you in fear of your life and the wellbeing of your family?" Given even a mild disposition to believe in ghosts and goblins, passing that test question with a "yes" response is altogether unremarkable. Furthermore, given even a slightly deficient education in science, it is not surprising that Lutz could truthfully answer "Yes" when Gugas asked him "During your 28 days in Amityville, did you experience unexplained flies and disturbing odors on several occasions?"

It is further unremarkable that Kathy Lutz, given once again even a mild disposition to believe in ghosts and goblins, could pass a lie-detector test with a "Yes" response to the questions "While in that Amityville house, were you embraced by an invisible being?" and "While in your Amityville bed did you actually feel the presence of an invisible being over you?"

Of somewhat greater relevance to the veracity of Anson's *True Story* was when Rice asked Kathy "While in that Amityville house did you actually see yourself as an old woman?" Some critics of the old-hag episode have hypothesized that Kathy might have been sleeping on a wrinkled pillowcase, which left fleeting furrows in her facial skin, or that the whole episode—like the levitations—might have been a case of dreaming while half awake. Being practitioners of Transcendental Meditation, it is clear both Lutzes were highly suggestible. I have already noted how my own research on hypnosis had found practitioners of "TM" to be easily hypnotizable. I found, moreover, that subjects under hypnosis or acting out post-hypnotic suggestions could easily pass a polygraph test. In the case of the Lutzes, my finding that autosuggestion can often be as powerful as heterosuggestion would seem to be quite relevant. Finally, we must wonder: Why was Lutz never asked the question "Did you ever see your wife as a ninety-year-old woman?" After all, in Anson's story, a much bigger fuss is made about what George, rather than Kathy, saw.

Two Important Questions

This leaves us with two questions of possible veridical significance that were asked of George Lutz: (1) "At the Amityville house, did you hear what sounded like a marching band tuning up in the middle of the night?" and (2) "After leaving Amityville, did you and Kathy both levitate at your mother-in-law's house?"

The first of these questions had clearly been tailored to match Lutz's previous testimony in the fraud trial, not what was written in Anson's *True Story*. Let us refresh our memory of some relevant details of the allegedly truthful tale:

> [George is in the backyard, with Harry asleep again.] George was about to reach down and shake the animal when he heard the marching band

strike up in his house. He ran back in through the kitchen. The drums and horns were blasting away in the living room. George heard the stomping of many feet as he tore through the hallway....

George took in great gulps of air. Then he realized there was something strange about the living room. Every piece of furniture had been moved. The rug had been rolled back. Chairs, couch, and tables had been pushed against the walls as if to make room for a lot of dancers—or a marching band! [*AH*-pb, pp. 157–8]

Was George having auditory hallucinations? Possibly. However, Paul Hoffman's accounts of *The Horror* do not make any mention of marching bands, making one suspect these episodes were fabricated sometime after the Lutzes had gone into business with Anson. In any case, what Lutz confessed to in court was an order of magnitude less dramatic:

Q You refer many places in the book, Mr. Lutz, do you not, to a marching band playing in the house at night?
A Yes.
Q And do you recall how many pieces were in the band?
A I never saw the band...I heard what appeared to be a number of different *instruments being tuned up* [emphasis added], not necessarily any kind of music, as such. The only way I can relate to it was years ago when I was in school there had been a marching band, and when they got together and tuned up....
Q Can you estimate the number of pieces in the band for us?
A No.
Q Did you notice whether any furniture in the living room had been rearranged to accommodate the marching band?
A It had not been....
Q Did you notice whether any furniture in the living room had been rearranged to accommodate the marching band?
A It had not been....
Q Is that true, that the drums, and horns were blasting away in the living room?
A Every time I remember hearing it, I was in bed and my family was in bed at the time. [*Lutz v Hoffman*, pp 59–61]

Readers are invited to draw their own conclusions about the significance of how every time Lutz thought he heard a band tuning up, he was lying in bed. Regarding the polygraph, it is certainly much easier to answer a question that matched what he had sworn under oath six months earlier (and would have been rehearsed many times in memory), than to answer a question about specific details within Anson's account. It is a pity Mr. Gugas didn't ask if the wall-to-wall carpeting had been rolled up.

This leaves us with one last question to examine—another question asked of George Lutz: "After leaving Amityville, did you and Kathy both levitate at your mother-in-law's house?" It will be recalled that in the earliest accounts of the Lutz story, there is no mention of the aerial *pas de deux* at the Conners home, only an Ocean Avenue episode in which Kathy slides across the bed "as if by levitation." It is likely that kernels of the levitation stories had been created for Jay Anson, and he in turn elaborated them into the detailed episodes we have already analyzed. However, a part of the account of the double flight needs to be repeated one last time to compare it to Lutz's testimony pertinent to the polygraph question under consideration. The following italicized words and phrases should be compared to Lutz's trial testimony given months before the polygraph test:

> *George awoke first.* He felt *as if he was having a dream*, because he had the sensation of floating in air! *He was aware of his body* being flown around the bedroom and *then landing softly back on the bed*. Then, *still in his dreamlike state*, George saw Kathy levitate off the bed. She rose about a foot and slowly began to drift away from him…George could only watch *Kathy fly higher toward the ceiling*. Then he felt himself being lifted, and again he had the sensation of floating…George looked down and saw [Kathy] was back on the bed, looking up at him. *He began to drift toward Kathy, then felt himself slowly settling back down on the bed beside her.* [*AH*-pb, pp. 252–253]

George leaves the bedroom, we are told, "*As though he was sleepwalking*." But then, being confronted by green slime coming up the steps toward them (something he disavowed under oath in the fraud trial), "George knew *he had not been dreaming*. It was all real" [*AH*-pb, p. 253].

A somewhat different picture emerges from Lutz's testimony under oath at the *Lutz v Hoffman* fraud trial:

> A Well, she certainly levitated. She certainly was above the bed. She was not two feet high at that time. There was another time she levitated much higher.
> Q How high was it the second time?
> A About seven feet.
> Q Were you with her?
> A Yes, I levitated, also.
> Q Was this in the middle of the night?
> A Yes.
> Q You were lying up in the bed?
> A *Not lying there. We were talking to each other* [i.e., both were awake and both were in the air at the same time], asking each other if we

believed what was happening at the time. There was no way for us to relate to it. We were just trying to understand what was going on.

Q How long were the two of you hanging in the air?

A Less than two feet [*sic*].

Q *After that, did you fall down to the floor together?*

A *No.*

Q What happened to you? Did you rise higher or did you come down to earth?

A *The next thing I remember, we were back in bed again.*

Q *You don't recall descending?*

A *No.*

Q That was about what time?

A That was at my mother-in-law's house in West Babylon.

Q And that is the truth, is it not?

A Yes. [*Lutz vs. Hoffman*, p. 57]

While Lutz's testimony contradicts many of the details of Anson's narrative, it is nevertheless an incredible tale he swore to the court "under the pains and penalties of perjury." Was Lutz perjuring himself? It would have been both easy and safe to lie about subjective states and private events that could neither be verified nor controverted. Even so, there is reason to think George might have actually believed what he was saying.

The Anson text quoted above allows for a real possibility that Lutz was indeed in a dream-like state in which he could not, for a few moments, determine what was real. It is also possible that physiological arousal—induced by a frightening dream—could have stamped in a false memory analogous to a post-hypnotic suggestion. This would have allowed him to testify honestly in support of a claim that violated the laws of physics—a claim that was not just false, it was *impossibly* false. Half a year later, after repeated retellings of the tale stamped the false memory even more securely into his brain, it would be no surprise at all for Lutz to pass a lie-detector test by affirming that he and his wife had levitated off a bed one ordinary night in West Babylon.

It is probably not an accident that the same question was not asked of Kathy Lutz, who allegedly took part in the same episode. (Curiously, Kathy was not asked about her night flights in the fraud trial either.) Could she have passed the test if she had been asked the same questions? Did the examiners have a reason not to do *too* thorough a test? Not an outrageous claim, as they had been hired by a publicity agent, for whom the desired outcome would have been obvious. Charles A. Moses, the publicist who hired them, can no longer be asked if there had been a desired outcome of the tests. In 2005, he died of a stroke in Burbank, California at the age of 82.

Sequels: Print

By the time I had begun to write the present book in the autumn of 1979, Prentice-Hall's hard-cover edition of *The Amityville Horror: A True Story* had been reprinted thirteen times. The Bantam paperback edition at the same time had been reprinted seventeen times, and the "Bantam movie edition"—released after the film—had already been reprinted ten times. Altogether, it has been estimated that the various editions of the original book sold over ten million copies. How much did it earn? The exact amount cannot be determined, but its magnitude must lie somewhere between the amount it would have earned if all ten million copies sold at an original sale price of around $2.25 and the amount it would have earned if all copies were sold at the $9.23 for which it now sells on Amazon—*i.e.*, between $22.5 million and $92.3 million dollars. The cumulative earnings probably lie closer to the lower figure than to the higher one—even considering how many copies were sold as the hard-cover edition, which almost surely sold for a price more than two or three times that of the paperback. Even so, earnings of thirty or forty million dollars would be a breath-taking statistic.

In addition to the hardcover and paperback editions, *The Amityville Horror: A True Story* was also serialized in the (New York) *Daily News* and possibly other newspapers under permission contracts with Prentice-Hall. The amount of the royalties earned by serialization could not be determined.

Two sequels to *The Amityville Horror* were written by John G. Jones: *The Amityville Horror II* (1982, Warner Books), and *Amityville: The Final Chapter*—"Based on the 7-year ordeal of George and Kathleen Lutz" (1985, A Jove Book). In both books, the Lutzes shared the copyright with the writer. I have been unable to find information on sales or earnings of either sequel.

The Ghosthunter Hans Holzer wrote three books relating to the house at 112 Ocean Avenue: *Murder in Amityville* (1979, Belmont Tower Books); *The Amityville Curse: Fact & Fiction* (1981, Barnes & Noble); and *The Secret of Amityville* (1985, TBS The Book Service, Ltd.).

Sequels: Film

Amityville's Horror first appeared in film in 1979, the year the present research began. *The Amityville Horror* was an immediate hit at the box office, grossing $86.43 million [*Internet Movie Database*, "The Amityville Horror"]

By the year 2020, at least twenty-five films directly or indirectly related to Anson's book had been produced:

- *Amityville II: The Possession* (1982) Gross $12.53 million.
- *Amityville 3-D* (1983) (also released as *Amityville III: The Demon*) Gross $6.33 million.
- *Amityville 4: The Evil Escapes* (1989)

- *The Amityville Curse* (1990)
- *Amityville: It's About Time* (1992)
- *Amityville: A New Generation* (1993)
- *Amityville Dollhouse* (1996)
- *The Amityville Horror* (2005 remake) Gross $65.23 million.
- *The Amityville Haunting* (2011)
- *The Amityville Asylum* (2013)
- *Amityville Death House* (2015)
- *The Amityville Playhouse* (2015)
- *The Amityville Terror* (2016)
- *Amityville: No Escape* (2016)
- *Amityville: Vanishing Point* (2016)
- *Amityville Toybox* (2016)
- *The Amityville Legacy* (2016)
- *Amityville Prison* (2017)
- *Amityville Clownhouse* (2017)
- *Amityville Exorcism* (2017)
- *Against the Night* (2017)
- *Amityville: The Awakening* (2017)
- *Amityville: Mr. Misery Rd.* (2018)
- *The Amityville Murders* (2018)
- *The Amityville Harvest* (2020)

At least one further Amityville-themed film is scheduled to be released before this book will go to print, and surely it will not be the last bit of "Devil's spawn" that will be released into the media pond. Broadcast television and Internet and cable streaming have proven to be even more successful media in which to propagate the Horror Anson hatched in Amityville. As I write, Amazon Prime is carrying *Devil's Road: The True Story of Ed and Lorraine Warren*—the demonologist and light-trance medium who were the catalyst that first moved me to investigate the paranormal claims of *The Amityville Horror: A True Story*.

Aftermath—*Dramatis Personae*

It has now been demonstrated beyond any reasonable doubt that *The Amityville Horror: A True Story* is a work of religiously-themed fiction—a passion play depicting not the suffering of Christ, but rather the imagined sufferings of a financially strapped family in an environment still nervously reacting to the film version of *The Exorcist.* It is now time to sum up the careers of the cast of characters who acted in the play.

The House at 112 Ocean Avenue—
the Stage of the Theater

Arguably, the house itself is the most important actor in Jay Anson's cast of characters. After reverting to the bank after being vacated by the Lutzes, the house was bought by James and Barbara Cromarty for $55,000, who then spent $25,000 on improvements. They promptly debunked many of the paranormal claims of the story. Whereas the house had originally been painted black with white trim, it quickly was painted white with black trim. Due to the annoyance of thousands of curiosity-seekers descending upon the property, the address was changed from 112 to 108 Ocean Avenue. Eventually, the iconic jack-o'-lantern front windows on the third floor were replaced with ordinary rectangular windows. Since being owned by the Cromartys, the house has been resold numerous times, its highest selling price being $950,000 in October of 2010. The swimming pool was removed, and a lovely sunporch was added to the back of the house, providing a beautiful view of the water. After having sold for nearly a million dollars in 2010, the house was sold for $605,000 in March of 2017, and the current "Zestimate" value of the house listed on the Zillow real estate webpage in 2020 was $782,563.

Jay Anson—
the Playwright

Born on November 4, 1921, Jay Anson did not live long enough to enjoy the full financial benefits of the Amityville enterprise. He died on March 12, 1980, at the age of 58. His net worth at the time of his death was $600,000

[Net Worth Post, "Jay Anson"]. In 2020 dollars, that is the equivalent of $1,440,000.

William Peter Blatty—
the Playwright's Muse

Born on January 7, 1928, the author of *The Exorcist* and other demon-themed novels and films, died of multiple myeloma in Bethesda, on January 12, 2020—just five days after his eighty-ninth birthday. His net worth at the time of his death was $5 million [Celebrity Net Wealth, "William Peter Blatty"].

Rev. Ralph J. Pecoraro—
the Possessed Priest

After leaving Amityville early in 1976, the priest known as "Father Mancuso" in Anson's book and "Father Delaney" in the first movie moved to California—apparently in the vicinity of San Francisco. According to Christopher Lutz, "Father Ray remained a part of our lives" for many years after relocation to California. Born in 1935, he died in 1987, aged 51 or 52. The place of his death and interment could not be determined.

Ed and Lorraine Warren—
the Ghost Hunters

It was a visit by the Warrens to Fulton-Montgomery Community College (SUNY) that first attracted the present author's attention to the story of *The Amityville Horror: A True Story*. Ed was born Ed Warren Miney on September 7, 1926. He died August 23, 2006, aged 79. Lorraine was born Lorraine Rita Moran on January 31, 1927. She participated in Daniel Lutz's film *My Amityville Horror* in 2012. She died April 18, 2019, aged 92. Her net wealth at the time of her death has been estimated at one or two million dollars. As this book goes to press, *Devil's Road: The True Story of Ed and Lorraine Warren* is still streaming on Amazon Prime.

George Lee Lutz and Kathleen Theresa Conners Lutz—
the Main Characters

After moving to California and investing in sequel books and films, the Lutzes divorced sometime in the late 1980s. Kathy, born on October 13, 1946, died of emphysema on August 17, 2004. George, born on January 1, 1947, died of heart disease on May 8, 2006. (Jay Anson failed to mention any New Year's Day celebration of George's birthday during the 28 days in the horror house.) The *Net Worth Post* estimated their joint net wealth at $17 million [*Net Worth Post*, "George Lutz," "Kathleen Lutz"]. If the estimate was made when the two last were still alive, that would be the equivalent of over $23 million in 2021.

Daniel Lutz—
Supporting Character

Daniel Edward Quaratino Lutz was born on October 26, 1965. Contrary to Anson's claim that Daniel was nine years old when the family moved into the demon house, he had recently turned ten. Little was known about his post-Amityville life until the release of his quasi-autobiographical film *My Amityville Horror*, in the spring of 2013 [Lutz, Daniel, Eric Walter, Andrea Adams, John Blythe, Ronald Puleio, and Michael S. Russo. *My Amityville Horror.* Released March 15, 2013 (Lost Witness Pictures, LLC, ©2012)]. In the film, forty-seven-year-old Daniel Lutz appears as an extremely angry, nervous, and severely emotionally disturbed man—a man who has been able to recover neither from the physical and emotional abuse suffered at the hands of his stepfather, George Lee Lutz, nor from the circus life ensuing from the movie *The Amityville Horror*.

In his film, Daniel describes violent conflicts with his stepfather even before moving into 112 Ocean Avenue—claiming that wooden-spoon beatings had commenced even before the beating alleged in Anson's book. In fact, he claims he was "beaten over fifty times with a wooden spoon" altogether. (Interestingly, the wooden-spoon beating appears to have been present in the earliest documentable form of the Amityville story—the typed notes of Laura DiDio, the Channel 5 News reporter who first discovered "the scoop" on the story.) He claims to have tried to kill George several times, but it isn't clear when or how those attempts might have occurred. Around the time the movie came out, he claims his parents "got a large advance to do a promotional tour [of the world] for close to a year."

"[I] wound up being dumped off at a Catholic Church monastery school. I had an authority problem … priests were beating the shit out of me, performing exorcisms … which they don't want to talk about." Daniel says he ran away "multiple times between [the ages of] twelve and fifteen." As will be shown in Chapter 39, Daniel not only confirms many of the outrageous claims of the book—some of which have been shown clearly not to have occurred—he magnifies many of them to comic proportions. When asked if he believes he was possessed at the time of the story, he replies, "I don't *believe* I was possessed; I *know* I was possessed."

Daniel claims to have left home at the age of "fifteen or sixteen" and led a homeless life "in the desert." He says George "left the scene" when he was about seventeen years old, and sometime thereafter he was reconciled to his mother. In fact, his film is "Dedicated to Kathleen Conners-Quaratino-Lutz." In the film, he repeatedly is seen playing several fancy electric guitars, producing a harsh, angry—indeed rebellious—type of rock music. One is left to wonder if he might have pursued a career as a musician.

Christopher Lutz—
Supporting Character

Christopher Lutz was seven years old at the time of the family's residence at 112 Ocean Avenue. He remained silent concerning the paranormal claims of his parents until February 11, 2012, when he participated in a telephone interview with ABC News' *Spooky South Coast Radio* program in New Bedford, Massachusetts [Lutz, C., "Inside the Amityville Horror"]. Lasting an hour and forty-one minutes, his rambling and sometimes incoherent testimony reveals an emotionally scarred man who never recovered from the wild publicity resulting from the publication of Anson's book and the 1979 release of the first film version of the story. In the interview, he tells of quarrels with his stepfather leading to his running away from home at the age of sixteen, somehow finishing high school, joining the army, changing his name from Lutz back to his birth name Quaratino, and supporting his mother during her terminal illness.

The interview creates the impression that one is listening to a highly superstitious person. When asked if he thinks the horror house was haunted, he replies, "Can you think of any reason for a house where six people were murdered *not* to be haunted?" When asked about his parents' practice of Transcendental Meditation, he launches into a dizzying lecture about mantras being the names of spirits that enter the body through chakras that are exposed by the cross-legged meditation posture, and substituting the names of demons for mantras can lead to possession.

When asked if his mother ever experienced "any paranormal experiences" before moving into 112 Ocean Avenue, he is coy: "That's relevant, but off the table," giving the impression he's saving information for a later exposé of his own. Immediately, however, he says "I don't want to say 'no' … I don't think Amityville was the start from it." Did anything happen? "Yeah, I do know that my parents did go through something that scared the crap out of them…and they continued to their grave saying something did happen."

When asked about the claims implied by the book and movie, he replies, "Everything that's been said *did* happen, I know *did not* happen. And so, I know things that the book said [happened], that *didn't* happen either." When asked about what specifically never happened, after saying "Not one piece of glass broke as far as windows [are concerned]," he becomes coy and gives no further details, merely asserting that "What I read in that book is *not* what happened."

The picture Christopher (Lutz) Quaratino paints of George Lutz is not very flattering. He claims his stepfather actually "was dealing with things in the occult, calling things up … when we left that house, that followed us." He indicates that George knew the names of demons and implies George was in fact trying to call up demons intentionally, not stupidly and innocently calling up their names as depicted in Anson's book. Interestingly, he reveals that the priest remained in contact with the family after everyone moved to California. "Father Ray [Ralph Pecoraro] continued to be a big part of our lives and counseled George on a number of things. One of those was specifically what he had been doing. And so, George stopped that, at the advice from that priest."

Apparently, the *Spooky South Coast* broadcast was not the first time Christopher Quaratino had publicly asserted the occult activities of his stepfather. He asserts that when he had previously claimed George was into occult activities, his stepfather had locked him up in a lawsuit in order to salvage a three-motion-picture deal he was negotiating with The Weinstein Company, newly founded by the now-disgraced movie mogul Harvey Weinstein. The lawsuit apparently ended with the death of George Lutz in 2006.

Altogether, the broadcast evokes the image of a deeply depressed man who is haunted, not by Amityville's Horror, but by the chaotic, socially, and psychologically disruptive publicity that resulted from the publication of the book and the release of the 1979 film. For reasons not disclosed, he has been estranged from his brother Daniel "for a long time." It is easy to feel sincere sympathy for this victim of post-traumatic stress syndrome—a stress inflicted not by something demonic, but rather by *a story* of something demonic.

Melissa (Missy) Lutz—
Supporting Character

The only member of the cast for whom I have been unable to discover reliable information is the five-year-old Missy Lutz—the counterpart of the girl Regan in *The Exorcist*, the child seen in the initial phases of demonic possession in Anson's story. Frances J. Armstrong, in her self-published *The Real Amityville Horror: The True Story Behind the Brutal DeFeo Murders*, says "The three children did not discuss the hauntings and events in the house publicly until recent years. Melissa is the only one who was [*sic*] remained completely silent. She did tell Rick Moran she recalls drawing a picture of Jodie, the demonic pig and giving it to her mother. Melissa is believed to have changed her name and does not speak about the hauntings" [pages not numbered]. Armstrong gives no references for any of the claims in her book, and so I have been unable to verify independently any parts of this quotation. I do not recommend her book.

Ronald DeFeo, Jr.— an Off-Stage Presence

We end this discussion of the Amityville cast of characters with the person whose arguably insane actions laid the premise for the play itself—Ronnie DeFeo. Ronald Joseph DeFeo, Jr. was born in Brooklyn, New York, on September 26, 1951. After he murdered his parents and four siblings on November 13, 1974, he was tried and found guilty on six counts of second-degree murder on November 21, 1975. He received six sentences of twenty-five years to life in prison at the Sullivan Correctional Facility in the town of Fallsburg, New York. He died in prison on March 12, 2021, at the age of 69. The cause of death was not immediately disclosed.

Daniel Lutz's *My Amityville Horror*

During the year 2012, with the collaboration of Eric Walter, Andrea Adams, John Blythe, Laura DiDio, Lorraine Warren, and others, Daniel Lutz produced a quasi-autobiographical film titled *My Amityville Horror*. Released to theaters on March 15 of 2013 and subsequently sold as a DVD, the independently produced film is important not only for what it reveals about Daniel Lutz and his over-the-top account of life in the horror house, but also for the number of TV interviews with the Lutzes that it incorporates and the very large number of still photographs dating back to the time of the Lutz residence in the Dutch Colonial house at 112 Ocean Avenue. Many of those pictures not only reveal further problems with Anson's scenario, they offer conclusive proof for some of the claims made by the present author and other skeptics.

Daniel's Tale

The tale told by Daniel Lutz is rambling, jerky, and at times incoherent; making it near impossible to present an organized analysis of his version of Anson's *True Story*. About the only generalization to be made is that he amplifies the claims of Anson's book and the Amityville movie to almost comic proportions. It must suffice, therefore, to simply list his remarks in the order they appear in his film.

- Daniel's birth name was Daniel Edward Quaratino, he was born in 1965 on October 26, and he left his mother to find his place in the world at the age of seventeen.
- He claims that George had a permit to carry a gun, that he owned Harley Choppers (plural) and Corvettes.
- He repeats the story of Harry nearly strangling on the kennel fence, and there were "garage problems."
- Flies were in his bedroom (not the sewing room) already on the day they moved in!
- George had beaten him with a wooden spoon "fifty times"—including on occasions predating their move to Amityville.

- He claims to have tried to kill George "several times," but does not say how the attempts were made.
- He claims he saw the garage door not ripped off its hinges but slamming up and down repeatedly.
- He claims to have seen an angry pig that looked like a cartoon character.
- He claims the little rocking chair in Missy's room was rocking back and forth by itself for twenty-five minutes!
- He says, "I don't *believe* I was possessed, I *know* I was possessed."
- He claims both his hands were crushed—"skin-on-skin"—by the window; they swelled up to five times normal, looking like a child's catcher's mitt; and seconds later his hands were back to normal, except for the pinky on his left hand. Contrary to Anson's book but agreeing with Hoffman, he wasn't taken to see a doctor.
- He claims that on the last night in the house, both he and his brother "shared a levitation experience" in their beds.

Probably the most consequential claim Daniel Quaratino Lutz makes (in agreement with his brother Chris), is that his stepfather was interested in occult and paranormal subjects before Amityville. Indeed, if we are to believe Daniel, when Daniel first moved into George's house, he saw a bookshelf filled with books on Transcendental Meditation, Buddhism, Satanic history, mind control, hypnosis, witchcraft, and other such topics. He claims he took a book about "sacrificing virgins" off the shelf and was reading it when Kathy caught him and angrily made him put it back on the shelf. Considering Daniel was just nine years old at the time he moved into George's house, it is questionable whether or not his reading skills would have been adequate to understand, remember, and accurately report the titles of the books George owned decades later.

According to the accounts of both Hoffman and Anson, after fleeing the Amityville house, the Lutzes took "crash courses" in the paranormal and supernatural. If that were true, clearly there would have been many books on topics such as those listed by Daniel. However, hypnosis and mind control don't leap immediately to mind as relevant for someone thinking about haunted houses. Given the repeated instances of the Lutzes making claims that turned out to be the exact opposite of the truth, it is not unreasonable to hypothesize that George was deeply involved in such topics well before the move to Amityville. Indeed, in the film Laura DiDio mentions hearing "reports and rumors" of George being "into the occult."

In his film, Daniel Lutz makes an extraordinary claim not yet discussed in this summary. He claims "George was into telekinesis, mind control, [astral] projection ... George moved objects telekinetically before they moved to Amityville." He goes on to recall a pre-Amityville scene where George was "in his garage with friends, and he moved wrenches [telekinetically] and put them down."

As with so many of the stories recounted by both Daniel and Christopher, this tale is told with a degree of sincerity characteristic of a person who really believes in what he is saying. It has all the hallmarks of false memories implanted by hypnosis. If Lutz in fact was trying to learn hypnosis, a child would be a perfect Guinea pig on whom to experiment. Except for especially young children, it is generally the case that the younger children are, the more suggestible they are. Older people are usually very difficult to hypnotize—if they can be hypnotized at all. Alas, the truth or falseness of this hypothesis must remain undetermined.

The Tales the Pictures Tell

One of the most valuable conclusions of the present book is that there was no kitchen door leading directly to the back yard, vitiating multiple episodes where George is in the back yard with Harry, sees a giant pig behind Missy in the upstairs bedroom window or hears a marching band inside the house, then rushes into the house through the kitchen door. Several photographs presented in the film clearly show that there was no external kitchen door at the time of the Lutz residency—just the double doors leading from the east wall of the dining room onto the patio overlooking the swimming pool, as indicated in the blueprints. Interestingly, they also show that unlike the rest of the black-shingled house, the shingles on the back side of the house were white—as is the case yet today when the entire house is now white with black trim. But the pictures reveal even further impossibilities of the episodes in question.

Several photographs of the front of the garage show the fenced-in kennel where Harry Lutz was always found sleeping or allegedly trying to hang himself. (The trapezoidal compound was the same fenced-in area where the DeFeo's dog Shaggy was kept and where Ronnie DeFeo tried to set things up so he would hang himself on the fence with his chain.) Anson's *True Story* requires the kennel to be on north side (pool side) of the garage-boathouse structure for George to fetch Harry from an alleged exterior kitchen door. Other pictures show that the kennel was not only located on the *south* side and southern part of the front of the garage, they show that another fence, running from the house along the north side of the driveway to the northwest corner of the garage, has no gates that would allow entry to the back yard from the driveway. *It would have been impossible for George Lutz to reach Harry's compound from any door in the kitchen wall*—or even from the north wall of the house, which the blueprints show would have been the shortest path between the kitchen and the back yard.

The film shows a picture of the basement furnace, which appears to be rather decrepit and perhaps unreliable for heating of the house. The same picture also shows a black, tall, double-door freezer beside the furnace, actually verifying Anson's placement of the freezer in the basement, not in the garage where the auction catalog listed it for sale during the auction of the Lutz's household possessions. Obviously, it must have been necessary to move such a heavy and bulky object out of the basement before the auction to allow rapid removal from the auction site.

DiDio's Bullet-Points and the Story They Tell

Laura DiDio, the Channel 5 News reporter who seems to have been the first to gain information from the Lutzes, makes numerous appearances in the film. Indeed, she seems to have been actively involved in the production of the film. In one of her appearances, the camera focuses on a page of the notes she typed up after her first meeting with the Lutzes. Though unavailable when this book was begun forty years ago, her notes document the earliest form of the Lutz story. Five bullet-point paragraphs are complete, and the nature of a sixth one can be deduced. For the most part, they would support the hypothesis that Lutz had already learned the *Exorcist* indicia required to indicate the onset of demonic possession. Importantly, the Lutz's claims at the time, with one exception, were moderate to the point of being downright boring and differed significantly from the details in Anson's story. Three of the points read:

- Kathy and George Lutz stated that they never wanted to leave the house to go visiting or even do such ordinary chores as shopping.
- The Lutzes [*sic*] sex life had been uncharacteristically non-existent after they moved into the house.
- Harry, the family dog, had spent an inordinate amount of time sleeping, unusual for a year-old animal. On one occasion when he wasn't dozing, the dog nearly strangled himself on his chain trying to climb over the fence and get off the property Lutz said. Other animals, they claimed, would not go on the property.

This point clearly shows that the Lutzes must have learned about the DeFeo dog-strangulation anecdote from Weber at a very early stage. Another bullet point—incomplete but easily interpreted—says "George Lutz could never get warm in the house and was always…" It would seem psychic cold was part of the Amityville tale from the beginning. Another bullet-point somewhat contradicts Anson's story, but partially comports with Paul Hoffman's version:

- The house worked differently on women than on men. Men were infested with violent reactions [*sic*], while women Kathy said were charmed by the house and overcome with a feeling of lassiditude [*sic*].

According to Hoffman, "When Kathy's sister-in-law visited, she reverted to childhood, spending all her time with the children in the third-floor playroom." This clearly is supported in a second, partial page of DiDio's notes that flash on the screen saying, "Kathy's sister-in-law gravitated to the /… / and reverted to childhood." Although Hoffman also mentions the episode with Kathy's ex-nun aunt that contradicts this bullet-point, Anson amplifies it and makes no explicit difference between men's and women's reactions to the house. Overall, the notes support the argument that Hoffman's account is much closer to "the true story" than is Anson's.

"Poltergeist Puke"

This leaves just one of the complete bullet points remaining to be discussed:

- The boathouse was a source of poltergeist activity, Lutz alleged. He had gone out to check it one night and found a green slime which he dubbed "poltergeist puke" oozing all over the place.

This constitutes the earliest version of how Weber's greenish-black fingerprint dust was transformed into green slime. The slime appears not in the house itself, but in the boathouse—again, clearly showing dependence on Weber's account of Ronnie DeFeo's obsession with the boathouse. Interestingly, it ties the green slime to things demonic explicitly, and shows a very early dependence upon *The Exorcist*, where "a thick and putrid greenish vomit began to pump from Regan's mouth in slow and regular spurts that oozed like lava over her lip and flowed in waves onto Merrin's hand" [*Exorcist*, p. 360].

Indebted to *The Exorcist* before Anson's Involvement

My Amityville Horror also flashes a picture of part of a newspaper article by a writer named John Huddy, titled "Amityville: Ghost Story or Chumps in the Night?" Repeatedly throughout the present book, evidence has been presented demonstrating Anson's debt to *The Exorcist*. It appears from this clipping, however, that George Lutz had already shaped the story to fit Anson's model before Anson had become part of the project. Huddy reports "Lutz takes all of this in stride. There will always be skeptics and those who laugh at the supernatural, the former engineer and surveyor says calmly. 'You know, people who don't believe in ghosts don't have much imagination. I had seen *The Exorcist* the year before we bought the house and I thought it was another silly movie,' Lutz says. 'My wife Kathy and I considered ourselves the original skeptics.'"

"Methinks the gentleman doth protest *too* much!" Just as religious apologists routinely claim atheist beginnings for their careers, so too it is practically formulaic for purveyors of the preternatural to proclaim their original skepticism. *The Exorcist* movie was released on December 26, 1973—slightly less than a year before the DeFeo murders on November 13, 1974. "The year before we bought the house" would accord with the time of the murders, not the time the film was likely being shown on Long Island. It is probable that Lutz had been greatly impressed by the film. When the murders occurred a year later, given the superstitious nature Lutz is revealed to have had in *My Amityville Horror*, he might genuinely have inferred a demonic dimension in the DeFeo story.

At What Cost?

This investigation into the facts surrounding *The Amityville Horror: A True Story* began as a purely academic exercise. It was intended to serve as an example for my students, demonstrating how to investigate haunted-house stories and similar paranormal and supernatural claims. In the beginning, I expected to find natural explanations for many of the phenomena reported in the book. Very soon, however, weather reports were obtained that conclusively showed the fictitious nature of many of the most extraordinary episodes in the "twenty-eight days of horror." When I learned of Anson's professional relationship with *The Exorcist*, I quickly changed my expectations. Instead of finding natural explanations, I now expected to discover details of how an elaborate hoax had been carried out. Nevertheless, throughout the investigations carried out over forty years ago, I had no emotional involvement in the case. It was all abstract, all academic. Even after I resumed work on the case in the following century, it had never occurred to me that there might be a deeply human dimension of the case that needed to be considered.

As I neared the end of the investigation, however, I became curious to know what had happened to all the characters who played a part in the Amityville story. Only then did I become conscious of the psychological trauma the hoax had inflicted upon the three Lutz children. Only as I was listening to Christopher Lutz's interview on Spooky South Coast Radio and viewing Daniel Lutz's video *My Amityville Horror* did it dawn on me: the Lutz children were—and still are—the victims of child abuse. Extreme, mental child abuse.

I was stunned as I listened to the sometimes incoherent, rambling reminiscences of two deeply disturbed men—men whose lives had been ruined by the demonic dementia induced by *The Exorcist* and its spawn *The Amityville Horror*. As I listened to their testimonies, a deep sense of shame swept over me as I realized that for decades, Missy, Chris, and Danny Lutz had seemed no more real—no more human, no more important—than the characters in any second-rate novel. I was deeply shaken as I listened to two men whose lives had been ruined. Men whose pursuit of happiness had been horrifically crippled by a superstition as old as Ur, as seminal as Sumer: the belief in demons. They had been psychologically wounded, not by demons, but *by the idea of demons*. Christopher and Daniel Lutz are living proof that teaching children that devils and demons are real is just as much a form a child abuse as is physical punishment.

I regret to say I was unable to find any reliable information concerning Melissa Lutz. It cannot be doubted that she too was acutely damaged by the story of Amityville's horror. Although I hope she has been able to escape any lingering trauma as serious as the abuse her brothers sustained, I am not sanguine. She was, in many ways, the focus of Amityville's Horror, and it seems probable that her life has been even more damaged than her brothers by the aftermath of the hoax.

A Thought Experiment

By the time I began writing the present book in 1979, the Amityville fraud had already generated several tens of millions of dollars in profit. Forty years ago, it could not have been imagined that at the beginning of the third decade of the following century, a scientifically impossible, theologically based fiction such as *The Amityville Horror: A True Story* would still be generating revenue. William Weber and the Lutzes could never have known the Devil's tale they concocted "over three or four bottles of wine" might possibly have generated as much as half a billion dollars-worth of time and money when all has been considered and evaluated. An exact estimation of the cumulative economy created by Anson's novel is beyond the scope of this book and might very well be impossible in principle. Nevertheless, the implications of a simple thought experiment might provide some sense of the order of magnitude of the economic and sociopolitical impact of the deception.

"Time is money," the old saying goes, and for millions of Americans forty hours of labor weekly are converted into their monetary equivalent. It is also clear that money in turn can be converted into energy. Every month, my money is converted into electricity, gasoline, natural gas, and food—the source of the biological energy needed for human labor. Given the conceptual equivalence of money, time, and energy, can we estimate the magnitudes and relevance of the corresponding post-Amityville sociopolitical economies that had emerged by January 6, 2021, when supporters of President Donald J. Trump attempted to overthrow the government of the United States? Let us examine the relevant facts and try to imagine the magnitudes and shapes of the economies in question.

The Time, Energy, and Cost Economies of the Books

Anson's book sold over ten million copies altogether in its various editions. The paperback presently sells on Amazon.com for $9.23—amounting to total sales of $92.3 million in present-day dollars, and it probably sold for around

$2.25—corresponding to $22.5 million if all copies had been sold in 1980. As noted earlier, the cumulative sales probably have been closer to the lower amount. But this amount does not take into account the tens of thousands of hardcover books sold. Rare today, they presently sell for $148.42 on Amazon. We must also consider the number of hours needed to write, edit, and typeset the book and the royalties and wages involved. Then there is the cost of the paper and ink consumed in the manufacture of the various editions of the book, as well as the time and wages required to produce them. We must not forget the energy and time consumed to ship the book to bookstores and mail-order customers. How much gasoline was consumed in trips to booksellers to purchase the fiction?

Outside of the physical costs, there is the question of how many human hours were wasted in reading the "true story"—hours that could have been spent on efforts for self-education or for improvement of human welfare. How many people were caused to turn away—and to what degree—from evidence-based decision making and turn instead to "faith-based" reasoning? How much did the book—and the alternative-facts universe it helped to spawn—weaken the degree to which human actions are based on science instead of evidence-free belief?

It is not clear how much money was involved in the production and sale of the six published sequels, let alone the various books relating loosely to Amityville and the DeFeo murders—books that frequently have mixed facts with more than a little fiction. All the questions just raised about Anson's book should be applied regarding its sequels and spin-offs.

The Time, Energy, and Cost Economies of the Films and Videos

In the case of the movies, the 1979 film *The Amityville Horror* grossed $86.43 million, and its 2005 remake yielded $65.23 million. By the year 2020, at least twenty-five spin-off films had been released, and a twenty-sixth film is scheduled for release before the present book will go to press. *The Conjuring*, a spin-off film featuring Ed and Lorraine Warren, grossed over $300 million. How much did all the movies together earn? How much money was expended in wages for the actors, directors, and production staff in their production? How much human time, money, and energy were spent on material required for production, manufacture, and distribution of the films? How much electricity was consumed by theaters and television sets required to present the films? How much gasoline was incinerated going to those presentations? How much carbon was released into the atmosphere?

It is impossible to know exactly how many radio and television interviews have been devoted all or in part to Amityville publicity and discussions of the story in support of a supernatural understanding of the world. Even so, that must be included in this thought experiment. How many other superstitions have been propped up by acceptance of Anson's fable as "a true story"? It rapidly has become clear that this thought experiment cannot be completed. Exponentially, its increasing complexity has raised more questions than could possibly be answered—questions relating to a near-infinity of possible factors needing to be evaluated if we were to answer the question of this chapter: *at what cost*?

Post-Truth Potlatch

Whatever the cost could prove to be, the "Amityville industry" by the fifth decade of its operation has involved the wastage of a vast amount of money, energy, and human time. It amounts to a Kwakiutl "potlatch," enlarged to nearly unimaginable dimensions. Like the nineteenth century potlatches of the Northwest Coast Indians, the Amityville industry (and the culture it has spawned) has involved the senseless destruction of the means of human subsistence and survival. While wanton destruction of wealth is the best-known characteristic of potlatches in the popular understanding, a more complete definition of the term might read, "a potlatch involves giving away or destroying wealth or items in order to demonstrate a person's wealth and power and to reaffirm human connections with the supernatural world."

A potlatch is, at its core, a religious rite. In a way, potlatches were like the holocaust sacrifices ("burnt offerings") practiced in the Temple of Yahweh in Jerusalem, where valuable animals and goods were burnt up completely to honor the Mosaic covenant—a human connection with the supernatural world.

The Socio-Political Cost

The Pre-Truth Era was an age before the emergence of science as a means for discovering "truth"—reliable information about what is real. In order to reliably make decisions of how best to respond to the daily challenges that threaten the survival of not only of individual human beings, but also entire societies, we must be able to differentiate between what is real and what is fantasy. The term "Truth Age"—the Age of Science—never existed before the commencement of the political ascendancy of Donald J. Trump, whose lies and "alternative facts" catalyzed the coining of the term "Post-Truth Era"—an era that even today is not yet ended, as fact-proof beliefs trample evidence-supported facts. The former president is still supported by millions of fundamentalist Catholic and Protestant Christians—people who have made faith a virtue and believe that the Christian Bible is literally true and factual. Not only do they believe such without evidence, they believe it *even against the evidence*.

In their Bible, the most important character—Jesus—is an exorcist who routinely casts out devils and demons believed to afflict humans with both physical and psychological illness. The Trump faithful live not just in the dangerous thought-world of the alternative facts and political propaganda of the Post-Truth Era that Donald Trump engendered, they are still living in the Pre-Truth Era of the Judeo-Christian scriptures. Thus, they reject not only the truths of human evolution and anthropogenic climate change, they are compelled to reject the truths of modern medicine and the science of embryology. Perhaps most alarmingly, they reject the findings of fact-based historical investigations. Many have convinced themselves that Blacks, because they have inherited "the curse of Ham," deserve to be "servants of servants" (*i.e.*, slaves, Gen 9:25). Not surprisingly, many of the Trump faithful believe in the supremacy of the white race.

The Christian Bible refers to demons or lesser devils sixty-one times. Not including references to Beelzebub, it refers to "the Devil" thirty-five times. There are thirteen references to demonic possession, and multiple reports that Jesus himself cast out demons or devils from people thus possessed. Like fundamentalist Catholics and Protestants, QAnon cultists believe their Bibles to be true in the literal sense. Because of their belief in Satan and his minions, many proved to be vulnerable to the Satanic conspiracy theories that led them to take part in the attempted *coup d'etat* in Washington, D.C. on January 6, 2021.

The insurrectionists who invaded the Capitol carried not only Trump flags, they carried Confederate flags and flags declaring the phrase "JESUS SAVES!" It seems highly likely that at least some of the maskless assailants believed Jesus would save them from demonic possession as well as from COVID-19; nevertheless, Jesus needed their paramilitary help.

The time is now long past for belief in the efficacy of the rite of exorcism—the casting out of devils or demons from human beings. Whether the exorcist be a priest, a pope, or Jesus himself, it is past time for the practice to stop. It is time now to drive out the very idea of devils and demons from the collective consciousness of civilized men and women. If a secular civilization is to endure, this is a moral as well as educational and political imperative.

In an age of rapidly deteriorating environmental conditions fueled by the thermal energy of global warming and the overpopulation that has driven it, the survival of civilization itself is no longer a certainty. Willful ignorance of the facts of science and history can be afforded no longer. We can't be sure that civilization can be saved even if everyone turns from faith-based to fact-based decision making. We *can* be sure, however, that global disaster awaits if we fail to navigate the turn successfully. Or if we fail to make the turn at all.

Image Credits

Fig. 1. Photograph by Stan Wolfson/Newsday RM via Getty Images; GettyImages-1026768664 Licensed Reproduction.

Fig. 2–4. Photograph by Frank R. Zindler.

Fig. 5–8. Reconstructed by Catherine E. Zindler from Images in the Public Domain.

Bibliography

Amityville Horror, The. American International Pictures, Cinema 77, 1979.

"'Amityville' Prisoner Seeks New Trial in Family's Killing." *New York Times,* Thursday, June 25, 1992.

Anson, Jay. *The Amityville Horror: A True Story* (hardcover edition). Englewood Cliffs, NJ: Prentice-Hall, 1977.

——— "The Amityville Horror: Did Demons Do It? First of a series." *New York Daily News*, Sunday, November 20, 1977. (Amityville Public Library photocopy of article)

——— *The Amityville Horror: A True Story* (paperback edition). New York, NY: Bantam Books, 1978

Armstrong, Frances J. *The Real Amityville Horror: The True Story Behind the Brutal DeFeo Murders.* Monee, Illinois: Self-published, 2017. .0

Associated Press. "Scalded, Roasted and Burned—Mother Charged with Putting Her Infant in 'Exorcist' Oven." *Schenectady Gazette*, Thursday, January 3, 1980.

Bailey, Paul. *Centennial of the Village of Amityville. Marking a Century of Achievement 1850–1950.* (Photocopy of Amityville Free Library copy of program for ceremonies taking place from Sunday to Saturday, July 23 to July 29, 1950)

Blatty, William Peter. *The Exorcist* (hardcover edition). New York, NY: Harper & Row, 1971.

——— *The Exorcist* (paperback edition). New York, NY: Bantam Books, 1972.

Bowles, Pete. "Lutz Family 'Horror' Suit Is Rejected." *Newsday*, September 11, 1979.

——— "Amityville Book Gets a Bad Review." *Newsday*, Wednesday, September 13, 1979.

——— "Out-of-Court Settlement in 'Amityville Horror' Case." *Newsday*, September 13, 1979.

Browder, Sue. "A guide to Ghosting in New England." *Newsday/The Island*, Sunday section, November 14, 1975.

Burstein, Patricia, and Sue Reilly. "The Amityville Horror Lives On—In a Snarl of Lawsuits and Suspicions." *People Magazine*, February 13, 1978: 28-31.

Carter, A.J., and Christopher M. Cook. "DeFeo Home Abandoned; buyer Calls It Haunted." *Newsday*, February 14, 1976.

Cassidy, Jerry. "Hosts of ghosts put Amityville tourist haunt on block." *New York Daily News*, February (day?), 1979. (photocopy of clipping in Amityville Free Library)

Celebrity Net Wealth, https://www.celebritynetwealth.com, accessed 6/3/21.

Conkey, Laura E., Ethel Boissevain, and Ives Goddard. "Indians of Southern New England: Late Period." In *Handbook of North American Indians, Vol. 15, Northea*st, edited by Bruce G. Trigger. Washington, DC: Smithsonian Institution, 1978.

"Death Threat Alleged at DeFeo Trial." *Newsday*, October 21, 1975.

"DeFeo Jury Into 2nd Day." *Newsday*, Thursday, November 20, 1975.

"DeFeo pleads not guilty! Cops find gun in canal." *Amityville Record*, November 21, 1974.

Dennis, Henry C. *The American Indian 1492–1976*. Dobbs Ferry, NY: Oceana Publications, 1977.

Drehsler, Alex, and Jim Scovel. "Amityville Horror: Is it fact or fiction?" *Newsday*, November 17, 1977: 4A-5A, 15A.

Fraser, C. Gerald. "Jay Anson, 58, Writer of 'Amityville Horror,' Dead on West Coast." *New York Times*, March 14, 1980.

Greene, Bob. "Strange encounters in a horrifying house." *Dallas Morning News*, March 6, 1978.

——— "Amityville house story a haunted hoax?" *Dallas Morning News*, March 8, 1978. (Reports on findings of Jim Scovel and Alex Drehsler)

Gugas, Chris, and Michael J. Rice. "Personal and Confidential Report on Polygraph Testing of George and Kathy Lutz," Letter from Professional Security Consultants—Polygraph and Security Specialists to Charles A. Moses, Charles A. Moses Company, 312 South Elm Drive #6, Beverly Hills, CA 90212, April 17, 1980.

Gupte, Pranay. "Six in Family Found Slain In Bedrooms in L.I. Home." *New York Times*, November 14, 1974.

——— "Surviving Son Held in Slayings of 6 in His Family at L.I. Home." *New York Times*, November 15, 1974.

——— "Slain Family Drugged, Police on L.I. Report." *New York Times*, November 18, 1974.

——— "DeFeos' Funeral Attended by 1,000." "Son Is Indicted on 6 counts of 2d-Degree Murder." *New York Times*, Tuesday, November 19, 1974.

Hevesi, Dennis. "Haunted by a Horror Story: The Cromartys want only to live quietly like other suburban families, but a best-selling book about their house, "The Amityville Horror," has turned their world upside down." *Newsday*, September 17, 1978.

Heyman, Harriet, and Milton Leebaw. "The Slayings on Long Island." *The New York Times*, November 17, 1974.

Hoffman, Paul. "Life in a Haunted House." "The ghosts in the $80,000 house in Amityville were too much even for an ex-Marine and his family." "It was haunted by the earth-bound spirits of those who had died in their sleep and didn't know they were dead." *New York Sunday News Magazine,* July 18, 1976: 8–9.

——— "Our Dream House Was Haunted. Lee and Kathy Lutz were delighted with their new home—in spite of its tragic history. Then strange and bizarre things began to happen." *Good Housekeeping*, 184 (April, 1977): 119.

Holzer, Hans. *Murder in Amityville*. New York, NY: Belmont Tower Books, 1979.

Homans, Mary A. *Amityville Past and Present.* Amityville, NY: Yesterday House, November 8, 1939. (Photocopy of typed manuscript in Amityville Free Library)

Hunter, Lois Marie. "The Shinnecock Indians." *The Hampton Chronicle*, Westhampton Beach, N.Y., 1960.

Internet Movie Database (IMDb). Accessed May 8, 2021. *https://www.imdb.com/list/ls097539998/?ref_=rls_3.*

Jones, John G. *The Amityville Horror II.* New York, NY: Warner Books, 1982.

——— *Amityville: The Final Chapter*. New York, NY: A Jove Book, 1985.

Kernan, Michael. "The Calamityville Horror" "A Family's Ghost Story Conjures Frightfully High Profits. Now Everyone's Haunting the Courtroom." *Washington Post*, September 16, 1979.

Klemensrud, Judy. "Behind the Best Sellers: Jay Anson." *New York Times Review of Books*, 83:28, January 22, 1978.

Lutz (Quaratino), Christopher. "Inside the Amityville Horror with Christopher (Lutz) Quaratino," *Spooky Southcoast.* ABC News, AM 1420, Feb. 11, 2012. https://www.youtube.com/watch?v=OlC3MMwg6jI

Lutz, Daniel, Eric Walter, Andrea Adams, John Blythe, Ronald Puleio, and Michael S. Russo. *My Amityville Horror.* Lost Witness Pictures, LLC. Distributed by MPI Media Group (DVD), 2013.

Lutz, Kathleen. "Exclusive: Wife Tells Chilling Story Behind: Our 28 Days of Horror in House Terrorized by Evil Spirits." *National Enquirer*, December 13, 1977.

Lutz v Hoffman, et al., 78 C 119 (Eastern District, NY September 10, 1979).

——— Trial Transcript. United States District Court Eastern District of New York. George Lutz and Kathleen Lutz, Plaintiffs, v Paul Hoffman, William Weber, Bernard Burton and Frederick Mars, Defendants. 78 C 119. Before: Honorable Jack B. Weinstein, U.S.D.J., Perry Auerbach, Marsha Diamond, and Nicholas Iannelli, Court Reporters. Four volumes, 459 pages.

——— Plaintiff's Answers to Interrogatories Propounded by Defendant, William Weber. Civil Action No: 78-C119.

——— Plaintiff's Trial Brief Marked Pleadings. 78 C 119 (JM) George Lutz and Kathleen Lutz, Plaintiffs, against Paul Hoffman, William Weber, Bernard Burton, Frederick M. Mars, Good Housekeeping, New York Sunday News, Hearst Corporation, and Does I through X inclusive, Defendants.

——— Defendants' Pre-Trial Memorandum of Law. Civil Action No. 78-C119. Frederic Block, Esq. Attorney for Defendants Burton, Weber and Hoffman.

Mason, Bill. "Books Cause Devilish Stir at School." *Newsday/The Island*, November 5, 1975.

McCollough, Kathy. "DeFeo house ghost vigil resumes." *Amityville Record*, July 22, 1976.

McDonald, John. "'Horror House' Is Haunted, But Not by Ghosts." *Newsday*, December 23, 1977.

Moran, Rick, and Peter Jordan. "The Amityville Horror Hoax," *Fate*, May 1978: 43–47.

Morris, Robert L. "Review: The Amityville Horror." *The Skeptical Inquirer/The Zetetic*, Vol. II, No. 2 Spring/Summer, 1978.

"Murder Confession Is Laid to a Beating." *New York Times*, Saturday, September, 27, 1975.

"Net Worth Post, George Lutz." Accessed May 8, 2021. *https://networthpost.org/net-worth/george-lutz-net-worth-2/*

"Net Worth Post, Jay Anson." Accessed May 8, 2021. *https://networthpost.org/net-worth/jay-anson-net-worth/*

"Net Worth Post, Kathleen Lutz." Accessed May 8, 2021. *https://networthpost.org/net-worth/kathy-lutz-net-worth/*

Page, Susan. "Gathering Pieces of a Long-Lost Montauk Culture." *Newsday*, November 6, 1975.

Pawel, Miriam. "Old Ghosts at Rest in Amityville." *Newsday*, Feb. 21, 1982.

Purdy, Seth Jr. "The History of 112 Ocean Avenue." Amityville, NY: Amityville Historical Society Museum, December 26, 1979.

Quest Associates. "Ed & Lorraine Warren: Seekers of the Supernatural." Media kit and sample press releases for the Warrens, 1979.

Reilly, Kevin. "DeFeo's Motive Still a Mystery." *New York Times*, Sunday, November 23, 1975.

"Residents blast DeFeo house circus." *Amityville Record*, August 26, 1976.

Roberts, Chris. "Exorcism and Demonic Possession Are Now Tools in the Culture Wars." Observer.com. January 3, 2019. https://observer.com/2019/01/pope-francis-exorcism-demonic-possession-culture-wars/

Roberts, George H. *Stars & Stripes*, Pacific edition, untitled, undated clipping from Amityville Public Library.

Rogo, D. Scott. "Amityville Horror or Hoax? *Human Behavior*, June 1978.

Rosenfeld, Neil S. "The Curious Haunt the DeFeo House." "Children gawk at the former DeFeo house as Frank Burger of Farmingdale photographs it." *Newsday*, February 16, 1976.

Ross, Peter. *A History of Long Island from Its Earliest Settlement to the Present Time. Volume III. Long Island: A History of Two Great Counties Nassau and Suffolk. Personal and Family History.* New York, NY: Lewis Historical Publishing Col., Inc., 1902.

"Scientific Truth Detector Shows Wife's Terrifying Story Is True." *National Enquirer*, December 13, 1977.

Smith, Don. "Medical Aide Describes Death of Mrs. DeFeo." "Bloodstains Tell Story" "Powder Burns on Body" *Newsday*, October 16, 1975.

——— "MD's Testimony Places DeFeo at the Scene." *Newsday*, October 17, 1975, page 25.

——— "Cop: DeFeo Altered Story." *Newsday*, Wednesday October 22, 1975.

——— "'I Left the Room in Awe of the Horror'" "Detective recalls DeFeo 'confession' to the murders of his father and brother." *Newsday*, Thursday, October 23, 1975.

——— "Cop: DeFeo Sought Insurance Funds." *Newsday*, October 24, 1975.

——— "Grandfather Has Kisses for DeFeo." Newsday, October 29, 1975.

——— "Issue Is Credibility at DeFeo Trial." *Newsday*, October 30.

——— "DeFeo Feared Loansharks, Witness Says." *Newsday*, Friday, October 31, 1975.

——— "DeFeo: I Killed Them in Self-Defense." Newsday, Thursday, November 6, 1975.

——— "I Killed a Dozen Others, DeFeo Says." *Newsday*, Friday, November 7, 1975.

——— "DeFeo Threatens Life of Prosecutor." *Newsday*, Saturday, November 8, 1975.

——— "Cellmate Says DeFeo Had Insanity Plan." *Newsday*, Tuesday, November 11, 1975.

——— "Doctor: DeFeo Knew It Was Wrong." Newsday, Thursday, November 13, 1975.

——— "Boy disputes DeFeo Claim About Fight." *Newsday*, Friday, November 14, 1975.

——— "'I Couldn't care Less,' DeFeo Says." *Newsday/The Island*, Tuesday, November 18, 1975.

——— "DeFeo Defended as Psychotic Killer." *Newsday/The Island*, Wednesday, November 19, 1975.

——— "DeFeo Guilty of Family Murder. Jury reported convinced by defendant's own testimony and his statements to police." *Newsday*, Saturday, November 22, 1975.

——— "DeFeo Sentenced." "DeFeo Called Menace, Gets 6 Life Terms." *Newsday/The Island,* December, 5, 1975.

Smith, Don, and A.J. Carter. "Lawyer Changes Story in DeFeo Trial." *Newsday/The Island,* Tuesday, November 4, 1975.

Smith, Don, and Sam Washington. "DeFeo a Heroin User, Cop Testifies." *Newsday*, Saturday October 18, 1975.

"Son, 24, Is Guilty in Murder of Six." "Conviction Follows Longest Trial in Suffolk County." *New York Times*, November 22, 1975.

"Still No Verdict in DeFeo Trial." *Newsday*, Friday, November 21, 1975.

Sullivan, Gerard, and Harvey Aronson. *High Hopes: The Amityville Murders.* New York, NY: Coward, McCann & Geoghegan, 1981.

"Summations Starting in DeFeo Case." *Newsday*, Monday, November 17, 1975.

Suplee, Curt. "Dolors to Dollars"; "Big Bucks and Big Questions in the Tale of a House Possessed"; "The book has become one of the biggest publishing successes of the year. More than 125,000 copies of the hardcover book are in print, and Prentice-Hall claims to have received more than 11,500 orders on a single day in November." *Washington Post*, December 9, 1977.

The New York Times. "Weather Reports and Forecast." December 18, 1975–January 15, 1976.

The Roman Ritual (Rituale Romanum): In Latin and English with Rubrics and Planechant Notation. Translated and Edited with Introduction and Notes by The Rev. Philip T. Weller, Caritas Publishing.

——— *Volume I. Sacraments and Processions.* Caritas Publishing, *1948.*

——— *Volume II. Christian Burial, Exorcisms, Reserved Blessings, Etc.* Caritas Publishing, *1950.*

——— *Volume III. The Blessings.* Caritas Publishing, *1945.*

"They Said It." "I killed them all. I killed them all in self-defense." *Newsday*, Sunday, November 9, 1975.

Tooker, William Wallace. *The Indian Place-Names on Long Island and Islands Adjacent with Their Probable Significations.* Edited, with an Introduction by Alexander F. Chamberlain. New York, NY: G.P. Putnam, 1911.

Van Gelder, Lawrence. "A Real-Life Horror Story." *The New York Times*, XXI Long Island, October 9, 1977.

Vecsey, George. "Neighbors Recall DeFeos As 'Nice, Normal Family.'" *New York Times*, Friday, November 15, 1974.

——— "L.I. Slayings Suspect Had Used Drugs." *The New York Times*, Saturday, November 16, 1974.

Weisman, Steven R. "Accused in Family's Murder, DeFeo Implicated in $19,000 Theft." *New York Times*, Sunday, November 17, 1974.

"We just wish it would end." *The Star Magazine/Newspaper*, July 24, 1979.

Welford, Sallyann. "Family finds only love & happiness inside the Amityville 'horror house,'" *The Star,* January 17, 1978.

Wick, Steve. "'Horror' House Suit Revived." *Newsday*, November 29, 1979.

Wikipedia. "The Amityville Horror," [*https://en.wikipedia.org/wiki/The_Amityville_Horror, accessed 1/24/21*]

"WNBC ghost house film ripped." *Amityville Record*, November 25, 1976.

www.ingramcontent.com/pod-product-compliance
Lightning Source LLC
Chambersburg PA
CBHW052108030426
42335CB00025B/2889

* 9 7 8 1 9 5 9 2 8 1 0 2 3 *